the best soups in the world

Also by Clifford A. Wright

ON COOKING

A Mediterranean Feast

Cucina Rapida

Cucina Paradiso

Italian Pure & Simple

Lasagne

Little Foods of the Mediterranean

Mediterranean Vegetables

Real Stew

Grill Italian

Some Like It Hot

Bake until Bubbly

ON POLITICS AND HISTORY

Facts and Fables: The Arab-Israeli Conflict

After the Palestine-Israel War: Limits to U.S. and Israeli Policy *with Khalil Nakhleh*

the best soups in the world

in the world

Clifford A. Wright

WILEY

JOHN WILEY & SONS, INC.

Copyright © 2010 by John Wiley & Sons, Inc. All rights reserved
Published by John Wiley & Sons, Inc., Hoboken, New Jersey
Published simultaneously in Canada

For general information on our other products and services or for technical support, please contact our Customer Care Department within the United States at (800) 762-2974, outside the United States at (317) 572-3993 or fax (317) 572-4002.

Wiley also publishes its books in a variety of electronic formats. Some content that appears in print may not be available in electronic books. For more information about Wiley products, visit our web site at www.wiley.com.

Visit the author at www.cliffordawright.com

Library of Congress Cataloging-in-Publication Data:

Wright, Clifford A.
  The best soups in the world / Clifford A. Wright.
     p.   cm.
  Includes index.
  ISBN 978-0-470-18052-5 (pbk.)
  1. Soups.   I. Title.
  TX757.W73 2009
  641.8'13—dc22   2008053454

Printed in the United States of America

10 9 8 7 6 5 4 3 2 1

Book design by Ralph Fowler / rlf design

For Najwa al-Qattan,

scholar, great mom,

reluctant cook

contents

acknowledgments

In the writing of any cookbook, it is the people who actually eat all the test preparations that go into perfecting the recipes who deserve the most thanks. They, after all, are the people who daily offer up their palates and provide crucial feedback, even concerning those not-so-great preparations that do not make it into the book. The others who deserve thanks are the people who provide advice on researching, writing, and editing recipes and on making a final selection that shows balance and breadth—especially important to a book that would offer the "best" in any category. So, many heart-felt thanks to my agent Angela Miller; my editor Justin Schwartz; my children Ali, Dyala, and Seri Kattan-Wright; to their mother, Najwa al-Qattan; and to my colleagues and friends Martha Rose Shulman, Deborah Madison, Russ Parsons, and Sarah Pillsbury.

the best soups in the world

introduction

In the dead of winter, rosy cheeks, cold hands, blown snow, and the icy chill are all forgotten the moment you stamp your boots in the mudroom and catch a whiff of a rich, thick, and hearty soup wafting in from the kitchen. Sometimes heaven is being hunched over a bowl of cabbage soup flavored with smoked bacon, kielbasa sausage, sour cream, and paprika, slurping with abandon. And in the summer, when the temperature hits the nineties, when green beans arrive in the market and tomatoes are bursting with ripeness, you make a simple yet delectable soup flavored with garlic, olive oil, celery, and fresh basil, or maybe a cold cucumber, yogurt, and walnut soup, or gazpacho.

Everyone remembers that "best" French onion soup they ate, with the slightly burnt cheese spilling over the edge of the bowl, or the spicy tang of the hot-and-sour shrimp soup at the neighborhood Thai restaurant. Oh, how you would love to make these soups at home! How hard could it be? Well, not so hard at all, and now you don't even have to look for a recipe. They're all here, all the classical, famous, and not-so-famous soups from around the globe. These are the best soups in the world (or should I say, those that could fit in this book). Whatever the season, a bowl of soup is a soul-satisfying experience.

One of my most poignant memories of real food is from a vacation I was on as a ten-year-old—a memory that inspired me to write this book. We were in Spain in the summer of 1961. I remember I had the most amazing soup. My parents took us to a wonderful restaurant. I had never been to such a place. It was elegant, or seemed elegant compared to the kind of restaurants we went to back home. The walls were a pale pastel gray, and the starched tablecloths were white. The tables were arranged in banquettes, which to this day I love to sit at. The waiter was better dressed than my dad.

My mother ordered vegetable soup for me. My heart sank because the only vegetable soup I knew was what I considered to be, even at age ten, the ghastly canned version, an unforgiving atrocity committed against what were once real vegetables. But what the waiter brought was something quite different. First of all, it was not red or clear or filled with perfectly diced overcooked vegetables. It was greenish and smooth—a velouté, I later learned. It was served in a very wide white bowl with a broad brim. And it was delicious: the most delicious thing I had ever eaten. I ate it with a funny little spoon that was halfway between a cereal bowl spoon and a baby spoon. It was a soup spoon. I had never eaten soup with a soup spoon.

Nearly fifty years later I finally told my mom about this memory, and she said, as if it had happened yesterday, "Oh, that must have been in Zaragoza; it was about ten in the evening and we couldn't find anywhere for you to eat until we finally found a restaurant that was open 'early.'" (Anyone who has been to Spain knows how impossibly late Spaniards eat supper.) She couldn't remember the name of the restaurant, but when my father died and I was cleaning out one of his closets I found a large brown envelope with all the hotel receipts from that trip in 1961. The restaurant was down the street from the Hotel Goya in Zaragoza, a hotel that still exists!

Soups are a basic food. They are enriching and satisfying. This book is a treasury of the favorite soups from world cuisines. Many of the recipes require no more than a trip to the supermarket and have great appeal because soups are comfort food. They're easy to make, can be an appetizer or a meal in themselves, freeze well, fit into a variety of personal diets, are light or filling (depending), and have a lot of culinary bang for the buck—one gets a heck of a lot of flavor out of something so simple. This is one of the reasons that soups have always been the first food of hard times.

Some recipes require ingredients found in ethnic markets. Today there are ethnic markets everywhere, and you should have no problem finding the somewhat specialized ingredients needed for the true taste. But even if you can't, on page 445 there is a complete listing of foods used in the book, and where on the Internet you can purchase them.

The central approach in my world of soups follows the comments of that great nineteenth-century French gastronome Grimod de la Reynière, who said, "Soup is to a dinner what the porch is to a building." The French chef Auguste Escoffier seconded him by suggesting that soup "in the manner of an overture in a light opera, should divulge what is to be the dominant phrase of the melody throughout."

Throughout this book, soups range from the ridiculously simple to the gastronomically sublime. To start, there is a vast repertoire of soup nomenclature, nearly all of which is rooted in the classical French cuisine of the famous chefs Marie-Antoine Carême (1784–1833) and Georges Auguste Escoffier (1846–1935). As useful as these classifications are, such as clear, puréed, bisque, and so on, they turn out to be limiting in a book such as this one, which deals with soups from around the world, not just French soups. You will not need to know the difference between a bouillon and a consommé to use this book with the greatest of joy.

There are soups made in restaurants and soups made at home, and the two soups are very different. For the most part, restaurant soups are based on stocks that can take days of preparation and involve several cooks and kitchen workers. Home soups are a much simpler affair, although home cooks can make complicated stocks, too, if they enjoy the process, are not pressed for time, and have good storage facilities. This book is a book of homemade soups, with a handful of so-called restaurant soups that can be successfully made at home.

First, though, what separates soups from stews and pottage? Basically, it all comes down to liquid. Except for fish stews, which are very soupy, a stew (which incidentally is both a noun and a verb, whereas soup is only a noun) can be thought of as a soup so thick the liquid has nearly disappeared. A stew can be eaten with a fork, whereas a soup can only be eaten with a spoon. Porridge or pottage is in between a soup and a stew; it's thick, but less thick than stew.

At its simplest, soup making does not require much—just a pot and water. But to make the full range of soups represented in this book, from bisques to veloutés, every home kitchen should have the following equipment. (I am not listing some items that are obvious and you already have, such as stew pots, pans, and knives):

Small pot (4-quart)

Large pot (8-quart)

Stock pot (20- to 22-quart)

Mortar and pestle

Blender

Food processor

Cheesecloth

Wok

Fine mesh wire strainers

Skimmer

Food mill

soup basics

homemade broth

The first decision soup cooks need to make is what they will use as their base when a recipe calls for broth. (I use the terms "broth" and "stock" interchangeably, as do many people, although technically there is a very small difference—not important to the home cook.) There are two options: make your own broth, or buy commercially available broth in the form of bouillon cubes, canned or cartoned broth or consommé, granules, or paste. I leave the choice to you, but can assure you that your own homemade broth will always taste better than a commercial broth, no matter what brand or kind. I know because I've tasted every commercial broth as research for this book. But, honestly, I use both; it depends on my time constraints, how spectacular I want my soup to taste, and whether I have, in fact, any homemade broth already made. Any recipe that relies on the broth itself as the centerpiece of the soup will clearly require homemade broth.

The foundation of all soups is water. Once you start flavoring or seasoning water you are making the foundation of all soups, not to mention gravies, sauces, and stews. In fact, a basic stock in French cuisine is called a *fonds,* or "foundation." Some soups require nothing but putting things in water and bringing them to a boil. Others require a foundation of broth or stock. Stock, broth, consommé, and bouillon tend to be used interchangeably for the same thing. A stock is a liquid seasoned by long simmering with meat, fish, or vegetables that is the basis for sauces, gravies, and soups. A consommé is a clear soup made from stock, clarified with egg whites and eggshells. It derives from the Latin word *consummare,* "to consummate or make perfect." Bouillon is a clear seasoned soup derived from the Old French word *boillir,* "to boil." The notion that bouillon was invented in the late eleventh century by Godfrey of Bouillon, one of the first Crusaders, is myth. A broth is a liquid in which meat, fish, vegetables, or cereal grains have been cooked. The word, derived from the Old English word *breowan,* "to brew," dates to before the twelfth century and is akin to the Old High German word *brod,* meaning "broth."

Some English-speaking writers make a distinction between broth and bouillon, but *bouillon* is simply the French word for broth. You've undoubtedly heard of broth, bouillon, stock, and consommé, and you will have read a variety of descriptions. Luckily, these are all the same thing as far as the mode of preparation—and this book—is concerned. The differences between them are minuscule, having to do with their purpose and flavor. Important mostly to restaurant chefs, these differences are not as important to the home cook. There is a distinction, if minor, between broth and stock. A broth is a clear liquid deriving its essence from a combination of meats, vegetables, and herbs that has simmered in water for a long time. Sometimes the meats themselves are combined, for example, beef and chicken. Stocks, called *fonds de cuisine* in French, meaning "foundations of cooking," are made in the same way as broths but are principally used by chefs for braising, stewing, and making sauces.

These classifications are rooted in French culinary culture, and there is nothing wrong with that. But increasingly, and this is especially true in the United States, a cookery is developing that can be called "international eclectic," and newer classifications need to be devised. Unfortunately, that's not so easy, but this book's chapter headings are my own attempt.

Traditionally, everything starts with stock, and chefs have devised general classifications for stocks, dividing them into two basic kinds: white stock and brown stock. White stock is made with white meats such as chicken and light-colored vegetables such as onions. Brown stock is made with dark meats like beef. The making of stock usually begins with scraps of meat on the bone that cannot be used for any other purpose (including cooked carcasses or fresh bones with a little meat on them), vegetable parings, and other bits of unspoiled food that are not attractive enough to serve on their own. Before I forget, let me say that you should never throw away the carcass of roast anything. The carcass makes for delicious soup making. French cooks often roast or sauté the meats they are using for their stocks to make the final product richer in taste and color; Italian (or for that matter, Thai) cooks, do not.

Supermarkets sell meat for stocks and soup making, packaging them as soup bones or marrow bones. Beef shank, neck bones, and oxtails all are good to use for soup making. To extract the maximum amount of flavor and gelatin from these bones they should be cut or cracked, which they usually are, but you can always ask the supermarket butcher to crack them further. A general rule of thumb is to use 1 quart of water for every pound of bones. For stock making at home to be worth your while, you need to use a large stock pot. My largest stockpot is 22 quarts. Any larger than that is not practical in a home kitchen, because your burner is too small and the range hood is too low. Two meats rarely used for stock making are lamb (too strong) and pork (too sweet). The ideal meats for nonspecialized all-purpose stock making are beef, veal, and chicken. Many cooks like a vegetable stock as their all-purpose stock.

Once your stock is made—and hereafter I will call it broth, following the language you will encounter in the recipes—there are three basic kinds of soups you can make. These divisions, though, are again derived from classical French cuisine, so it's difficult to apply them to all of the soups in this book, which are from around the world. The first kind of soup is clear soup, the second is thick soup, and the third is bulky soup. Miso soup or consommé is an example of the first, cream of mushroom is an example of the second, and minestrone is an example of the third. There are further divisions, such as purées, cream soups, and veloutés, under thick soups, as well as bisques, chowders, and international soups.

Now a few words about consommé. Consommé is a clarified beef broth, and a double consommé is a clarified broth made with broth rather than water. A consommé is consummate, meaning it's supposed to be perfect—and perfect means clear, without any fat globules or cloudiness from particles, and only slightly gelatinous. Making clear soup, or consommé, involves a process of clarifying the basic stock.

The first step is to make the stock, then refrigerate it in order to remove the fat that solidifies on top. Measure the stock, then pour it into a clean saucepan or stockpot with a mixture of one lightly beaten egg white, one eggshell broken into smaller pieces, and

2 teaspoons cold water per quart of stock. Place the stockpot on a burner and stir over medium-low heat until it comes to a boil. Boil for two minutes, then turn the heat off, cover, and let rest for twenty minutes. Strain into a large bowl, another pot, or storage container through a fine mesh strainer lined with a triple layer of cheesecloth.

But it is not always necessary to go through these steps to make a clear consommé. If you use care and patience, you can make a fine clear consommé by keeping the liquid just below a boil, the water only shimmering on top. Skim the foam that rises often and thoroughly, then strain slowly and carefully through multiple layers of cheesecloth. And don't forget, as a home cook, you can make a less-than-perfect consommé and no one will fire you. The basic consommé recipe is on page 20, with one variation on page 21, but there are literally hundreds of different consommés, and once you make the basic recipe you can become as inventive as you want.

Clear soups, or consommés, can have things added to them, while thick soups are made by puréeing vegetables, poultry, or fish in a blender or food processor or passing it through a food mill. Cream soups are purées that have had cream or milk added to them; if they are made with shellfish, they're called bisques.

In soup making, it is important not to salt or pepper until the end of cooking. If you salt at the beginning of the process, before the inevitable reduction of the liquid through evaporation, the result will be a far too salty and even inedible broth. Pepper is never added at the beginning of the cooking process, because the pepper, after long cooking, becomes tasteless and acrid. Peppering at the end gives the soup a burst of fresh, spicy flavor that perfumes the dish perfectly. (I sometimes violate this rule and you should feel free to do so, too.)

commercial broths

There is no denying that store-bought broths are a great convenience, no matter how much foodies pooh-pooh them. I use them whenever I don't have homemade broth around. But I have to admit that one of the wonderful, unexpected benefits of writing a book about soups is that I always had plenty of my homemade broth in the refrigerator or freezer, and I just loved that.

But let's be honest: we all will use a commercial broth when necessary. Store-bought broths come in a variety of styles, from cubes, paste, and granules to powder, condensed soup base, and liquid broth in cartons. You may be surprised by which brand from the following list won our blind taste test. Here are the broths tasted, with their salt content in milligrams per serving in parentheses. All the broths were chicken broths. The taste test covered low-, no-sodium, and fat-free broths, and all broths were tasted at room temperature. Salt content was ignored, and the broths were judged on fullness of chicken flavor.

BOUILLON CUBES

Tone's (1070 mg)

Knorr (1270 mg)

Maggi (1100 mg)

LIQUID OR CONDENSED BROTH IN CARTON, OR CANS

Pacific Natural Foods (70 mg)

Imagine (570 mg)

Health Valley (330 mg)

Organics (570 mg)

Wolfgang Puck (720 mg)

Kitchen Basics (490 mg)

Pritikin (290 mg)

Swanson (570 mg)

Campbell's Condensed (770 mg)

Streit's (790 mg)

Shelton (60 mg)

College Inn (930 mg)

Butterball (840 mg)

GRANULATED

Herb-Ox (0 mg)

Wyler's (800 mg)

PASTE

Superior Touch "Better Than Bouillon" (750 mg)

In our blind taste test with eight people, four of whom are food professionals and all of whom are cooks, the hands-down winner was Campbell's Condensed, shocking all of us. Swanson, Streit's, College Inn, Knorr, and Wyler's were distant seconds. But, in the judgment of the tasters, *all* commercial broths were woefully inferior to homemade broth, and although Campbell's won the taste test, it would not have been the choice of these cooks.

an odd, irregular, and abbreviated cultural history of soups

In Iraq, sometime around 1500 BC, an unknown scribe scratched into three clay tablets the first known written culinary recipes. The cuneiform tablets are written in Akkadian, a language of ancient Babylonia, and are part of the Yale Babylonian Collection. They are unrelated to each other except for their content and the fact that they may have been discovered together. Jean Bottéro, a French scholar, translated the recipes in *The Oldest Cuisine in the World: Cooking in Mesopotamia*, published by University of Chicago Press in 2004. Tablet A has twenty-five soup recipes. Twenty-one of the recipes are for meat broths and four are for vegetable broths.

Athenaeus (about AD 170–230), a Greek writer from Egypt who lived in Rome, wrote about soup, especially lentil soup, throughout his massive work on food known as the *Deipnosophistae* (Professors at the dinner table). If his lentil soup tasted anything like the lentil soup on page 244, then it's no wonder.

In the Roman cookery book Apicius, compiled in the late fourth century AD, soups come into their own. His barley soup, although odd by today's standards, could be made by a cook today. Crushed barley is boiled in water with oil and a bouquet garni of dill, dry onion, savory, and pork leg until well flavored. A pesto of cilantro and salt is stirred in; it is then creamed and stirred into another pot over the pork leg, and another pesto made of pepper, lovage, pennyroyal,

cumin, and dried cicely is added. Finally, honey, vinegar, reduced grape must, and *liquamen*—a kind of ancient Roman sauce of fish entrails similar to today's Thai fish sauce, and a key ingredient in all Roman cooking—is stirred in.

In the Middle Ages, soup came to have connotations for students, monks, and the military that may strike you as surprising. Students of the Middle Ages were not at all like the college students of today. They were dirt poor and had lives more like beggars. Students in Spain thought the worst misery was begging for their supper, which they called "going on the soup." In Spanish picaresque novels, poor rascals become antiheroes. They were known as the *sopistas*, the "soup eaters," living off the handouts of *sopa boba* at monastery doors. Two of the earliest picaresque novels are the anonymous *Lazarillo de Tormes*, published in 1554, and Francisco de Quevedo's *La Vida del Buscón*, written in 1608. These novels about down-and-out rascally youths are preoccupied with how to get food.

Soups were also often breakfast in the Middle Ages. We have a record from 1569 of a typical weekly menu of a farmhand at a royal estate in Saxony, in northwestern Germany: Sunday morning is meat soup; Monday morning is beer soup and some bread and cheese; Tuesday morning is soup; Wednesday morning is soup and buttermilk; Thursday, Friday, and Saturday mornings are all soup.

In early modern Provence, the students at the Papal school in Tret ate cabbage soup 125 days out the year. Monks of the time, even when their order did not insist on a vow of poverty, ate rather poorly, and when they did eat, soup was a prominent part of their diet. A menu from the dining room of the Benedictine monastery Santa Maria delle Vergini in Bitonto, Apulia, in southern Italy, during a week in June 1751, shows Monday's lunch was cabbage and chicory soup, Tuesday's lunch was onion soup, and Thursday's lunch was cabbage and chicory soup again. At about the same time, in France, the word *restaurant* was first used to designate a rich and fortifying bouillon. By the end of the eighteenth century the word had come to refer only to the establishment where bouillon was served: in 1765, on the rue des Poulies, near the Louvre in Paris, a certain *boulanger,* Champ d'Oiseux, served *restaurants,* that is, broths, under a Latin motto: *Venite ad me, omnes qui stomacho laboratis, et ego vos restaurabo* (Come to me all who feel the pangs of hunger, and I will restore you).

Soups and soup makers came to have a prominent symbolic role in the armies of the Ottoman Empire. The Ottoman rulers had imported slaves—often young Christian boys from lands conquered by the Ottomans—to Istanbul, as well as to Egypt, where they were integrated into the military and became the elite guard known as the Janissary Corps. The Janissaries eventually became strong enough to be king makers, and they engaged in numerous revolts against some minister or another and, in several instances, the sultan himself. They were organized on the model of a kitchen. The *kazan-i şarif,* or sacred cauldron of *şorba* (soup), was the emblem of the whole Janissary corps, and the Janissary headgear was ornamented with a spoon. High-ranking officers were called *şorbadji* ("soupiers" or "soup makers"). The corps was composed of battalions (*orta*), and each battalion had two or three great *kazan*s, "cauldrons," to feed the battalion, which could number between one hundred and five hundred troops. Typically the cauldrons were for cooking soup or pilaf. The head cook of each battalion kitchen was the most influential officer in the battalion. Important meetings were held in the kitchen around the cauldron. The Janissaries, who eventually became quite powerful, would "overturn the cauldron" when displeased by the sultan, symbolizing a rejection of the sultan's food, and hence his policies, and signaling the beginning of a rebellion. To this day, "overturning the cauldron" is an expression in Turkish meaning the expression of displeasure. The Janissaries became so strong, and such a privileged class, that Christian parents soon begged to have their children enlisted.

The word "soup" comes from the Old English and Old French word *sop*, which is nothing but bread soaked in liquid—either water, broth, or wine. You will find some of these old-style soups in the Grain-Based Soups chapter (page 283). Before you start cooking, here's a piece of advice for when you've messed up or have leftovers that don't look appealing: put them all in a blender with a little cream, water, or fresh tomato juice (or all three), purée, and voilà, you've just created a masterpiece!

Soup making requires a major decision on your part based on balancing taste and convenience. For the best taste, you will want to make your own broth. In this chapter are easy recipes for the best-tasting broths in the world. Broth making is not hard, and broth freezes well, so you can make a large volume at once. Mind you, there's not a lot of work involved, but you do need to simmer the pot for many hours. If time or inclination does not allow you to make homemade broth then you must use commercially made broths you find in your supermarket.

basic
broths

beef broth

THIS ITALIAN-STYLE BEEF BROTH, or *brodo,* is an all-purpose broth that can be used for any recipe calling for beef broth, Italian or otherwise. A good broth is the foundation for sauces, soups, and many stews. Broth freezes well and can be made in advance. For recipes calling for veal broth, replace the beef with veal shoulder and other bones; for lamb broth, replace with lamb neck and shoulder; and for vegetable broth, omit the meat and add a bunch of spinach or Swiss chard and one cut-up leek. French cooks make the broth richer by first frying the bones in a skillet or roasting the bones in an oven. See the recipe for Rich Veal Broth (page 12). **[Makes 2 to 3 quarts]**

4 pounds cracked beef marrow, shin, and/or shank bones, with meat on them
1 large sweet onion, with its skin, cut into eighths
1 carrot, cut up
1 celery stalk, cut up
1 leek, split lengthwise, washed well, and cut up
10 black peppercorns
Bouquet garni, tied together in cheesecloth, consisting of 3 sprigs fresh parsley,
    1 sprig fresh thyme, 2 fresh sage leaves, and 1 bay leaf
4 quarts water
Salt and freshly ground black pepper to taste

1. Place all the ingredients except the salt and pepper in a stockpot, bring to a boil over high heat, then reduce to a simmer. Skim the surface of foam until no more appears. Partially cover and simmer over low heat for 4 to 6 hours.

2. Pour the broth through a cone-shaped strainer (chinois) or whatever strainer you have and discard all the bones, meat, vegetables, and bouquet garni. Now pour the broth through a strainer lined with cheesecloth into a clean pot or bowl. Taste the broth and season with salt and pepper to your liking.

3. To de-fat the broth, let it rest in a refrigerator until the fat congeals on the top and can be lifted off by scooping with a spoon. If not using the broth immediately, transfer into 1-quart plastic containers and refrigerate for up to 1 week or freeze for up to 6 months.

Variation: Preheat the oven to 425°F. Place the beef bones in a roasting pan and roast until golden brown, about 45 minutes. Continue with Step 1.

beef broth for asian soups

[Makes 2 quarts]

5 pounds beef shank or beef bones, with meat on them
2 quarts water
One 2-inch piece fresh ginger, peeled and cut into 4 pieces
15 black peppercorns
Salt to taste

Place the beef shank in a large pot and add the water, ginger, and black peppercorns. Bring to just below a boil over high heat, reduce the heat to medium, skim
the surface of foam, then cook until the meat is falling off the bones, about 4 hours.
Strain the broth through a cone-shaped strainer (chinois) or whatever strainer you
have, discarding all the bones; the meat can be taken off and used in other soups.
Strain the broth again through a cheesecloth-lined strainer into a clean pot or
bowl. The broth only needs to be salted before using. If not using the broth immediately, transfer into 1-quart plastic containers and refrigerate for up to 1 week
or freeze for up to 6 months.

basic broths

rich veal broth

IN FRENCH they call this kind of broth *fond brun de veau* (brown veal foundation, or base) because it forms the base for sauces, soups, and stews. To make this a rich beef broth, simply replace the veal with beef. It is best to start making the broth in the morning. Although I don't always use my own broth, when I do make broth, it is usually on a Sunday morning, and I prepare it, lazily, all day, simmering, straining, cooling, and storing it over the entire day so it ends up not feeling like a lot of work. **[Makes 2 to 3 quarts]**

4 pounds cracked veal marrow bones with shin and/or shank bones,
   with meat on them
1 large onion, cut into eighths
1 carrot, sliced
1 leek, split lengthwise, washed well, and cut up
2 celery stalks, cut up
10 black peppercorns
Bouquet garni, tied together in cheesecloth, consisting of 3 sprigs fresh parsley,
   1 sprig fresh thyme, 2 fresh sage leaves, and 1 bay leaf
4 quarts water
Salt and freshly ground black pepper to taste

1. Preheat the oven to 425°F.

2. Put all the meat in a roasting pan and place in the oven until well browned, about 45 minutes.

3. Transfer the meat bones and their juices and all the other ingredients including the water—but not the salt and pepper—into a stockpot, bring to a boil over high heat, then reduce to a simmer. Skim the surface of foam with a slotted skimmer until no more appears. Partially cover and simmer over low heat for 4 to 6 hours. Strain now or turn the heat off and let sit 2 hours.

4. Pour the broth through a cone-shaped strainer (chinois) or whatever strainer you have into another large pot or 2 large bowls and discard all the bones, meat, vegetables, and bouquet garni. Now pour the broth through a fine wire mesh strainer lined with cheesecloth into a cleaned stockpot. Season with salt and pepper. The broth is ready to use now, although most cooks prefer to de-fat the broth, so go on to Step 5.

5. To de-fat the broth, pour it into a more convenient receptacle and let it rest in a refrigerator until the fat congeals on the top and can be lifted off, usually overnight. You can use a spoon or spatula to scoop it off. If not using the broth immediately, transfer into 1-quart plastic containers and refrigerate for up to 1 week or freeze for up to 6 months.

basic broths

chicken broth

THIS NICE HOMEMADE BROTH can be used for any recipes calling for chicken broth. For duck broth, replace the chicken with a roasted duck carcass, and for rabbit broth, replace with rabbit bones. For recipes calling for a rich chicken broth, a darker stock, first roast the chicken bones in a 425°F oven until golden. Some French chefs also use veal bones to make their chicken stock, while Chinese chefs use pork bones and chicken feet as well. Norman chefs might add turnips and parsnips to the stock, which gives it a flavor typical of that region.

[Makes 3 to 4 quarts]

8 pounds chicken bones, with some meat
2 carrots, sliced
3 celery stalks, with leaves, sliced
1 large onion, peeled, halved, and separated into layers
1 leek, washed well and cut up
10 black peppercorns
Bouquet garni, tied in cheesecloth, consisting of 6 sprigs fresh parsley,
    6 sprigs fresh thyme, 6 sprigs fresh marjoram, 2 sprigs fresh sage,
    and 1 bay leaf
2 cups dry white wine
5 quarts cold water
Salt and freshly ground black pepper to taste

1. Place all the ingredients, except the salt and pepper, in a stockpot, and bring to a boil over high heat. Reduce the heat to a simmer and skim off the foam until no more appears. Partially cover the pot and simmer over low heat for 3 hours.

2. Pour the broth through a cone-shaped strainer (chinois) or whatever strainer you have and discard all the bones, vegetables, and bouquet garni. Now pour the broth through a cheesecloth-lined strainer into a clean pot or bowl. Season to taste with salt and pepper. Place the broth in the refrigerator until the fat congeals and remove by scooping it off with a spoon. If not using the broth immediately, transfer into 1-quart plastic containers and refrigerate for up to 1 week or freeze for up to 6 months.

the best soups in the world

chicken broth for asian soups

[Makes 2 quarts]

One 3-pound stewing chicken or 3 chicken carcasses
9 cups cold water
One 2-inch piece fresh ginger, peeled and cut into 4 slices
8 scallions, trimmed and cut in half

1. Place the chicken or chicken carcasses in a large pot and cover with 8 cups water. Bring to just below a boil over high heat, then, before it starts to bubble, reduce the heat to low, pour in the remaining 1 cup cold water and add the ginger and scallions, and then simmer for 3 hours, skimming the surface of foam as it rises.

2. Strain the broth into another pot or bowl. Strain again through a cheesecloth-lined strainer and reserve. If using whole chicken, remove the skin and bones and save the meat for another soup. If using chicken carcasses, you can discard them. If not using the broth immediately, transfer into 1-quart plastic containers and refrigerate for up to 1 week or freeze for up to 6 months.

fish broth

THIS FISH BROTH is one that I use for soups and even for cooking certain risottos. Ask the fishmonger for some fish carcasses. He should give them to you for free, although some may charge. Try to mix up the fish, using three or four kinds, a couple from white-fleshed fish and one or two from dark-fleshed fish, and get a head, which provides so much flavor.

[Makes 2 quarts]

6 pounds mixed fish carcasses, including at least 1 or 2 fish heads

3 quarts cold water

2 cups dry white wine

2 carrots, peeled and cut up

2 celery stalks, sliced

1 onion, quartered

10 black peppercorns

Bouquet garni, tied in cheesecloth, consisting of 10 sprigs each fresh parsley
   and thyme, 6 sprigs fresh marjoram, and 1 sprig fresh sage

Place all the ingredients in a large pot. Bring to a boil over high heat, then reduce the heat to low and simmer for 4 hours, skimming the foam that forms on the surface. Strain the broth through a strainer into a large bowl or another large pot. Line the strainer with cheesecloth and strain the broth again into the large bowl or pot. If not using the broth immediately, transfer into 1-quart plastic containers and refrigerate for up to 1 week or freeze for up to 6 months.

the best soups in the world

vegetable broth

ONE CAN MAKE VEGETABLE BROTHS in an infinite variety of ways, but this recipe is simple and works just fine as a bouillon and as a broth for any recipe calling for one. I prefer to stay away from the use of cruciferous vegetables such as cabbage, broccoli, and Brussels sprouts when making vegetable broths. Feel free to add potato or carrot peelings and leafy greens such as Swiss chard or spinach for a greener broth. **[Makes 8 cups]**

3 quarts water
1 leek, split lengthwise, washed well, and cut up
1 carrot, cut up
1 small onion, quartered
2 scallions, cut up
1 celery stalk, cut up
6 sprigs fresh parsley
10 blades fresh chives (half bunch)
6 sprigs fresh thyme
6 black peppercorns

Place all the ingredients in a large pot. Bring to a boil over high heat, then reduce the heat to low and simmer for 4 hours, partially covered. Strain the broth, discarding the vegetables, and it's ready for use. If not using the broth immediately, transfer into 1-quart plastic containers and refrigerate for up to 1 week or freeze for up to 9 months.

basic broths

clear
soups

This chapter is filled with clear soups, that is, soups based on a clear broth with the addition of garnishes such as custards, stuffed vegetables, dumplings, meatballs, crêpes, and so on. Because the foundation of all these soups, the thing that makes them special, is the broth, it is most important that these broths be homemade, using the recipes in the Basic Broths chapter (page 9). You could, of course, use commercial broths, but realize that if you do, the soups in this chapter won't seem so special, and they may not taste as I've described them in the recipe.

consommé

A CONSOMMÉ IS A LIGHT, almost clear meat stock with an intense, heightened flavor—that is, a clarified broth. In classical French cuisine it is the base for many other soups and can take tens of different garnishes, of which I provide one example in the next recipe. Consommé, which means to complete or make perfect or boil down, is indeed the consummate French soup. The famous French chef Auguste Escoffier offered nearly a hundred consommé recipes in his *Le guide culinaire,* many of which are fantastically complicated recipes meant only for hotel or restaurant kitchens. The albumin of the meat and the egg white will turn the stock into a clear liquid. To degrease broth or consommé, refrigerate it for several hours until a layer of fat forms on top, then remove it. There's something slightly old-fashioned about making and serving a consommé, but I think it's a nice recipe to have in your repertoire.

[**Makes 2½ quarts**]

1½ pounds beef round, all fat removed, chopped very fine

Giblets from 1 chicken (except for the liver), chopped very fine

1 small carrot, peeled and cut into tiny dice

3 leeks, white part only, split lengthwise, washed well, and chopped

1 large egg white

2½ quarts beef broth

1. Place the beef, chicken giblets, carrot, leeks, and egg white in a large stockpot, cover with the beef broth, and stir. Bring to a boil slowly over medium heat, stirring quite frequently. As soon as it reaches a boil, reduce the heat to low and simmer, partially covered, for 1¼ hours.

2. Soak a swath of cheesecloth in water and wring it out, then cover a fine mesh strainer with the cheesecloth and strain the broth into a clean pot or bowl. If not using immediately, transfer into 1-quart plastic containers and refrigerate for up to 1 week or freeze for up to 6 months.

consommé à la royale

THIS CONSOMMÉ is just one of the many ways this light soup can be served—and one of the most classic ways, too. *Royale* is a French culinary term meaning a molded custard, usually used in consommé, but also in other fancy preparations. The other garnishes that can be used in consommés are innumerable. **[Makes 4 servings]**

2 large eggs
½ cup whole milk
6½ cups Consommé (page 20), hot
1 teaspoon finely chopped fresh parsley, chervil, or chives
Pinch of salt
Pinch of ground nutmeg

1. Preheat the oven to 325°F.

2. In a bowl, beat the eggs, then strain them through a fine mesh strainer into a pot. Add the milk and ½ cup hot consommé (make sure it is not boiling) to the eggs. Season with the herbs (saving a pinch for garnishing at the end), salt, and nutmeg. Pour this mixture into two 4-inch ramekins or a small cake pan that can fit inside a larger pan such as a baking casserole or roasting pan and fill the large pan with water until it is three-quarters of the way up the sides of the ramekins.

3. Bake until the custard sets, when a toothpick pushed into the middle of the custard comes out clean, about 40 minutes. Cool completely, then carefully unmold and cut into even strips. Cut the strips into decorative shapes such as diamonds or squares or—if you have the patience or the molds—hearts or stars.

4. Bring the remaining consommé to a boil, then turn the heat off. Place the custard shapes in individual bowls, ladle the soup over them, and serve with a sprinkle of parsley if desired.

crêpes in chicken broth

DURING CARNIVAL, in the mountains around Teramo in the Abruzzo, a region of Italy about halfway down the peninsula, this traditional soup called *scrippelle 'mbusse* (or *'nfuss*) is made with eggy crêpes stuffed with pecorino and Parmesan cheese and soaked in boiling chicken broth. In the countryside, pork skin is often used to flavor the chicken broth. The name of the soup means "soaked crêpes" in Abruzzese dialect. In Italian the crêpe used here is actually called *frittatina,* which means a thin and small frittata, indicating that the crêpes are eggier than a normal crêpe. Although it can be made with beef broth, chicken broth is more common. In older recipes the batter was made with water, while today milk is more common. There are various rules of thumb for this dish, but as there are so many recipes and interpretations, I'm striving for what I ate once and loved. Some cooks put the cheese into the crêpe batter; others don't. The crêpes should be rolled up like cigars. Another rule of thumb is two tablespoons flour for every egg, although I use a tad more. The parsley can be put into the broth instead of the batter, but I prefer it in the batter. Some cooks add chopped prosciutto di Parma, but I believe that must be a restaurant introduction.   **[Makes 8 servings]**

6 large eggs

1½ cups whole milk

¾ cup plus 2 tablespoons all-purpose flour

2½ tablespoons finely chopped fresh parsley

1 cup (2 ounces) freshly grated Parmesan cheese (preferably imported Parmigiano-Reggiano)

¾ teaspoon salt

Pinch of ground nutmeg

Pork lard (preferably) or vegetable oil for greasing

1 cup (2 ounces) freshly grated pecorino cheese

2 quarts chicken broth

1. In a bowl, beat the eggs until frothy. Add the milk, flour, parsley, 1 tablespoon Parmesan cheese, salt, and nutmeg. Beat some more, then set aside at room temperature for 20 minutes. The consistency should be like crêpe batter, that is, like a heavy buttermilk.

2. Heat a 7-inch crêpe pan, cast-iron skillet, or nonstick skillet over high heat, then rub the surface of the pan with a little lard or oil, using a paper towel, so there is only a film on the surface. Pour in enough batter, about 3 tablespoons, to cover the bottom of the pan, twirling the pan as you do it so the batter covers the entire bottom. The batter should be thin enough to spread rapidly, not slowly like pancake batter. Use the first crêpe as a test case. Once the crêpe is in the pan, cook until the top surface looks dry, then flip and cook the other side, about 1 minute in all. As they finish cooking, set the crêpes aside, making sure that they cool before placing another one on top of them. Alternatively, separate them with sections of plastic wrap as you continue cooking. The crêpes can be frozen at this point if desired or left at room temperature if using the same day.

3. Sprinkle some of the remaining Parmesan and the pecorino cheese on each crêpe, then roll them up tightly like a handmade cigar. Arrange 2 crêpes in each serving bowl, side by side, bending them if you must.

4. Bring the chicken broth to a boil then ladle over the crêpes so the liquid only comes up to about one-third of the crêpe. Cover and let the crêpes absorb the broth and serve hot.

meat- and cheeseball spoon-drop soufflé soup

MY ENGLISH TRANSLATION of this renowned Sicilian soup called *sciuscieddu* is quite a mouthful I realize, but that's what it is—and so is the soup. Everything about this dish from Messina in Sicily is open to question: the origin and meaning of the name, whether it is a soup or a stew, whether it should be made in a workingman's style or in an aristocratic way, where it is from, and even its spelling, which may appear as *sciuscieddu* or *susceddu* or *ciusceddu*. Perhaps the famous Roman version of this soup served on Easter throughout Italy, *stracciatella*, meaning "little rags," which is better known, derives from the Sicilian. Vincenzo Mortillaro's Sicilian-Italian dictionary, published in 1881, provides a number of origins for the word *sciuscieddu*, the most likely being that the word derives from the Sicilian verb *ciusciari*, "to puff up." Theories abound. The Sicilian culinary expert Giuseppe Coria proposes that the name comes from the Latin *juscellum*, a liquid *minestre*. Another proposal is that the word is onomatopoeic, sounding like its cooking. Anna Pomar, author of some excellent Sicilian cookbooks, disagrees with some of her colleagues that the soup is Arab derived, and claims it is "without a doubt French." But cookbook authors Tomasso d'Alba and Fiammetta di Napoli Oliver are of the opinion that the dish is Arab-influenced, as is Enzo Siena, former head of the Syracuse delegation of the Accademia Italiana della Cucina. If this is so, perhaps it is related to the Arab soup *shūrbat al-qīma,* a meatball soup where the meatballs are first fried in fat and then made with tomato paste, parsley, and cinnamon. I relate all this history so you can truly appreciate this delicious and impressive soup, which your guests will surely ask about—and now you have a story you can tell them. **[Makes 6 servings]**

1¼ pounds ground beef
½ cup freshly grated pecorino or caciocavallo cheese
¼ cup dry bread crumbs
Salt and freshly ground black pepper to taste
5 large eggs
2 tablespoons extra-virgin olive oil
1¾ cups ricotta cheese
4 cups beef broth
Ground cinnamon for sprinkling

1. Preheat the oven to 350°F.

2. In a bowl, mix the ground beef, half the grated cheese, the bread crumbs, salt, pepper, and 1 beaten egg. Knead the meat well and make little meatballs not more than 1 inch across, forming them with wet hands so they don't stick.

3. In a nonstick skillet, heat the olive oil over low heat, then cook the meatballs, shaking the pan occasionally, until browned, about 15 minutes. Remove the meatballs with a slotted spoon and leave to drain on some paper towels.

4. Separate the 4 remaining eggs, putting the whites in one bowl and the yolks in another. Mix the yolks with the ricotta cheese. Whisk the egg whites until they form peaks, then delicately add to them the remaining grated pecorino cheese until well mixed.

5. In a deep, flame-proof baking casserole, bring the beef broth to a boil over high heat. Drop the meatballs into the boiling broth, and then the egg yolk–and–ricotta cheese mixture, using a large serving spoon. When the broth returns to a boil, turn the heat off, sprinkle the top with cinnamon, and pour in the egg white mixture. Place the casserole in the oven and bake until the top is firm, hot, and bubbling, 20 minutes. Serve hot.

SICILIAN SOUP PROVERB

Think of this wisdom, an old Sicilian proverb, when you make your soups.

Li conzi fannu li minestri sapuriti; ma piu si conza piu si sconza.

"Seasoning gives soups flavor, but the more one seasons the more one spoils."

soup of stuffed lettuce leaves

THIS SOUP OF STUFFED LETTUCE leaves poached in a rich beef broth is called *leitûghe pinn-e* in the Ligurian dialect spoken in Genoa or *zuppa di lattughe ripiene* in Italian. Although it is one of the most famed soups in Italy, it is rarely made in the home today because it is complex and labor intensive. But it is so good that you will never be unhappy with the result, and your guests will be simply astounded. It may make sense to make this recipe over a period of two or three days to lessen the workload; furthermore, you need to give yourself time to find all the ingredients. Another version of this soup is the one I had at the Ristorante Mario Rivaro in Genoa, where the *lattughe ripiene in salsa rossa* consisted of lightly poached lettuce leaves stuffed with a very fine and delicately chopped veal-and-Parmesan mixture with spices. The bundles of stuffed lettuce were poached in a rich beef broth and served with red kidney beans that were cooked in a soupy tomato sauce with lots of garlic. It will be easier to remove the marrow from the marrow bones if they are at room temperature. I usually cut them out using a butter knife and a demitasse or baby spoon. **[Makes 6 servings]**

the best soups in the world

1½ teaspoons all-purpose flour

6 ounces veal sweetbread, soaked in cold water to cover for 1 hour

Juice of ½ lemon

5 tablespoons unsalted butter

¼ pound plus 3 tablespoons veal or beef marrow (from about
    2 pounds of marrow bones)

½ pound beef chuck, diced tiny

1 carrot, peeled and finely chopped

1 celery stalk, finely chopped

6 tablespoons finely chopped fresh parsley leaves

¼ cup dried mushrooms, soaked for 30 minutes in ½ cup tepid water,
    drained, liquid saved, and chopped

2 large ripe tomatoes, cut in half, seeds squeezed out, and grated against the
    largest holes of a standing grater down to the peel

1 cup water

Salt to taste

½ cup dry white wine

6 cups beef broth

1 large green leaf lettuce, 12 large lettuce leaves set aside, heart finely chopped

1 small onion, finely chopped

3 tablespoons finely chopped veal fat (cut from the shoulder used below)

Freshly ground black pepper to taste

¼ teaspoon freshly ground nutmeg

¼ pound boneless veal shoulder, chopped

2 cups fresh bread crumbs

2 large eggs

1 cup freshly grated Parmesan cheese (preferably Parmigiano-Reggiano)

6 slices Italian bread, toasted

1. Place the flour in a small cast-iron skillet without any fat and heat over medium-high heat, stirring occasionally, until lightly browned, about 2 minutes. Set aside.

2. Drain the sweetbread. Pour the lemon juice into a pot of water and bring to a near boil over medium-high heat. Reduce the heat so the water is only shimmering, add the sweetbread, and poach until it is white and firm, about 20 minutes. Drain, cool, chop, and set aside.

3. In a large, heavy, flame-proof casserole, melt 2 tablespoons of the butter with 3 tablespoons of the bone marrow over medium-high heat. Add the diced beef chuck, half the carrot, half the celery, half the parsley, the mushrooms and their soaking liquid, the tomatoes, water, and 2 teaspoons salt. (If you like, you can put 3 or 4 marrow bones from which you've scooped out the marrow into the casserole.) Stir, reduce the heat to medium, and cook, stirring occasionally, until denser, 15 minutes. Add the white wine and cook for 15 minutes. Add the beef broth and cook for 20 minutes. Pass the mixture through a food mill, return to the casserole, and cook for another 30 minutes. Set the broth aside and keep warm until needed in Step 9.

4. Bring a pot of water to a very gentle boil over high heat, then reduce the heat so the water is only shimmering. Remove the lettuce leaves carefully and blanch them, one at a time, in the shimmering water until barely wilted, about 10 seconds. Drain and set aside, handling them carefully so they don't rip.

5. In a large, heavy, flame-proof casserole, prepare the stuffing by melting the remaining 3 tablespoons butter over medium heat, then add the onion, the remaining carrot, celery, and parsley, and the veal fat, and cook, stirring occasionally, until the onion is translucent, about 8 minutes. Season with salt, pepper, and nutmeg and stir.

6. Add the chopped veal, ¼ pound veal marrow, and the sweetbread to the casserole with the stuffing. Reduce the heat to medium-low and stir in the chopped lettuce

heart and browned flour. Cook, stirring occasionally, until the stuffing has a rich, deep, appetizing color and aroma, about 30 minutes.

7. Pour 1 cup of the reserved broth into the casserole with the stuffing and cook, stirring, until thick and gooey, about 30 minutes. Add the bread crumbs to the casserole. Stir well and transfer to a bowl. Let cool for 15 minutes, then stir in the eggs and ½ cup Parmesan cheese.

8. Lay a lettuce leaf in front of you and cut off the hard white part with a paring knife. Place a heaping tablespoon of stuffing on the end nearest you. Fold over once away from you, then tuck in the two sides and continue rolling until you have a neat, tight, bundle. Continue with the remaining lettuce leaves, placing them on a tray or plate until you are finished.

9. Reheat the reserved broth in the first casserole in Step 3 over medium heat. Place the lettuce bundles in the broth with tongs, then poach them, covered, making sure the broth doesn't boil but just bubbles very gently, until firm and very hot, 20 minutes.

10. Place a slice of toasted bread in each soup bowl, lay 2 stuffed lettuce bundles on top, then ladle in the broth the lettuce poached in, sprinkle with the remaining ½ cup Parmesan cheese, and serve.

tortellini in brodo

TORTELLINI IN BRODO, a soup of homemade broth and (hopefully) homemade tortellini stuffed with either meat or cheese, is very much a soup equated with Bologna in Emilia-Romagna. This particular version popular in the spring also has lamb, white beans, and asparagus to complement the tortellini. When you hear people waxing ecstatic about this soup, they remember soup whose tortellini and broth were lovingly made by their mother's hand. I suggest you do the same, at least for the broth (pages 10 and 14).   **[Makes 6 servings]**

1 cup (½ pound) small dried white beans
Salt to taste
½ pound asparagus tips
¼ cup extra-virgin olive oil
1 pound boneless lamb sirloin, diced
1 medium onion, finely chopped
4 large garlic cloves, finely chopped
¼ cup finely chopped fresh rosemary
3 tablespoons dry white wine
4 cups chicken broth
4 cups beef broth
1 pound store-bought or homemade cheese tortellini
Freshly grated pecorino cheese to taste

1. Place the white beans in a large pot and cover by 4 inches with cold water. Bring to a boil, salt lightly, and cook until tender, 45 to 50 minutes. Drain and set aside.

2. Bring a pot of lightly salted water to a boil and cook the asparagus until tender, 6 to 7 minutes. Drain and set aside.

3. In a flame-proof casserole or a pot, heat the olive oil over high heat, then brown the lamb, stirring, for about 3 minutes. Remove the lamb with a slotted spoon. Add the onion, garlic, and rosemary and cook, stirring frequently, until the onion is softened, about 4 minutes. Return the lamb to the casserole, add the white wine, and cook until it is evaporated by half, 2 to 3 minutes. Pour in the chicken and beef broth and bring to a near boil over high heat, then reduce the heat to low and leave to simmer while you cook the tortellini.

4. Bring a large pot of abundantly salted water to a vigorous boil and add the tortellini. Cook until tender, about 15 minutes. Drain well and add to the broth, heat for a couple of minutes, and serve with pecorino cheese.

small rice balls in broth

IF THESE RICE BALLS in broth, called *badduzzi di risu 'nto brodu* in Sicilian, seem familiar, it is because the recipe for the rice is identical to *risotto alla milanese,* the traditional accompaniment to osso buco. The rice balls are also quite similar to *arancine* (the deep-fried stuffed rice balls served as a snack in Sicily), except here the *badduzzi di risu* are floured and have a lighter, tempura-like look. These delicate rice balls will fall apart in the broth, as they should.

[**Makes 8 servings**]

Pinch of saffron, crumbled

1 to 2 pounds beef or veal marrow bones, at room temperature

¼ cup unsalted butter

1 small onion, finely chopped

⅓ cup dry white wine

2 cups Arborio rice, washed well in a strainer

10 cups beef broth

¼ cup freshly grated pecorino or caciocavallo cheese

¼ pound fresh mozzarella cheese, cut into tiny cubes

Sunflower seed oil or vegetable oil for deep frying

3 large eggs

All-purpose flour for dredging

Freshly grated Parmesan cheese for sprinkling (optional)

1. Soak the saffron in 1 tablespoon of tepid water. Extract 3 tablespoons of the marrow from the bones with a small spoon or knife and set aside.

2. In a large pot, melt 2 tablespoons of the butter over medium-high heat, then add the onion and marrow and cook, stirring often, until the onion is translucent, about 3 minutes. Add the wine and cook, stirring occasionally, until it is reduced to a few tablespoons. Stir in the rice and cook over medium-low heat for 3 minutes.

3. Meanwhile, in another pot, bring the broth to a boil and add 1 cup of the broth to the pot with the rice; it will sizzle. Stir once and let cook until the broth is almost all absorbed, shaking the pot once in a while. Continue in this manner, 1 cup at a time, until you have used 3½ cups of broth. Stir very gently and shake until the rice is al dente. This should take about 20 minutes. Keep the remaining broth very hot over low heat.

4. Add the saffron by sprinkling over the rice and stir gently. Remove from the heat and gently stir in the remaining butter and the grated cheese. Cover and let stand for a few minutes. Uncover and spread the rice on a large platter to let it cool completely.

5. Shape the rice into small balls the size of a walnut, putting a cube of mozzarella cheese into the center and molding the rice around the cheese, sealing it completely.

6. In a deep-fryer or an 8-inch saucepan with a wire fry basket, preheat the frying oil to 360°F.

7. In a shallow bowl, beat the eggs and spread some flour on a piece of wax paper. Roll the balls in the beaten egg and then in the flour. Deep-fry them until golden and set aside as they finish cooking, keeping them warm.

8. Bring the remaining broth to a boil over high heat, then ladle into individual bowls. Place 4 rice balls in each bowl and sprinkle some grated Parmesan cheese on top, if desired.

cambodian stuffed cabbage roll soup

IN THIS KHMER (CAMBODIAN) RECIPE from the countryside, cabbage leaves are filled with a stuffing of ground pork and bean thread noodles seasoned with fish sauce. It's called *salor spee kdop nhoat sach chrouk,* a phrase you will probably never have to use even though you may make this soup more than once. It's a soup the villagers make for special occasions. This recipe is adapted from Mylinh Nakry. You can serve steamed rice on the side.

[Makes 4 servings]

FOR THE CABBAGE STUFFING

1 green cabbage

6 scallions, trimmed, 4 cut in 2-inch slices, 2 finely chopped

1 pound ground pork

2 ounces bean thread noodles, soaked in very hot water until soft, then drained and chopped

1 tablespoon Thai or Vietnamese fish sauce

1 teaspoon sugar

½ teaspoon salt

¼ teaspoon freshly ground black pepper

Toothpicks

FOR THE BROTH AND GARNISH

4 cups chicken broth

2 tablespoons Thai or Vietnamese fish sauce

1 tablespoon sugar

¼ teaspoon salt

1. In a stockpot, cover the whole cabbage and the green part of 2 sliced scallions with water. Bring to a boil over high heat, covered, then reduce the heat to medium and cook until the cabbage leaves can be pulled off the head without ripping, about 15 minutes. Drain, saving 2 cups of the cooking water. When the cabbage is cool enough to handle, peel off the leaves, discarding any that rip or fall apart.

2. In a bowl, add the pork, bean thread noodles, fish sauce, sugar, salt, black pepper, and the 2 finely chopped scallions, mix well, and set aside.

3. Place a cabbage leaf in front of you and cut out the white central rib. You will still have a whole leaf but with the hard white rib cut out. Take a piece of cabbage, lay it flat, spoon about 2 tablespoons of the pork stuffing on top, and fold the edge over once. Fold the sides in and roll up like an egg roll. Secure the cabbage rolls with a toothpick. You should have 12 to 14 roll-ups.

4. Place the rolled-up cabbage leaves in a large pot and pour in the chicken broth and the 2 cups reserved cabbage water. Bring to below a gentle boil over medium heat, about 15 minutes, then reduce the heat to low and simmer, covered, until the rolls are soft and the meat cooked through, 40 minutes. Season the soup with the fish sauce, sugar, and salt. Garnish with the remaining sliced scallions and serve.

clear soups

wonton soup

WONTON SOUP IS A CLASSIC of Chinese restaurants, but it is also a classic of Chinese cuisine, period. You may never have considered making your own wonton soup, given how easy it is to order at Chinese restaurants, but don't pass this by, as it's rewarding. *Wonton* means "swallowing a cloud," which should give you an idea about what the wontons should resemble in look and taste. The wonton wrappers are easily found in supermarkets, usually refrigerated with other Asian products like tofu. Although you can use store-bought broth, I highly recommend your own homemade chicken broth for this wonderful soup. The actual manipulation of the wonton wrapper into its shape may seem difficult, but it isn't really; it just sounds difficult. You can use the method described below or twist the stuffed wonton to seal so that it looks like a drawstring purse. Restaurants often use larger wontons but with the same amount of stuffing as here. **[Makes 4 to 6 servings]**

the best soups in the world

FOR THE FILLING AND WONTONS

½ pound boneless pork tenderloin, chopped very finely

1 tablespoon soy sauce

1 tablespoon oyster sauce

1 teaspoon sherry

¼ teaspoon sesame oil

½ teaspoon sugar

1 scallion, trimmed and finely chopped

1 teaspoon cornstarch

¼ teaspoon salt

⅛ teaspoon freshly ground white pepper

40 wonton wrappers (about 3½ inches square)

FOR THE BROTH

7 cups Chicken Broth for Asian Soups (page 15)

1 scallion, trimmed and thinly sliced

¼ teaspoon sesame oil

1. In a bowl, mix the pork, soy sauce, oyster sauce, sherry, sesame oil, sugar, scallion, cornstarch, salt, and white pepper together until well blended.

2. Stuff the wontons by laying a wrapper in front of you. Keep the other wontons covered with a damp kitchen towel so they don't dry out and become brittle. Moisten all the edges of the wonton wrapper with water using your finger. Place a heaping teaspoon of wonton filling in the center of the wonton and fold the wrapper in half lengthwise, making sure the ends meet evenly. Press down firmly on the ends to seal. Push down the edges of the filling with your thumbs to keep it in the center. Holding the wonton with your thumbs while it's still on the work surface, fold the wonton wrapper over one more time to make it a narrow tube. Pull the ends up and hold in place between your thumb and index finger. Bring the two ends together so that they overlap, then press to seal the corners using wet fingers. The finished product should resemble a nurse's cap. Repeat with the remaining wontons.

3. Bring water to a boil in a 10-quart pot over high heat, then boil the wontons, making sure they are not crowded in the pot, until they rise to the top and the filling is cooked through, 6 to 7 minutes. Remove from the pot with a slotted spoon.

4. In a large pot, bring the chicken broth to a boil over high heat. Add the wontons and bring the soup back to a boil. Add the scallion, then remove from the heat and add the sesame oil, stirring. Ladle into soup bowls and serve.

sichuan clear beef soup

EVEN THOUGH THIS SOUP is so simple, it is quite pleasing to eat and has wonderful tastes that are not obvious because the soup is clear. It is important that you use home-made beef broth—or if that's not possible, then sodium-free commercial beef broth—for this soup, which cooks for so long. The Sichuan peppercorns can be ordered from www.adrianascaravan.com, or you can replace them with crushed pink peppercorns.

[**Makes 4 servings**]

One ¾-pound piece beef brisket
8 cups Beef Broth for Asian Soups (page 11)
2 scallions, trimmed and cut into 4 pieces
One 2-inch piece fresh ginger, peeled and cut into 4 slices
1 tablespoon rice cooking wine
½ teaspoon salt
½ teaspoon Sichuan peppercorns

1. Place the beef brisket in a pot of boiling water and boil until there is a lot of foam, about 10 minutes. Skim off the foam. Remove the beef and cut into ½-inch cubes.

2. In another pot, bring the beef broth to a boil over high heat, then add the cubed beef brisket, scallion, ginger, rice cooking wine, salt, and Sichuan peppercorns. Reduce the heat to medium and cook, covered, until very tender, about 3½ hours. There should be about 5 cups of broth. Strain the soup through a cheesecloth-lined strainer into a clean soup pot. Remove all the pieces of meat and transfer them to the soup pot with the broth. Discard all other material in the strainer. Heat the broth for a few minutes, then serve hot.

the best soups in the world

duck soup # 1

CHINESE-STYLE DUCK SOUPS are always made with leftover roast duck. There are many different duck soups, but this one and the one on page 122 are two of my favorites. Actually, I love duck soup so much that I often make it from scratch, meaning I'll roast a duck simply to have the duck carcass for these recipes. The roast duck meat I use for making sandwiches, tossing with pasta, or laying on top of risotto. The dried shrimp is sold near Mexican condiments in the international aisle of most supermarkets. I call for spring onions, which are young onions pushing out of the ground in the spring; they are not scallions, an entirely different species in the same family. If you can't find spring onions, use onions or scallions.

[**Makes 4 servings**]

FOR THE BROTH

1 roasted duck carcass and neck (see boxed copy, page 38)
4 spring onions or 6 scallions, trimmed and cut into 2-inch lengths
1 celery top
6 sprigs cilantro (fresh coriander)
1 lemongrass stalk, outer leaves trimmed and split lengthwise
One 1-inch piece fresh ginger, peeled and split in half
10 black peppercorns
12 cups water

FOR THE SOUP

1 pound bok choy, cut into 2-inch segments
2 tablespoons rice wine vinegar
1 tablespoon dried shrimp
Salt and freshly ground black pepper to taste

1. Place the broth ingredients in a stockpot and bring to a boil over high heat. Reduce the heat to low, skim the surface of foam, and simmer for 2 hours. Turn the heat off and strain. Strain again through a cheesecloth-lined strainer into a large saucepan.

2. Bring the duck broth to a boil over high heat. Reduce the heat to medium-high, add the bok choy, rice wine vinegar, and dried shrimp, and boil for 15 minutes. Check the seasoning and add salt and pepper, then serve hot.

ROAST DUCK

It might seem crazy to roast a duck simply to have a roasted carcass to make Chinese-style duck soup, but hey, duck is great, and now you don't have to look up a recipe.

One 5-pound duck, fatty parts in cavity removed

1. Preheat the oven to 350°F.

2. Wipe the duck inside and out with a damp cloth or several folds of paper towel. Place the duck, breast-side up, on a rack in a roasting pan filled with a couple inches of water. Roast until tender and golden brown. Add more water to the drip roasting pan as it evaporates. Check by moving a leg up and down; if it moves easily in its joint, it's done. A 5-pound duck should take about 2½ hours.

3. Let the duck cool and drain. Bone and cut the bird into 2-inch sections. The meat can be served hot or room temperature, and the carcass saved for Duck Soup #1.

the best soups in the world

miso soup

ALTHOUGH MISO SOUP IS NOTHING BUT A BASIC BROTH—a fermented soybean paste soup—nearly every ingredient for this soup must be bought from a Japanese or Korean market. Do give your local supermarket a try first, though: in our ever more diverse culture, the foods it carries are changing rapidly. If you have no luck, the place to head is www.asianfoodgrocer.com, a terrific source for all Asian foods. Of course, it's also fun to go to a Japanese market, and unlike years ago when ethnic markets only served their own immigrant populations, today they serve everyone and foods are usually labeled in English. This miso soup starts with a basic stock called *ichiban dashi,* which is water flavored with dried kelp and dried bonito. Once you've made that, the miso goes in and you've got your soup.

[**Makes 4 servings**]

2 quarts water

3-inch square dried kelp (*kombu*)

1 cup dried bonito flakes (*katsuobushi*)

½ cup miso (fermented soybean paste)

6 ounces silken tofu, cut into ¼-inch dice

1 scallion, trimmed and cut into thin slices

1. In a pot, bring the water to a boil over high heat. Add the dried kelp and let the water come to a boil again. Remove the kelp with a slotted spoon and discard. Stir in the dried bonito flakes and turn the heat off. Let the water steep until the dried bonito flakes drop to the bottom of the pot. Skim the surface with a slotted spoon or skimmer.

2. Pour the soup through a fine wire mesh sieve covered with a kitchen towel or double thickness of cheesecloth set over another pot. You should have about 6 cups of liquid. Discard the cheesecloth with the dried bonito.

3. Set aside ½ cup of the liquid. Place a sieve over the pot and rub the miso through the sieve with the back of a wooden spoon, moistening with some of the stock you've set aside to help it go through the sieve. Bring the stock to a near boil over medium heat. Add the tofu and cook for 1 minute. Pour the soup into individual soup bowls, add the scallion, and serve hot.

chunky meat soups

This chapter has meat soups—beef, buffalo, lamb, pork, chicken, and so forth—with or without the addition of vegetables and/or dairy. The Chunky Vegetable Soups chapter on page 87 has vegetable soups, with or without the addition of meat and/or dairy.

blackfoot bison
and blackberry soup

THE BLACKFOOT NATION is a confederation of three distinct Native American tribes—the Pikuni, the Kainai, and the Siksika. The Blackfoot were nomadic; they ranged from the northwest portion of the Great Plains, from the northern part of the Saskatchewan River of western Saskatchewan and southern Alberta in Canada to the Yellowstone River in central Montana, an area that includes the headwaters of the Missouri River. They followed the herds of buffalo, which was their primary food. They roasted buffalo, made it into pemmican (jerky), and boiled it in rawhide pouches filled with very hot stones. The spicebush berries (*Lindera benzoin*) called for in this recipe cannot be found in supermarkets, but they can be collected in the wild, even in Prospect Park in Brooklyn, where "Wildman" Steve Brill, author of *The Wild Vegetarian Cookbook,* finds them. (For the would-be foragers out there, you can identify them by looking at www.wildmanstevebrill.com/Plants.Folder/Spicebush.html.) Rendered buffalo suet can sometimes be found at farmers markets. Suet is simply the hard fat around the kidneys that is used to make tallow. You can use beef fat, sliced from any cut, in its place. I've called for salt and pepper, but that is not traditional among the Blackfoot, who did not know black peppercorns. I've adapted this soup from Patricia Solley's *An Exaltation of Soups: The Soul-Satisfying Story of Soup, As Told in More Than 100 Recipes* and made it a little more manageable. A curiosity, it is nonetheless very good, but is not a soup you are likely to serve to a big dinner party. **[Makes 4 small servings]**

1½ tablespoons rendered buffalo suet or beef fat or bacon fat,
    cut into bite-size cubes if solid

1 pound buffalo or beef top round, cut into 1-inch cubes

2 cups buffalo or beef broth

½ cup sliced spring onions or scallions

2½ cups (about ¾ pound) fresh blackberries or
    one 12-ounce bag frozen blackberries

¼ teaspoon crushed spicebush berries or juniper berries

1 tablespoon honey or maple syrup

Salt and freshly ground black pepper to taste

4 teaspoons very finely chopped onions

1. In a large pot, melt the fat over medium-high heat, then cook the meat, stirring, until browned on all sides, about 5 minutes. Pour in the broth, ⅓ cup of the onions, 2 cups of the blackberries, and the spicebush or juniper berries. Bring to a boil over high heat, then reduce the heat to low and simmer until the meat is tender, about 45 minutes.

2. Season the soup with the honey, salt, and pepper. Ladle into bowls and garnish with the remaining berries and chopped onions.

chunky meat soups

shchi

BEFORE PETER THE GREAT (1672–1725) popularized French cuisine, there was no word in the Russian language for soup. Although there were many soups, each was known by its own name; there was no general category called "soups." One of these old soups was *shchi* or *schi,* a famous soup of Russia not well-known outside of the motherland. In the winter it is made with sauerkraut and in the summer with fresh cabbage, although it can have both at any time of year. *Shchi* is basically a dense sour soup of meat, fish, or mushroom broth with different smoked meats, sausages, pickles, and vegetables. The quantity of ingredients will determine the density of the soup. Cabbage, greens, sauerkraut, and other vegetables can all go into a *shchi.* Its sourness or piquancy is created by the amount of pickles, sauerkraut, vinegar, sour cream, tomatoes, or *kvas* (a sour but refreshing drink made from fermented wheat or rye) used, and most cooks believe the soup needs to sit for up to two days before serving to achieve that unique taste. *Shchi* is usually cooked in the oven, or at least on very low heat.

The history of *shchi* may reach back to the tenth century in pre-Christian times, about the time that cabbage was being introduced. *Shchi* is the title of a moralistic tale by the great Russian novelist Ivan Turgenev that inspects, with heartbreaking and ironic poignancy, the utter separation between master and serf in nineteenth-century Russia. There are many Russian proverbs that invoke *shchi,* such as "boil *shchi* to have guests in the house," "people don't go away from good *shchi*," and "a good wife is not the one who speaks well, but who cooks *shchi* well." When Russians call someone "a professor of sour *shchi*," they mean he's a fraud. As with borshch, *shchi* transcends class: it was eaten with meat by the czars, and by the serfs with cabbage and onion; it was the favorite soup made by that famous Communist klutz in the kitchen, Lenin, and in the Orthodox monasteries it was the principal meal. *Shchi* is served with sour cream and fresh bread. **[Makes 8 servings]**

the best soups in the world

2 pounds beef ribs

2 ounces beef suet (preferably) or unsalted butter (½ stick)

1 large carrot, peeled and chopped

1 green cabbage (about 2 pounds), cored and shredded

5 teaspoons salt and more as desired

¾ pound boiling potatoes, peeled and cubed small

1 onion, chopped

1 small turnip, peeled and chopped

¾ pound tomatoes, cut in half, seeds squeezed out, and grated against the
largest holes of a standing grater down to the peel

½ pound sauerkraut

1 small fresh parsley root or celery root (celeriac), peeled and chopped

Freshly ground black pepper to taste

¼ cup finely chopped fresh parsley

2 bay leaves

1 cup sour cream for garnish

1. Place the beef in a large pot and cover with 2 quarts water. Bring to a boil over high heat, then reduce the heat to low and simmer, skimming the surface of foam as it appears, until the beef is tender and almost falling off the bone, about 2½ hours. Add water as needed to keep the amount at 2 quarts.

2. Meanwhile, in a flame-proof casserole, melt half the beef suet over medium-high heat, then add the carrot, cabbage, and 3 teaspoons salt and cook, stirring, until the cabbage is wilted, about 10 minutes. Once the ribs have been cooking for 2½ hours, add the cabbage to the pot. Bring to a boil over high heat again, then add the potatoes, reduce the heat to low, and cook, stirring occasionally, until almost tender, about 45 minutes.

3. Meanwhile, in the same casserole, melt the remaining half of the beef suet over medium-high heat, then add the onion, turnip, tomatoes, sauerkraut, and parsley root and cook, stirring, until it looks soft, about 10 minutes.

4. Transfer the contents of the casserole to the soup pot, bring to a boil over medium-high heat, then reduce to medium-low heat and cook until everything is tender, about 30 minutes. Season with the remaining salt, pepper, parsley, and bay leaves and cook for 5 minutes. Serve the soup hot and garnish each bowl with a big dollop of sour cream.

EVERYTHING YOU WANT
TO KNOW ABOUT BORSHCH

As far as its exact origin, the consensus leans toward the Ukraine. But it is a soup proudly claimed by Russians, Belorussians, Poles, Latvians, Lithuanians, and Eastern European Jews. It is eaten in all the countries that border these regions and is found as far afield as Anatolia, where it is called *borç*. There are a great many recipes and no one true recipe. Some people claim that Ukrainians don't use beets; others add everything from catsup to beans. Generally, in the Ukraine, borshch contains many different ingredients—as many as twenty—and the combinations and proportions vary according to region, season, and family tradition. In the end, however, beet roots predominate.

Borscht, spelled with a "t," became popular in New York by way of immigrating Eastern European Jews, who, as they settled into their new lives in America and had families, began to vacation at huge summer resorts in the Catskill Mountains of upstate New York, entertained by comedians who called the whole area the Borscht Belt. Olga Timohina, the food editor of russianfoods.com, points out that in the Ukraine and Russia, borshch is in a class by itself. In Russia, nobody calls it soup; they call it borshch. Most commentaries suggest that borshch, one of the most popular dishes in Russia, appeared toward the end of the eighteenth century. The word "borshch" is said to derive from the word for hogweed (*Heracleum sphondylium*), a lacto-fermented wild vegetable; it is thought that originally the soup was made with hogweed, which became old-fashioned as beets became more popular in the eighteenth century.

The soup with beets took the name *barszcz,* which had earlier been attributed to hogweed. One Polish historian, R. Ładowski, wrote in 1783 that "the vulgar people use hogweed to make a soup called *Barszcz.*" Although it contains meat, smoked sausages, vegetables, mushrooms, and other ingredients—including cabbage, onions, carrots, potatoes, tomatoes, spinach, and sorrel—it is one of its minor ingredients (in relative volume), the red beetroot, that gives the soup its famous blood-red color. (A white borshch without beets is still made in Poland.) It was also a soup that transcended class to become a true national dish. The rich would have theirs with meats, and the poor would have theirs with vegetables. It acquired a sour taste because of the use of vinegar or *kvas.* In earlier times the soup was eaten with pancakes or different porridges.

borshch

BORSHCH (BORSCHT) IS A FAMOUS SOUP throughout Eastern Europe, particularly in the Ukraine, Russia, Poland, and among the Jews of those lands. The tart flavor of a borshch usually comes from the beets, prepared for fermentation several days in advance of the soupmaking. (Some cooks take a short cut and use pickle brine, vinegar, rhubarb juice, lemon juice, or beet *kvas,* a fermented beet juice that can be store-bought in many Slavic countries.) The blood-red color comes from the beet roots. Some recipes call for pork instead of beef; others make an entirely vegetable version. In the end, this recipe just tastes great.

[Makes 8 servings]

1 pound beef shank or ribs

1 pound pork spareribs

½ pound beef marrow bone

1 pound beef soup bones (such as neck)

2½ quarts water

2 medium onions, chopped

2 carrots, 1 cut up, 1 grated

½ small celery root (celeriac), peeled and diced

2 tablespoons unsalted butter

3 large red beetroots, peeled and grated

2 tomatoes, peeled and chopped

3 tablespoons white wine vinegar

6 large garlic cloves, 1 chopped and 5 mashed in a mortar

½ pound smoked Polish kielbasa, diced

½ pound green cabbage, shredded

4 small boiling potatoes (such as Yukon Gold), peeled and cut into french fries

1 tablespoon salt or more to taste

1 teaspoon freshly ground black pepper or more to taste

¼ cup finely chopped fresh parsley

¼ cup chopped fresh dill

3 scallions, trimmed and finely chopped

½ cup sour cream

1. Place the beef, pork, marrow bone, and soup bones in a large pot and cover with the water. Bring to a boil over high heat, skimming the surface of foam as it appears, then reduce the heat to low. Add 1 onion, 1 cut-up carrot, and the celery root and continue to simmer over low heat until the meat is not quite falling off the bones,

2 hours. Remove the beef and pork from the soup, cut off all the meat from the bones, return the meat to the soup, and discard the bones. Remove the marrow from the marrow bones and return the marrow to the soup.

2. Meanwhile, in a pot, melt 1 tablespoon butter over medium heat, then add the grated beetroot, a ladleful of the beef broth, and the tomatoes. Reduce the heat to low and simmer, partially covered and stirring occasionally, for 1 hour, adding another 1 or 2 cups of broth to keep it from drying out. Add the vinegar and stir.

3. Meanwhile, in a skillet, melt the remaining tablespoon of butter over medium heat, then cook the remaining onion, the carrot, and 1 chopped garlic clove, covered, and stirring occasionally, until softened, about 10 minutes.

4. Bring the beef broth to a boil over medium-high heat. Add the kielbasa, cabbage, and potatoes and cook for 5 minutes. Add the onion, carrot, and garlic from the skillet and cook for another 10 minutes. Add the beetroots and cook another 5 minutes. Season with salt and pepper. Stir in the mashed garlic and heat for a couple of minutes, then serve with the parsley, dill, scallions, and a dollop of sour cream as garnish.

PEELING TOMATOES

There are two methods for peeling tomatoes; the one you should use depends on how the tomatoes will be used. If they are to be whole or coarsely chopped, then plunge them into boiling water for one to two minutes, then remove them. Slit the peel with a paring knife, and it will pinch right off. If the recipe calls for finely chopped tomatoes or the tomatoes are meant to become saucy anyway, there is an easier method: cut each tomato in half, squeeze the seeds out, and grate the flesh against the largest holes of a box grater down to the peel.

georgian beef and apricot soup

THIS GEORGIAN SOUP from the Trans-Caucasian area of the former Soviet Union is called *yaini*. It's a soup known by the neighboring Armenians as well. The soup's broth is an integral part of the final dish, so you can't use a commercial broth. The flavors are wonderful, and the dried apricot provides that slight touch of sweetness that you can't quite put your finger on. Everyone loves this soup. **[Makes 4 servings]**

1 pound beef chuck or brisket, in one piece

2 medium onions, quartered and ½ small onion, finely chopped

2 carrots, cut up

10 sprigs fresh parsley

10 sprigs cilantro (fresh coriander), plus 2 tablespoons finely chopped cilantro for garnish

10 sprigs fresh dill

2½ teaspoons salt and more to taste

¼ pound (1 stick) unsalted butter

1 medium tomato, peeled (page 48), seeded, and coarsely chopped

1 pound boiling potatoes (such as Yukon Gold), peeled and cut into 1-inch cubes

2 ounces dried apricots, quartered

Pinch of freshly ground black pepper

1. Bring a large pot with 2 quarts of water to a boil over high heat and add the beef, quartered onions, carrots, parsley, cilantro, and dill. Skim the surface of foam as it appears and after it has reached a boil, reduce the heat to low and simmer, partially covered, for 1 hour. Remove the beef, cut it into a dice, and return it to the pot. Simmer, partially covered, until tender, about 4 hours.

2. Remove the diced beef and set aside. Strain the broth. You should have 4 cups of broth. If you don't, add water until you do. Season the broth with salt and set it aside.

3. In a heavy, flame-proof casserole, melt the butter over high heat. Add the chopped onion and cook, stirring frequently, until softened, 4 to 5 minutes. Stir in the tomato and cook, stirring, until its liquid has evaporated, about 3 minutes. Pour in the reserved broth, then add the reserved diced beef and the potatoes and apricots. Season with black pepper and more salt, if desired, and bring to a boil over high heat. Reduce the heat to medium, cover, and cook, without stirring, until the potatoes are tender but not falling apart, about 20 minutes. Correct the seasoning if necessary. Serve hot with the chopped cilantro sprinkled on top of each serving.

avgolemono meatball soup

THE TRADITIONAL GREEK EMULSION of eggs and lemon is known as avgolemono, and it is used not only in this soup but with fish soup and even stuffed grape leaves. It has a light, refreshing taste and yet is deeply satisfying. This soup is called *youvarlakia avgolemono* in Greek. The mixture of eggs and lemon, thought of as so typically Greek, is also known in Turkey and is probably a result of French culinary influence within the past hundred years. The only tricky part—and it's not *that* tricky—is making sure that the egg doesn't solidify from the heat, so always blend while whisking or stirring. You can use lamb in place of beef for the meatballs and mint instead of dill and olive oil instead of butter—they'll all taste great. You can also make the soup with chicken breast. **[Makes 6 servings]**

1 pound ground beef

1 small onion, finely chopped

¼ cup short grain rice

3 tablespoons finely chopped fresh parsley

2 tablespoons finely chopped fresh dill

2 tablespoons extra-virgin olive oil

Pinch of ground cinnamon

1 teaspoon salt

½ teaspoon freshly ground black pepper

All-purpose flour for dredging

5 cups beef broth

¼ cup unsalted butter

2 large eggs

¼ cup freshly squeezed lemon juice

1. In a bowl, mix together the ground beef, onion, rice, parsley, dill, olive oil, cinnamon, salt, and pepper. Knead the mixture for a minute, with wet hands to prevent sticking, until well blended. Then form into meatballs about an inch in diameter. As you finish making the meatballs, roll them in a platter filled with some flour until coated on all sides and set aside in the refrigerator until needed, unless you are cooking right away.

2. In a pot, bring the broth and butter to a boil over high heat, add the meatballs a few at a time (so the broth stays at the boil), then reduce the heat to low, cover, and simmer until the meatballs are cooked through and the rice is tender, about 30 minutes.

3. Meanwhile, in a small bowl, beat the eggs, then whisk in the lemon juice a little at a time, beating constantly. Add a ladleful of hot broth to the lemon and egg mixture, beating all the time. Now add the lemon and egg mixture to the meatball soup, stirring the whole time, and as soon as it's added remove from the heat and serve.

THE OGBONO SOUP OF NIGERIA

This strangely black and mucilaginous soup is popular in Nigeria and a favorite among the Ibos in the east, who deem it incomplete without the addition of stockfish (usually air-dried cod). *Ogbono* soup, also spelled *agbono* or *apon* (and pronounced o-bo-no), is so-called for its use of ground *ogbono* seed as a thickener. *Ogbono* are the whole or crushed kernels or nuts of a plant called the bush mango or wild mango tree (*Irvingia gabonensis* or *Irvingia wombolu*), which is unrelated to the mango fruit and native to the tropical Atlantic coast region of Africa. In Cameroon and Gabon, *ogbono* goes by the names *etima, odika,* or *dika*. *Ogbono* may be the most powerful of all African soup thickeners; it is best to add it to the soup in small amounts, stirring to avoid creating lumps, until the desired consistency is obtained. Outside of Africa, *ogbono* is available in West African markets in packages, or through Internet sources such as www.asiamex.com. Another important addition to this soup are the fermented locust bean (*Parkia biglobosa*) paste balls called *iru* in Yoruba and *ogili-igala* in Ibo, but better known in other parts of West Africa as *dawadawa* or *soumbala* in Mali and Burkina Faso.

The soup is made with goat, beef shank, onion, smoked fish, stockfish, red palm oil, and an inhuman amount of chile, as well as the ingredients mentioned above. If you are interested in a recipe you can write the author through www.cliffordawright.com. Because of how piquant the soup is, it is usually served with the appropriately bland cassava *fufu* (page 148), a sticky paste made from pounded fermented cassava mixed with water.

spicy beef soup from indonesia

KNOWN AS *RAWON*, this is a simple, highly flavored soup whose spice paste is traditionally made with a fruit unavailable to North Americans called *kluwek* (*Pangium edule* Reinw). It is the fruit of the kepayang tree. *Kluwek,* sometimes called black nut or football fruit, is a rare, seasonal, and expensive fruit-nut and the ingredient that gives the soup its black color; in fact, the soup is sometimes translated into English as "black soup." I've used walnuts in its place. *Soto rawon* is popular enough that one can find commercial soup mix packets of *rawon* in Indonesian markets in cities such as Los Angeles. Bean sprouts are a typical garnish for the soup, but I prefer clover sprouts because the sprout is thinner and the texture more pleasant. You can find them in your supermarket.   [**Makes 4 servings**]

the best soups in the world

FOR THE SPICE PASTE

4 small shallots, very finely chopped

2 large garlic cloves, very finely chopped

4 macadamia nuts or cashews, finely crushed

4 walnuts, shelled and crushed

2 fresh red finger-type chiles

FOR THE SOUP

2 tablespoons vegetable oil

2 bay leaves, preferably fresh

1 teaspoon grated lime zest or 4 kaffir lime leaves

¾-inch cube fresh ginger or galangal, lightly crushed

1 lemongrass stalk, outer leaf removed and crushed (bruised)

2 teaspoons salt or more if desired

Freshly ground black pepper to taste

¾ pound beef brisket, cut into ¾-inch cubes

8 cups water

¼ pound clover sprouts, broccoli sprouts, or bean sprouts for garnish

Fresh basil leaves for garnish

1. Place the spice paste ingredients in a food processor and run until a paste is formed, scraping down the sides when necessary. (You may have to do this multiple times.) Transfer the spice paste to a smaller mini–food processor and continue processing into a finer paste, or alternatively, transfer to a mortar and pound with a pestle. If you don't have either a mini-processor or mortar, continue even longer in the food processor while scraping down more often.

2. In a wok, heat the oil over high heat, then add the spice paste and cook, stirring quickly, until sizzling vigorously, about 2 minutes. Add the bay leaves, lime zest, ginger, lemongrass, salt, and pepper and cook, stirring quickly, for 1 minute. Add the beef cubes and cook, stirring, until they turn color, about 1 minute.

3. Meanwhile, in a large pot, bring 6 cups water to a boil over high heat, then add the stir-fried ingredients, reduce the heat to low, and cook until the meat is tender and the flavor of the spices have permeated the soup, about 3 hours. At some point during the cooking time, add the remaining 2 cups water. Serve garnished with the sprouts and basil.

chunky meat soups

żurek

ŻUREK (**PRONOUNCED JHOO-REK**), or *żur* for short, is a sour Polish soup flavored with bacon and fermented rye juice called *kwas,* which gives the sour taste. The Russians also use *kvas* in their cooking. A modest version of the soup is made around Lent, but after fasting is done it becomes the rich soup represented in this recipe. The soup is made differently from region to region in Poland, but all recipes start with making fermented rye flour about five days in advance, as I ask you to do in this recipe. But it's worth it. Sometimes, especially in restaurants, the soup will be served in an individual rye bread round that has been hollowed out, and you can eat the bread as well. The Polish smoked bacon called for is known as *szalona* and can be bought in Polish delis or on-line at www.polisheats.com or www.janeksfinefoods.com.   **[Makes 6 servings]**

the best soups in the world

FOR THE *KWAS* (FERMENTED RYE JUICE)

3 ounces (½ cup) wholemeal rye flour
2½ cups boiling water
¼ garlic clove, chopped

FOR THE SOUP

6 cups vegetable broth
¼ pound Polish *szalona* smoked bacon (preferably) or slab bacon, diced
1 cup finely chopped onion
4 ounces button (white) mushrooms, sliced
1¼ cups sour cream
1 large garlic clove, finely chopped
4 teaspoons salt or more to taste
1 teaspoon freshly ground black pepper
1 pound boiling potatoes, peeled and diced
¼ pound smoked kielbasa, diced
1 tablespoon prepared horseradish (optional)

1. To make the *kwas*: Several days before you plan to make the soup, place a large glass jar and its lid in a large pot, cover with water, bring to a boil over high heat, and boil for 5 minutes to sterilize the jar. Remove the jar and lid from the pot using tongs; do not touch with your hands. Add the rye flour to the jar and mix with a little of the boiling water to form a paste. Let sit for 5 minutes, then add the remaining water and the garlic. Cover the top with a section of muslin or several

folds of cheesecloth and use a rubber band or string to secure it around the mouth of the jar. Let sit in a warm place to ferment for 4 to 5 days. Strain and store in an airtight container for up to 2 weeks.

2. To make the soup: In a large pot, bring the broth to a boil over high heat, then add the bacon and onion, reduce the heat to low, and simmer for 10 minutes. Add the mushrooms, 1¾ cups of the reserved fermented rye juice, the sour cream, and the garlic. Add the salt and pepper and simmer for 20 minutes. Add the potatoes and kielbasa, increase the heat to medium so the broth is bubbling gently, and cook until the potatoes are tender, about 45 minutes. Stir in the horseradish, if using, and season with more salt and pepper, if desired. Serve hot.

ABOUT AFRICAN SOUPS

So many African soups utilize plants unavailable to us that it is just not practical to offer a recipe. Furthermore, African soups are more like stews, and they mix everything under the sun, such as beef, fish, seeds, and vegetables. But I offer this *egusi* soup anyway, more as a curiosity than anything else. If you are inclined to experiment and explore a foreign cuisine—and shop via the Internet—this is an instructive recipe. This popular soup of Nigeria, Sierra Leone, and their neighboring West African countries is adapted from a recipe by Dennis Deen-Sie Sawaneh, the author of the *Sierra Leone Cookbook*.

The soup gets its name from the *egusi* seeds that are its essential thickener. *Egusi* seeds are nothing but the seeds of a wild watermelon (*Citrullus lanatus*). They are sometimes mistakenly identified as the seeds of the colocynth (*Citrullus colocynthis*). One can use pumpkin seeds with equal taste authenticity in this recipe, as well as cultivated watermelon seeds.

Another essential ingredient is bitterleaf (*Vernonia amygdalina*), a plant whose young shoots and leaves are eaten as potherbs or in soups after first being washed to remove some bitterness. African cooks also use *ukazi* or *afang* leaves (*Gnetum african*), the shiny, dark green foliage of the creeping plant cultivated mostly in Calabar and Igbo land in southern Nigeria (these plants are used in much of the cooking of the region). Another plant's leaves, *utazi* (*Crongromena*

(continued)

ratifolia), are also used in this soup. Both *ukazi* and *utazi* leaves are bitter tasting pale green leaves used for flavoring Pepper Soup (page 73) and used very sparingly. All are substitutes for or used in addition to bitterleaf.

Every ingredient mentioned above, and in the ingredient list below, can be bought online at www.afrikan-food.com, www.jbafricanmarket.com, or www .asiamex.com, as can the very authentic red palm oil, a must for a true West African soup. It can be eaten with *fufu* (page 148) or rice.   [Makes 6 servings]

1 pound beef round or chuck, cut into ¾-inch cubes

Salt and freshly ground black pepper to taste

½ pound salt cod or dried stockfish, soaked in water to cover for
    24 hours, then drained

½ pound African dried or smoked fish or smoked canned oysters or
    smoked canned mussels

8 cups water or more as needed

1 fresh red finger-type chile

½ pound tomato, peeled and seeded

½ small onion

½ cup red palm oil

6 ounces ground shelled watermelon seeds (*egusi*) or pumpkin seeds

1 beef bouillon cube

½ pound fresh spinach, sorrel, or bitterleaf leaves, finely shredded or
    1 small bag (about 15 grams) dried cut *ukazi* leaves

Salt to taste

1. Toss the beef cubes with some salt and pepper. Place the beef, whole piece of salt cod, and African smoked or dried fish (but not the canned oysters or mussels if using) in a large pot and cover with the water. Bring to a boil over high heat, then cook until slightly tender, about 45 minutes. Remove from the water with a slotted spoon or skimmer and set aside. Remove and discard any bones or skin from the salt cod and African dried fish.

2. Place the chile, tomato, and onion in a blender and blend until smooth.

3. In a flame-proof casserole or large pot, heat the red palm oil over medium-high heat. Add the beef, salt cod, African dried fish, and the vegetables from the blender, reduce the heat to medium-low, and cook until tender and bubbling, about 25 minutes. Add the ground watermelon or pumpkin seeds, the beef bouillon cube, and the canned oysters or mussels if you have not used African dried fish, and cook for another 10 minutes. Add the fresh spinach or dried bitterleaf to the soup and cook for about 5 minutes if using spinach and 1 hour if using dried bitterleaf. Add some water if necessary to make it more liquid. Stir and taste for salt.

tofu, spinach, and ham soup

ALTHOUGH IT DOESN'T SEEM to be substantial, this soup from Shanghai can leave you quite satisfied. In place of the Chinese ham, I find Smithfield ham to be excellent, or use any similar cooked ham. The combination of the dried wood ear mushrooms and the fresh mushrooms is particularly pleasant. The dried wood ear mushrooms are not as hard to find as you would think; just look in your supermarket. **[Makes 4 servings]**

¼ ounce (10 grams) dried wood ear mushrooms
2 tablespoons cornstarch
4 cups Chicken Broth for Asian Soups (page 15)
2 ounces button (white) mushrooms, cut in half and thinly sliced
½ pound firm tofu, cut into ½-inch cubes
1 chicken bouillon cube, crushed in a mortar
½ teaspoon freshly ground black pepper
2 ounces cooked ham (such as Smithfield), shredded or finely and thinly sliced
6 ounces baby spinach leaves or regular spinach leaves, cut very coarsely
1 tablespoon soy sauce
1 teaspoon sesame oil

1. Soak the dried mushrooms in hot water to cover (about ¾ cup) until completely soft, 20 to 40 minutes. Drain and reserve the liquid in a small bowl and stir the cornstarch into the mushroom liquid.

2. In a pot, bring the chicken broth to a boil over high heat. Add the button and wood ear mushrooms, tofu, bouillon cube, and pepper. After a minute, when the broth returns to a boil, add the ham, spinach, soy sauce, and mushroom liquid mixture. Reduce the heat to low and simmer for 5 minutes. Drizzle in the sesame oil and serve.

lamb trotter soup

IN THE EARLY 1970s I was living in Switzerland, and on spring break friends and I drove to Istanbul and then to Athens. As we drove through Thessalonica early one morning, I learned how cold April can be in the Mediterranean. Many years later I rediscovered the lamb soup we ate then and loved so much. My now vague memory of the soup was jump-started by a recipe given to me by Nikos Stavroulakis, whose *Cookbook of the Jews of Greece* is a classic of culinary anthropology. This recipe from the Jews of Salonika (Thessalonica) was made in the winter for stevedores. It is a purely proletarian dish served as an early morning meal by special shops in the harbor, where steaming cauldrons of *patsas* that had been cooking all night would fortify the workers before their long day. The *patsas* can be served for breakfast. This soup is perfect if you've roasted a leg of lamb the day before and have leftover meat still on the bone. **[Makes 4 to 6 servings]**

the best soups in the world

5 pounds lamb bones, with some meat on them (preferably
    leftover roast leg bone)

3 quarts water

4 garlic cloves, thinly sliced

3 tablespoons extra-virgin olive oil

Juice from 2 lemons, plus extra for serving

Salt and freshly ground black pepper to taste

Finely chopped fresh parsley leaves or dill

Sliced or chopped garlic for garnish (optional)

1. Put the lamb bones in a large pot and cover with the water. Bring to a boil over high heat and once it is boiling furiously, remove the foam from the surface with a skimmer. Keep the water at a boil and add the thinly sliced garlic, olive oil, lemon juice, salt, and pepper.

2. Reduce the heat to very low, using a heat diffuser if your stove's burner does not have a very low simmer control. Cover and place a heavy cleaver, pot, or some other heavy object on the lid to keep it tightly covered. Simmer overnight, about 12 hours.

3. Serve the soup in individual bowls with parsley or dill, more lemon juice, and sliced or chopped garlic, if desired.

spicy lamb trotter soup

THERE IS A SOUP CALLED *HARQMA* (sometimes transliterated as *hergma)* that is known and loved throughout the Maghrib, from Morocco to Tunisia. The name *harqma* actually refers to different dishes in different regions: a lamb tagine with wheat and chickpeas; a soup of butcher's scraps; a ragoût of tripe, feet, and heart; and also this rich and hot soup from Tunisia. It is typically eaten during Ramadan, when soul-satisfying foods for breaking the fast after sunset are the norm. My recipe is based on the way I've had it in Tunis, adjusted a little. The recipe calls for lamb feet, which is what gives it such a magnificent flavor. You don't have to eat them, of course—they're for flavor, although I do pick at them, looking for scrumptious morsels. They can be ordered through a good butcher, but the best place to buy them are halal meat markets, which can now be found everywhere. **[Makes 6 servings]**

¼ cup extra-virgin olive oil

2 pounds lamb feet

2 pounds lamb shanks

Salt and freshly ground black pepper to taste

2 tablespoons *harīsa* (page 62)

2 quarts water

2 large eggs

2 tablespoons freshly squeezed lemon juice

1. In a large stockpot or casserole, heat the olive oil over medium-high heat. Season the lamb feet and shanks with salt and pepper. Add the feet and shanks to the pan and brown on all sides, 4 to 5 minutes. Stir in the *harīsa*; once it has melted and blended with the oil, add the water. Bring to a boil, reduce the heat to low, cover, and cook until tender, about 2½ hours.

2. Strain the soup through a cone-shaped strainer (chinois), or any strainer you have, into a clean stockpot. Pull off and chop any meat from the shank and put it back into the broth. Discard the feet and bones.

3. Break the eggs into a bowl and whisk in the lemon juice. Whisk a ladle of hot soup into the egg mixture. Once it is blended, whisk in another ladle of soup. Now whisk the entire egg mixture back into the soup. Strain again and discard all bits of gristly meat and fat. Return the soup to the stockpot and serve hot.

chunky meat soups

HARĪSA

Harīsa is a chile and spice paste and the most important prepared condiment used in Tunisian and Algerian cooking. Although commercially made versions are available, you should make your own, as it's easy and better. De arbol chiles is the name for the common dried red finger-type chiles you'll find in the supermarket.

[Makes 1 cup]

¼ pound dried guajillo chiles
1 ounce dried de arbol chiles
5 large garlic cloves, peeled
2 tablespoons water
2 tablespoons extra-virgin olive oil
½ teaspoon freshly ground caraway seeds
¼ teaspoon freshly ground coriander seeds
1½ teaspoons salt
Extra-virgin olive oil for topping off

1. Soak the chiles in tepid water to cover until soft, about 1 hour. Drain and remove the stems and seeds. Place in a food processor with the garlic, water, and olive oil. Process until a purée, stopping occasionally to scrape down the sides.

2. Transfer to a mixing bowl and stir in the caraway, coriander, and salt. Store in a jar and top off with olive oil, covering the surface of the paste. The *harīsa* must always be covered with olive oil to prevent spoilage, so whenever you use some always make sure to top it off with a little olive oil. Properly stored in the refrigerator, it will keep for 6 months to a year.

the best soups in the world

turkmen boiled soup

TURKMENISTAN IS A FORMER SOVIET REPUBLIC that became independent with the break-up of the USSR. It is bounded to the south by Iran, to the west by the Caspian Sea, and to the north by Kazakhstan and Uzbekistan. Most Turkmen soups are thick, main course affairs, just a hair soupier than a stew. There are two kinds of soups in Turkmen cuisine: fried soups and boiled soups. This one, called *chektyrma,* is a boiled soup. The recipe is adapted from one by Tanya Zilberter, a researcher at the Mediterranean Institute of Neurobiology (Inmed) at Marseilles, France. **[Makes 4 servings]**

5 cups water

1 pound boneless lamb stew meat, cut into ½-inch cubes

2 medium onions, finely chopped

¾ pound tomatoes, peeled (page 273) and chopped

1 pound spinach, leaves only, washed well and chopped

2½ teaspoons salt

1½ teaspoons hot paprika

Pinch of saffron

3 large garlic cloves, finely chopped

3 tablespoons finely chopped fresh parsley

1 tablespoon finely chopped fresh mint

¼ teaspoon dried mint

1. In a pot, bring the water to a boil over high heat, then add the lamb, reduce the heat to medium and boil gently, partially covered and stirring occasionally, until tender, about 1¼ hours.

2. Add the onions and tomatoes and continue to boil over medium heat, partially covered and stirring occasionally, for 20 more minutes. Add the spinach and cook for 8 minutes. Season with the salt, paprika, and saffron, and remove the pot from the heat. Add the garlic, parsley, and fresh and dried mint, stir to mix well, cover, and let rest for 15 minutes before serving.

chunky meat soups

palóc soup

THIS SOUP, CALLED *PALÓCLEVES* in Hungarian, is named for the people inhabiting the north-central part of Hungary called the Palóc. The Palóc country extends from the Mátra to around the Rima and Sajó valleys, and from the Bükk Hills west to the marshes of the Ipoly, an area immediately south of the Slovak border. The Palóc speak a distinct Hungarian dialect, which is unusual in a country where there are no regional dialects. Some ethnologists think that they came from western Siberia and merged with the Magyar tribes that came to settle Hungary in the dim past. To this day many Palóc in the smaller villages still wear their native costumes, and if you've ever seen a Hungarian tourism brochure depicting gaily dressed "peasants" dancing, the photo is probably of the Palóc. One village, Hollókö, is a UNESCO World Heritage Site. This soup is traditionally made with mutton, but both lamb and beef are used too. This recipe is from János Mohácsi of the Budapest University of Technology and Economics. **[Makes 4 to 6 servings]**

2 tablespoons pork lard (preferably) or unsalted butter

1 small onion, chopped

1 teaspoon hot paprika

1 pound boneless leg of lamb or beef stew meat, cut into small cubes

5 cups water

¼ teaspoon caraway seeds

1 small bay leaf

1 tablespoon salt

½ teaspoon freshly ground black pepper or more to taste

1 pound green beans, trimmed and cut into 1-inch pieces

3 boiling potatoes (about ¾ pound), peeled and diced

2 tablespoons all-purpose flour

2 tablespoons sour cream

1. In a pot, melt 1 tablespoon of the pork lard over medium-high heat, then add the onion and cook, stirring, until translucent, about 4 minutes. Remove the pot from the heat and sprinkle with the paprika.

2. Add the meat, 1 cup of the water, the caraway seeds, bay leaf, 1 teaspoon salt, and pepper to the pot, cover, return to low heat, and braise, stirring occasionally, until almost tender, about 1 hour. Add the green beans and cook for 10 minutes. Add the potatoes, the remaining 2 teaspoons salt, and the remaining 4 cups of water and simmer over medium-low heat, partially covered, until the potatoes are soft, 1 to 1¼ hours.

3. Meanwhile, in a small skillet, melt the remaining 1 tablespoon of lard over medium heat, then add the flour, stirring to form a roux, and cook for 1 minute. Add the sour cream and stir until blended. Turn this roux into the soup and stir to blend well. Serve hot.

chunky meat soups

uzbek meat soup with rice

THIS UZBEK SOUP called *mastava* always starts with frying the meat, followed by the addition of fresh tomatoes in the summer and tomato paste in the winter, so choose accordingly. The soup will be most flavorful if you use mutton, but given that mutton must be ordered and is not regularly sold in supermarkets, lamb will do just fine. (You can even use beef.) When cutting up the meat for the soup, don't remove all the fat from the pieces; keep a little for flavor. As this is a thick and filling soup it need not accompany anything, although a green salad would be nice afterward. *Mastava* is one of the most common soups made in the Uzbek home.

This soup is well-known in Central Asia. In Afghanistan, the people, some of whom are Uzbeks, call it *maushawa,* and they eat it either as a starter or as a main meal. Theirs is made with meat *qorma* (stew meat) or meatballs (*kofta*) and tends to be spicy hot. They use dill as a seasoning herb and beans and chickpeas. In Tajikistan, they make theirs, called *mastoba,* with big pieces of mutton that are fried first with tomatoes and other vegetables. Then water is added, it is cooked for twenty minutes, and rice and the sour-milk product called *katyk* are added. **[Makes 4 servings]**

the best soups in the world

7 tablespoons vegetable or safflower seed oil

1 pound boneless leg of lamb or beef top round, cubed small

1 medium-large yellow onion, chopped

2 carrots, peeled and diced

4 plum tomatoes (about ¾ pound), peeled (page 273) and chopped, or
   one 6-ounce can tomato paste

6 cups lamb broth, beef broth, or water

¾ cup long grain rice

3 potatoes (about ¾ pound), peeled and diced small

2½ teaspoons ground cumin

4 teaspoons salt or more to taste

1 teaspoon freshly ground black pepper or more to taste

2 cups yogurt or sour cream

½ cup chopped cilantro (fresh coriander)

1. In a large flame-proof casserole or pot, heat the oil over medium-high heat, then cook the meat, stirring, until browned on all sides, about 5 minutes. Add the onion and carrots and cook, stirring frequently, until the vegetables are tender, about 10 minutes. Add the tomatoes and stir.

2. Stir in the broth and bring to a boil over medium-high heat. Add the rice and potatoes and cook, stirring occasionally, for 10 minutes, then add the cumin, salt, and pepper and stir well. Continue cooking until the potatoes are tender, about another 5 minutes. Ladle into individual bowls and serve with a dollop of yogurt and the chopped cilantro as garnish.

chunky meat soups

tripe in broth

LECCE IS A CHARMING BAROQUE CITY in the Salento Peninsula of the southern Italian province of Apulia, otherwise known as the heel of the Italian boot. One of the sweetest places to sample typical Leccese cooking outside of the home is at the Trattoria Casareccia, where I first tasted this soup listed on the menu simply as *trippa*; I thought it just amazing. The kind of tripe used was not the common honeycomb tripe, which is the second stomach of a ruminant (a cud-chewing animal), but the flat and smooth first stomach called paunch, the famous *gras-double* of the French, called *rumine* in Italian. It was cooked so long it almost melted in my mouth—a phenomenon not usually associated with eating tripe. The cook had cut the cooked tripe into small pieces and stewed them a bit in a light broth of tomato purée and olive oil with zucchini and celery that had been chopped tiny, softened, and sprinkled with parsley. It was utterly delicious.

You will need to make this soup over three days—but it's worth it if you love tripe. As you need to be around the kitchen to keep replenishing the water while the tripe is cooking it may be most convenient to make this over the weekend. I usually start on a Friday night, boil for about four hours, turn the heat off, then start boiling again the next morning around 6 AM and boil for fourteen hours. I also usually make more than I need so I can keep cooked tripe in the freezer. If you don't like tripe the effort is probably not worth it, but if you do, the reward is great. **[Makes 4 servings]**

2 pounds beef tripe

3 tablespoons extra-virgin olive oil

1 large garlic clove, crushed

Salt to taste

½ cup dry white wine

Water as needed

½ cup tomato purée

¼ cup finely diced zucchini

¼ cup finely diced celery stalk

2 tablespoons finely chopped fresh parsley

1. Two days before you plan to serve, wash the tripe and cut off any fat. Place the tripe in a large stockpot, cover by many inches with cold water, and bring to a boil over high heat. Boil until very tender, about 20 hours of boiling divided over two 10-hour days, replenishing the water whenever it has dropped by half. For its overnight rest, leave the tripe in its boiling water, covered; it will stay warm most of the night, then continue cooking in the morning. Remove the tripe, reserving

2 cups of the cooking water, let the tripe cool, then cut into strips. Let the reserved cooking water cool and once the fat has solidified on top, remove and discard it.

2. In a pot, heat 2 tablespoons of the olive oil with the garlic over medium-high heat, and as the garlic turns light golden, remove and discard. Add the tripe and salt and cook, stirring, for 2 minutes. Add the wine and cook until bubbling, then add 3½ cups water and bring to a boil over high heat. Reduce the heat to low, add the tomato purée, and simmer, stirring occasionally, for 3 hours, adding a little water if necessary.

3. Add the 2 cups of reserved cooking liquid and cook for 1 hour. Add the zucchini and celery, season with salt if necessary, and continue cooking for another hour. Sprinkle on the parsley, drizzle with the remaining 1 tablespoon of olive oil, and serve.

MAGERITSA—THE GREEK EASTER SOUP

Easter Sunday is the most important and meaningful holiday among the Greek Orthodox. On Saturday, Easter eve, the housewife would traditionally take this soup—resurrection soup—to be blessed by the priest. She might begin making the soup in the late afternoon, as many families prefer the late-night services. When they return from church the *mageritsa* (other transliterations exist) can be eaten, breaking the long fast following midnight services on Easter eve. This soup, with its dark colors and aroma, uses all parts of the lamb that have not been grilled.

It is interesting to observe the making of *mageritsa*—the braiding of the intestines, the washing and cutting up of organ meats, and so on. One starts by boiling the lamb's head and feet for the broth. The brain is removed and used in this soup, while other parts are used for other dishes. The remaining lamb stock is seasoned with scallions, parsley, dill, and celery leaves, and then the heart, lungs, and liver, all cut into little bite-size pieces, are simmered, too. After a while, the intestines are braided and cut up, simmered with some rice and aniseed. The brains are returned to the broth and avgolemono is stirred in to finish the soup.

So why do I not provide a recipe for *mageritsa*? Because I am, like you, a home cook who doesn't live in Greece and who doesn't have special suppliers who can bring that lamb head, lung, heart, intestine, and stomach to my kitchen. One could make a *mageritsa* soup without all the "parts," but then there would be nothing special about it; it would simply be lamb broth.

menudo

MENUDO IS A TRIPE SOUP popular in northern Mexico. Although menudo is found elsewhere in Mexico, it is usually associated with the state of Sonora, which borders the United States. Menudo is typically made for New Year's Day and is a traditional cure-all for hangovers. Because tripe is one of the less desirable meats, and because it takes a very long time to cook, menudo has always been associated with poor people as well as with restaurants, because it can be made in very large batches, and their kitchens are going all the time. Menudo is very popular among Mexican-Americans, especially in southern California, New Mexico, and Texas, where it is offered as a breakfast item in restaurants at least once a week. This recipe uses precooked beef honeycomb tripe. Place the tripe in a large stockpot of water and bring to a boil over high heat. Boil until tender, which will take about twenty hours (you can do this in stages over two days). Replenish the water periodically. This parboiled tripe can now be frozen if you like. This recipe is based on my favorite menudo, which I had at Super Cocina restaurant in the City Heights section of San Diego, California. You might think the beef foot is optional, but do try to procure one because there's a heck of a lot of flavor there

.   [**Makes 8 to 10 servings**]

3 large dried ancho chiles

2 pounds precooked beef honeycomb tripe (see the instructions in the
    Tripe in Broth recipe on page 68)

1 beef foot (about 4 pounds), split

1 large onion

4 large garlic cloves, peeled and lightly crushed

¼ teaspoon black peppercorns

4 teaspoons salt or more to taste

4 quarts water

One 29-ounce can Mexican-style hominy

1 teaspoon dried oregano

FOR THE GARNISH

Corn or flour tortillas, warmed

Chopped serrano chiles

Finely chopped onion

Lemon wedges

Mexican hot sauce

1. In a cast-iron skillet without any fat, toast the dried ancho chiles over medium-high heat until blackened and some seeds are spilling out, about 5 minutes. Remove, let cool, and split open. Remove and discard the seeds and stem. Grind the remaining chile sections in a spice grinder or coffee mill until a powder.

2. Place the precooked tripe, beef foot, onion, garlic, peppercorns, salt, and chile powder in a large stockpot and cover with the water. Bring to a boil over high heat, then reduce the heat to low and simmer until the foot is tender, about 2½ hours.

3. Remove the beef foot from the pot and cut off the tender fleshy parts if there are any. Chop the meat coarsely and return to the pot. Discard the bony and gristly parts. Add the hominy and simmer over low heat, uncovered, for 3 more hours. Correct the salt and stir in the oregano. Serve hot with the garnishes.

TURKISH CURE FOR HANGOVERS

İşkembe Çorbası is the famous tripe soup from Istanbul. Pronounced ish-kem-beh chor-bas-uh, it is a tripe soup like no tripe soup you can imagine. It has a long history: We know that during the lifetime of the greatest Ottoman sultan, Süleyman I the Magnificent (1494–1566), the denizens of Istanbul could buy food for takeout—often for the midday meal— at a variety of shops about the city. One of the most popular cookshops was the *işkembeci,* the tripe merchant's shop, where one could buy prepared takeout tripe soup. Today, many Istanbulu will have an *işkembe çorbası* late at night as they are returning home from a night out on the town. In fact, it is rarely made at home. Folklore has it that this soup is a comforting antidote for an anticipated hangover.

PHILADELPHIA PEPPER POT SOUP

The common story of the origin of this soup is that George Washington instructed his cook to feed his soldiers, who were encamped at Valley Forge through the winter of 1777–78 after their defeat in the Battle of Germantown while the British enjoyed the comforts of Philadelphia. The cook only had some tripe and odds and ends and developed this soup. That story is surely apocryphal as there is plenty of evidence that pepper pot soup was popular in Philadelphia before the war. Philadelphia had a large population of free African-Americans, many of whom made a living as street vendors. They were depicted by a young German artist named John Lewis Krimmel, who had four paintings at the 1811 annual art exhibit of the Pennsylvania Academy of the Fine Arts. One of his paintings is called *Pepper-Pot: A Scene in the Philadelphia Market*. It was this painting of a black woman street vendor selling pepper pot soup to white customers that brought public attention to Krimmel as the first Philadelphia artist to approach street scenes as the subject of fine art. The year before, a book of woodcuts called *The Cries of Philadelphia* (Philadelphia, 1810) was published; in it there was an illustration of a black woman selling her pepper pot with the cry "pepper pot, smokin' hot!" In this illustration all the customers are black. The illustration is quite charming; you can find it at www.pbs.org/wgbh/aia/part3/3h251.html

It seems most likely that pepper pot soup was an African-American soup, probably derived from the callaloo soup of the West Indies. The West Indian cooks loved hot and spicy food, so it's likely that the soup from eighteenth-century Philadelphia had plenty of cracked black peppercorns in it and perhaps even the chile of the West Indies, the Scotch bonnet chile, a chile nearly identical to the habanero chile. Pepper pot soup, a thick, spicy soup made of vegetables and tripe, ox feet, or other cheap meats, was unique to Philadelphia. I do not believe it exists any longer, and I do not believe there is any restaurant that sells it. Although people from Philadelphia know of it, none seem to make it or know how to make it. (Interested readers can write the author via www.cliffordawright.com for an untested recipe.)

pepper soup

THIS SIMPLE GAMBIAN SOUP is said to be a cure-all for the common cold. No kidding, I think it might be true! The spiciness from the chile alone will clear up your sinuses instantly. In Gambia, and Ghana too, they also add *utazi,* a bitter-tasting pale green leaf (*Crongromena ratifolia*) used very sparingly for flavoring pepper soups. For seasoning salt, any supermarket seasoning salt will do, but I think the best of them is Knorr's Aromat, which incidentally is popular in West Africa. It is very nice to spoon in some cooked rice right before serving. This recipe is adapted from a Gambian couple named Ebrima and Kiki Touray, and they do call for a Knorr bouillon cube and seasoning salt. **[Makes 4 servings]**

1 pound chicken thighs on the bone, skin removed and
    each cut into 4 pieces
8 cups water
1 tablespoon freshly ground black pepper
1 tablespoon cayenne pepper
1 tablespoon seasoning salt
½ teaspoon garlic salt
1 chicken bouillon cube
One 6-ounce can tomato paste

1. Place the chicken in a large pot, add the water, and bring to just below a boil over high heat, making sure the water never comes to a boil and is only shimmering on the surface. Cook for 10 minutes, then add the black pepper, cayenne, seasoning salt, garlic salt, and chicken bouillon cube. Reduce the heat to low and simmer until there are about 3 cups of broth left, about 1½ hours; at no time should the broth be boiling.

2. Add the tomato paste and stir it in until blended. Cook until the broth is fully blended and slightly thicker, about 10 minutes.

chunky meat soups

mulligatawny soup

THIS CLASSIC SOUP of the British Raj, the colonial regime of India from the eighteenth to twentieth centuries, is considered an example of Anglo-Indian cooking, the British extrapolation of Indian dishes. Although popular in North America and Australia, the original soup was not as complex as it has become today in many recipes. After all, we are talking about British cooking here, and the British love of curry. Curry has become such a part of British cooking that today the English think of curry as English in the same way Americans think of pizza as American. The name of the soup derives from the Tamil words *mulaga,* which means "pepper," and *tanni,* which means "water" or "broth." Hence, a peppery broth. It likely is derived from a *rasam* (page 246). This recipe is adapted from the one described by Dr. William Kitchiner in *The Cook's Oracle,* published in London in 1818.   [**Makes 6 servings**]

1 pound chicken breast on the bone

½ pound chicken thigh on the bone

8 cups water

2 small onions, chopped

1 teaspoon powdered turmeric

¾ teaspoon ground ginger

¼ teaspoon ground cumin

¼ teaspoon ground coriander

¼ teaspoon ground black mustard seeds

¼ teaspoon freshly ground black pepper

⅛ teaspoon cayenne pepper

2 tablespoons unsalted butter

3 teaspoons salt or more to taste

the best soups in the world

1. Place the chicken in a large pot and cover with the water. Bring to just below a boil over high heat, never letting the water bubble, then reduce the heat to low and simmer for 1¼ hours.

2. Add 1 chopped onion and the turmeric, ginger, cumin, coriander, mustard seeds, black pepper, and cayenne and simmer until the meat is nearly falling off the bone, about 30 minutes.

3. Remove the chicken from the broth, reserving the broth in the pot, and when cool enough to handle, remove all the chicken meat, discarding the bones and skin. Chop the chicken into smaller than bite-size pieces.

4. In a large skillet, melt the butter over medium heat, then cook the remaining onion, stirring, until translucent, about 5 minutes. Add the chopped chicken, season with up to 1 teaspoon salt, and cook until heated through, about 5 minutes. Transfer the contents of the skillet to the reserved broth and stir. Add 2 teaspoons salt or more to taste and simmer for 10 minutes. Serve hot.

CZARINA—POLISH DUCK BLOOD SOUP

I've always wanted to make this but, darn, my supermarket was all out of duck's blood. Seriously, I find this an intriguing soup, and I figured that since I love roasted duck and I do like blood sausage, why not duck blood soup? First, one must collect the blood of a freshly killed duck and stir in some vinegar, then seal the receptacle and refrigerate until ready to use. The stock is made with duck wings, neck, backbone, heart, and gizzard with about 2 quarts of cold water, which is brought to a boil and simmered with black peppercorns, cloves, allspice, bay leaf, and the standard soup greens. After it is strained it is simmered again with 2 cups of dried prunes, apples, pears, and raisins. Then it is thickened with the duck blood and some flour, heated a bit, and served with noodles or dumplings. Sounds good to me!

coconut chicken soup

THIS REFRESHING YET RICH northern Thai soup is called *tom kha gai.* It is quite easy to prepare, and much of the flavor comes from the garnishes stirred with the soup after it is cooked: the fresh lime juice, the chiles, the cilantro leaves, and the *nam prik pao,* a roasted chile curry paste that can be bought in most supermarkets. The Thai red curry paste, fish sauce, and canned coconut milk called for in the ingredient list are all sold in the international aisle of your local supermarket, or you can try to get all the Thai ingredients called for through the fun, online Thai supermarkets at www.importfood.com and www.templeofthai.com.

[Makes 4 servings]

One 14-ounce can coconut milk

6 thin slices fresh galangal or 4 slices fresh ginger

2 lemongrass stalks, tough outer portion removed, tender portion only,
  chopped and crushed in a mortar

5 fresh kaffir lime leaves, torn in half, or 1 tablespoon grated lime zest

¾ pound boneless and skinless chicken breast, thinly sliced

5 tablespoons Thai or Vietnamese fish sauce

2 tablespoons palm sugar or granulated sugar

½ cup fresh lime juice

1 teaspoon Thai red curry paste

¼ cup coarsely chopped cilantro (fresh coriander)

25 fresh green bird's-eye chiles or 15 fresh green Thai chiles or
  8 green serrano chiles, crushed in a mortar with the pestle

1. In a wok or large pot, combine 1 cup of the coconut milk with the galangal, lemongrass, and lime leaves and bring to a boil. Add the chicken, fish sauce, and sugar, reduce the heat to medium, and simmer until the chicken is white and firm, about 4 minutes. Add the remaining coconut milk and heat to just below boiling, about 3 minutes.

2. Divide the lime juice and curry paste into individual serving bowls and ladle the soup over them. Garnish each bowl with the cilantro and crushed chile peppers. Serve immediately.

CORIANDER AND CILANTRO

Just a note so there's no confusion: fresh coriander and cilantro are the same thing. For some unknown reason "cilantro," the Spanish word, has come to refer to the leaves of the coriander plant, while "coriander" is used to refer to the seeds, which are used as a spice. And how do we refer to the coriander plants' roots? Well, we don't have to worry about it unless Thai food becomes unbelievably popular in the American kitchen. Right now it's "coriander roots," but you're not likely to find it anyway, unless you've got a plant in your garden.

turkey soup

ON THE FOURTH FRIDAY AND SATURDAY of every November, in countless homes in America, smart cooks are serving this all-American post-Thanksgiving soup. It begins with that beautiful roasted turkey carcass, which goes into a stockpot and is covered with water and made into a flavorful broth. At that point a variety of ingredients can go in. Leftover turkey of course, and any leftovers you think will make a nice soup. The basic idea is to try not to add new things, but only utilize leftovers. This particular turkey soup is the one we make, using leftover turkey meat (half dark meat and half white), cut-up leftover green beans with pine nuts, and sweet potatoes if there are any left. The amount of water you use depends on how much leftovers you have. The water should just barely cover all the ingredients in the pot.

[**Makes 4 servings**]

½ leftover roasted turkey carcass, meat pulled off and diced
   (about ½ pound meat)

1 small onion, quartered

2 scallions, cut up

1 celery stalk, cut up

4 large garlic cloves

6 sprigs fresh parsley

6 sprigs cilantro (fresh coriander)

1 sprig fresh sage

10 black peppercorns

3 ounces cooked green beans

1 tablespoon pine nuts, toasted in a skillet over medium heat until golden

¼ cup finely shredded white cheddar cheese

1. Place the turkey carcass in a large stockpot with the onion, scallions, celery, garlic, parsley, cilantro, sage, and peppercorns. Cover with water, bring to a boil over high heat, then reduce the heat to low and simmer for 4 hours. Strain the broth and transfer into a clean pot.

2. Bring the broth to a boil over high heat, add the turkey meat, green beans, and pine nuts, and turn the heat off. Cover and let sit for 10 minutes, then serve with some cheese.

   Note: If you do have leftover roast sweet potatoes, dice about 6 ounces and add them to the soup at the same time as the green beans.

chunky meat soups

cock-a-leekie

THIS CLASSIC SCOTTISH CAPON AND LEEK SOUP, also called cocky-leeky, is one I first began researching when I was responsible for several dishes for a Robert Burns party some years ago. Scotland's best-loved bard is Robert Burns, and for two hundred years Burns Suppers have been held in his honor, the dinner usually starting with this soup. I ended up writing a recipe for and preparing a haggis instead, and we all had a rousing, ribald time. But here is the famous cock-a-leekie. There are several ideas about its origins. Patricia Solley's *An Exaltation of Soups,* published in 2004, tells us that as early as 1598 the traveler Fynes Morrison recorded that it was served at a knight's house with "boiling fowl" (meaning "cock") and prunes. But a close look at the text reveals that it doesn't mention leeks at all, just the chicken and prunes in broth. The British dramatist Samuel Foote mentions cock-a-leekie soup clearly in his play *The Maid of Bath,* which was published in 1771. It's also reported that the late eighteenth-century French statesman and gastronome Charles Maurice de Talleyrand recommended that the prunes should be cooked with the soup but removed before serving. Sir Walter Scott, in "St. Ronan's Well," also chimed in about the soup, exclaiming: "Such were the cock-a-leekie and the savoury minced collops . . . ." The Scots say the dish came about as a way of dispensing with the loser of a cockfight. Some say cock-a-leekie is just an adaptation of a fourteenth-century English dish called ma-leachi, "ma" meaning fowl, but I've not been able to verify that suggestion, as the word in Old English for chicken is either "henn" for a hen or "cocc" for a cock. The recipe calls for you to wrap the chicken in cheesecloth, which is only done to make its retrieval from the pot easier. If you can use a capon for this recipe, all the better.

[**Makes 8 servings**]

One 4-pound chicken

10 leeks, split lengthwise, washed well, and cut into 1-inch slices, using the
   white and green parts of 5 and only the white part of the other 5

2 small onions, 1 quartered, 1 chopped

1 bouquet garni, tied in cheesecloth, consisting of 1 clove,
   1 whole nutmeg, and 1 sprig fresh parsley

3 quarts water

12 prunes

2 tablespoons salt or more to taste

2 teaspoons freshly ground black pepper or more to taste

¼ teaspoon ground allspice

3 tablespoons finely chopped fresh parsley for garnish (optional)

1. Pull off the easily reachable pieces of fat from the opening to the chicken's body cavity, then place the fat in a skillet and render over low heat so that you have at least ¼ cup of fat. Remove from the heat.

2. Truss the chicken, then wrap it in cheesecloth and tie off with a long section of kitchen twine with which to pull up the chicken from the pot later. Place the chicken in a large stockpot with the 5 leeks with white and green parts, 1 quartered onion, and the bouquet garni, making sure the kitchen twine hangs over the edge of the pot so you can retrieve it once the chicken is cooked. Cover with the water and bring to a near boil over high heat. As the water begins to shimmer, reduce the heat to low and cook until the chicken is nearly falling apart, about 2 hours. Remove any foam with a skimmer as it appears.

3. Remove the chicken from the broth by lifting with the kitchen twine and set aside to cool. Remove and discard the cheesecloth and twine. Strain the broth through a strainer and return it to a large pot or stockpot.

4. Set the skillet with the rendered chicken fat over medium heat, then add the remaining chopped onion and cook, stirring, until translucent, about 5 minutes. Add the remaining 5 leeks with white part only and cook, stirring, for 5 minutes. Transfer to the chicken broth.

5. Remove and discard the skin and bones of the chicken and shred or slice the chicken meat into smaller pieces. Place the cut-up chicken into the chicken broth with the prunes, salt, pepper, and allspice and simmer for 30 minutes. Serve hot with the parsley as garnish, if desired.

chunky meat soups

kurdish chicken and yogurt soup

THIS LIGHT-TASTING AND REFRESHING SOUP came to me by way of a mere description, but it sounded easy to make, and it is. This is a Kurdish soup called *dowjic,* and you will find its hint of lemon just delightful mixed with yogurt and gently poached chicken shredded like silk. The broth you make first will yield a quart more then you need for this recipe, so freeze it for later and you can make the Chilean Cabbage Soup some other time (page 88).

[**Makes 6 servings**]

One 3-pound chicken, quartered
5 sprigs fresh parsley
1 celery stalk, quartered
½ carrot, halved lengthwise
One ½-inch-thick slice onion
1 cinnamon stick
1 bay leaf
4 cloves
10 black peppercorns
3½ quarts water
½ cup medium grain rice
2 teaspoons salt or more to taste
1 pound (2 cups) plain whole yogurt
Juice from 1 lemon
3 tablespoons chopped fresh basil
1 teaspoon freshly ground black pepper

the best soups in the world

1. Lay a large swath of cheesecloth on a work surface before you. Lay the chicken quarters on the cheesecloth, then put the parsley, celery, carrot, onion, cinnamon, bay leaf, cloves, and black peppercorns on top of or stuck in between the pieces of chicken. Fold the cheesecloth over to cover the chicken and tie off with kitchen twine in three places. Place in a stockpot and cover with the water. Bring to a near boil over high heat, making sure the water never boils but only shimmers on top at most, then reduce the heat to low and simmer until the meat falls off the bone, about 2 hours.

2. Remove the chicken from the pot and discard the cheesecloth and seasoning ingredients. Discard the bones and skin of the chicken and shred the remaining meat with your hands or two forks and set aside. Strain the chicken broth into a large, clean pot. Remove 8 cups for this recipe and freeze the rest for another use.

3. In a large pot, bring the 8 cups chicken broth to a boil over high heat, then add the rice and 2 teaspoons salt and boil until tender, about 12 minutes. Reduce the heat to low and simmer.

4. Meanwhile, in a bowl, beat the yogurt until smooth. Add the lemon juice and stir to blend, then add about a ladleful of the hot chicken broth to the yogurt mixture and stir it in, too. Once the rice is tender, stir the yogurt into the chicken broth until well blended. Stir in the reserved chicken and the basil and simmer just long enough so that everything is hot, about 5 minutes. Correct the salt and stir in the pepper. Serve hot.

DILLIGROUT SOUP

There is no real recipe for dilligrout soup because we don't really know the meaning of the word. It is a soup that commemorates the coronation of William the Conqueror, Duke of Normandy, who crowned himself King of the English at Westminster Abbey on Christmas Day 1066 following his victory at the Battle of Hastings a few months before. A lavish banquet was prepared for the coronation by the royal cook, a man named Tezelin. Tezelin created a simple white soup called dilligrout. William was so pleased with the soup that he presented Tezelin with one of the two manors then extant at Addington during the time of the Domesday Book, our source for this story.

Dilligrout seems to have been related to a typical medieval European food known as blancmange (which means "white food"), a kind of chicken and almond pudding. This soup was likely made with pounded chicken and almond, sugar, and spices. As far as the derivation of the word goes, no one knows, but it does seem to be related to "grout," an old form of grits or groats, which was a kind of coarse meal made from barley or rye; the word also refers to the malt used in beer making.

chicken tinola

IN THE PHILIPPINES, CHICKEN *TINOLA* is a kind of cross between a soup and a stew. Many Filipinos consider this the ultimate comfort food. You'll probably agree. The dish usually utilizes chile leaves, which are both difficult to find (unless you've got your own chile plant) and a little bitter, so it's perfectly authentic to replace them with bok choy, spinach, or lettuce leaves. Filipinos would normally leave the chicken on the bone in large chunks, but I like to remove the meat from the bone after it has poached. Serve hot with steamed rice and use any of the garnishes. Rice is eaten, always on the side, with nearly every Filipino meal.

[**Makes 4 servings**]

10 cups water

1 cup medium grain rice

1 tablespoon vegetable oil

4 large garlic cloves, crushed

½ cup chopped onion

½-inch piece fresh ginger, peeled and cut into thin strips

2 pounds chicken breast and thigh on the bone, cut into 4 to 6 pieces

1 tablespoon Thai or Vietnamese fish sauce

1 small ripe papaya, peeled and sliced thin

1 teaspoon salt or more to taste

1 cup baby spinach leaves or bok choy

FOR THE GARNISHES

Chopped scallions

Chopped fresh red chiles

Chopped fresh green chiles

Chopped cilantro (fresh coriander) leaves

Quartered limes

Thai chili sauce

the best soups in the world

1. In a pot, bring the water to a boil over high heat and add the rice. Cook the rice until tender, about 12 minutes. Strain the water into a bowl and reserve and set the rice aside, keeping it warm.

2. In another pot, heat the oil over high heat, then cook the garlic, stirring, until it starts to turn brown, about 1 minute. Add the onion and ginger and cook, stirring, until softened, about 3 minutes.

3. Add the chicken pieces and fish sauce, cover, reduce the heat to low, and cook, turning several times, until the chicken has turned color, about 10 minutes. Add the reserved rice water and simmer, without letting the water come to a boil, until the chicken is tender, about 30 minutes.

4. Add the papaya and cook until tender, about 5 minutes. Just before removing from the heat, season with salt and add the spinach or bok choy leaves. Serve with the reserved rice on the side and some or all of the garnishes.

chunky meat soups

chicken and oyster mushroom soup

THIS CHICKEN AND MUSHROOM SOUP is on many menus in Thai restaurants. It has a luscious taste and should be slightly salty, a bit sour, and as hot as you want it, although I've written the recipe so it's a bit mild. One note though: you must use oyster mushrooms; otherwise, it will be a different dish. Coriander roots can only be found in Thai markets, but the rest of the ingredients can be found at the Thai online supermarket www.importfoods.com.

[Makes 4 servings]

2 lemongrass stalks, outer leaf removed, chopped

3 shallots, chopped

2 cilantro (fresh coriander) roots (preferably), or six 1-inch pieces of cilantro stems, chopped

15 dried bird's-eye chiles, crushed or 2 dried red finger-type chiles, crumbled

2 cups chicken broth

2 cups coconut milk (page 191)

½ teaspoon salt

1 teaspoon palm sugar or granulated sugar

10 very thin slices galangal (about ½ ounce) or 5 very thin slices ginger

3 kaffir lime leaves or 1 teaspoon grated lime zest

¼ pound boneless chicken breast, sliced ¼ inch thick

3 ounces oyster mushrooms, sliced

3 tablespoons Thai or Vietnamese fish sauce

1 tablespoon freshly squeezed lime juice

1 tablespoon coarsely chopped cilantro (fresh coriander) leaves

1. In a mortar, pound the lemongrass, shallots, cilantro roots, and half the chiles with the pestle until crushed but not a paste.

2. In a pot, bring the chicken broth and coconut milk to a boil over high heat, then season with salt and sugar. Add the galangal and lime leaves. When the broth returns to a boil, reduce the heat to low, add the chicken and mushrooms, and simmer without the broth bubbling until the chicken is white and firm, about 8 minutes.

3. Meanwhile, in a bowl, stir together the fish sauce, lime juice, remaining chiles, and cilantro. Place this mixture in a soup tureen or individual soup bowls, then ladle the soup on top and serve.

the best soups in the world

This chapter consists of chunky vegetable soups made either entirely of vegetables or mostly with vegetables with some meat, chicken, and/or dairy. Here you'll find the classic French onion soup, rich in browned onions and melted cheese, which you can now do at home. There are lots of soups with cabbage that are rewarding and easy to make. Try Chinese Simple Vegetable Soup, made with bok choy, carrots, scallions, and dried black mushrooms, and you'll see where it got its name. The Bohemian-style potato soup with mushrooms and caraway may just become one of your favorites.

chunky
vegetable
soups

chilean cabbage soup

THIS SIMPLE RECIPE YIELDS A LOT MORE FLAVOR from its humble ingredients than you might expect. It makes for a very nice lunch soup. The cabbage should be shredded as for coleslaw.   [**Makes 6 servings**]

3 tablespoons unsalted butter

1 small green cabbage or Savoy cabbage (about 1 pound),
    cored and shredded

1 large boiling potato (such as Yukon Gold or white rose),
    peeled and cut into shoestring fries

1 leek, white and light green parts only, split lengthwise, washed well,
    and thinly sliced

5 cups chicken broth

2 teaspoons salt

½ teaspoon freshly ground black pepper to taste

1 cup coarsely crumbled or chopped Mexican *queso fresco* or
    Muenster cheese

In a pot, melt the butter over medium-high heat, then cook the cabbage, potato, and leek, stirring and tossing, until the cabbage has wilted, about 4 minutes. Add the chicken broth and season with salt and pepper. Reduce the heat to medium, cover, and cook until thickened, about 30 minutes. Stir in the cheese, cook until it is slightly melted, 2 to 3 minutes, then serve.

the best soups in the world

french garlic soup, housewife-style

THE ORDINARY HOUSEWIFE in the Middle Ages would hardly have exotic spices from the East for her soups, but she did have garlic. Garlic and onions were so abundant in the local Provençal *horta* (garden) that they were the only products commonly transported any distance. The other *ortolagia* (garden produce varieties) were consumed locally. Garlic was indispensable for *soupe aïgo bouïdo à la menagerie,* or *aïgo bouïdo,* as this soup is called for short. Oil and water or water and bread soups are very old preparations, and in Provence they are often dubbed "housewife-style," as is the soup called *aïgo-sau d'iou,* "water and salt," a fish soup made with water and salt plus a mixture of small white fish, onions, potatoes, tomatoes, garlic, herbs, and olive oil. These kinds of soups are notable for being filling, economical, and delicious. **[Makes 6 servings]**

2 quarts water

1 cup extra-virgin olive oil

15 garlic cloves (about 1 head), crushed

Bouquet garni, tied in cheesecloth, consisting of 8 sprigs fresh parsley,
     8 sprigs fresh thyme, 8 sprigs fresh marjoram, and 1 sprig fresh sage

4 teaspoons salt

¼ teaspoon freshly ground black pepper

6 to 12 slices French bread, toasted golden or not

Finely chopped fresh parsley, for garnish

1. In a large pot or flame-proof casserole, bring the water to a boil over high heat with the olive oil, garlic cloves, bouquet garni, salt, and black pepper and boil for 5 minutes. Reduce the heat to low and simmer for 1 hour.

2. Place 1 to 2 slices of bread in each bowl and ladle the broth over. Sprinkle with parsley and serve.

soupe bourguignonne

THIS OLD-FASHIONED SOUP from Burgundy has all the richness one would expect from a deep, full-bodied red Burgundy wine, its essential ingredient. The only tricky part is making the potato balls, as they may fall apart in the broth, although thankfully that does not affect the taste. Don't be tempted to use flour to bind the potato balls, as that would only make them heavier tasting. This soup's rich flavors make it ideal for a winter repast.

[Makes 4 servings]

10 ounces pearl onions

3 tablespoons unsalted butter

¼ pound slab bacon, diced

¼ cup all-purpose flour

3 cups beef broth

1 cup water

1 cup red Burgundy wine

Bouquet garni, tied in cheesecloth, consisting of 4 sprigs each
    fresh parsley, thyme, and tarragon, and 1 bay leaf

1½ teaspoons salt or more to taste

½ teaspoon freshly ground black pepper or more to taste

2 potatoes (1 pound), peeled and finely grated

1 large egg, beaten

the best soups in the world

1. Bring a pot of water to a boil, then add the onions and boil for 3 minutes to loosen their skins. Drain, cool under cold water, and slice off the root end. Squeeze the onions and the peel will slip right off and the onion will pop out. Set the onions aside.

2. In a large pot, melt the butter over medium heat, then cook the bacon and onions, stirring frequently, until the onions are light golden and the bacon a little crispy, about 10 minutes. Add the flour and stir until a roux is formed, for about a minute, then slowly add the beef broth, water, and wine and stir or whisk to blend. Add the bouquet garni and bring to a boil. Reduce the heat to low and simmer for 30 minutes. Season with 1 teaspoon salt and ¼ teaspoon black pepper.

3. Grate the potatoes into a bowl, then with your hands squeeze out as much liquid as you can. Place the grated and squeezed potatoes in a bowl and stir in the beaten egg, ½ teaspoon salt, and ¼ teaspoon black pepper. Form the mixture into tight 1-inch-diameter balls with the help of a spoon and add to the soup. Cook over low heat until the potato balls rise to the surface, about 20 minutes. Carefully ladle the potato balls out with a slotted spoon and transfer to individual soup bowls. Ladle the broth over the top and serve.

belorussian sauerkraut soup

THIS SOUP, CALLED *KAPUSNIK*, is on old Belorussian recipe, but sauerkraut soups are popular throughout eastern Europe. The soup is traditionally served with baked potatoes on the side. Belorussians eat lots of potatoes and pork, and they love mushrooms of any kind. Bilberries, cranberries, wild strawberries, whortleberries, and other berries find their way into prepared dishes. The plum jam needed here, curiously, does not seem to be common in American supermarkets (I had a hard time finding the one I did, a Bonne Maman Damson plum preserve), so you can replace it with boysenberry jam, or order some delicious Amish-made plum jam from www.shakersprings.com. **[Makes 4 servings]**

10 ounces button (white) mushrooms

5 cups water

1 tablespoon pork lard (preferably) or unsalted butter

¾ pound sauerkraut, drained

1 carrot, chopped

1 medium onion, chopped

2 tablespoons plum jam

1 teaspoon all-purpose flour

1 teaspoon sugar

1½ teaspoons salt

1. Preheat the oven to 325°F.

2. Thinly slice ½ pound of the mushrooms, add them to a pot of water, and bring to a boil over high heat, then boil for 8 minutes. Cover, turn the heat off, and leave until needed. Shred or crumble the remaining 2 ounces of mushrooms and set aside.

3. In a flame- and oven-proof casserole, melt the pork lard over medium heat, then cook the sauerkraut, stirring and turning occasionally, until the strands separate and glisten, about 5 minutes. Add the carrot and onion and cook, stirring, until the onion is softened, about 6 minutes.

4. Bring the mushroom stock with the sliced mushrooms back to a boil over high heat, then pour into the casserole and bring to a boil, cooking until the carrot is almost soft, about 6 minutes. Add the shredded mushrooms, plum jam, the flour blended with some mushroom stock, sugar, and salt. Stir, cover, and place in the oven until thickened and stewlike, about 1 hour. Serve hot.

the best soups in the world

spinach-stem soup of the turkish jews

WHEN THE JEWISH AND MUSLIM POPULATIONS of Spain were expelled, beginning in 1492, a sizable group of Jews were welcomed in Muslim lands, especially Ottoman Turkey. Although a few displaced families made their fortunes in Istanbul and Smyrna, most Jews were very poor and would have appreciated an inexpensive and nutritious soup such as this one, called *ravikos,* made from spinach stems. It is likely this soup made the journey from Spain, because according to Esther Benbassa's *Cuisine judéo-espagnole* and Meri Badi's *La cocina judeo-española,* a Spanish soup called *ravikos* was made for Shabbat, the Sabbath day. The stems are cooked with water or broth, chopped tomatoes, a little rice, lemon juice, olive oil, and paprika. You can use the leaves for another dish, stir them into a Wonton Soup (page 34), or use them in Spinach Soup with Miniature Meatballs (page 114).   [**Makes 4 servings**]

1¼ pounds spinach stems, cut into ½-inch lengths (save the
    leaves for another soup)
1 tomato, chopped
Juice from ½ small lemon
2 tablespoons extra-virgin olive oil
½ teaspoon paprika
4 cups water
1 tablespoon rice
Salt to taste

Place the spinach stems, tomato, lemon juice, olive oil, and paprika in a saucepan, then pour in the water, bring to a gentle boil over medium heat, and cook, covered, for 10 minutes. Reduce the heat to low, add the rice, and cook, uncovered, until the rice is tender, 12 minutes. Season with salt and serve hot.

chunky vegetable soups

dogon onion soup

AS WE APPROACHED the home of the Dogon people of Mali in West Africa, the two-hundred-kilometer-long escarpment called the Falaise de Bandiagara rose before us. At two thousand feet high, this gigantic north-south running cliff face is brightly illuminated as the sun sets, its reddish-orange glow bathing garden plots nestled along the meandering streams at the cliff's base. As we passed in our four-wheel drive, farmers righted their bent backs to look and wave, leaning on their long, crooked staffs. The Dogon are a people technologically only two or three generations out of the Stone Age who live a simple life that rests on a complex set of cosmological beliefs. They live in tiny, hobbitlike villages at the base of the cliff, and the idyllic gardens we passed were onion fields. There were so many fields, and so intense was their smell, that the air was redolent of sweet onions. Onions are the major cash crop of the Dogon, although "cash crop" is a misnomer, as the Dogon live in a barter and subsistence economy and would be happier if you paid for your onions with kola nuts rather than money.

That evening we stayed in a trekker's auberge in the hamlet of Sangha, where we ate an onion soup that I declared the best—and frankly, the onioniest—I had ever had. This recipe is my attempt to re-create it. I cobbled it together by asking questions of my Bambara-speaking guide, Youssouf Mariko, who asked his (and our) Dogon-speaking guide, Ouma Sangara, who asked the auberge's Dogon cook. Needless to say, much was likely lost in translation, so this recipe is based on lots of experimentation, as well as my detailed on-the-spot notes about the taste of the dish.

Strangely, this soup, with only one ingredient to speak of, was the hardest recipe in this book to perfect. The foundation is a rich, deep-brown onion broth. Two things are key for the success of this dish, and there's no point in making it unless you fulfill these conditions: first, you'll need sweet onions with their skins for the broth, and second, you'll need smallish spring sweet onions (not scallions), that is, young onions pulled in the spring before they mature, with bulbs not more than two inches in diameter. The reason you need sweet onions for the broth is because you use the skins, and the skins of storage onions are more bitter than sweet onions skins. **[Makes 6 servings]**

5 pounds sweet onions (such as Vidalia, Walla Walla, or Maui),
     quartered or cut into sixths, with their skins
3 quarts water
2 pounds spring onions, bulb only, half finely chopped and
     half thinly sliced
5 teaspoons salt or more to taste

1. Place the quartered sweet onions in a large stockpot and cover with the water. Bring to a boil over high heat, then reduce to low, and simmer for 4 hours. Strain the broth and discard the onions. Return 8 cups of broth to the pot and bring to a boil again over high heat.

2. Place the chopped and sliced spring onions in the pot, season with salt, reduce the heat to medium, and cook until softened, about 30 minutes. Serve hot.

chunky vegetable soups

mushroom and chile soup

TOM KAENG HET is one among many types of mushroom soups that Thai cooks make. There are numerous edible fungi in Thailand, and many of them would be completely unfamiliar and intimidating to an American cook. Your best choice is to use oyster mushrooms and wood ear mushrooms, both of which are available in better American supermarkets; they taste good and distinctive. If your market has it, use fresh lemon basil leaves for the garnish, as they provide a delicate and fragrant touch. Nearly all the more unusual ingredients called for can be found in the international food aisle of your supermarket, or you can check the Internet sources on page 445.   **[Makes 4 to 6 servings]**

¼ cup dried bird's-eye chiles or dried whole red chiles, chopped
 or crumbled
2 tablespoons chopped lemongrass, tender part only
½ teaspoon salt
1 cup water
3 whole salted anchovies or 6 anchovy fillets
3 cups vegetable broth
3 ounces oyster mushrooms, cut up smaller
2 ounces wood ear mushrooms, cut up smaller
2 tablespoons Thai or Vietnamese fish sauce
½ cup coarsely chopped loosely packed fresh basil leaves
4 to 6 thin slices fresh ginger

1. In a mortar, pound the chiles, lemongrass, and salt until a paste. Bring the water to a boil with the salted anchovies or anchovy fillets and once they break down completely and there is only ¼ cup of liquid remaining, turn off the heat and strain, saving the liquid.

2. In a pot, bring the vegetable broth to a boil with the anchovy liquid and the chile mixture. Add the mushrooms and fish sauce, reduce the heat to low, and simmer until the mushrooms are tender, about 10 minutes. Remove from the heat and serve garnished with some basil and a slice of ginger.

chinese simple vegetable soup

THE REALLY WONDERFUL THING about this soup is that something so simple and easy can be so satisfying. It is made with finely julienned vegetables, and the finer and more evenly you cut them, the better. The soup is always made with water, not broth. You can, of course, put in more vegetables (spinach or fresh mushrooms, for example), but remember that the soup is supposed to be simple. **[Makes 4 to 5 servings]**

2 tablespoons peanut oil
1 bok choy, cut into strips
2 small carrots, peeled and julienned
1½ celery stalks, julienned
1 scallion, trimmed, cut into 2-inch slices, and slices julienned
6 cups water
¼ cup dried black mushrooms
1 tablespoon soy sauce
1 teaspoon rice cooking wine
1½ teaspoons salt
½ teaspoon freshly ground black pepper

In a pot, heat the oil over medium-high heat, then add the bok choy, carrots, celery, and scallion and cook, stirring, until a little softened, about 3 minutes. Add the water, dried mushrooms, soy sauce, and rice wine. Stir, season with salt and pepper, and bring to a boil over high heat. Reduce the heat to low, cover, and simmer for 8 minutes. Serve hot.

chunky vegetable soups

korean bean paste soup

ALTHOUGH THIS SOUP, called *toenjang chigae* (fermented soy bean paste soup), is named for a main ingredient, it has an equal amount of other ingredients, such as *myŏlch'i changguk*, the base of stock made from dried anchovies, Korean red chile paste (*koch'ujang*), Korean red adzuki bean paste (*p'at komul*), tofu, and zucchini. This is a great example of three-alarm Korean cooking. I usually make this soup in the late fall for a satisfying, full-flavored, luscious cold-weather treat. For a totally uncompromising soup you can order all the ingredients needed from www.kgrocer.com or www.ikoreaplaza.com, and I recommend you do so, because this is a soup not to be missed at its best. It's also a great introduction to Korean cooking, if you've never tried it. (When searching at these sites, you may need to use English language search words such as "hot pepper paste" for *koch'ujang*). **[Makes 4 servings]**

3 cups water

10 dried anchovies

1 teaspoon sesame oil

¼ cup chopped onions

¼ cup (about 6 large garlic cloves) chopped garlic

1 ounce ground beef

1 tablespoon Korean red adzuki bean paste (*p'at komul*)

¼ cup Korean chile paste (*koch'ujang*)

1 green jalapeño chile, seeded and cut into ½-inch slices

½ medium zucchini, peeled, split lengthwise, and sliced
  into thin half-moon slices

¼ pound firm tofu, diced

1 scallion, trimmed and chopped

1. Add the water and dried anchovies to a pot, bring to a boil over high heat, reduce the heat so the water is only bubbling gently, and cook for 30 minutes. Drain the broth, discarding the anchovies and setting the broth aside.

2. In a pot, heat the sesame oil over medium heat, then add the onions and garlic and cook, stirring, until softened, about 4 minutes. Add the ground beef and red adzuki bean paste and cook, stirring, until the beef is browned, about 2 minutes. Add the reserved anchovy broth and bring to a boil over high heat. Add the Korean chile paste and sliced chile and stir to mix. Add the zucchini and cook, stirring, for 5 minutes, then add the tofu and cook for 2 minutes. Add the scallion and cook for 1 minute, then serve.

chunky vegetable soups

portuguese kale soup

IT MAY BE CALLED Portuguese kale soup, or *caldo verde,* but this dish is a classic of Portu-
guese-American cookery as found from Fall River and New Bedford, Massachusetts, east to
Cape Cod, where many Portuguese immigrants settled in the late nineteenth century. This
version is my attempt to approximate the one I ate regularly at P. J.'s Dairi-Burger in Wellfleet
on the Cape during our summer vacations. The key ingredient here, besides freshness, is the
fresh linguiça sausage. Supermarkets usually carry it on the East Coast, but elsewhere you
may need to substitute the fully cooked version, and if you can't find that, then sweet Italian
sausage or kielbasa. **[Makes 4 to 6 servings]**

¼ cup extra-virgin olive oil

½ pound (about 1 link) fresh Portuguese linguiça or chourico, casing removed

1 large onion, chopped

4 cups chicken broth

2 cups water

1½ pounds russet potatoes, peeled and thinly sliced

1 pound kale leaves, heavy stems removed, laid on top of one another, rolled up,
    and sliced ¼ inch thick

2½ teaspoons salt or more to taste

½ teaspoon freshly ground black pepper or more to taste

1. In a large pot, heat the olive oil over medium heat, then add the sausage and onion and cook, stirring occasionally and breaking up the sausage but leaving largish chunks, until the onion is softened, about 10 minutes.

2. Add the chicken broth, water, potatoes, and kale. Bring to a boil over high heat, then reduce to low and simmer, partially covered, until the potatoes are softened and almost falling apart, about 1½ hours. The potatoes are meant to fall apart and thicken the broth. Season with salt and pepper and serve. Break up the potatoes further in your bowl to make it thicker.

IKE'S HOME-STYLE VEGETABLE SOUP

It is not well-known that President Dwight D. Eisenhower was a talented home cook. This is his charming vegetable soup recipe, in his own words, from the archives of the Dwight D. Eisenhower Presidential Library in Abilene, Kansas:

"The best time to make vegetable soup is a day or so after you have fried chicken and out of which you have saved the necks, ribs, backs, uncooked. (The chicken is not essential, but does add something.)

"Procure from the meat market a good beef soup bone, the bigger the better. It is rather a good idea to have it split down the middle so that all the marrow is exposed. I frequently buy, in addition, a couple of pounds of ordinary soup meat, either beef or mutton, or a combination of both.

"Put all this meat, early in the morning, in a big kettle. The best kind is of heavy aluminum, but a good iron pot will do almost as well. Put in all the bony parts of the chicken you have saved. Cover with water, something on the order of five quarts. Add a teaspoon of salt, a bit of black pepper and, if you like, a touch of garlic (one small piece). If you don't like garlic, put in an onion. Boil all this slowly all day long. Keep on boiling until the meat has literally dropped off the bone. If your stock boils down during the day, add enough water from time to time to keep the meat covered. When the whole thing has practically disintegrated, pour out into another large kettle through a collander [sic]. Make sure that the marrow is out of the bones. I advise you to let this drain through the collander for quite a while as much juice will drain out of the meat. Shake the collander well to help get out all of the juice.

"I usually save a few of the better pieces of meat to be diced and put into the soup after it is done. Put the kettle containing the stock you now have in a very cool place, outdoors in the wintertime or in the icebox; let it stand all night and the next day until you are ready to make your soup.

"You will find that a hard layer of fat has formed on the top of the stock which can usually be lifted off since the whole kettle full of stock has jelled. Some people like a little bit of fat left on, and I know a few who like their soup very rich and do not remove more than about half of the fat.

"Put the stock back into your kettle and you are now ready to make your soup.

"In a separate pan, boil slowly about a third of the teacupful of barley. This should be cooked separately since it has a habit, in a soup kettle, of settling to the bottom and if your fire should happen to get too hot it is likely to burn. If you cannot get barley use rice, but it is a poor substitute.

"One of the secrets of making good vegetable soup is not to cook any of the vegetables too long. However, it is impossible to give you an exact measure of the vegetables you should put in because some people like their vegetable soup almost as thick as stew, others like it much thinner. Moreover, sometimes you can't get exactly the vegetables you want; other times you have to substitute. When you use canned vegetables, put them in only a few minutes before taking the soup off the fire. If you use fresh ones, naturally they must be fully cooked in the soup.

"The things I like to put into my soup are about as follows:

> 1 quart of canned tomatoes
> ½ teacupful of fresh peas
> If you can't get peas, a handful of good green beans cut up very
>   small can substitute.
> 2 normal sized potatoes, diced into cubes of about half-inch size
> 2 or 3 branches of good celery
> 1 good sized onion (sliced)
> 3 nice sized carrots diced about the same as the potato
> ½ cup of canned corn
> a handful of raw cabbage cut up in small pieces

"Your vegetables should not all be dumped in at once. The potatoes, for example, will cook more quickly than the carrots. Your effort must be to have them all nicely cooked but not mushy, at about the same time.

"The fire must not be too hot, but the soup should keep bubbling.

"When you figure the soup is about done, put in your barley, which should now be fully cooked, add a tablespoonful of Kitchen Bouquet and taste for flavoring, particularly salt and pepper and, if you have it, use some onion salt, garlic salt, and celery salt. (If you cannot get Kitchen Bouquet, use one teaspoonful of Worcestershire Sauce.)

"Cut up the few bits of the meat you have saved and put about a small handful into the soup.

"While you are cooking the soup, do not allow the liquid to boil down too much. Add a bit of water from time to time. If your stock was good and thick when you started, you can add more water than if it was thin when you started.

"As a final touch, in the springtime when nasturtiums are green and tender, you can take a few nasturtium stems, cut them up in small pieces, boil them separately as you did the barley, and add them to your soup. (About one tablespoon after cooking.)"

croatian cabbage soup

DUBROVNIK, A BEAUTIFUL AND QUAINT medieval city on the Dalmatian coast of Croatia, has a cuisine heavily influenced by the Italians, who are, after all, just across the Adriatic. The further inland and north you go, the more pronounced the Hapsburg influence in the cooking, as we see in this soup called *supe od kupuse* (cabbage soup), with its use of pork sausages, paprika, and sour cream. (The further inland, south, and east you go, into Bosnia, the greater the Turkish influence, evidenced by the use of olive oil and yogurt.) This delicious soup is best in the late fall. **[Makes 4 servings]**

¼ pound smoked bacon, cut into small pieces
2 tablespoons pork lard (preferably) or unsalted butter
1 medium onion, chopped
1½ pounds Savoy cabbage, cored and chopped
1 tablespoon paprika
Salt and freshly ground black pepper to taste
2 quarts water
2 fresh or smoked Polish kielbasa sausages (¾ to 1 pound)
1 tablespoon all-purpose flour
1 large egg yolk
2 tablespoons sour cream
2 tablespoons freshly squeezed lemon juice

1. In a large flame-proof casserole, cook the bacon over medium-high heat, stirring, until it has been sizzling a bit, about 10 minutes. Reduce the heat to medium and cook, stirring, until crisp, about another 10 minutes, but keep your eye on the bacon.

2. Add 1 tablespoon of the lard and once it has melted, add the onion. Cook over medium heat, stirring occasionally, until translucent, about 6 minutes. Add the chopped cabbage and sweat for 5 minutes, tossing with the bacon fat until it is well coated. Season with the paprika, salt, and pepper.

3. Pour in the water and boil gently until the cabbage is soft, about 30 minutes. In a pot, boil the sausages separately in water to cover for 10 minutes. Drain and slice the sausages and set aside.

4. In a small pot, melt the remaining tablespoon of lard over medium-high heat and make a roux by stirring in the flour. Cook the roux for 1 minute, then add the sliced sausages. Dilute the roux with 2 ladlefuls of the cabbage broth (about 1 cup), stirring to blend. Pour the roux and sausages into the casserole and stir. Cook, stirring occasionally, for 10 minutes.

5. In a small bowl, beat the egg yolk, sour cream, and lemon juice together. Slowly add several tablespoons of the cabbage broth to the egg mixture and beat it in. Pour the egg mixture into the soup and stir several times before serving. Serve hot.

chunky vegetable soups

slovak sauerkraut soup

THE BEST-KNOWN SLOVAK SOUP IS *kapustnica,* a hearty wintertime sauerkraut soup rich in flavor from a variety of smoked pork products and dried mushrooms and related to similar soups throughout Slavic lands. In Slovakia (once eastern Czechoslovakia and independent since it split from the Czech Republic in the 1990s) a cook would serve it with *bryndzové halušky,* dumplings made with a sheep cheese similar to feta.

Sauerkraut soup is made in most of eastern Europe and is called *kapusniak,* whether it's made by Poles, Belorussians, or Jews. Sauerkraut is as common in the Polish kitchen as the potato is in the American one. Each culture makes the soup a wee bit differently, and there are many recipes. Some cooks use eggs and milk or cream. Some serve it with potato dumplings. The Polish version is simpler than this Slovak one, which seasons the sauerkraut with pork spareribs, dried mushroom, and onion. Serve this soup with fresh rye bread. It tastes even better when reheated, so don't cut back on the yield. The soup is a delight for a filling lunch on a cold day.

In the 1970s I lived in Yorkville on Manhattan's Upper East Side, where a small Hungarian neighborhood still existed. That's where I fell in love with *hurka,* the Hungarian farmer's sausage made with rice and liver that I use in this soup. You can order it at Otto's Import Store & Deli in Burbank, California, found online at www.hungariandeli.com.

[Makes 6 servings]

1 pound smoked ham hock

1 pound pork spareribs (preferably smoked), separated if on the rack

3 quarts water

2 cups (1 pound) sauerkraut, drained

1 large onion, chopped

6 prunes, pitted and cut in half

1 cup dry white wine

One 6-ounce can tomato paste

2 large garlic cloves, finely chopped

1½ ounces dried porcini or shiitake mushrooms, soaked in water to cover
  for 30 minutes, drained, and chopped

1 teaspoon caraway seeds

1 teaspoon dried marjoram

1 pound smoked Hungarian farmer's sausage (*hurka*) or
  smoked Polish kielbasa, cut in half

2 tablespoons unsalted butter

2 tablespoons all-purpose flour

1 teaspoon hot paprika

1. Place the ham hock and spareribs in a large pot and cover with the water. Bring to a boil over high heat, then reduce the heat to low and cook, skimming the surface of foam and adding water if it is evaporating, until the meat can fall off the bone, about 3 hours. Remove the meat and dice, discarding the bones and fat.

2. Return the meat to the pot and add the sauerkraut, onion, prunes, wine, tomato paste, garlic, mushrooms, caraway, and marjoram. Bring to a boil over high heat, then reduce the heat to low and simmer for 1¾ hours.

3. Add the sausage and continue cooking over low heat for 45 minutes. Remove the sausage, cut it into slices, return it to the soup, and simmer while you prepare the roux.

4. Meanwhile, in a small skillet, make the paprika roux, called *zaprazka*. Melt the butter over medium heat, then stir in the flour and paprika to form a roux. Cook, stirring, for 1 minute, then add to the soup, and stir to blend. Serve hot.

chunky vegetable soups

cabbage soup
with flanken

A FAMOUS SOUP of the Polish Jews is cabbage soup with flanken. *Flanken* is a Yiddish word meaning "flank," and in this case the meat is cut from the short ribs on the side of the beef. Interestingly, the word is used today by all butchers for this cut, not just Jewish butchers. This classic all Jewish grandmothers know how to make. Some cooks add apples or beets or use ketchup instead of tomatoes. Others remove the flanken and eat it separately as a second course with mustard or horseradish sauce, but I prefer to return the cut-up meat to the soup. This recipe is adapted from a rare book, *Cooking the Polish-Jewish Way,* published in 1988 by a now-defunct state publishing house in Poland (where it is called white cabbage soup), with recipes collected by Eugeniusz Wirkowski. The soup is eaten with black bread.

[**Makes 8 servings**]

the best soups in the world

2 pounds flanken (narrow-cut beef short ribs)

1¼ pounds beef soup bones with some meat on them (optional)

8 cups water

2 tablespoons rendered beef fat or unsalted butter

½ pound onions, chopped

One 2½-pound green cabbage, cored, cut in half, and shredded

One 28-ounce can crushed tomatoes

¼ pound (¾ cup) raisins

½ cup freshly squeezed lemon juice

¼ cup brown sugar

3 teaspoons salt

1 teaspoon freshly ground black pepper

1. Place the flanken and beef bones, if using, in a stockpot, cover with the water, and bring to a boil over high heat, skimming the surface of foam as it appears. Reduce the heat to low and simmer, partially covered, until the meat falls off the bone, about 2 hours. Remove the bones and cut off all the meat. Discard the bones and return the meat to the soup.

2. In a skillet, melt the rendered beef fat over medium-high heat, then add the onions and cook, stirring occasionally, until the onions turn light golden, 6 to 7 minutes.

3. Transfer the onions to the soup with the cabbage and tomatoes and simmer over medium-low heat until softened, about 1 hour. Add the raisins, lemon juice, sugar, salt, and pepper, cook for 5 minutes, then serve.

cabbage and potato soup

THIS CABBAGE AND POTATO SOUP, or *minestra di cavoli e patate,* from Sardinia is typically eaten as a first course. The pig's foot and skin provide flavoring but are removed from the soup before eating, although you can cut up the skin and eat it if you like, as it is delicious. If you are unable to procure pig's foot and skin, you can use a prosciutto hock or an end piece of about ¼ pound and the skin that is usually still attached to a piece of salt pork. I have found many of these items at Whole Foods markets, but any good Italian market should have them. The soup is finished by boiling, which will emulsify the olive oil and broth, making for a flavorful *minestra.*   [**Makes 4 servings**]

1 pig's foot (¾ pound)
¼ pound piece pork skin
4 quarts water
½ pound Savoy cabbage, cut into large pieces
½ pound potatoes, peeled and cubed small
6 tablespoons extra-virgin olive oil
1 small onion, chopped
3 large garlic cloves, finely chopped
1 sun-dried tomato, cut or ripped into 8 pieces
3 tablespoons finely chopped fresh parsley leaves
3 tablespoons finely chopped fresh basil leaves
Salt and freshly ground black pepper to taste

1. Place the pig's foot and pork skin in a large pot and cover with 2 quarts of the water. Bring to a boil over high heat and boil 30 minutes. Drain, clean the pot (or use another one), and return the pig's foot and skin.

2. Add the cabbage to the pot with the pig's foot and skin, cover with the remaining 2 quarts of water, and bring to a boil over high heat. Boil until the cabbage has wilted some more, about 5 minutes, then add the potatoes, reduce the heat to medium-low, and cook until tender, about 20 minutes.

3. Meanwhile, in a skillet, heat the olive oil over medium-high heat, then add the onion, garlic, dried tomato, parsley, and basil and cook, stirring occasionally, until softened, about 4 minutes. This mixture is called a *soffritto* in Italian. Transfer the *soffritto* to the cabbage, taste, season with salt and pepper, then cook over high heat, stirring occasionally, for 5 minutes. Serve hot.

chunky vegetable soups

cabbage and sausage soup

THIS RUSTIC SOUP from the Abruzzo region of Italy is called, simply enough, cabbage soup (*zuppa di cavoli*), but my goodness, how much better it is than that! One of the key ingredients is the pork skin used for flavoring. Outside of ordering it from a butcher or in an ethnic market, which is what I usually do, you can also use the pork skin left on pork shoulder roasts or salt pork sold in your local supermarket. Don't skip it or the pancetta, or you'll be wondering what all the fuss is about. **[Makes 6 servings]**

2 ounces pork skin, prosciutto skin, bacon skin, or salt pork skin

5 tablespoons extra-virgin olive oil

2 ounces pancetta, solid pork fat, or salt pork

1 large garlic clove, finely chopped

2 tablespoons finely chopped fresh parsley

¾ pound hot Italian sausage, casing removed and meat crumbled

1 head green cabbage (about 1¾ pounds), cored, quartered,
    and thinly sliced

2 quarts water

Salt to taste

1 tablespoon freshly ground black pepper or to taste

6 slices Italian bread, toasted

Freshly grated pecorino cheese to taste

1. Bring a small pot of water to a boil over high heat, then cook the skin until softened, about 45 minutes. Drain, dice the skin, and set aside.

2. In an earthenware soup pot (preferably) or any large pot, heat the olive oil over medium-high heat, then cook the pancetta, garlic, and parsley, stirring frequently, until it begins to get crispy, about 6 minutes. Add the sausage and continue cooking, stirring and breaking up the lumps with a wooden spoon, until it loses all its pinkness, about 3 minutes.

3. Add the cabbage and water, season with salt and pepper, increase the heat to high, and as soon as it reaches a boil, reduce the heat to low, add the diced pork skin, cover, and simmer until the cabbage is tender, about 30 minutes.

4. Place the bread slices in the soup bowls, ladle the hot soup on top, and serve with the pecorino cheese.

the best soups in the world

UKAZI SOUP

The food of southern Nigeria is both rich in green leafy vegetables you've never heard of and always spiced thermonuclearly. Ukazi soup is so-named for the *ukazi* or *afang* leaves (*Gnetum african*), the dark green shiny foliage of the creeping plant cultivated mostly in Calabar and Igbo land in southern Nigeria. The leaves of another plant, *utazi* (*Crongromena ratifolia*), are also used; they are pale green and bitter-tasting and usually used, very sparingly, for flavoring pepper soup. They are sometimes a substitute for bitterleaf (*Vernonia amygdalina*), yet another leafy green used in Nigerian cooking. Go to www.jbafricanmarket.com or www.asiamex.com and you will find all the African ingredients you need to cook authentically; it's a fun experience, and you'll feel like quite the traveler.

The names of the following ingredients used in this soup are in the Igbo language: Colocynth seeds (*Citrullis colocynthis*) are called *egusi*. *Achi* are the ground protein-rich legumes of *Brachystegia eurycoma,* a tree native to Africa; they are used as a soup thickener. *Ukpo* are the seeds of the legume known as hamburger bean or horse-eye bean (*Mucuna sloanei*), ground to use as a thickener. The soft bamboo is *achara* (*Bambusa vulgads*). The dried small fish called *ngara-azu* are mostly known in the United States as an aquarium fish, *Aulonocara stuartgranti Ngara*. Crayfish are called *ayiya*. The *azu okpo,* or dried fish, is a squeaker or kind of catfish. Stockfish is called *okporoko*. The mangove oyster is called *mgbe* (*Crassostrea gasar*). Beef jerky is known as *kai* and is usually made from goat. Also used in the soup is oxtail, chiles, red palm oil, and melon ball biscuits called *aku agbo,* although I'm not sure what they actually are.

What do you do with all this? It all goes into a soup pot and simmers. And you don't need to know much more than that for an African soup.

spinach soup with miniature meatballs

THIS DELIGHTFUL LEBANESE SOUP is called spinach soup, *shūrbat al-sabānakh* in Arabic, but the memorable tastes are, in fact, the cardamom-flavored broth with its miniature meatballs. This is one time when a homemade broth is the way to go. But if you decide on using commercial broth, and if you have some time, put about a pound of lamb neck bones into the beef broth. This will enhance the commercial broth considerably (use 7 cups instead of the 6 cups specified in the ingredient list). You can save the spinach stems to make Spinach Stem Soup of the Turkish Jews (page 93). **[Makes 6 servings]**

½ pound ground lamb

1 tablespoon finely chopped fresh parsley

¼ teaspoon ground cinnamon

1½ teaspoons salt

¼ teaspoon freshly ground black pepper

6 tablespoons clarified unsalted butter or unsalted butter

2 tablespoons all-purpose flour

6 cups beef or lamb broth

6 cardamom pods, shelled, seeds crushed lightly

1 pound spinach, washed well, trimmed of heavy stems, and
    leaves very finely chopped

the best soups in the world

1. In a bowl, combine the lamb, parsley, cinnamon, ½ teaspoon of the salt, and the pepper until well blended. Form into small balls about the size of a hazelnut, keeping your hands wet with cold water to avoid sticking.

2. In a skillet that can hold all the meatballs in one layer, melt the clarified butter over medium-high heat, then cook the meatballs, shaking the pan so the meatballs don't stick, until browned all over, about 3 minutes. Remove the meatballs and set aside. Add the flour to the skillet and cook over medium-high heat, stirring, until it is browned.

3. Pour 1 cup of the meat broth into the skillet and scrape the bottom of the pan with a wooden spoon to collect any bits of flour or meat, then transfer to a pot with the cardamom. Pour the remaining 5 cups of broth into the pot and heat over medium heat, stirring, until it comes to a boil, about 12 minutes. Reduce the heat to low and simmer for 5 minutes.

4. Meanwhile, place the chopped spinach in a small pot with 1 cup of water, bring to a boil over medium heat, then boil for 3 minutes. Drain the spinach, add the spinach and meatballs to the soup, check the seasoning, add 1 teaspoon salt if necessary, then simmer for 5 minutes and serve.

chunky vegetable soups

daikon and pork soup

THIS SOUP FROM SICHUAN PROVINCE in China is typically served at the end of the meal in order to cleanse the palate of the rich tastes of the main dishes. Fuchsia Dunlop tells us in *Land of Plenty* that the name of this soup is *lian guo tang,* which means something like "even the soup in the cooking pot." She speculates that it may refer to the fact that the soup pot was brought to the table to finish the meal. Generally, a soup for the end of a meal will not be very salty, and the radish and pork will be lifted out of the broth and dipped in the relish. This dish is searing hot and will certainly cleanse your palate—and probably more. The Sichuan peppercorns and Sichuan chile bean paste can both be ordered from www.asiamex.com and www.adrianascaravan.com. The chile oil is sold in the international food aisle of your supermarket, and you might find the Sichuan chile bean paste there too. (When searching on these sites you may need to search in English for "hot bean paste" or "Szechwan" for Sichuan). **[Makes 6 servings]**

2 quarts water

1 pound boneless pork butt or shoulder, in one piece

1-inch cube fresh ginger

2 scallions, trimmed and cut in half

1 teaspoon Sichuan peppercorns

3 tablespoons peanut oil

1 cup halved and seeded dried whole red chiles

3 tablespoons Sichuan chile bean paste

2 tablespoon soy sauce

1 tablespoon chile oil

½ teaspoon red chile flakes

1 pound daikon, cut into 2-inch pieces and thinly sliced

Salt and freshly ground black pepper to taste

1. In a large pot, bring the water to a boil over high heat and add the pork. After a few minutes, skim the foam from the top and add the ginger, 3 of the scallion halves, and ½ teaspoon Sichuan peppercorns. Reduce the heat to medium and simmer until the pork is almost cooked, about 20 minutes. Remove the pork and set aside to cool. Strain the broth, remove all solid particles, and reserve the liquid. Finely chop the remaining ½ scallion and set aside for the garnish.

2. In a wok, heat the peanut oil over medium heat, then add the chiles and remaining ½ teaspoon Sichuan peppercorns and cook, stirring, until a little darker, about 30 seconds. Remove with a skimmer and set aside. Add the chile bean paste and cook, stirring, until the oil is deep red, about 1 minute. Transfer to a medium-size bowl.

3. Add the chiles to the bowl with the chile paste, along with the soy sauce, chile oil, and red chile flakes, and mix well. Divide this mixture between 6 soup bowls. Slice the pork into very thin slices.

4. Return the broth to a boil over high heat, add the daikon, reduce the heat to low, and simmer until tender, about 12 minutes. Add the pork and simmer for 2 minutes. Season with salt and pepper. Ladle the soup into the bowls, garnish with the remaining chopped scallion, and serve.

sichuan turnip and bacon soup

SICHUAN FOOD IS ALMOST ALWAYS associated with spicy heat. But not all preparations from the Sichuan province of China are blisteringly hot. This soothing dish is mild and quite delicious in cold weather. If you would like it hot, simply add six dried red chiles and remove them at the end of the cooking. In Sichuan the cook would typically make this soup with pork belly—in other words, raw bacon—but as that is hard to find unless you special order it or live near an Asian market, I suggest a piece of parboiled slab bacon. The Sichuan peppercorns can be ordered from www.adrianascaravan.com.　**[Makes 4 to 5 servings]**

One 6-ounce piece slab bacon or thick-cut bacon or raw pork belly

6 cups Chicken Broth for Asian Soups (page 15)

1 teaspoon Sichuan peppercorns

½ teaspoon salt (only if using homemade broth)

4 small turnips (¾ pound), each cut into sixths

4 scallions, trimmed

1-inch cube fresh ginger, peeled and cut into 5 slices

1 teaspoon melted chicken or duck fat (preferably) or peanut oil

1. Bring a pot of water to a boil over high heat, then boil the bacon for 5 minutes if using slab or sliced bacon and 15 minutes if using pork belly. Remove the bacon and cut into large, thin slices.

2. In a large pot, bring the chicken broth, Sichuan peppercorns, and salt to a boil over high heat, then add the turnips, reduce the heat to low, and simmer until softened, about 25 minutes. Add the bacon, scallions, and ginger and cook until heated through, about 15 minutes. Remove and discard the ginger slices and scallions. Serve with a sprinkle of melted duck or chicken fat.

pork sparerib and watercress soup

THIS SIMPLE SOUP packs a lot of taste because one starts off with a very flavorful broth and then enriches that by simmering in it pork spareribs and ginger. It is finished with watercress and a touch of sesame oil, for a perfect soup. **[Makes 4 servings]**

4 cups Chicken Broth for Asian Soups (page 15)
½ pound pork spareribs, cut into 1-inch segments with a cleaver
Two 2 × ¼-inch-thick slices fresh ginger
1 bunch watercress
2 medium tomatoes, quartered
Salt
½ teaspoon freshly ground black pepper
1 teaspoon sesame oil

1. In a pot, bring the chicken broth to a boil over high heat, then reduce to low, add the spareribs and ginger, and simmer, skimming the surface of foam, until tender, about 1 hour.

2. Remove the bottom third of the watercress stems and discard. Cut the remaining watercress into 1-inch segments. Add the watercress, tomatoes, salt (if necessary), and pepper to the soup and simmer until softened, 30 minutes. Turn the heat off, pour in the sesame oil, and serve hot.

chunky vegetable soups

chayote soup from nicaragua

THE MILD-TASTING CHAYOTE is a member of the family of curcubits, the same family as pumpkins. But chayotes are different because their fruit are classified as pepo—berrylike, with a hard rind that can be peeled. The fruit can range in color from pale green to ivory, and the shape is round to pear shape. Like the tomato, the fruit of the chayote was treated as a common vegetable by the Mayas and Aztecs, in its native Central America. This soup from Nicaragua is relatively simple to make. It's also a common soup in Morelos, Mexico, but without the chicken. **[Makes 4 servings]**

½ pound boneless and skinless chicken breast

Salt to taste

2 large chayotes (about 1¼ pounds), peeled and sliced ¼ inch thick

2 tablespoons unsalted butter

1 medium onion, finely chopped

1 garlic clove, finely chopped

1 tablespoon all-purpose flour

4 cups chicken broth

½ teaspoon freshly ground white pepper or more to taste

FOR THE GARNISH (OPTIONAL)

2 tablespoons chopped cilantro (fresh coriander) leaves

½ small avocado, diced

the best soups in the world

1. Place the chicken breast in a pot of water and turn the heat to high. As the water begins to bubble slightly on the edges turn the heat to low, salt lightly, and poach the chicken until white and firm without ever letting the water reach a boil, about 20 minutes. Remove the chicken and let it rest until cool enough to handle. Pull the chicken apart with your fingers, shredding it as you do.

2. Bring a large pot of salted water to a boil over high heat, then reduce the heat to low and simmer the chayotes until tender, about 20 minutes. Transfer the chayotes to a blender and blend, using about 1 cup of the cooking water so the blades turn well, until a smooth purée is formed.

3. In a pot, melt the butter over medium-high heat, then add the onion and garlic and cook, stirring, until softened, 4 to 5 minutes. Add the flour and cook, stirring, for about 1 minute. Add the chicken broth and cook, stirring occasionally, until the mixture is smooth. Add the chicken and chayote mixture, season with 1 teaspoon salt and the pepper, and simmer, covered, until very hot, about 5 minutes. Serve with the cilantro and avocado, if desired.

chunky vegetable soups

duck soup #2

THIS CHINESE SOUP is one reserved for when you have leftover roast duck. Winter melon, called *dong qua*, is a traditional ingredient in some famous Chinese soups. It is not a melon but a gourd, and a member of the squash family. As its texture and taste is close to squash or cucumber, those are the vegetables I use when none is locally available. Winter melon can be ordered at www.friedas.com. **[Makes 6 servings]**

1 tablespoon vegetable oil

2 scallions, trimmed and white and green parts finely chopped

¼ pound roasted boneless duck breast, chopped into ½-inch pieces

1-inch cube fresh ginger, peeled and finely chopped

¼ pound winter melon, opo squash, or cucumber, peeled and
    thinly sliced into 1½ × ¾-inch lengths

6 cups chicken or duck broth

1 tablespoon rice wine

1 teaspoon cornstarch blended with 1 teaspoon water

1½ teaspoons salt

½ teaspoon freshly ground black pepper to taste

In a wok, heat the oil over medium-high heat, then add the scallions and cook, stirring constantly, for 1 minute. Add the duck and ginger and cook, tossing, for 1 minute. Add the winter melon and cook, stirring, for another 2 minutes, then add the chicken broth, rice wine, cornstarch, salt, and pepper and cook until the soup is clear and beginning to bubble on the edges of the wok, 3 to 4 minutes. Serve immediately.

flemish leek soup

PREISOEP, **SIMPLY "LEEK SOUP"** in Flemish, means so much more than that to the Belgians. What seems a mere leek soup can actually be quite a meal, because some cooks make the beef broth with meaty bones which, after they're tender and used up for the broth, are reserved for a second course. My recipe, which is based on numerous leek soups I've had in Oost-Vlaanderen, treats the dish just as a soup and is a little less complicated for that reason. I cut the leeks and potatoes finer than they do in Flanders. If you can find young, spring leeks (ramps), the soup will be even better.　　　　　　　　　　**[Makes 6 servings]**

¼ cup unsalted butter

1 pound leeks, white and light green parts only, split lengthwise,
    washed well, and thinly sliced

1 pound boiling potatoes, peeled and cubed small

6 cups beef broth

1 teaspoon salt

½ cup heavy cream

6 slices French bread, toasted and buttered

1. In a large pot, melt the butter over medium-high heat, then add the leeks and cook, stirring, until softened, about 3 minutes. Add the potatoes, beef broth, and salt. Bring to a boil over high heat, reduce the heat to medium-low to keep the liquid barely bubbling, and cook, stirring occasionally, until tender, about 45 minutes.

2. Stir in the cream, and once the soup nearly returns to a boil, serve. Place a piece of bread in each soup bowl and ladle the soup over the bread.

french onion soup
au gratin

WHY CALL IT ONION SOUP when you can capture an entire culture with the proper full name, *soupe à l'oignon gratinée traditionnelle des Halles de Paris* (onion soup au gratin in the traditional style of the Halles of Paris). Les Halles was once the most important wholesale food market in Paris, perhaps the whole of France, and it is commonly believed that it was in this great market that onion soup was invented, although the Lyonnais may disagree. This recipe is in fact how they do it at Au Pied de Cochon, a famous restaurant in Les Halles founded in 1946. Apparently, I ate there in 1957 when my family lived in France, but of course I have no memory of that, as I was six years old . . . or maybe I do, because I'm crazy about onion soup.

This is a classic soup of French bistros, but it is ideally suited for the home cook as well. In former times French housewives would have enriched the soup with some port, brandy, and egg yolk. Onion soup is something of a misnomer, as the soup is really a bread, cheese, and onion soup, thick and luscious. The one trick is to make it slowly: prepare slowly and cook slowly. Some cooks use beef broth or cook the onions in wine, but I prefer this simpler recipe. If you could make this in four or six individual oven-proof bowls as instructed below, all the better; otherwise, use an oven-proof tureen. **[Makes 4 servings]**

10 tablespoons unsalted butter, at room temperature

2 pounds yellow onions, thinly sliced

1 teaspoon sugar

1 tablespoon all-purpose flour

2 teaspoons salt

½ teaspoon freshly ground black pepper

5 to 6 cups water or beef broth

1 bay leaf

Sixteen ¼-inch-thick slices French baguette

2 cups (about ½ pound) freshly shredded Gruyère cheese

1. In a large, deep, flame-proof casserole, melt 5 tablespoons of the butter over medium-low heat, then add the onions and sugar and cook, stirring occasionally, until the onions are caramelized, about 35 minutes. Stir in the flour, cook for 1 minute, then season with salt and pepper.

2. Add the water and bay leaf, reduce the heat to medium-low, and simmer until the onions look melted, about 45 minutes more. Taste, and if it is bitter add a little water.

3. Meanwhile, preheat the oven to 400°F.

4. Melt the remaining 5 tablespoons butter in a large 12-inch skillet over medium heat, then cook the bread slices until golden on both sides, about 3 minutes a side. Remove and let cool.

5. Remove and discard the bay leaf from the soup. Arrange 2 slices of bread on the bottom of each individual, oven-proof soup bowl. Use a slotted spoon to remove the onions from the casserole and divide the onions into eighths. Spread ⅛ of the onions over the bread in each bowl, then layer each with ¼ cup of the cheese. Continue layering the 4 bowls with the remaining bread and onions. Ladle in the broth so the bread, cheese, and onions are soaked. Layer ¼ cup of cheese on top of each bowl. Bake until the cheese is melted and golden and crusty on top, about 20 minutes. Serve hot.

south bohemian potato soup

IN THE FOOTHILLS of the Czech mountain ranges (Krkonoše, Šumava) a variation appears on the popular Czech potato soup *bramborova polevka jihoceska*. This specialty, called *kulajda* (pronounced koo-lie-dah), is a thick soup made with sour milk or heavy cream, potatoes, forest mushrooms, and poached eggs and seasoned with dill. It's rich, delicious, and a perfect example of Czech cooking.   [**Makes 4 to 6 servings**]

¾ pound boiling potatoes (such as Yukon Gold), peeled and cubed
4 cups water
1 small onion, chopped
1 teaspoon caraway seeds
1 small bay leaf
½ pound small button (white) mushrooms, quartered
1 tablespoon salt
2 cups sour cream
¼ cup all-purpose flour
4 large eggs
2 tablespoons chopped fresh dill

1. In a large pot, add the potatoes, water, onion, caraway seeds, and bay leaf. Bring to a boil over medium heat and cook until the potatoes are tender, about 20 minutes. Add the mushrooms and stir. Season with salt.

2. In a small bowl, stir together the sour cream and flour, add it to the soup, and bring to a boil again.

3. Carefully break one egg after the other into the bubbling soup, and spread the egg white with a fork, stirring, and trying not to break the yolk (it doesn't matter much if you do). As soon as the whites solidify sprinkle the dill and serve.

the best soups in the world

moravian pickle soup

THIS SOUP IS CALLED *polevka okukova Moravska,* which means "Moravian cucumber soup" in Czech. But what you actually use are sweet gherkins, which give the soup an intriguing and delicious taste. As they spoon some soup, your guests won't quite be able to put their finger on what it is they like so much, which makes it a delightful prelude to, for example, roast duck or roast pork shoulder. Moravia is a region that straddles the Czech Republic and Slovakia.

[Makes 4 servings]

½ pound boiling potatoes (such as Yukon Gold), peeled
    and cubed small

5 cups water

1¼ teaspoons caraway seeds

2½ teaspoons salt or more to taste

¾ cup diced sweet gherkins and 2 tablespoons brining
    liquid from the pickle jar

1 cup sour cream

½ cup all-purpose flour

2 tablespoons finely chopped fresh dill

1 teaspoon sugar

1. In a large pot, add the potatoes, water, caraway seeds, and 2 teaspoons salt. Bring to a boil over medium heat and cook until the potatoes are almost tender, about 20 minutes. Stir in the gherkins and the juice from the jar.

2. In a bowl, blend together the sour cream and flour with a fork, then add to the soup and whisk until blended. Reduce the heat to low and simmer until the potatoes are tender, about 20 minutes. Stir in the dill, sugar, and ½ teaspoon salt. Serve hot.

chunky vegetable soups

palace soup

THIS TURKISH DISH is called *saray çorbası,* or "palace soup," and the name most likely refers to the soup made in one of the Ottoman palaces (or what some inventive cook imagines was made in the palace kitchens). The palace of the Ottoman sultan was described as a bottomless pit of food because it fed a huge palace population and the sultan didn't care about expense. In 1527, there were 5,457 palace servants to feed. The Topkapı Palace alone had several kitchens, and by the mid-sixteenth century the number of cooks in the imperial kitchens numbered 1,570. I've seen very few recipes for this soup, and the two I'm familiar with are radically different. In Berrin Ardakoç's *Türk sofrası: Alaturka-alafranga yemek ve tatlı kitabı* (1993), the soup is made with red lentils, onions, parsley, and mint, while Irfan Orga's recipe, which I've adapted here from her *Turkish Cooking* (1963), is made with mushrooms. Orga's recipe is unusual in its use of wine and croutons, leading me to believe it is French influenced.

[**Makes 4 servings**]

3 tablespoons unsalted butter

2 tablespoons all-purpose flour

2½ cups turkey or veal broth

1 pound small button (white) mushrooms, cut in half

1 cup half and half

5 egg yolks

1 cup dry white wine

1 teaspoon salt

½ teaspoon freshly ground white pepper or more to taste

1 cup croûtons made from French bread fried in olive oil (see box)

3 tablespoons finely chopped chives

the best soups in the world

1. In a pot, melt 1 tablespoon of the butter over medium heat, then add the flour and cook, stirring, to form a roux, about a minute. Slowly pour in the turkey or veal broth, stirring constantly.

2. Meanwhile, in a skillet, melt the remaining 2 tablespoons butter over medium-high heat, then add the mushrooms and cook, stirring, until browned and sticking to the pan, 6 to 7 minutes. Add a little broth to the skillet to loosen the bits on the pan, then transfer the mushrooms to the pot and bring the broth to a boil over medium heat, cooking for about 35 minutes in all. Remove from the heat and add the half and half.

3. In a bowl, beat the egg yolks with the wine, then add to the soup and let heat, stirring constantly, for 2 minutes. Season with salt and white pepper. Roll the croûtons in the chives and serve with the soup.

MAKING HOMEMADE CROÛTONS

Cover the bottom of a large skillet with $1/16$ inch of olive oil. Heat the oil over medium heat for a few minutes, then add French bread cut into ¾-inch cubes. Cook, stirring or tossing frequently, until the cubes of bread are golden brown, 5 to 7 minutes. Remove from the skillet and set aside. Optionally, you can add a crushed garlic clove to the heating oil and then remove and discard it before you add the bread.

hungarian mushroom soup

IF YOU LOVE MUSHROOM SOUP, this Hungarian soup called *Magyaros gombaleves,* which simply means "Hungarian mushroom soup," will definitely please. It's not as rich as a cream of mushroom soup, but it's very savory and delicious. It's always made with white button mushrooms. The recipe is adapted from one by János Mohácsi. **[Makes 4 servings]**

1 tablespoon pork lard or unsalted butter

½ pound white button mushrooms, thinly sliced

1 small onion, chopped

½ bunch fresh parsley, leaves only, chopped

1 tablespoon all-purpose flour

2 teaspoons salt or more to taste

½ teaspoon hot paprika

4 cups beef broth

½ cup sour cream

In a pot, melt the lard over medium-low heat, then cook the mushrooms, covered, stirring occasionally, until softened, about 10 minutes. Add the onion and cook, stirring occasionally, until all the water has evaporated, about 6 minutes. Add the parsley, flour, and salt, stir together for 1 minute, and sprinkle with the paprika. Pour in the broth and stir well. Add the sour cream, stir or whisk well so the sour cream doesn't clump, and continue to cook until hot but not boiling, about 10 minutes. Serve hot.

the best soups in the world

chunky legume soups

What's a chunky legume soup? Well, it's one in which beans are whole or coarsely mashed, and it probably numbers among your favorite soups. Many of those favorites will be found here. You've heard of the famous U.S. Senate bean soup, but have you ever made it? It's one of the most satisfying you'll ever have. If you go for spicy-hot then you'll love the kick of an African peanut soup. And if gorgeous fresh greens and beans are your style, you'll find great recipes for soups with those ingredients here, too.

u.s. senate bean soup

THIS FAMOUS SOUP is on the menu of the U.S. Senate dining room every day. The story of the soup has never been settled, and several tales compete for authority. According to the first, Senator Fred Dubois of Idaho introduced the soup to the menu at the beginning of the twentieth century. Another story suggests that in 1903 it was requested by Senator Knute Nelson of Minnesota, who was fond of bean soup. A third story is that it was introduced by Senator Henry Cabot Lodge of Massachusetts sometime between 1918 and 1924. Finally, one popular and colorful favorite is that it was Joseph G. Cannon, Speaker of the House, 1903–1911, who one day entered the dining room, looked at the menu, and exclaimed "Thunderation, I had my mouth set for bean soup! From now on, hot or cold, rain, snow or shine, I want it on the menu every day." The Senate's web site posts two recipes. The one attributed to Dubois includes mashed potatoes and makes a five-gallon batch. The recipe served in the Senate today does not include mashed potatoes, but does include a braised onion. Now, it should be admitted that most reports concerning the bean soup served in the Senate dining room suggest that it unfortunately leaves a lot to be desired, so I've taken some liberties to assure a delicious soup.   **[Makes 8 servings]**

2 cups (about 1 pound) dried white navy beans, soaked
    overnight in cold water to cover and drained
2 quarts hot water
1½ pounds smoked ham hocks (1 or 2)
2 tablespoons unsalted butter
1 medium onion, chopped
1 tablespoon salt or more to taste
1 teaspoon freshly ground black pepper or more to taste

1. Place the beans in a large pot with the water and ham hocks, set over low heat, cover, and simmer, stirring occasionally, until the meat is falling off the bone, about 3 hours. Remove the ham hocks, and when they are cool enough to handle, cut off all the meat, dice it, and return it to the soup. Discard the bone, skin, and fat.

2. Meanwhile, in a skillet, melt the butter over medium-high heat, then add the onion and cook, stirring frequently, until golden, about 6 minutes. Add the onion to the soup, bring to a boil over high heat, season with salt and pepper, and serve.

sixteen-bean soup

THE SIXTEEN BEANS for this popular American soup are now available in convenient packages of the appropriate proportions. Remember that anything between seven beans and sixteen beans is going to taste more or less the same, so don't worry about exactness on that count. The prepackaged beans are a blessing—you don't have to buy sixteen one-pound bags of different beans. I use both the smoked ham hock (although raw is fine too) and the pig's ear for flavoring, but you don't need the pig's ear. The cooking time will depend on the age of the beans, so allow an hour more than described in the method even though you might not need it (in which case the soup can rest). **[Makes 6 servings]**

1 smoked ham hock (about 1 pound)
1 pig's ear (optional)
One 1-pound package 16-beans soup
1 tablespoon salt
1 teaspoon freshly ground black pepper
1 teaspoon chili powder
1 teaspoon hot paprika
2 bay leaves
1 cup diced celery
1 cup diced onion
3 large garlic cloves, finely chopped

1. Place the ham hock, pig's ear, if using, and beans in a large pot, cover just barely with cold water, and bring to a boil over high heat. Add the salt, pepper, chili powder, paprika, and bay leaves, reduce the heat to low, and simmer, partially covered, until the ham hock is tender but not falling off the bone, about 2½ hours. Remove the ham hock and let cool.

2. Add the celery, onion, and garlic to the pot and cook, partially covered, until the beans are completely tender, about 1½ hours more. Remove the pig's ear and discard. Remove the meat from the ham hock, dice it, and return the meat to the soup, discarding the bone. Check the seasoning, simmer for 20 minutes, then serve.

chunky legume soups

french canadian
pea soup

IT SEEMS THAT EVERY CULINARY CULTURE has a great pea soup: the Berliners (page 136), the English (page 233), the Dutch (page 135), and we Americans, known for the split green pea soup with cut up frankfurters our kids grow up on (page 234). The French-Canadian *soupe aux pois* is Canada's great pea soup, made with dried yellow peas. The best version comes from Quebec, where it is made with dried peas, a whole chunk of salt pork, and some herbs for flavor, often *herbes salées* (salted herbs). Traditionally, the soup is not puréed and is made with yellow peas—not green as it is in the United States. There is a version from Newfoundland that is similar, but with more root vegetables and, sometimes, dumplings. All the ingredients are put in a pot and cooked slowly until done, then the salt pork is removed and diced or sliced to be returned to the pot. The soup is excellent reheated. If you can't find yellow split peas in your supermarket, they are always sold in Indian markets under the Hindi name, *chana dal.*   [**Makes 4 servings**]

1 cup (½ pound) dried split yellow peas

¼ pound salt pork, in one piece

1 small onion, chopped

2 tablespoons grated carrot

¼ cup chopped celery

2 tablespoons finely chopped fresh parsley

1 small bay leaf

½ teaspoon dried savory

6 cups water

2 teaspoons salt

½ teaspoon freshly ground black pepper or more to taste

1. Place the dried peas, salt pork, onion, carrot, celery, parsley, bay leaf, and savory in a large pot, then pour in the water. Bring to a boil over high heat, reduce the heat to low, and simmer, partially covered, until very tender, about 3 hours. Add a little more water if it is becoming too thick, because it should always be soupy.

2. Remove the salt pork, dice small, and return to the soup. Discard the bay leaf, season with the salt and pepper, and serve hot.

dutch pea soup

THE NATIONAL SOUP of the Netherlands is *erwtensoep* or "pea soup." The Dutch cook says it should be so thick that a spoon stands upright in it. This was how it was made in the Dutch navy and came to be called navy pea soup. It's popular in cold weather, beginning in the fall when inns and restaurants start advertising their pea soup, usually eaten with frankfurters, bacon, or sausage. It is customarily served with rye bread (*roggebrood*) and cheese or butter. The meat may be put on the rye bread and eaten with mustard. It is not uncommonly seen in small cups at the so-called *koek en zopie,* outlets on frozen canals, where it is offered as a hearty snack to skaters. Typically, this pea soup would be served as a main course, but my recipe is written so that you can serve it as a first course, followed by a light main course. Double the recipe if you intend it as a main course. Nearly all markets sell pigs' feet, and you probably wonder who buys them and what they're for. Soup and stew makers buy them, for flavor—one does not eat them. Slow cooking releases the natural gelatin in pigs' feet, providing a level of flavor not otherwise attainable. **[Makes 4 servings]**

¾ cup dried split green peas

6 cups water

1 pig's foot, split

1 medium onion, thinly sliced

½ celery stalk with the top leaves, chopped

2 small potatoes (about ½ pound), peeled and diced

1½ teaspoons salt or more to taste

1 frankfurter or veal knockwurst, thinly sliced diagonally

1. Place the peas in a large pot with the water and pig's foot. Bring to a boil over high heat, then reduce the heat to low and simmer, stirring occasionally and partially covered, until dense, about 3 hours. Add the onion, celery and its leaves, potatoes, and salt and simmer, stirring occasionally, for another 30 minutes.

2. Add the frankfurter and cook 10 minutes over low heat. Discard the pig's foot and serve hot.

EAT YOUR SOUP OR FADE AWAY

Every German child knows the story of Suppenkaspar, the little boy who faded away because he refused to eat his soup.

berlin-style yellow pea soup

THIS FAMOUS SOUP is sold everywhere in Berlin, from cafeterias to restaurants. I haven't been in Germany since the 1970s, but I well remember being in the dreary Berlin train station on my way to Leipzig on a cold February day and enjoying a hot, steaming yellow pea soup. There are two secrets to this soup, if one can call it that: first, use a nice mixture of what are known as pot vegetables, which give German soups and stews that typically rich fragrance and taste; second, finely dice or chop them—meaning not more than three millimeters across. Use whatever vegetables you can find from the list below: the more the merrier. The hard-to-find whole yellow peas are sold in Indian markets under the name *toor dal* or *chana dal* (a name also used for split chickpeas). Use yellow split peas if you can't find the whole ones. This recipe is adapted from Mimi Sheraton's *German Cookbook* (1965).

[**Makes 6 servings**]

½ pound (1 cup) whole or split dried yellow peas, soaked overnight
    in cold water to cover

2 quarts water

½ pound smoked slab bacon, cut into thick strips

3 tablespoons rendered bacon fat or unsalted butter

1 medium onion, very finely chopped

1 large carrot, finely diced

1 celery stalk with leaves, finely chopped

1 small celery root (celeriac), peeled, rinsed, and finely diced

1 fresh parsley root, peeled and finely diced

1 small parsnip, peeled and finely diced

1 leek, white and light green parts, and three-quarters of dark green part,
    split in half lengthwise, washed well, and thinly sliced

3 fresh parsley sprigs, finely chopped

3 tablespoons all-purpose flour

2 large boiling potatoes (about 1 pound), peeled and cubed small

½ teaspoon dried marjoram

½ teaspoon dried thyme

2½ teaspoons salt and more to taste

Freshly ground black pepper to taste

¼ pound smoked sausage or frankfurters, cut in half lengthwise and
    sliced (optional)

1. In a large pot, add the drained yellow peas, water, and bacon and bring to a boil over high heat. Cover, reduce the heat to low, and simmer for 1 hour.

2. Meanwhile, in a large skillet or flame-proof casserole, heat the bacon fat over medium heat, then add the onion, carrot, celery stalk, celery root, parsley root, parsnip, leek, and parsley and cook, stirring occasionally, until softened, about 15 minutes. Sprinkle with flour and stir until it is absorbed and browned.

3. Add the flour-vegetable mixture to the soup, along with the potatoes, marjoram, thyme, salt, and pepper. Cover and simmer until the peas are softened but retain their shape, about 1 hour. Do not strain or purée. Remove the bacon, cut into small pieces, and return to the soup. If you want to use smoked sausage or frankfurter as a garnish, slice and heat in the soup.

chunky legume soups

fava bean and chickpea soup from andalusia

DRIED BEANS ARE POPULAR EVERYWHERE in the Mediterranean. They also have a flavor a tad different than the fresh bean, which means they are ideal in earthy and deeply flavorful soups such as this Spanish one from Granada in Andalusia called *potaje de habas secas,* which means, very simply, dried bean soup. Although this is easy to make, there is some long simmering involved, to extract all the wonderful flavor that makes the soup so rich and delicious. To get that richness you will need to use the pork parts listed in the ingredient list, although you don't eat them. You can save the spinach stems for Spinach Stem Soup of the Turkish Jews (page 93). **[Makes 8 servings]**

1 cup (about ½ pound) dried fava beans, soaked in water to cover for
    at least 6 hours, drained

½ cup (about ¼ pound) dried chickpeas, soaked in water to cover for
    at least 6 hours, drained

2 onions (1 small and halved, 1 medium and cut into 1-inch squares)

1 carrot, peeled and halved (½ in one piece, ½ chopped)

2 bay leaves

1 tablespoon salt and more to taste

6 tablespoons extra-virgin olive oil

8 large garlic cloves, finely chopped

3 ounces slab bacon, diced

2 teaspoons sweet paprika

½ teaspoon ground cumin

½ teaspoon dried thyme

1 smoked ham hock

1 pig's ear (optional)

1 pig's foot, split

12 cups beef broth

1 link (6 ounces) Spanish- or Portuguese-style linguiça sausage,
    mild Italian sausage, or fresh Polish kielbasa, casing removed
    and meat crumbled

1 pound spinach, heavy stems removed, washed well, and
    ripped into smaller pieces

Pinch of saffron threads, crumbled

½ teaspoon freshly ground black pepper and more to taste

4 large hard-boiled eggs, shelled and halved

8 toasted French or Italian country bread slices, lightly
    smeared with olive oil

1. Place the fava beans, chickpeas, small halved onion, whole carrot half, and 1 bay leaf in a large pot and cover with cold water by 4 inches. Bring to a boil over high heat, then reduce to medium, season with 1 tablespoon salt, and cook until tender, about 1¼ hours. Don't worry if the fava beans begin to split apart. Drain the fava beans and set aside. Discard the onion, carrot, and bay leaf.

2. In a large flame-proof casserole or pot, heat 5 tablespoons olive oil over medium heat, then add the cut-up medium onion, chopped carrot half, garlic, and diced bacon and cook, stirring occasionally, until the onion is softened, about 5 minutes. Add the paprika, cumin, thyme, and remaining bay leaf and cook, stirring, for 1 minute. Add the ham hock, pig's ear, if using, and the pig's foot, then pour in the beef broth and bring to a boil over high heat. Reduce the heat to low and simmer, partially covered, until the meat is falling off the bone, about 3 hours. Remove the ham hock, ear, and foot. Remove any edible meat from the ham hock, cut into small pieces, and return it to the soup. Discard the remaining ham hock, ear, and foot.

3. In a skillet, heat the remaining 1 tablespoon olive oil over medium heat, then cook the sausage, breaking the meat up further with a wooden spoon, until browned, about 8 minutes. Transfer the sausage to the soup, using a slotted spoon to leave the fat behind, and add the spinach, reserved fava beans, and saffron. Season the broth with more salt, if needed, and the pepper. Continue to simmer the broth for another 15 minutes. Serve with the hard-boiled eggs and bread slices as garnishes.

hungarian bean and ham hock soup

THIS RICH, RIB-STICKING SOUP is a perfect foil for cold weather. Perhaps you can imagine yourself in Hungary in the winter, in a small pub with a fire roaring, as you sip this *bableves csülökkel*. Typically, dried speckled beans are used, but you can use any dried red or white bean. Parsley root is unfortunately not carried in all supermarkets, so feel free to use celery root (celeriac) instead. You can soak the ham hock and beans together. I usually make this soup on a weekend when I have the time to cook leisurely. The recipe is from János Mohácsi of the Budapest University of Technology and Economics.   **[Makes 4 to 6 servings]**

1 pound smoked ham hock

6 ounces (about 1 cup) dried speckled beans or pinto beans

1 whole small onion

1 large garlic clove

8 cups water

Salt to taste

1 carrot, peeled and sliced

1 small fresh parsley root or celery root (about ¾ pound), peeled, quartered, and sliced

1 tablespoon pork lard (preferably) or unsalted butter

1 tablespoon all-purpose flour

½ teaspoon hot paprika

1 cup sour cream

1. Soak the ham hock and beans in water to cover for 8 hours, then remove the ham hock.

2. Place the ham hock in a large pot with the whole onion and garlic and cover with the water. Bring to a boil over high heat, then reduce to low, partially cover, and cook until the skin is tender, about 2½ hours. Remove and discard the onion and garlic and season with salt if necessary (taste first, as you probably will not need to as the ham hock is salty).

3. Add the drained beans, carrot, and parsley root and continue to simmer until they are tender, 1½ to 2 hours. Remove the ham hock, cut the meat off and chop, then return the meat to the soup and discard the bone.

4. Meanwhile, in a small skillet, melt the pork lard over medium-high heat, then stir in the flour for about a minute to form a roux. Stir in the paprika, then stir in the sour cream. Transfer this to the soup and bring the soup to a boil. Serve hot.

chunky legume soups

harīra

HARĪRA **IS A TRADITIONAL SOUP** made in Morocco to observe the breaking of the daily fast during Ramadan, the ninth and holiest month of the Muslim calendar, which celebrates the first revelation of the Quran. It has been said that the soup was originally a Berber dish and that it is known in Algeria, too. In tenth-century Tunisia, even, the soup known as *samāsāhiyya* was essentially this recipe.

There are many variations of this soup, not only because there are many families of many different economic classes but also because the Islamic calendar is lunar, so Ramadan falls during different times of the year, and thus the seasonality of the ingredients changes. A summer Ramadan soup will be different from a winter one. This soup is made when Ramadan falls between October and December.

The first decision is whether you want a version with or without meat. The cooking should be slow and long. I usually buy a six-rib rack of lamb loin chops, remove the sirloin (which will yield the ¾ pound of meat you need for this recipe), and add the rack to the soup for extra flavoring. Both are traditional.

Harīra is found throughout the Maghrib, but it is this Moroccan version which seems to be the most famous. Traditionally, one eats dates and elaborate honey cakes called *shabā'k* (or *shabā'kiyya*) or *mahalkra* along with it. Some cooks add pasta or rice, chicken liver or gizzards, dried fava beans, or yeast (in which case the flour mixture in Step 4 is not used) in addition to the elements below. Also added are rare spices such as *boldo* (*Peumus boldus* syn. *Boldea fragrans, Peumus fragrans*), called *balduh al-faghiya* in Arabic, the berry of a slow-growing evergreen that is used in place of caraway. The tomato mixture in Step 2 and the flour and water mixture used in Step 4 is known as the *tadawīra* in Morocco.

A great souvenir of Morocco are the little earthenware bowls used to eat *harīra*. Soups in Morocco tend to be supper dishes, heavy and filling, and not a first course. When soup is served as a first course, it most likely reflects a French influence.   [**Makes 8 to 10 servings**]

¼ cup clarified butter (preferably) or butter

¾ pound lamb sirloin, fat removed, cut into ½-inch cubes

1 pound onions, finely chopped

2 celery stalks with their leaves, finely chopped

1½ cups finely chopped cilantro (fresh coriander, from about 2 bunches)

1 cup finely chopped fresh parsley (from about 1 bunch)

1 tablespoon sweet paprika

2½ teaspoons freshly ground black pepper

1 teaspoon turmeric

1 teaspoon ground ginger

1 teaspoon ground cinnamon

2½ quarts water

2 pounds ripe tomatoes, cut in half, seeds squeezed out, and grated
   against the largest holes of a standing grater down to the peel, or
   one 28-ounce can crushed tomatoes

1 tablespoon tomato paste

½ teaspoon saffron threads, lightly crumbled in a mortar

One 15-ounce can chickpeas, drained

½ cup brown lentils

2 tablespoons salt and more to taste

⅓ cup fine semolina flour

Juice from 2 lemons

2 large eggs

1. In a large stockpot or flame-proof casserole, melt the clarified butter over medium-high heat, then add the lamb and cook, stirring, until browned on all sides, about 5 minutes. Add the onions, celery, 1 cup of the cilantro, the parsley, paprika, pepper, turmeric, ginger, and cinnamon and continue cooking, stirring, for 4 minutes.

2. Pour in the water and bring to a boil over medium-high heat. Reduce the heat to low and simmer, covered, for 20 minutes. Add the tomatoes, tomato paste, and saffron, stir, and simmer for 10 more minutes.

3. Add the chickpeas and lentils to the soup, season with 2 tablespoons salt, add the remaining cilantro leaves, and cook, stirring occasionally, until the lentils are tender, about 40 minutes.

4. Blend 1 cup cold water with the semolina flour until smooth. Add this mixture to the soup in a slow stream, whisking out any lumps. Cook for 5 minutes while stirring. Add the lemon juice and cook for 5 minutes. Beat the eggs in a bowl and add them to the soup, stirring constantly, slowly, and very gently to create ribbons and not pieces, and cook until they congeal, about 5 minutes. Check for salt and serve hot.

black-eyed pea and coconut soup

AFRICAN SOUPS TEND TO BE more like stews and are usually eaten as the main course. This soup from Tanzania called *supu ya maharage na nazi* (soup of beans and coconut) shows typical Swahili influence in its use of coconut. The recipe is adapted from Bea Sandler's in *The African Cookbook*. She made the preparation thinner than is typical, and I've followed her there. The use of curry powder reflects the influence of the Indian community in East Africa. I recommend the garam masala from www.penzeys.com; it is a bit more authentic tasting than supermarket curry powder, which tends to be heavy on the turmeric.

[**Makes 4 servings**]

1 cup dried black-eyed peas

3¼ teaspoons salt

¼ cup long grain rice

3 tablespoons unsalted clarified butter (preferably) or unsalted butter

¾ cup chopped onion

¾ cup chopped green bell pepper

1 teaspoon garam masala or curry powder

¼ teaspoon cayenne pepper

1 cup chopped, peeled (page 273), and seeded tomato

2 cups coconut milk (page 191)

3 cups water

4 teaspoons shredded unsweetened coconut

the best soups in the world

1. Place the black-eyed peas in a pot of cold water to cover by 4 inches and bring to a boil over high heat. Add 1 teaspoon salt and boil until tender, 30 to 40 minutes. Drain, saving 1 cup of the cooking liquid.

2. Bring ½ cup water to a boil in a small pot, then add the rice and ¼ teaspoon salt and boil until the rice is softened or the water is absorbed. Turn the heat off, drain if any liquid is left, or set aside if absorbed.

3. In a large pot, melt the butter over medium heat, then add the onion, bell pepper, garam masala, 1 teaspoon salt, and cayenne and cook, stirring occasionally, until softened, about 8 minutes. Add the tomato and cook, stirring, for 2 minutes. Add the cooked black-eyed peas and reserved 1 cup of cooking liquid, the coconut milk, and the water and cook until it returns to a bubble, about 10 minutes. Add the cooked rice and 1 teaspoon salt and serve with the shredded coconut on top of each bowl.

peanut soup

PEANUT SOUP IS FAMOUS THROUGHOUT West Africa and is the African soup that shows up most often in American venues, probably because here one just dumps in peanut butter. The real thing is a little more involved, as you will make your own "peanut butter," which is roasted and mashed peanuts without any additions. But don't fret, I'm not going to send you out on a mission here, just to a local whole, natural, or organic foods market that has its own peanut grinder. If you must buy commercial peanut butter, read the label and make sure it only contains peanuts. The soup, which should be thick and smooth, is usually eaten as a main course, like a stew, with *fufu* made from mashed plantains or African yams. (See page 148.) If using commercial peanut butter, add it during the last five minutes of cooking. Red palm oil is essential for West African food, so for a true African taste you should make every effort to get it. You can buy it online at www.jbafricanmarket.com or www.afrikan-food.com.

[**Makes 4 servings**]

14 ounces cassava (yucca or manioc), ñame, malanga, or sweet potato

3 cups vegetable or chicken broth

2 tablespoons red palm oil or walnut oil mixed with ¼ teaspoon paprika

1 cup unsweetened peanut butter

1 small onion, finely chopped

1 small green bell pepper, finely chopped

1 small carrot, peeled and finely chopped

1 garlic clove, crushed

1 habanero chile, finely chopped

2 teaspoons salt

1 teaspoon freshly ground black pepper

½ teaspoon cayenne pepper

1. Place the cassava in a pot and cover with cold water. Bring to a boil over high heat, then boil until tender, about 40 minutes. Drain and mash in a food processor or with a potato masher and set aside.

2. In a pot, add the chicken broth and red palm oil, bring to a boil over high heat, then reduce the heat to low. Add the peanut butter and simmer, stirring occasionally to break it up, for 15 minutes. Add the onion, bell pepper, carrot, garlic, habanero chile, cassava, salt, pepper, and cayenne and cook, stirring occasionally, until the vegetables are tender, about 40 minutes. Serve hot.

FAMOUS PEANUT SOUPS OF AFRICA

Pépé supi is a spicy peanut and chile soup with fish—one of many peanut soups in Africa—eaten from the Ivory Coast and Ghana to the Congo. West African cooks usually use beef or tripe in this soup. In Guinea this soup is really nothing but a very hot fish bouillon given to an invalid. But everywhere it is known as an excellent antidote to a hangover. There are several traditional ingredients that go into making the soup, some quite impossible to find in North America. The first, *pébé* or *pépé,* is no problem: this is simply peanut butter. The mongongo nut (*Ricinodendron rautanenii*) is called *njansau* and has a thin, edible flesh and pleasant tasting fat- and protein-rich kernel contained in a hard pit. It comes from a large, dioecious, deciduous tree that grows wild on sandy soils in southern Africa and plays a central role in the diet of the Kung San, food gathering and hunting people of the Kalahari desert. It is also used in the cooking of Gambia, Ivory Coast, Congo, and Cameroon. *Esèsè* (*Tetrapleura tetraptera* Taub) is the fruit shell, fruit pulp, and seed, containing varying amounts of protein, lipids, and minerals, of a plant used in Nigeria and elsewhere in West Africa. In the eastern parts of Nigeria, the fruits are used to prepare soups for mothers from the first day of delivery to prevent postpartum contractions, while in the southern parts it is used in the preparation of pepper soup. In the Ivory Coast and the Congo cooks use this spice for *pépé supi*. It is served with rice or a semolina *fufu* (page 148) and chiles. The soup can be made with chicken, guinea hen, or another meat if desired.

FUFU

Fufu, a West African dish, is nothing but a glutinous mass of starchy food pounded into a sticky ball that is then used as a kind of utensil to eat other foods. There isn't one *fufu*, but many, made from fermented cassava flour, plantains, African yams, semolina, rice, and a few other starchy foods. *Fufu* is always bland, because the foods you eat with it are highly spiced and very piquant. This recipe is for plantain *fufu*. The plantains must be very ripe, meaning the skins must be black. If you buy plantains in the market and their skins are yellow, it may take up to two weeks sitting in your kitchen for them to reach the proper ripeness, so make sure you buy the ripest available. [Makes about 2 cups]

 2 very ripe plantains, peeled and sliced
 2 tablespoons red palm oil

Bring a saucepan of water to a boil over high heat, then add the plantains and cook for 10 minutes. Drain well, place the plantains in a food processor, and blend with the red palm oil until completely smooth. Serve hot or reheat later.

congolese peanut vegetable soup

ONE OF THE MOST SURPRISING THINGS I found when I was in Africa was just how often food is cooked out of doors. Not just street food like kebabs and fritters, but everything from soups to couscous, and not always for public consumption. I imagine this is because of the heat and the lack of well-ventilated indoor kitchens. I can easily imagine this spicy-hot nourishing soup from the Congo being cooked on the banks of the river described by the anonymous author in the *Afropop Worldwide Cookbook* (found on www.afropop.org), from which the recipe is adapted. As he or she relates, "This was one of my favorite soups while I lived on the banks of the Kwilu river, in the Congo (formerly Zaire). It is a quick (20 minute or less) soup that is different each time." The red palm oil will give the soup a distinctly African taste; you can order it from www.jbafricanmarket.com or www.afrikan-food.com. The hot sauce is called *pili-pili* in the Congo, but Africans in America will tell you that there are plenty of good hot sauces made here, such as Melinda's Habanero XXXtra Hot Sauce found in many supermarkets. Start with a teaspoon and then work up to a tablespoon, because it is very piquant.

[**Makes 4 to 6 servings**]

149

chunky legume soups

3 tablespoons red palm oil or peanut oil

1 medium onion, thinly sliced

1 garlic clove, finely chopped

6 cups chicken broth

½ cup unsweetened smooth peanut butter

½ pound kale or collard greens, heavy stems removed and chopped coarsely

½ pound Swiss chard or mustard greens, heavy stems removed and
  chopped coarsely

2 teaspoons salt or more to taste

1 to 3 teaspoons habanero chile–based hot sauce or to taste

1. In a pot, heat the oil over medium heat, then add the onion and cook, stirring, until translucent, about 5 minutes. Add the garlic and cook, stirring, for 1 minute.

2. Add the chicken broth and peanut butter and cook, stirring to blend and dissolve the peanut butter, for about 3 minutes. Bring to a boil over high heat, add the kale, then reduce the heat to medium-low and cook for 5 minutes. Add the Swiss chard and continue cooking until all the greens are softened and tender, about 15 minutes. Add the salt and habanero sauce, stir well, and serve.

fava bean soup

THIS *SOUPE DE FÈVES* is one that Odette Cocula, a neighbor of my father's when he lived in his adopted village of Frayssinet, near Cahors in the Lot department of France, would prepare for him occasionally in the springtime. It's a hearty soup typical of the region. You'll need about 4 pounds of fava bean pods to yield 3 cups of double-peeled beans.

[**Makes 8 servings**]

3 tablespoons rendered duck fat (preferably), chicken fat, or unsalted butter

1 medium onion, finely chopped

2 leeks, white part only, split lengthwise, washed, and sliced

3 large garlic cloves (2 whole, 1 cut in half)

1 tablespoon tomato paste or 1 ripe plum tomato, peeled and finely chopped

2 medium russet potatoes (about ¾ pound), peeled and diced

10 cups chicken broth

3 cups double-peeled fresh fava beans (see Note)

Salt and freshly ground black pepper to taste

8 slices French or Italian country bread

1. In a large pot or flame-proof casserole, melt the duck fat over medium-high heat, then add the onion, leeks, and 2 whole garlic cloves and cook, stirring frequently, until softened, about 15 minutes.

2. Stir in the tomato paste and cook for 1 to 2 minutes. Stir in the potatoes and chicken broth and simmer for 1 hour. Use a potato masher to slightly crush the vegetables. Add the fava beans and cook for 5 minutes, then season with salt and pepper.

3. Toast the slices of bread in a preheated broiler or a countertop oven. Rub the bread on both sides with the cut side of the remaining garlic clove. Place a slice of bread in a soup bowl and ladle the soup on top. Serve hot.

Note: Double-peeled fava beans means that the bean is taken out of its pod and its skin is pinched off after being dropped in boiling water for a couple of minutes to loosen it.

chickpea and swiss chard soup

THIS QUICK AND SIMPLE SOUP is called *potaje de Carteya,* which means nothing more than that it is a soup from Nueva Carteya, a small town of about five thousand people in the province of Córdoba in Spain's southern region of Andalusia. Swiss chard is probably the Córdobans' favorite leafy green vegetable and chickpeas their favorite legume, and in this soup they form a perfect marriage. It is best to mix everything together at the last minute. The soup is meant to be thick. **[Makes 5 to 6 servings]**

Two 15-ounce cans cooked chickpeas (3 cups), with its liquid
1 pound Swiss chard, heaviest part of stem removed and washed well
¾ pound spinach, heavy stems removed and well washed
4 large garlic cloves, 3 finely chopped, 1 sliced
5 tablespoons extra-virgin olive oil
¼ pound white part of Italian or French bread, cut into small cubes
1 long mild green chile (such as peperoncino or Anaheim chile), seeded and finely chopped
1 teaspoon sweet paprika
Salt to taste
3 tablespoons good quality sherry vinegar

1. In a pot, cook the chickpeas in a cup of salted water and their own liquid over medium heat until softened, 20 to 30 minutes. Keep warm.

2. In another pot, place the Swiss chard and spinach with only the water from their last rinsing, cover, and turn the heat to high. Once the water is bubbling and the greens are a little wilted, cook for 2 minutes. Drain the greens, chop coarsely, mix with the sliced garlic, and set aside.

3. In a large skillet, heat the olive oil over medium heat, then add the chopped garlic, bread, chile, and paprika and cook, stirring, until the bread is golden, about 20 minutes. Season with salt and pour in the vinegar. Once the vinegar has evaporated, mix the chickpeas, greens, and cooked bread together and serve.

sicilian beans and greens soup

THE VUCCIRIA, with its close-quartered warrens and noisy hustle-bustle, is the old street market of Palermo. Although it's something of a tourist attraction, all kinds of foods can be found in the Vucciria, from local vegetables such as *giri* (a leafy Sicilian green), Swiss chard, *sparacelli* (broccoli), and dandelion to sweet Tunisian eggplants, swordfish, and pine nuts. Since vegetables are popular in Sicily, they find their way into many soups, such as this *minestra di verdure e legumi* (soup of greens and legumes). I usually serve this soup during the winter or early spring and will do so at a dinner party.   **[Makes 8 servings]**

2 quarts lightly salted water

½ cup (about ¼ pound) dried fava beans, soaked for 8 hours in
    water to cover, drained

½ cup (about ¼ pound) dried white beans, soaked for 8 hours in
    water to cover, drained

2 medium onions, cut into eighths and layers pulled apart

1 carrot, peeled and coarsely chopped

1 celery stalk, coarsely chopped

1 bay leaf

1 fennel (bulb, stalks, and some leaves), coarsely chopped

3 green cabbage leaves

2 large Swiss chard or beet leaves

3 Belgian endive leaves

Salt and freshly ground black pepper to taste

1 cup Arborio rice

Extra-virgin olive oil for drizzling

Freshly grated Parmesan cheese for sprinkling (optional)

1. Bring the water to a boil over high heat in a large pot. Add the dried beans, onions, carrot, celery, and bay leaf. After the water returns to a boil, reduce the heat to low and simmer until tender but not mushy soft, 1 to 1¼ hours, but keep checking.

2. Add the fennel, cabbage leaves, beet leaves, and endive. Season with salt and pepper and simmer for 25 minutes, uncovered.

3. Add the rice. Cover and cook until the rice is tender, about 15 minutes. Serve with a generous amount of olive oil with each serving. You can sprinkle some Parmesan cheese on top, too.

chunky legume soups

vegetable soup

THE ITALIAN WORD *MINESTRA* today refers to soup or to a first course, but in the fifteenth century it was an elemental food, almost like a stew, that also could contain pasta. At sea, rice was reserved for meatless days, and made into *minestra* with fava beans and chickpeas moistened with vinegar and olive oil. Fifteenth-century Sicilian documents referring to military rations confirm that fresh vegetables were substituted for meat on Sicilian galleys. This was totally opposite of the Spanish galleys, which had only meat and no fresh vegetables. Although no longer associated with seamen, this soup slowly evolved into recipes such as this, from which a simple list of ingredients elicits an extraordinary taste. Because every cook makes *minestra di verdure* in a different way, there is no standard recipe.

[Makes 6 servings]

the best soups in the world

3 quarts water

1 cup (about ½ pound) dried fava beans

1 cup (about ½ pound) dried white beans (such as navy, cannellini, or
    great northern)

2 medium onions (about 1 pound total), finely chopped

2 carrots, peeled and finely chopped

1 celery stalk, finely chopped

1 small Savoy cabbage (about 1 pound), cored and chopped

1 Belgian endive, chopped

1 head Boston lettuce, chopped

Salt and freshly ground black pepper to taste

Freshly grated Parmesan cheese for sprinkling

Extra-virgin olive oil for drizzling

1. Bring the water to a boil in a large pot. Add the fava beans and boil for 5 minutes. Remove the fava beans with a slotted spoon or skimmer and, when cool enough to handle, pinch off the skin of the fava beans. Return the fava beans to the boiling water again with the white beans, onions, carrots, and celery and cook, partially covered, until the beans are half cooked, about 30 minutes.

2. Add the cabbage, endive, and lettuce, season with salt and pepper, and cook until the beans are fully tender, 15 to 20 minutes. Transfer to a tureen or individual serving bowls, sprinkle with some cheese, and drizzle with olive oil before serving.

chunky legume soups

persian greens and barley soup

THERE IS A LOT OF SOAKING in this Persian recipe called *aash-e jo*. You can soak the rice and barley together, and all the peas and beans can be soaked together, but separately from the rice and barley. The *kashk* (or *kishk*) can only be found in Middle Eastern groceries, or you can order it from www.sadaf.com. *Kashk* is a thickened milk or yogurt product made from the whey left over from cheese-making mixed with wheat flour or bulgur and fermented. It is popular in the Middle East and comes as a thick liquid or in a dried powdered form. The liquid form is used in this soup, and it can be approximated by mixing 2 cups of sour cream with 2 tablespoons of tahini, for a less authentic taste. The so-called Persian chives, also used in Korean cooking, are simply thicker and heavier chives, and are sold mostly at farmers markets or ethnic markets. There is a lot of chopping involved in this recipe, so feel free to use a food processor, but if you do make sure you process in short pulses and not continuously. The leaves of the herbs should amount to about 5 ounces each.

[Makes 6 to 8 servings]

½ cup (about ¼ pound) dried chickpeas, soaked 8 hours in water to
    cover, drained

½ cup (about ¼ pound) red kidney beans, soaked 8 hours in water
    to cover, drained

½ cup (about ¼ pound) dried brown lentils, soaked 8 hours in water
    to cover, drained

4 quarts cold water

½ cup (about ¼ pound) pearl barley, soaked 8 hours in water to
    cover, drained

½ cup (about ¼ pound) long grain rice, soaked 8 hours in water to
    cover, drained

½ pound fresh spinach leaves, rinsed well and finely chopped

2 bunches fresh parsley, leaves only, finely chopped

2 to 3 bunches cilantro (fresh coriander), leaves only, finely chopped

3 bunches Persian chives (preferably) or 8 bunches regular
    chives, chopped

2 bunches fresh dill, finely chopped

2 cups *kashk* (see above) or sour cream mixed with 2 tablespoon tahini

2 tablespoons salt or more to taste

2 teaspoons freshly ground black pepper or more to taste

3 tablespoons vegetable oil
4 medium onions, thinly sliced
1 tablespoon dried mint
1 teaspoon turmeric powder

1. Place the dried chickpeas, kidney beans, and lentils in a large pot and cover with the water. Bring to a boil over high heat, then reduce to low and simmer for 1 hour. Add the barley and rice and continue to cook, partially covered and stirring occasionally, for another 30 minutes.

2. Add the spinach, parsley, cilantro, chives, and dill, and cook, stirring occasionally, until all the ingredients are tender, well blended, and looking very mushy, about 3½ hours. The soup should now be thick like a minestrone and not watery.

3. Remove from the heat and stir in the *kashk,* salt, and pepper. Stir and keep warm.

4. Meanwhile, in a large skillet, heat the oil over medium-high heat, then add the onions and cook, stirring, until golden brown, about 15 minutes. Stir in the mint and turmeric and cook for 1 more minute. Serve the soup hot, garnished with the seasoned fried onions.

Note: If the soup sits a while before serving or if you are eating leftovers, you may want to add a little hot water before serving if it has become too thick.

chunky legume soups

lentil and mint soup

IN TURKEY, soups are favorite preparations during winter. One forgets how cold it gets in the Mediterranean, and these soul-satisfying soups are quite perfect for warming up and feeling good about exorcizing that piercing chill. In this recipe, called *ezo gelin çorbası* and known as the bride's soup because it is made for the soon-to-be-married young maiden, red lentils, thought of as "soup" lentils by Turkish cooks because they disintegrate rapidly, are balanced by the earthy taste of cracked wheat and the mellow hint of mint.

[Makes 4 to 6 servings]

1 cup red lentils, rinsed

2 quarts vegetable broth or veal and chicken broth

1 medium-large onion, grated

½ cup medium or coarse bulgur (#3 or #4), rinsed

¼ cup unsalted butter

1 tablespoon tomato paste diluted in ¼ cup water

Salt to taste

1 teaspoon hot or sweet paprika

1 tablespoon dried mint

In a large pot, add the lentils, broth, onion, bulgur, butter, tomato paste, and salt. Bring to a very gentle boil over high heat, about 5 minutes, then reduce the heat to very low and cook until the lentils and bulgur are tender and the soup has a creamy consistency, about 1 hour. Stir in the paprika and mint, cook for 5 more minutes, and serve.

the best soups in the world

For the soups in this chapter you'll want your blender and food processor at the ready, because that's the easiest way to make smooth vegetable soups. I recommend making the classic American tomato soup offered here—you'll be surprised how much better your homemade one is than canned. There's the surprising spinach soup called *paparòt* from northern Italy and a luscious tortilla soup that will be better than anything you've had at a restaurant.

smooth
vegetable
soups

tortilla soup

EVERY MEXICAN RESTAURANT in the United States offers this wonderful Oaxacan soup, called *sopa de tortilla*. But why go out, when you can make an excellent one at home that everyone will love? All you need are some day-old tortillas. If your tortillas are not day-old, cut them into strips and let them dry in the hot oven for about five minutes. Pasilla chiles are sold in the supermarket, but some markets label them as poblano chiles; they are long and very dark green. **[Makes 6 servings]**

2 cups vegetable oil

12 tortillas, at least a day old, cut into thin strips

3 fresh pasilla chiles

3 large tomatoes (about 1¼ pounds), quartered, or
    one 28-ounce can whole tomatoes with their purée

1 small white onion, quartered

2 large garlic cloves

8 cups chicken broth (if using fresh tomatoes) or
    4 cups (if using canned tomatoes)

Salt to taste

FOR THE GARNISH

¼ cup chopped cilantro (fresh coriander) leaves

1 cup crumbled Mexican *queso panela* cheese or any
    soft white farmer-type cheese

1 avocado, pitted and diced

1. Preheat the oven to 450°F.

2. In a skillet, heat the oil over medium-high heat for 10 minutes, then carefully add the tortilla strips and fry, turning and removing with tongs, until golden brown, about 40 seconds or less. Set aside to drain on some paper towels.

3. Add the chiles to the hot oil and fry until they blister golden, 1 to 2 minutes. Drain on paper towels. Let the oil cool down, then discard all but 2 tablespoons. Peel the skin off the chiles, remove their stems and seeds, cut into strips, and set aside.

4. Place the fresh tomatoes, onion, and garlic in a baking pan and roast in the oven, turning once or twice, until blistered black all over, about 45 minutes for the tomatoes and onion and about 20 minutes for the garlic. (If using canned tomatoes, do not roast.) Remove from the oven, peel the tomatoes and garlic, and purée in a blender until smooth, adding a little water if necessary to get the blades turning. (If using canned tomatoes, purée with the onion and garlic.)

5. Heat the reserved 2 tablespoons of vegetable oil in the skillet over medium heat, then add the purée and simmer, stirring constantly, until bubbling, about 6 minutes. Transfer the purée to a pot and add the chicken broth, reserved pasilla chiles, and salt. Bring to a boil over high heat, then reduce the heat to low and simmer for 20 minutes.

6. Place the tortilla strips in individual serving bowls, then ladle some soup on top and serve with the garnishes of cilantro, cheese, and avocado.

smooth vegetable soups

tomato soup

WHY IN THE WORLD would anyone buy this in a can? Why indeed, you'll ask after making tomato soup from scratch. Canned tomato soup is so insipid that when Andy Warhol was asked why he chose a can of Campbell's Tomato Soup as his subject matter, he famously replied, "I was looking for something that was the essence of nothing and the soup can was it." A real tomato soup, on the other hand, is the essence of everything and is very easy to make. The secret, if it can be called that, is to make it only in summer, when garden fresh tomatoes, preferably your own, are bursting with ripeness. Tomato soup is usually served hot, garnished with croûtons or not garnished at all. It can be eaten cold too, although I tend to make gazpacho (page 430) instead when I want a cold tomato soup. This soup will seem boring and tasteless if made in the winter with supermarket tomatoes, so you must use your own homegrown or farmers market tomatoes during the summer months. For a winter tomato soup, see page 204. **[Makes 4 servings]**

4 pounds ripe tomatoes

2 tablespoons unsalted butter

1 small onion, finely chopped

1 teaspoon salt and more to taste

Freshly ground black pepper to taste

Croûtons for garnish (optional, page 129)

the best soups in the world

1. Cut the tomatoes in half and squeeze the seeds out in one quick shake over the sink or garbage pail, then grate the tomato against the largest holes of a standing grater down to the peel, using the peel to protect your hand.

2. In a large pot, melt the butter over medium heat, then add the onion and cook, stirring, until softened, about 4 minutes. Add the tomatoes to the pot, reduce the heat to medium-low, and simmer, partially covered and stirring occasionally, until bubbling for a while and fragrant, about 50 minutes. If your tomatoes weren't juicy to begin with you will need to add about 1 cup of water.

3. Pass the tomatoes through a food mill or push through a strainer into a clean pot to remove any remaining seeds. Season with salt and simmer for 5 minutes. Serve with freshly ground black pepper and croûtons if desired.

smooth vegetable soups

white garlic soup with bread and cheese

ONE USUALLY THINKS OF FRENCH CUISINE as ultrasophisticated, but we sometimes forget that there is peasant-based regional cooking all over the country. These styles are rarely encountered in American restaurants. This garlic soup from the southwestern region called the Perigord is a good example of such hearty, simple French cooking. Called *tourin blanchi à l'ail,* or *tourin* for short, it is made with goose fat and water, an egg and bread—and that's it. It's a simple and very white soup, so you may want to sprinkle some chopped parsley on top if you are serving it to guests. Sometimes the soup is made with sorrel or tomatoes or verjuice. It's a dish as native to Perigord as bouillabaisse is to Marseilles.   [**Makes 4 servings**]

164

1 tablespoon goose fat (preferably), duck fat, pork lard, or butter

6 large garlic cloves, finely chopped

2½ tablespoons all-purpose flour

5½ cups water

2 teaspoons salt

¼ teaspoon freshly ground black pepper

1 large egg, separated

1 tablespoon white wine vinegar

4 slices French country bread

2 ounces shredded Gruyère cheese

1. In a flame-proof casserole, melt the fat with the garlic over medium heat until sizzling for about a minute. Add the flour and stir constantly to blend into a roux. Slowly pour in the water, whisking or stirring as you do, then season with the salt and pepper. Bring to a boil over high heat, then reduce to medium and cook for 20 minutes.

2. Add the egg white to the soup and cook, stirring constantly, for 15 minutes. Meanwhile, in a small bowl, stir the egg yolk with the vinegar, then stir in a ladle of the soup broth. Return this mixture to the soup and remove from the heat.

3. Place the bread in individual bowls or in a tureen, sprinkle the cheese on top, then soak with a couple of ladlefuls of soup. Then pour the remaining soup over and serve very hot.

smooth vegetable soups

purée crécy

THIS FAMOUS SMOOTH CARROT SOUP of France is claimed by two of three Crécy's in France: Crécy-la-Chapelle in the Seine-et-Marne department and Crécy-en-Ponthieu in the Somme department. Both towns are known for their carrots, and any French preparation with the description *Crécy* is made with carrots. Crécy-la-Chapelle is famous today as the location of Disneyland Paris, and Crécy-en-Ponthieu is famous as the site of one of the most famous military battles in history. It was there in 1346 that the English king Edward III defeated the far stronger French army under Philip VI by the judicious use of longbowmen, ushering in the return of the infantry soldier after several centuries of battlefield dominance by cavalry. There's no record of carrots on the battlefield. So what about carrots? Young carrots, newly pulled from the ground, are of course best here. **[Makes 4 servings]**

¼ cup (½ stick) unsalted butter

1 pound young carrots, peeled and cut into ¼-inch-thick rounds

1 small onion, chopped

1 leek, white part only, split lengthwise, washed well, and chopped

4½ cups water

¼ cup long grain rice

2½ teaspoons salt or more to taste

Freshly ground black pepper to taste

2 cups chicken or veal broth

FOR THE GARNISH

Croûtons (page 129)

Chopped fresh chervil

1. In a pot, melt the butter over medium-high heat, then reduce the heat to very low. Add the carrots, onion, and leek, and cook, covered, stirring occasionally, until semisoft, about 20 minutes. Add the water, rice, and salt and bring to a boil over high heat. Reduce the heat to low and simmer, uncovered, for 20 minutes.

2. Transfer the soup to a blender, in batches if necessary, and purée. Return the purée to a clean pot. Add the broth and heat over medium heat for 20 minutes. Add some black pepper, check the salt, and serve hot with croûtons and chervil.

smooth vegetable soups

almond and saffron soup

THE ROOTS OF THIS SOUP, called *sopa de almendras,* can be traced to the sixteenth-century cookbook of Ruperto de Nola, chef to King Ferdinand V (1452–1516), the Spanish ruler of Naples. That book has a similar recipe for almond soup with onions, cinnamon, and sugar. The *Libro del arte de cozina* (Book of the art of cooking) by Diego Granado Maldonado, published in 1599, also has a recipe, although it probably was copied from de Nola. Earlier still, we can see the genesis of these flavors in the sauces used in medieval Arab cookery. Take, for instance the description of *ibrāhīmiyya* in the medical synopsis of the eleventh-century doctor Ibn Jazla, who tells us it is prepared in the same way as *zīrbāj:* a boiled meat with cinnamon, sesame oil, chickpeas, wine vinegar, sugar water or sugar, sweet almonds, corian-der, rue, and saffron. In Algeria today, a *maraqat dajāj bi'l-lawz* is a chicken stew with almond and saffron sauce that harkens back to this medieval combination. This thick, creamy green soup typical of Granada is rich and flavorful. The preparation begins with a *sofrito* of almonds, garlic, and parsley. Some people like to sprinkle chopped egg or a few drops of very fine sherry vinegar on top before serving. **[Makes 4 servings]**

½ pound blanched whole almonds

½ cup extra-virgin olive oil

½ cup finely chopped fresh parsley leaves

2 large garlic cloves

Pinch of saffron threads, crumbled

5¼ cups water

1 teaspoon freshly ground black pepper

1½ teaspoons ground cumin

Salt to taste

¾ pound Italian or French bread, crust removed, soaked in water,
    squeezed dry, and mashed

1 large hard-boiled egg, shelled and chopped fine

1 cup cubed toasted bread (optional)

Blanched slivered almonds (optional)

1. In a large flame-proof casserole or pot, add the whole almonds, olive oil, parsley, and garlic. Set over medium heat and cook, stirring and shaking the pan occasionally so the garlic doesn't burn, until the almonds are a bit browned, about 12 minutes. This is the *sofrito*. As you do this, steep the saffron in ¼ cup of tepid water.

2. Transfer the *sofrito* to a food processor or blender. Add the black pepper, cumin, and steeped saffron and season with salt. Process the mixture until blended and smooth.

3. Return the mixture to the casserole or pot and cook for 1 minute over medium heat. Add the bread and continue cooking for 3 to 4 minutes, stirring a few times. Add the remaining 5 cups of water, reduce the heat to low, and cook, covered and stirring occasionally, until thickened, 1 hour.

4. Pass the soup through a food mill or fine wire mesh strainer, return to the casserole or pot, and simmer over very low heat until creamy and smooth, about 45 minutes. Serve hot garnished with the chopped egg and the bread cubes and slivered almonds, if using.

vegetable soup
from the truck farms

THIS *PURÉ HORTELANO* is a soup purée from the farmlands around low-lying Málaga in Andalusia. It gets its name from the local *huertas,* the vast irrigated commercial vegetable gardens of the region. There is a family of Spanish dishes called *hortalizas,* made with the vegetables harvested from the *huertas,* which are something like truck farms. The salicornia (*Salsola kali*) called for in this recipe is a green twiglike plant that is also known as saltwort, sea grape, sea asparagus, Jamaica samphire, marsh samphire, and poor man's asparagus. It is grown in marshy areas near the sea. In Spain, a similar plant is glasswort (*barilla*), which was once used to make glass. Although you may be able to find salicornia in gourmet greengrocers or farmers markets, you can replace it with laver (*Porphyra umbilicalis*), a sea vegetable most often found dried in whole food stores. You can also order salicornia from www.melissas.com. **[Makes 4 to 6 servings]**

2 quarts vegetable or chicken broth

2 cups whole salicornia, ends trimmed, or 1 ounce dried laver or seaweed

1 head romaine lettuce, central ribs removed and leaves chopped

10 ounces spinach, heavy stems removed, washed well, and chopped

4 cups diced Italian or French bread, white part only

1 leek, white and light green parts only, split lengthwise, washed well, and chopped

¼ cup chopped fresh chives

Salt and freshly ground black pepper to taste

2 tablespoons bacon fat (preferably) or unsalted butter

4 to 6 slices Italian or French bread with crust

1 hard-boiled large egg, shelled and finely chopped

1. In a large pot, place the broth, salicornia, lettuce, spinach, cubed bread, leek, and chives and season with salt and pepper. Cover, set over medium heat, and cook for 30 minutes. Reduce the heat to low and cook for another 30 minutes.

2. Pass the mixture through a food mill, pressing as much liquid out of the vegetables as possible. Discard the vegetable pieces that do not pass through the food mill. Return the soup to the pot and cook for 1 hour over low heat, uncovered. Keep the soup warm until needed.

3. When you are ready to serve, melt the bacon fat in a large skillet over medium-high heat and cook the bread slices until golden on both sides. Place a slice of bread in each serving bowl with a tablespoon or so of the chopped egg, ladle the soup over, and serve.

paparòt

THIS INTERESTING SPINACH SOUP from Friuli-Venezia Giulia, the region of northeastern Italy, is far more exciting than its humble list of ingredients would indicate. It is made with cornmeal flour as a thickening agent. *Paparòt,* in the dialect of Friuli, means "pulped" (in other words "pulped soup") and indicates that the spinach is treated like a pesto but is pulped by chopping, rather than pounding in a mortar. The cornmeal to use is the one used for polenta; I prefer the slightly coarse one, because I enjoy the resulting gruel-like texture. This soup is surprisingly rich and filling. **[Makes 4 servings]**

2¼ pounds spinach, heavy stems removed and washed well
3 tablespoons unsalted butter
1 tablespoon extra-virgin olive oil
1 garlic clove, finely chopped
½ cup cornmeal for polenta
6 tablespoons all-purpose flour
4 cups chicken broth
2 teaspoons salt or more to taste
1 teaspoon freshly ground black pepper

1. You should have about 1½ pounds of spinach after you remove the heavy stems. Place the spinach with only the water adhering to it from its last rinsing in a large pot, cover, turn the heat to high, and steam until the leaves wilt, about 5 minutes. Strain the spinach, pushing out excess water with the back of a wooden spoon, and save this water. Chop the spinach very finely or pulse in a food processor.

2. In a pot, melt the butter with the olive oil and garlic over low heat. Once melted, add the spinach and cook, gently stirring, for 4 minutes.

3. In a bowl, combine the cornmeal and flour, then stir in a ladleful or two of the chicken broth to form a smooth batter with no lumps. Pour the remaining chicken broth into the spinach, bring to a near boil over high heat, then reduce the heat to low and stir in the cornmeal batter slowly, stirring continuously. Add ½ cup of the reserved spinach liquid and cook, partially covered and stirring frequently, until it is thickened and gooey, and the cornmeal is tender, 20 to 25 minutes. Season with salt and pepper and serve.

asparagus soup

THIS IS *ZUPPA DI ASPARAGI* from Calabria, the region otherwise known as the toe of the Italian boot. It is popular in the late spring, when wild asparagus can be gathered. The soup should look creamy. **[Makes 4 to 6 servings]**

1 pound asparagus, trimmed, stem end peeled, and cut into 1-inch lengths
¼ cup extra-virgin olive oil
2 large garlic cloves, crushed
1 quart beef or vegetable broth
Salt and freshly ground black pepper to taste
4 large eggs
¼ cup freshly grated pecorino cheese
3 tablespoons finely chopped fresh parsley
4 to 6 slices toasted Italian bread

1. Bring a pot of lightly salted water to a boil. Reduce the heat to medium, add the asparagus, and simmer until tender, 12 to 15 minutes. Drain and set aside.

2. In a flame-proof casserole, heat the olive oil with the garlic over medium heat, stirring constantly, until it is sizzling, about 3 minutes. Add the asparagus and broth and season with salt and pepper. Stir and let it cook for 6 to 7 minutes.

3. Meanwhile, in a bowl, beat the eggs together with the pecorino cheese and parsley. Arrange the slices of bread in individual bowls. Whisk a ladleful of soup into the egg mixture, beating constantly. Reduce the heat to low. Pour the egg mixture into the broth, whisking constantly for 3 to 5 minutes. Ladle the soup into the bowls on top of the bread and serve hot.

smooth vegetable soups

AN EGYPTIAN SOUP OF JEW'S MALLOW

The recipe is Egyptian, but a main ingredient is Jew's mallow (*Corchorus olitorius*), also called by its Arabic name *mulūkhiyya,* a green-leafed mucilaginous vegetable that is enormously popular in the Middle East. Its after-cooking viscous texture will remind you of mashed okra, although the two plants are from different families. The leaf itself is tasteless, but in Egypt, it is so popular among farm workers that it can be thought of as an Egyptian national vegetable. If you witness two Egyptians waxing poetic about *mulūkhiyya,* you will feel as if you're not privy to a common secret.

Generally, Egyptians cook *mulūkhiyya* as a soup enriched with a broth of duck, goose, chicken, or rabbit, with lots of garlic and spices. The fresh *mulūkhiyya* is usually chopped until nearly a purée with a mezzaluna, or what the Egyptians call a *makhrata*, a two-handled curved knife. When the *mulūkhiyya* is stirred into the broth it only cooks for a short period, until it is "suspended" in the broth and before it falls to the bottom of the pot. Do not chop the leaves before the step calling for it, otherwise the viscosity will ruin the vegetable.

One may encounter many different transliterations for *mulūkhiyya,* such as *melokheya, milookhiyya, miloukia, mlukhiyyeh, mlukhiyyi, moulouhiyee, moulou-khia, melohkia, molokhiya, melokhiyya, and melookeya.* Fresh *mulūkhiyya* is found seasonally at some farmers markets. Frozen chopped *mulūkhiyya* is found in Middle Eastern markets.

This is not a popular soup among gringos, as it is quite hard to get past the texture. It is definitely an acquired taste: Egyptian cooks often add mastic, an aromatic tree resin, to the pot, to mask any unpleasant odors that might come from the meat. This recipe is adapted from my book *Mediterranean Vegetables.*

[Makes 6 servings]

the best soups in the world

One 4-pound rabbit, duck, or chicken, cut into 4 pieces
   (if using duck remove as much fat as possible)
10 cups water
1 medium onion, quartered
½ teaspoon mastic grains (optional)
1 cinnamon stick
Seeds from 4 cardamom pods
1 bay leaf
1 teaspoon peppercorns
4 teaspoons salt
1 garlic bulb, cloves separated and peeled

2 pounds fresh or frozen *mulūkhiyya* (or ¼ pound dried), stems removed,
   leaves washed thoroughly, and dried thoroughly

3 tablespoons extra-virgin olive oil

¼ cup finely chopped cilantro (fresh coriander)

¼ teaspoon cayenne pepper

1 loaf Arabic flatbread, toasted brown and broken into pieces

1. Place the rabbit, duck, or chicken in a stew pot and cover with the water. Add the onion, mastic, if using, the cinnamon stick, cardamom seeds, bay leaf, and peppercorns. Bring to just below a boil over high heat, 15 to 18 minutes, reduce the heat to very low, cover, and poach until firm, about 45 minutes. Season with 2 teaspoons of the salt. Remove the meat and reserve. Strain the broth through cheesecloth and return to the pot, saving ½ cup for the rabbit.

2. In a mortar, pound the garlic (there should be about 15 cloves) with the remaining 2 teaspoons salt and set aside. Bring the broth to a boil, add the *mulūkhiyya,* and cook uncovered until it remains suspended on the top, 8 to 10 minutes (20 to 30 if using dried *mulūkhiyya*).

3. In a small skillet, heat the olive oil over medium-high heat, then cook the garlic mash until light golden, 1 to 2 minutes. Stir into the broth with the cilantro and a dash of cayenne. Serve with the toasted Arabic bread.

Note: The rabbit can be eaten afterward with some rice pilaf by baking it in a 375°F oven until light golden, about 15 minutes, with the reserved ½ cup of broth.

purée of swiss chard and romaine soup

THIS SOUP IS SO GREEN you'll slurp it crazily simply for its color—but it's deliciously smooth and healthy as well. The flavor is as soothing as the texture, and the romaine lettuce keeps the heartier taste of dark green Swiss chard under control.　　　　**[Makes 6 servings]**

8 cups water

¾ pound (about 3) baking potatoes, peeled and halved

1 carrot, peeled and cut into 1-inch pieces

3 tablespoons extra-virgin olive oil

1 tablespoon unsalted butter

1 medium onion, chopped

½ celery stalk, chopped

½ pound Swiss chard, washed well

¼ pound romaine lettuce leaves

Handful of arugula leaves

1 tablespoon chopped fresh tarragon

¼ cup mascarpone cheese

2 tablespoons salt

1 teaspoon freshly ground black pepper or more to taste

Fried croûtons for garnish (page 129)

Chopped fresh parsley for garnish

1. In a pot, add the water, potatoes, and carrot, bring to a boil over high heat, reduce the heat to medium, and cook until tender, about 15 minutes.

2. Meanwhile, in a skillet, heat the olive oil with the butter over medium-high heat, then add the onion and celery and cook, stirring, until translucent, about 5 minutes.

3. Remove the potato and carrot from the boiling water, mash them both, and set aside. Add the Swiss chard, lettuce, arugula, and cooked onion and celery to the boiling water and cook until the chard stems are softened, 15 to 20 minutes. Transfer the greens and their water and the tarragon to a blender and blend until a purée. Add the mashed potato, carrot, and mascarpone cheese and blend by pulsing for a few seconds several times.

4. Return the purée to the pot and heat over medium heat until very hot. Season with salt and pepper and serve immediately with croûtons and chopped parsley.

smooth vegetable soups

purée of sunchoke soup

THE SUNCHOKE IS more famously known as the Jerusalem artichoke, an appellation I don't care for because I almost always have to tell those to whom I am serving it, "No, it's not an artichoke." The sunchoke is a tuber related to the sunflower. It is native to Canada and portions of the eastern United States. It first entered Europe around 1607. In Italy, it came to be known as the *girasole articiocco,* the "sunflower artichoke." It has long been assumed that "Jerusalem" was a corruption of *girasole.* But historically, "Jerusalem artichoke" was used before *girasole* and may be a corruption of *Terneuzen,* the Dutch town whence the sunchoke was introduced to England. In their book *The L.L. Bean Book of* New *New England Cookery* (1987), Judith and Evan Jones tell us that Jerusalem artichoke soup is an old Yankee first course known as Palestine soup. It probably is an old Yankee dish, but I've only known it to be called Palestine soup by the famous French chef Auguste Escoffier (1846–1935). The Joneses' finish the soup with watercress, while Escoffier garnishes it with diced bread fried in butter. To prepare the sunchokes for cooking, simply brush them clean in water rather than peeling them.

[**Makes 4 servings**]

the best soups in the world

1 pound sunchokes (Jerusalem artichokes)

¼ cups unsalted butter

3 cups chicken broth

1 teaspoon crushed roasted blanched hazelnuts

1½ teaspoons corn starch

½ cup whole milk

½ cup water

Salt and freshly ground black pepper to taste

2 tablespoons sunflower seeds, dry roasted in a cast-iron skillet (optional)

1. Place the sunchokes in a food processor and grind until they look finely chopped.

2. In a large pot, melt 2 tablespoons of the butter over medium-high heat, then add the sunchokes and cook, stirring, until they smell nutty and start to stick, about 5 minutes. Add the broth and hazelnuts, reduce the heat to low, and simmer until bubbling and tender, about 40 minutes.

3. In a small bowl, dilute the corn starch in the milk and water. Pass the soup through a food mill into a pot and add the diluted cornstarch. Season with salt and pepper. Bring to a boil, then add the remaining butter, and divide into soup bowls. Garnish with the sunflower seeds, if using, and serve.

smooth vegetable soups

BLANCHING AND ROASTING NUTS AND SEEDS

In cooking, nuts such as almonds and hazelnuts are almost always used blanched, which removes their skins (they can be bought that way). Almonds are blanched by plunging them in boiling water for about five minutes, until their skins can be pinched off. Hazelnuts must be roasted to remove their skins: place them in a 400°F oven for about fifteen minutes, or until the skins can be scraped off. Other nuts, such as pine nuts, and seeds are sold skinned, and they can be pan roasted by shaking in a cast-iron skillet without using any fat for a few minutes, until they turn golden.

ROMANIAN SOUPS

Romanians have a taste for a kind of soup called *ciorba*, a word derived from Turkish. *Ciorbas* are a rich variety of sour soups, far more sour than what one finds in most other countries, although they are found throughout the Balkans. Traditionally, the element that makes these soups sour is the juice of fermented wheat bran. Today, the labor-intensive art of making the fermented juice is dying. Romanian cooks are looking for shortcuts and using other souring agents, such as unripened green grapes, green plums, green sorrel leaves, sour grape vine leaves, sour apple juice, and sauerkraut juice. These are also easy to buy in supermarkets. But the flavor of a *ciorba* made with sour fermented wheat bran juice is unique and improves over time, so large quantities were always made.

romanian spinach soup with french toast

THIS ROMANIAN DISH, called *supa de spanac,* is a kind of purée of spinach soup with a French toast known as *friganele.* It's really delicious, partly because the French bread fried in lard is so appealing. **[Makes 4 to 6 servings]**

3 quarts water

2 pounds spinach, heavy stems removed and washed well

1 lemon slice

2½ teaspoons salt or more to taste

1 tablespoon butter

½ cup sour cream

1 teaspoon all-purpose flour

FOR THE FRENCH TOAST

2 tablespoons pork lard (preferably) or butter

1 large egg

1 cup milk

1 teaspoon sugar

¼ teaspoon salt

Eight to twelve ½-inch-thick slices French baguette

smooth vegetable soups

1. In a large pot, bring the water to a boil over high heat, then add the spinach and cook, covered, until wilted, about 5 minutes. Remove from the heat and process the spinach and 2 quarts of the spinach water in a blender, in batches if necessary, until smooth and liquid. Return to the pot.

2. Bring to a boil again over high heat, then add the lemon slice, salt, and butter and boil for 1 minute. Meanwhile, in a small bowl, mix the sour cream with the flour and add to the soup, whisking or stirring until well blended. Keep the soup warm while you make the French toast.

3. In a large skillet, melt the lard over medium-high heat. Meanwhile, in a bowl, beat the egg, milk, sugar, and salt. Dip the bread into the egg and moisten on both sides. Cook in the hot lard until golden brown on both sides, about 5 minutes. Ladle the soup into individual bowls and place two slices of French toast on top and serve.

vegetable soup
from aragon

IN CASE YOU HAVE NOT READ the introduction to this book, let me repeat the story behind this soup, which is as close to my heart as a food can be. One of my first memories of "real" food is from when I was on vacation with my parents in Spain in 1961 as a ten-year-old. All I remember was that I had a soup that was extraordinarily delicious—so delicious I recall it fifty years later. I have no memory of where we were in Spain, just that the starched tablecloths were white and my mother ordered a vegetable soup for me. This was my worst nightmare, because the only vegetable soup I knew was that which I considered, even at age ten, ghastly—the canned variety, an unforgivable atrocity visited on once-tasty vegetables. But what the waiter brought was something quite different. First of all, it was not red or clear with chunks in it. It was greenish and smooth—a purée, as I later learned. It was served in a very wide white bowl with a broad rim.

Nearly fifty years later, I told my mom about this memory for the first time, and she responded as if it had happened yesterday, "Oh, that must have been in Zaragoza, because it was about ten in the evening and we couldn't find anywhere for you to eat until we finally found this restaurant that was open 'early.'" (Anyone who has been to Spain knows how impossibly late Spaniards eat supper.) This memory had been so important to me that I just couldn't believe I hadn't thought of asking her about it before, and I was surprised and gratified at the vividness of her recollection. The soup was a *puré de verduras,* a notable dish in Aragon, as the vegetable farms around Zaragoza produce some of the finest vegetables in Spain.

[**Makes 4 servings**]

the best soups in the world

½ pound green beans, trimmed and cut into ½-inch lengths

2 carrots, sliced

2 medium potatoes (about 10 ounces), peeled and cubed small

1 turnip (about 10 ounces), peeled and cubed small

1 celery stalk, left whole

2 quarts water

1 small zucchini, peeled and sliced

1 small leek, white and light green parts only, split lengthwise, washed well,
    and thinly sliced

4½ teaspoons salt

2 tablespoons extra-virgin olive oil

1 small onion, chopped

⅓ cup heavy cream

French or Italian bread, diced and fried in olive oil until golden

1. Bring a pot of water to a boil over high heat, then add the green beans and cook until softened, about 8 minutes. Drain and set aside.

2. Place the carrots, potatoes, turnip, and celery in a large pot and cover with the water. Bring to a boil over high heat, then add the zucchini and leek and cook at a boil until softened, about 10 minutes. Strain the vegetables, saving the cooking liquid. Remove and discard the celery stalk.

3. Place the green beans in a food processor and process until very finely chopped. Place the remaining cooked vegetables in the food processor and run until puréed, adding a little of the reserved cooking water to help the blade spin. Transfer the puréed vegetables to the pot, season with the salt, and stir well.

4. Meanwhile, in a skillet, heat the olive oil over medium-high heat, add the onion, and cook, stirring constantly, until softened and golden, 4 to 5 minutes. Transfer the onions to the pot.

5. Pour in 3 cups of the reserved cooking liquid and bring the soup to a near boil over high heat. Reduce the heat to low, stir in the cream, and simmer until very hot, 15 to 20 minutes. Serve with the fried bread.

THE SOUP EATERS

The odd assortment of rogues in Spanish society during the Middle Ages often became characters in literature. In the picaresque (derived from the word for "rogue's den") novel, the poor rascals become antiheroes. They were known as the *sopistas,* the "soup eaters" living off the handouts of *sopa boba* at monastery doors. Two of the earliest picaresque novels were the anonymous *Lazarillo de Tormes,* published in 1554, and Francisco de Quevedo's *La Vida del Buscón,* written in 1608. These novels about down-and-out rascally youths are preoccupied with how to get food. In *Lazarillo de Tormes,* poor Lazarillo works for an evil priest who gives him one onion every four days. Lazarillo finds a tinkerer to make a copy of the key to the priest's bread box. But he can eat only mere crumbs, like a mouse, so he will not be found out.

stinging nettle soup

MY FIRST ENCOUNTER with stinging nettles was while chasing my kids through a field in Frayssinet, a little village in the Lot region of France, where my father had a place during his retirement years. My legs and hands were soon stinging from brushing against the plant. When a neighbor told me that locals make *soupe d'ortie* (nettle soup) with it, I wondered who in the world would want to eat this stuff. But I did have some in an omelet, and thought it really amazing. I learned that once you cook them, they lose their sting. In the Lot, they make nettle soup very simply, with potato, onion, garlic, and water. This Bulgarian recipe is different and quite delicious. I've adapted the recipe from Maria Kaneva-Johnson's *The Melting Pot: Balkan Food and Cookery* (1995). She tells us that in Bulgarian it is called *chorba ot dzhourkana kopriva,* which means "nettles mashed with a wooden mallet." The soup is poured into a bowl with *sirene*, a Bulgarian cheese made from either sheep's or cow's milk and very similar to feta. Some people use finely ground walnuts instead, but I think the cheese is marvelous. The most likely place you will find nettles, outside of a field, is in a farmers market, so ask the farmer if they are stinging, because not all nettles are. If they are, then you must clean them with gloves or under water as you remove the leaves. **[Makes 3 to 4 servings]**

the best soups in the world

4 quarts water

Salt to taste

1 pound fresh nettles, leaves only, washed very well

3 tablespoons unsalted butter

6 tablespoons all-purpose flour

2 ounces feta cheese, crumbled

Garlic vinegar or white wine vinegar for sprinkling (optional)

1. In a large pot, bring the water to a boil over high heat, salt lightly, add the nettles, and cook for 1 minute after it returns to a boil. Turn the heat off and leave the nettles in the pot for 5 minutes. Strain the nettles, saving 3 cups of the cooking water, place the nettles in a food processor, and purée.

2. In the pot, melt the butter over medium-high heat, then add the flour and stir constantly for 2 minutes to form a roux. Remove from the heat, stir in the nettles, then slowly stir in 2½ cups of the reserved cooking water. Return to a low heat and simmer for 2 minutes. Correct the seasoning and add the remaining cooking water if the soup is too thick; it should be soupy and creamy looking. Place the cheese in a soup bowl, ladle the soup over the cheese, and serve. Sprinkle some vinegar at the table, if desired.

smooth vegetable soups

smooth
creamed
soups

Smooth creamed soups are velvety—without chunks of meat or vegetables—and use milk or cream to create a rich, creamy effect. These tend to be the most luscious of all soups, because they are subtle, elegant, and have a lasting, satisfying flavor. There are some here I'm sure you've never had, such as cream of plantain soup, and which you will find memorable. Others, such as cream of mushroom soup, you may have had only out of a can, and once you've made your own—which is so simple—you'll never go back. There are others here that are surprisingly easy to make (especially considering the payoff in terms of taste), such as the various potato and leek soups from different cultures. These will easily slip into your soup-making repertoire.

hearts of palm soup

IN NORTH AMERICA we think of hearts of palm as something to add to a tossed salad, but in Costa Rica (and many other Latin American countries) they go into this smooth and mild soup, along with some leeks and milk. It's very simple to make, and canned hearts of palm are readily available in all supermarkets. [**Makes 4 servings**]

2 tablespoons unsalted butter

1 leek, white and light green parts only, split lengthwise,
    washed well, and thinly sliced

1 tablespoon all-purpose flour

1 tablespoon cornstarch

¼ teaspoon freshly ground white pepper and more to taste

One 14-ounce can hearts of palm, drained and cut into ½-inch pieces

2 cups chicken broth

1 cup whole milk

Salt to taste

Sweet paprika for garnish

1. In a large pot, melt the butter over low heat, then add the leek and cook, stirring occasionally, until softened, about 3 minutes. Add the flour, cornstarch, and white pepper, stir to mix, and cook for 1 minute. Add the hearts of palm and the chicken broth and cook, stirring, until well blended and soft, about 5 minutes.

2. Transfer to a blender, in batches if necessary, and process to a smooth purée. Return to a clean pot, add the milk, then bring to a boil over high heat. Reduce the heat to low and simmer for 2 minutes. Season with salt and more pepper. Ladle into individual soup bowls, sprinkle lightly with paprika, and serve.

cream of avocado soup

THIS *SOPA DE AGUACATE* is from Atlixco, an area of Mexico where many avocados grow. It's creamy smooth, very flavorful, and not too hot—a nice dish to serve before chicken, pork, or salmon. For a spicier soup, you can add a small, finely chopped habanero chile. Some Mexicans eat this soup cold, like a gazpacho, but I think it's much better hot.

[Makes 8 servings]

3 large ripe avocados, peeled, pitted, and diced

1½ cups heavy cream

¼ cup dry sherry

1 tablespoon fresh lime juice

1 tablespoon grated onion

2 garlic cloves, mashed in a mortar with 1 teaspoon salt until mushy

1 teaspoon freshly ground dried ancho chile or ½ teaspoon chili powder

1 tablespoon salt

1 teaspoon freshly ground white pepper

6 cups chicken broth

3 corn tortillas, quartered and fried in oil until crisp

Cilantro (fresh coriander) leaves for garnish

1. Place the avocados in a blender with the cream, sherry, lime juice, onion, and garlic and blend at high speed for 30 seconds. Season with the ancho chile, 1 teaspoon salt, and the white pepper.

2. Bring the chicken broth to a boil in a large pot over high heat. Reduce the heat to low and, once the broth is only simmering, add the avocado purée. Whisk the soup until smooth, taste, and add the remaining salt if desired. Serve hot, garnished with the corn tortilla pieces and coriander leaves.

cream of plantain soup

IN CUBA, ONE HARDLY SEES a table without plaintains in some form, and we think of it as an age-old fruit of the Caribbean. But the plantain is an Old World food that only arrived in the Caribbean after Columbus's voyages. It was likely the Portuguese who, in the 1500s, introduced bananas and plantains to the Americas from West Africa, to which they probably had been brought earlier by Arabs from further east. In our supermarkets plantains are almost never sold ripe, so count on buying them anywhere from two to ten days in advance. When they are ripe their skins will be mottled black and they will start to feel squishy. This Cuban soup is called *sopa de crema de platano con cilantro* and it is ever so slightly sweet, so I recommend a savory dish to follow, such as garlic chicken or roast chicken. **[Makes 6 servings]**

3 large plantains, peeled and cut into ½-inch slices
Juice from ½ lemon
3 tablespoons unsalted butter
1 medium onion, chopped
6 large garlic cloves, finely chopped
4 cups chicken broth
2 teaspoons salt and more to taste
½ teaspoon freshly ground black pepper or more to taste
¾ cup evaporated milk
½ cup fresh or canned coconut milk (page 191)
3 tablespoons freshly squeezed lime juice (from about 2 limes)
1 teaspoon grated orange zest
⅓ cup finely chopped cilantro (fresh coriander)

1. Place the sliced plantains in a bowl with the lemon juice and toss to prevent their discoloring.

2. In a large pot, melt the butter over medium heat, then add the onion and 5 garlic cloves and cook, stirring frequently, until yellow, 7 to 8 minutes. Add the plantains and chicken broth and bring to a boil over high heat. Reduce the heat to low, season with salt and pepper, and simmer until the plantains are softened, about 25 minutes.

3. Transfer the soup mixture to a blender, in batches, and purée until almost smooth, in five 2-second pulses. Caution: don't over process or it will be ruined. Return the soup to the pot, add the evaporated milk and coconut milk, and heat over low heat for 5 minutes.

4. Meanwhile, rinse the blender clean, then add the lime juice, orange zest, cilantro, and remaining garlic and blend until smooth. If necessary, add a little soup to get the blender blades to move. Pour into the soup, stir, and serve.

COCONUT MILK AND COCONUT CREAM

You will encounter these two ingredients in this book and they may seem utterly mystifying, but they are both very simple to make at home. Coconut cream, or thick coconut milk, refers to the very thick, almost solidified liquid that rises to the top after the first pressing of the boiled grated or shredded coconut is steeped. Coconut milk, or thin coconut milk, is the liquid left from this first steeping and the liquid left over after repeated pressings of the same coconut gratings with more boiling water. Although it is best to make these with freshly grated coconut, one can also use dried unsweetened grated coconut, usually available at Indian markets (the shredded coconut found in supermarkets is sweetened and not appropriate). Many supermarkets now sell canned coconut milk, which is not as good as freshly made (the canned product uses preservatives and flour as a thickener, and its taste is a little "off"), but you can still use it without harming the overall taste of the dish. To make 2 cups of coconut milk, soak 2 cups of shredded coconut in 3 cups boiling water. This same amount will produce about ¼ cup of coconut cream. Both must be refrigerated and will go bad if not frozen after several days.

crema de chile poblano

CHILE NOMENCLATURE DRIVES CHEFS NUTS because there is so much variation. The poblano chile, for example, a plump, heart-shaped, dark green chile about four inches long when mature, is called an ancho chile when it is dried. In California, supermarkets (for some completely mysterious reason) call the poblano chile a pasilla chile, which is in fact another skinnier, longer, and darker variety. *Poblano* means "from Pueblo," and this soup originates in the Mexican state of that name. Some cooks add cooked shrimp or roasted almonds to the soup as garnish. The Mexican *crema* and cheese can be found in many supermarkets.

[**Makes 4 servings**]

¾ pound russet potato, peeled and cubed large

6 poblano or pasilla chiles

3 large garlic cloves, unpeeled

2 tablespoons unsalted butter

1 medium onion, chopped

6 cups chicken broth

¾ pound Mexican *crema,* crème fraîche, or sour cream

5 ounces Mexican *queso panela* or *queso fresco* or mozzarella, cut into strips

1. Preheat the oven to 425°F.

2. Place the potato in a pot and cover with cold water. Bring to a gentle boil over medium heat, then cook until tender, about 35 minutes in all. Drain and mash the potato or pass it through a strainer.

3. Place the chiles and garlic in a baking pan and roast until the garlic is softened, about 30 minutes, and the chiles are blistered all over, about 35 minutes. Remove from the oven and let cool. Peel the garlic and chiles and discard the chile seeds. Place 5 chiles and the garlic in a food processor and run until mushy. Add the potato and run in pulses until blended. Cut the sixth chile in strips and set aside.

4. In a pot, melt the butter over medium heat, then add the onion and cook, stirring, until translucent, about 5 minutes. Reduce the heat to low, add the poblano-potato mixture, and cook, stirring, for 15 minutes. Add the chicken broth and cook over low heat for 30 minutes.

5. Ladle the soup into individual serving bowls and add some strips of the remaining chile, a dollop of *crema,* and a slice of cheese. Serve hot.

pasilla chile and pork soup

THIS SMOOTH SOUP is enhanced by the roasting of the vegetables and the type of chiles used. Ideally, you will find pasilla chiles for this recipe, but if you don't then you can use Anaheim (New Mexico), poblano, or peperoncino chiles. All these are mildly hot. You do not want to use very hot chiles, such as serranos or jalapeños, in this soup. Adding to our confusion about chiles is the fact that some supermarkets in the western United States call poblano chiles pasilla chiles. A pasilla, more correctly, is a distinct and very flavorful chile used in moles. In Mexico, it is called *chile negro,* or *chile chilaca* when fresh. It is a narrow, very dark green chile, while the poblano (called ancho chile when dried) is dark green (but lighter colored than the pasilla), short and squat, and heart-shaped; it is the chile used for *chile rellanos.*

[Makes 6 servings]

2 fresh pasilla or poblano chiles

1 medium white onion

4 large garlic cloves

2 cups canned crushed tomatoes

4 cups chicken broth

2 tablespoons roasted ground almonds

1 tablespoon extra-virgin olive oil

½ pound pork belly or fatty part of pork shoulder, diced

1 Mexican-style chorizo sausage (about 5 ounces), casing removed and meat crumbled

1 zucchini, peeled and diced small

1 teaspoon dried oregano

1 teaspoon ground cumin

⅛ teaspoon ground cloves

1 teaspoon salt or more to taste

½ teaspoon freshly ground black pepper or more to taste

½ cup sour cream or Mexican *crema*

1 tablespoon freshly squeezed lime juice

Crumbled Monterey Jack cheese or Mexican *queso panela*

Cilantro (fresh coriander) leaves for garnish

1. Preheat the oven to 425°F.

2. Place the pasilla chiles, onion, and garlic on a baking tray and roast until the garlic is soft, 20 minutes, and the chiles are blistered black and the onion is soft and golden, about 35 minutes. Remove from the oven, peel off the blistered skin of the chile, and place them all in a blender with the crushed tomatoes, 1 cup of chicken broth, and the almonds and blend until smooth.

3. In a pot or flame-proof casserole, heat the olive oil over medium heat, then cook the pork, turning occasionally, until brown and crispy, about 10 minutes. Remove the pork from the pot with a slotted spoon and set aside. Discard all but 1 tablespoon of the fat. Reduce the heat to low, add the sausage, and cook, stirring occasionally, until it turns color, about 3 minutes. Add the zucchini and cook, stirring, for 5 minutes. Return the pork to the pot with the oregano, cumin, and cloves and cook, stirring, for 5 minutes more.

4. Add the remaining chicken broth and the vegetable purée from the blender, season with the salt and pepper, and stir. Add the sour cream and lime juice and bring to a boil over medium-high heat, stirring or whisking to blend the sour cream. Reduce the heat to medium-low and cook for 10 minutes. Serve the soup garnished with crumbled cheese and cilantro leaves.

LATIN AMERICAN KIDS' DISLIKE FOR SOUP

The hugely popular Latin American comic strip "Mafalda" was created by the Argentine cartoonist Quino (the pseudonym of Joaquin Salvador Lavador) in 1964; it continued until 1973. But the character Mafalda, an unconventional little girl who hates soup, cares about humanity, loves the Beatles, and has quirky friends, lives on in many reprints and collections. "Mafalda" is still immensely popular in Latin America. Mafalda's dislike of soup, according to a 1998 study, appears to have been adopted by her fans, especially kids.[*] Children between the ages of seven and eleven in Latin America were asked about their frequency of reading "Mafalda" and their fondness for soup. Only 4 percent of the children who read "Mafalda" every day liked soup, while 55 percent of those who read the comic once a year liked soup.

the best soups in the world

*"Pan Latin-American Kids Study," Audits & Surveys Worldwide, Inc.

ecuadorian peanut soup

IN ECUADOR THIS SOUP is called *sopa de mani*. It is made by blending peanuts with potatoes, and the taste is simply heavenly. But you need to make sure the peanuts are not granular, otherwise they will tickle your throat. If you decide to use peanut butter in their place, make sure that it is 100 percent pure peanut butter with no additives.

[**Makes 4 to 6 servings**]

1 pound boiling potatoes (such as red bliss or white rose), peeled and quartered
2 tablespoons unsalted butter
1 medium onion, finely chopped
1 cup roasted unsalted peanuts, skins removed and finely ground until
    nearly a paste
4 cups chicken broth
1 cup half-and-half
2 teaspoons salt or more to taste
½ teaspoon freshly ground black pepper or more to taste
2 tablespoons chopped fresh chives

1. Place the potatoes in a pot and cover with water. Turn the heat to medium-high and once the water comes to a boil in about 15 minutes, turn the heat down to medium and cook until fork tender, about 20 minutes more. Drain the potatoes and then mash well.

2. In a skillet, melt the butter over medium-high heat, then add the onion and cook, stirring, until translucent, about 5 minutes. Place the onion in a food processor with the peanuts and 1 cup of broth and process until smooth, about 2 minutes of processing. Add the mashed potatoes and process in short pulses until smooth, but for no more than 15 seconds of processing.

3. Return the contents of the food processor to the pot, stir in the remaining 3 cups of the broth, and heat over medium heat, covered, for 15 minutes. Stir in the half-and-half, season with the salt and pepper, and simmer just long enough to heat through, about 5 minutes. Serve garnished with the chives.

pumpkin soup

THIS PURÉE OF PUMPKIN SOUP is popular in New England for Thanksgiving. It looks creamed but in fact uses very little cream. Like many chowders, you will find that this soup tastes even better the next day—so much so that I instruct you here to cool it and reheat later. Typical garnishes are drizzled olive oil, roasted red bell pepper, chopped chervil or parsley, Parmesan cheese, and oyster crackers. Of these, Parmesan cheese is my favorite.

[**Makes 6 servings**]

4½ pounds fresh pumpkin, seeds discarded, or 4 cups pumpkin purée

Extra-virgin olive oil for brushing

2 tablespoons unsalted butter

2 large shallots, finely chopped

1 tablespoon all-purpose flour

4 cups chicken broth

Salt and freshly ground black pepper to taste

½ cup heavy cream

Ground nutmeg for garnish

1. Preheat the oven to 350°F.

2. If using fresh pumpkin, brush the flesh side of the pumpkin with olive oil, then bake until easily pierced with a fork, about 1½ hours. Remove the pumpkin and discard the skin. Purée the pumpkin flesh in a food processor.

3. In a pot or flame-proof casserole, melt the butter over low heat, then add the shallots and cook, stirring occasionally, until softened, about 10 minutes. Stir in the flour and cook, stirring, to form a roux, about 2 minutes. Slowly pour in the chicken broth while whisking thoroughly to blend.

4. Add the pumpkin purée, stir to mix well, and continue cooking for 15 minutes. Season with salt and pepper and stir in the cream. Cook for another 5 minutes. Let cool in the saucepan, then refrigerate overnight and reheat in a pot the following day. Dust the top with nutmeg and use any of the garnishes mentioned in the introduction if desired.

Variation: Add 1 roasted red bell pepper to the pumpkin purée in Step 2 or 1 roasted red bell pepper diced as a garnish.

cream of mushroom soup

THIS RECIPE IS WHAT cream of mushroom soup could have tasted like in 1933. By 1934, the Campbell's Soup Company had canned a condensed cream of mushroom soup, and thereafter few people made it from scratch. But this you should try. It's a very intense mushroom soup and utterly delicious. I say *"could* have tasted like in 1933" because the shiitake mushrooms, Marsala wine, and crème fraîche called for here were little known in Depression-era American kitchens. **[Makes 6 servings]**

¼ cup unsalted butter

1¼ pounds white or shiitake mushrooms, brushed clean and sliced

3 tablespoons all-purpose flour

1½ cups hot milk (any kind)

2 tablespoons dry Marsala wine

4 cups hot chicken broth

½ cup crème fraîche (preferably) or sour cream

½ cup heavy cream

1 teaspoon lemon juice

Salt and freshly ground black pepper to taste

1. In a pot, melt the butter over medium heat, then add the mushrooms and cook, stirring, until browned and softened, about 15 minutes. Reduce the heat to low, add the flour and cook, stirring, until it has blended with the mushrooms, about 2 minutes. Slowly add the hot milk, stirring until it is all absorbed, then simmer for 15 minutes.

2. Stir in the Marsala wine, then add the chicken broth and simmer for another 15 minutes. Place the mushroom mixture in a blender, in batches if necessary, and run for 2 minutes or until smooth. Transfer the blended mixture back to the pot and stir in the crème fraîche and heavy cream. Simmer over a low heat for 35 minutes. Season with lemon juice, salt, and pepper and serve.

cream of celery soup

CREAM OF CELERY SOUP is an American favorite probably introduced in Michigan in the 1870s. Although celery was domesticated in the Mediterranean, eighteenth-century London is where celery soup shows up on the menus of clubs and restaurants. The vegetable was not widely known in America until a Scotsman, George Taylor, began its mass cultivation in the 1850s in Kalamazoo, Michigan, where the rich, mucky organic soil was ideal for the plants. At first, celery was a novelty sold by vendors to passengers on trains passing through Kalamazoo. But it wasn't long before the simple celery soup of London became a smooth cream of celery soup, common enough for the Campbell's Soup Company to condense and can in 1913. You can serve the soup garnished with celery leaves, parsley leaves, or butter-fried croûtons (page 129), if desired. **[Makes 4 servings]**

3 cups water

1½ cups chopped celery

1 small potato, peeled and diced

1 small carrot, peeled and diced

½ small onion, chopped

3½ teaspoons salt

2 tablespoons unsalted butter

2 tablespoons all-purpose flour

⅛ teaspoon freshly ground white pepper

3 cups whole milk, hot

1. In a pot, add the water, celery, potato, carrot, and onion, bring to a boil, season with 3 teaspoons of the salt, and cook at a boil, stirring once or twice, until tender, about 20 minutes. Transfer the vegetables and the remaining liquid to a blender in batches and blend until smooth.

2. In a pot, prepare a thin béchamel (white) sauce: melt the butter over medium heat, then stir in the flour to form a roux, season with ½ teaspoon salt and the white pepper, and cook, stirring, for 1 minute. Remove the pot from the heat, then slowly pour in the milk, stirring constantly. Return the pot to medium heat and cook, stirring frequently, until the sauce thickens a bit and is bubbling, about 12 minutes.

3. Transfer the smooth celery purée to the pot with the béchamel sauce. Stir well to blend and reheat over medium heat for about 5 minutes. Correct the seasoning if necessary and serve.

smooth creamed soups

cream of carrot with ginger soup

OUR FAMILIAR ORANGE CARROT, the only color a carrot should have, many feel, was first cultivated in seventeenth-century Holland, so it's unlikely a cream of carrot soup existed before then. Until then it seems likely that people ate wild carrots, which are white. More than likely it was the French who created a cream of carrot soup. In any case, although we don't know whose idea it was to add ginger, this delicious soup became popular in American restaurants in the 1980s. It's quite easy to make at home, and it appeals to many palates.

[**Makes 6 servings**]

2 tablespoons unsalted butter

2 medium onions, coarsely chopped

1½ pounds young carrots, peeled and sliced

3 tablespoons chopped fresh ginger

6 cups hot chicken broth

1 cup whole milk

1½ cups half-and-half

3 teaspoons salt or more to taste

½ teaspoon freshly ground black pepper

FOR THE GARNISHES (CHOOSE ONE)

Croûtons fried in butter (page 129)
Chopped cilantro (fresh coriander) leaves

the best soups in the world

1. In a pot, melt the butter over low heat, then add the onions and cook, stirring, until slightly softened, about 15 minutes. Increase the heat to medium-low, then add the carrots and ginger and cook, stirring frequently, until the carrots are softer, about 20 minutes.

2. Add the chicken broth to the pot, bring to a boil over medium heat, then cook, stirring occasionally, for 20 minutes. Remove the soup from the heat and add the milk. Transfer to a blender and blend, in batches if necessary, until it forms a purée. Return the soup to the pot, add the half-and-half, season with the salt and pepper, and cook until very hot without letting it come to a boil. Serve hot with one of the garnishes.

cream of tomato soup

THERE ARE TWO FAMOUS American tomato soups: one is a winter cream of tomato soup using canned tomatoes and cream, and the other a summer tomato soup using fresh ripe tomatoes (page 162). I suppose the most famous tomato soup is the one Andy Warhol used as a subject for his 1960s pieces featuring Campbell's tomato soup cans (among others). This recipe is soothing and delicious. If you don't have ripe fresh tomatoes available, then use good-quality canned tomatoes. I have clearer memories of the grilled cheese sandwich that always accompanied cream of tomato soup, because the soup my mom gave me always came out of a can. This, however, is the real thing, and quite amazing. Older recipes call for baking soda to prevent the milk from curdling, but in this recipe I use cream.

[Makes 4 servings]

3 tablespoons unsalted butter

1 small onion, chopped

1 tablespoon all-purpose flour

1½ pounds ripe tomatoes, fresh or canned, peeled (page 273), seeded, and chopped

2 cups chicken broth

1 teaspoon sugar

1 teaspoon salt or more to taste

¼ teaspoon freshly ground black pepper or more to taste

3 tablespoons heavy cream

1. In a pot, melt the butter over medium heat, then add the onion and cook, stirring, until softened, 7 to 8 minutes. Stir in the flour, then add the tomatoes, chicken broth, sugar, salt, and pepper and bring to a boil over high heat. Reduce the heat to low, and simmer, partially covered, for 25 minutes.

2. Let the soup cool for a few minutes, then transfer to a blender, in batches if necessary, and blend until smooth. Return to a cleaned pot and stir in the cream. Heat over medium heat until the soup is hot and serve.

the best soups in the world

cream of red kidney
bean soup

THIS QUICK AND EASY SOUP uses a can of dark red kidney beans, which give the soup an appetizing purple haze, flecked ever so minutely with specks of red. I usually garnish with croûtons, but you can also use thin slices of cooked Italian sausage, chopped chives, or chervil.

[Makes 4 servings]

2 tablespoons extra-virgin olive oil
1 tablespoon unsalted butter
1 small onion, chopped
1 large garlic clove, finely chopped
One 16-ounce can red kidney beans, undrained
3 cups chicken broth
½ cup heavy cream
1 teaspoon salt
½ teaspoon freshly ground black pepper
½ cup croûtons (page 129)

1. In a pot, heat the olive oil and butter over medium-high heat, then add the onion and garlic and cook, stirring, until translucent, about 4 minutes. Stir in the kidney beans and their liquid and heat for a couple of minutes, then add the chicken broth and cook for 5 minutes. Remove from the heat and let cool for 10 minutes.

2. Transfer the soup to a blender, in batches if necessary, and blend for about 2 minutes. Return to the pot, stir in the cream, and heat over medium heat. Season with the salt and pepper and serve with croûtons.

cream of kohlrabi and green bean soup

KOHLRABI IS THE SWOLLEN CORM—the turniplike part of the stem just above ground level—of a plant in the cabbage family, but its taste is not at all like cabbage. Kohlrabi has a curious shape that I swear reminds me of the first Russian satellite, Sputnik. Originally a Mediterranean vegetable, it is not well-known. In this creamy soup, the vegetables are the real stars, but it's the truffle oil and walnut oil that put it over the top. Truffle and walnut oils can be found in Italian markets and in supermarkets among the oils or in the gourmet foods aisle.

[**Makes 4 servings**]

the best soups in the world

6 cups water

Salt to taste

2 kohlrabies, trimmed, peeled, and cut into french-fry shapes

½ pound green beans, trimmed

6 tablespoons heavy cream

4 teaspoons freshly squeezed lemon juice

1 teaspoon truffle oil

½ teaspoon freshly ground black pepper

1 cup croûtons (page 129, but cooked in 2 tablespoons extra-virgin
   olive oil and 1 tablespoon walnut oil)

1. Bring the water to a boil in a pot, salt lightly, then add the kohlrabies and green beans and cook until tender, 13 to 15 minutes.

2. Transfer the vegetables and liquid, in batches if necessary, to a blender and purée until smooth. Return to a clean pot and cook over medium heat for 10 minutes. Add the cream, lemon juice, truffle oil, 4 teaspoons salt, and pepper and heat for another 5 minutes over medium heat. Serve the soup hot with the croûtons.

cream of brussels sprouts soup

THE COMMENT I RECEIVE THE MOST about this soup is, "This is great, and I don't even like Brussels sprouts." So without a doubt, this is how you introduce people to Brussels sprouts. This soup is based on a similar one, called *kohlsprossensuppe,* that I had when I lived in Salzburg, Austria, through the fall and winter of 1977. I found it thoroughly enjoyable then and still like to make it during colder weather. **[Makes 6 servings]**

1 pound Brussels sprouts, trimmed
¼ cup unsalted butter
6 tablespoons all-purpose flour
4 cups chicken broth
2 large egg yolks
1 cup heavy cream
Salt and freshly ground black pepper to taste
1 tablespoon chopped fresh chervil or parsley
2 tablespoons hazelnut oil (optional)
3 tablespoons crushed roasted hazelnuts (optional)

1. Bring a large pot of lightly salted water to a boil over high heat, then add the Brussels sprouts and boil until tender when pierced by a fork, about 20 minutes. Drain, saving 2 cups of the cooking water, and set aside the Brussels sprouts.

2. In a pot, melt the butter over medium-high heat, then stir in the flour to form a roux and cook, stirring constantly, until golden, about 2 minutes. Slowly pour in the 2 cups of reserved cooking water and the chicken broth. Cook, stirring frequently, until smooth, about 5 minutes. Add the Brussels sprouts, reduce the heat to low, and simmer, stirring occasionally, for 30 minutes. Pass the soup through a food mill into another pot. If you don't have a food mill, process briefly in a blender.

3. In a small bowl, stir together the egg yolks and cream. Stir the cream mixture into the soup and heat over medium heat, making sure it does not bubble or boil. Season with salt and pepper and garnish with the chervil and hazelnut oil and hazelnuts, if desired. Serve hot.

roasted garlic soup

ONE THINKS OF GARLIC as the quintessential Mediterranean condiment or spice, but in the Middle Ages the English were fond of garlic, the French and Italians only used it in sauces, and city folk thought it a primitive peasant food. This recipe is a modern one, and although you might think the garlic would be overwhelming, it's not. This is a very smooth, creamy soup that is delicious and filling. Make sure you use very dry sherry and not cream sherry, which will discolor the soup and give it an odd taste. **[Makes 4 servings]**

4 garlic heads, left whole, top quarter of nonstem end sliced off

3 tablespoons extra-virgin olive oil

6 tablespoons unsalted butter

1 medium onion, chopped

3 leeks, white part only, split lengthwise, washed well, and chopped

6 tablespoons all-purpose flour

4 cups hot chicken broth

6 tablespoons very dry sherry

1 cup heavy cream

2 teaspoons freshly squeezed lemon juice

1½ teaspoons salt

½ teaspoon freshly ground white pepper

2 tablespoons chopped fresh chives

1. Preheat the oven to 350°F.

2. Place the garlic heads in a small, shallow baking dish, cut side up, and drizzle with the olive oil. Bake until golden and soft, 50 to 60 minutes. Remove the garlic from the oven and when cool enough to handle, squeeze out the garlic. Chop the garlic.

3. In a pot, melt the butter over medium heat, then add the onion, leeks, and garlic and cook, stirring, until softened and mushy, about 8 minutes. Reduce the heat to low. Stir in the flour to form a roux, then cook, stirring occasionally, until pasty and thick, about 10 minutes.

4. Pour the hot broth and sherry into the pot in a slow stream while stirring constantly, then simmer, stirring occasionally, until bubbling, about 20 minutes. Turn the heat off and let cool for 15 minutes.

5. Transfer the soup to a blender and purée, in batches if necessary. Return the soup to the pot. Add the cream and simmer until thickened, about 10 minutes. Add the lemon juice and season with salt and white pepper. Serve garnished with chives.

czech smooth potato soup

IF YOU DIDN'T KNOW BETTER you might think the only soups Czechs eat are those with potatoes, bacon, beer, cream, or leeks. Well, it's true there is a theme to Czech soup cookery, and any time you put potatoes and bacon together with cream you are going to have one delicious soup. This is called *bramborova lisovana polevka,* or "smooth potato soup," and although from the ingredients it sounds quite rich, the final effect is not heavy at all. You could, of course, replace the pork lard with butter, but I recommend the lard for an authentic taste. The ideal bread to use is soft poppy-seed rolls. **[Makes 4 servings]**

1¼ pounds all-purpose potatoes, peeled and cubed

5 cups water

3 teaspoons salt or more to taste

¼ cup pork lard or unsalted butter

1 cup diced slab bacon (about ¼ pound)

2 soft bread rolls (4 to 5 ounces), sliced

1 cup heavy cream

1 large egg yolk

3 tablespoons chopped fresh parsley

1. Place the potatoes in a pot with the water and 1 teaspoon salt and bring to a boil over high heat, then reduce to medium and cook until tender, about 35 minutes in all. Remove the potatoes without dumping the water, pass the potatoes through a food mill or sieve, and return to the potato water in the pot.

2. Meanwhile, in a skillet, melt the lard over medium heat, then add the diced bacon and cook, stirring, until crispy, about 8 minutes. Remove the bacon with a slotted spoon and set aside. Cook the bread slices in the skillet until golden on both sides, about 2 minutes in all. Remove and set aside.

3. In a small bowl, mix the cream and egg yolk, then stir into the soup and heat over low heat for a few minutes, until the soup is very hot but not bubbling. Add the remaining 2 teaspoons of salt, stir, then taste and add some more if necessary. Add the bacon and parsley, stir, and serve with the slices of fried bread.

russian swiss chard soup

IT'S A WONDER that this Russian favorite known as *shchav* isn't better known. Well, it is hard to pronounce. In Russia, it's quite a famous soup. *Shchav* means "sorrel," so you can make the soup with sorrel, but Swiss chard is traditional as well. This soup is also known elsewhere in eastern Europe—in the Ukraine, Poland, and among eastern European Jews. Once you taste it you'll have a new perspective on that otherwise tough, leafy green vegetable considered spinach's poor relation. **[Makes 4 to 6 servings]**

2 tablespoons unsalted butter
1 pound Swiss chard, washed well, stems sliced, and leaves chopped
2 tablespoons all-purpose flour
1½ cups chicken broth
½ cup sour cream
Salt and freshly ground black pepper to taste
2 large eggs, hard-boiled, shelled, and cut in half

1. In a flame-proof casserole, melt the butter over medium heat, then add the Swiss chard stems and cook, covered and stirring once or twice, for 4 minutes. Add the leaves and cook covered, stirring occasionally, for 4 minutes more.

2. Sprinkle with the flour and stir until blended. Slowly pour in the chicken broth and sour cream and cook, covered and stirring once or twice, until slightly thickened, about 4 minutes.

3. Transfer the soup to a blender and process until it is puréed. Transfer to a pot, season with salt and pepper, heat for a few minutes, and serve with the egg halves as a garnish.

belgian lettuce and pea soup

THIS SMOOTH, FLAVORFUL SOUP is made with the soft buttery lettuce known as Boston head lettuce or, appropriately, butter lettuce. In Belgium, where this dish is much appreciated, it is called *soupe mosane,* meaning soup from the Meuse, the great river valley that was the scene of heavy fighting in World War I. Be careful with the salting, as your ham may be saltier than expected. **[Makes 4 servings]**

¼ cup unsalted butter
1 head Boston lettuce, shredded
4 scallions, trimmed and sliced
1 celery stalk, chopped
6 cups water
½ pound (2 cups) fresh or frozen peas
½ pound cooked ham, in one piece
1 teaspoon thyme
1 bay leaf
1 teaspoon salt
½ teaspoon freshly ground black pepper
½ cup heavy cream
2 tablespoons finely chopped fresh parsley

1. In a large pot, melt the butter over medium-low heat, then add the lettuce, scallions, and celery and cook, stirring, until softened, about 10 minutes. Add the water, peas, ham, thyme, bay leaf, salt, and pepper and bring to a boil over high heat. Reduce the heat to low and simmer for 1 hour.

2. Remove the ham and cut into small pieces. Strain the broth. Place the vegetables in a blender and purée using some of the broth to help the blade turn. Return the broth and the puréed vegetables to the pot along with the ham. Add the cream, heat to just below a boil over medium heat, then serve with parsley.

smooth creamed soups

basler mehlsuppe

IN THE EARLY 1970S I lived in Basel, Switzerland, for a year. The trolley from my home to school wound its way through the city's historic center, and sometimes I would alight there to shop, meet friends, or have some lunch. In the winter, a *Basler mehlsuppe* was a most welcome soup—smooth, richly flavorful, and very satisfying even if very simple. The soup uses a hard raw whole-milk cheese called *Sbrinz* made in the Swiss cantons around Lucerne. When it's young it has the consistency of Gruyère, which is what I now most often use. When it's older it's a grating cheese like Parmesan. You can order *Sbrinz* via the Internet at www.igourmet.com. I've adapted this recipe from Marianne Kaltenbach's *Aechti Schwizer Chuchi: Schweizer Kuchenrezepte Rund ums Jahr* (1977).　　**[Makes 4 servings]**

¼ cup all-purpose flour

¼ cup (½ stick) unsalted butter

1 pound onions, halved and very thinly sliced

6 cups beef broth

¾ cup dry red wine

¼ teaspoon dried marjoram

Pinch of ground nutmeg

Salt to taste

½ teaspoon freshly ground black pepper

3 ounces *Sbrinz* cheese (or other Swiss cheese such as Gruyère or
    Emmentaler or domestic Swiss cheese), shredded

¼ cup heavy cream

1 tablespoon finely chopped fresh parsley

1 tablespoon finely chopped fresh chives

1. Place the flour in a cast-iron skillet without any fat, turn the heat to medium-high, and cook the flour, shaking the pan or stirring almost constantly, until it is dark brown, about 8 minutes; as the flour darkens, make sure it doesn't burn and turn black by stirring a little faster. Remove from the skillet and let cool.

2. In a pot, melt the butter over medium-high heat, then add the onions and cook, stirring, until translucent, about 8 minutes. Stir in the flour and mix well. Add the beef broth slowly, stirring the whole time. Add the red wine, bring to a boil over high heat, then reduce the heat to low and cook for 1 hour. Season with the marjoram, nutmeg, salt, and pepper.

3. Transfer the soup to a blender and run until a smooth purée is formed. Return to the pot and check the seasonings. Bring the soup to a boil over high heat, then serve with the shredded cheese. Garnish the soup with the cream, parsley, and chives.

lobster mushroom and hazelnut butter soup

THIS UNIQUE AND QUITE EXTRAORDINARY SOUP called *potage aux oronges et aux noisettes, magnificat* (a praiseworthy Caesar mushroom and hazelnut soup) is from the Franche-Comté, the Alpine French province next to Switzerland, and is made with Caesar mushrooms called *oronges*. These are *Amanita caesarea*, the thin orange-capped mushrooms very popular among gourmets of France and Italy, but not at all so in North America because of their similarity to poisonous varieties of *Amanita*, which are in fact known as death's heads. In this recipe you can play it safe with lobster mushrooms or chanterelles. The powdered dried mushroom called for in the ingredient list can be made by placing dried mushrooms in a coffee mill or spice grinder. **[Makes 8 servings]**

¼ pound (1 stick) butter, at room temperature

3 ounces blanched hazelnuts (about ½ cup), ground fine in
    a food processor

¾ pound lobster mushrooms or chanterelle mushrooms, julienned

2 heads Boston lettuce, greenest leaves removed and used for
    salad, remaining lettuce shredded

1 tablespoon salt

1½ teaspoons freshly ground black pepper or more to taste

½ teaspoon sugar

¼ cup medium or long grain rice

1 veal knuckle or 2 beef oxtails (about 1½ pounds in all)

1 medium onion, chopped

½ teaspoon dried mushroom powder

6 cups water

4 cups whole milk

1 teaspoon truffle oil

2 large egg yolks, lightly beaten

½ cup heavy cream

1. Place half the butter in a food processor with the ground hazelnuts and process until it forms a nut butter. Remove the hazelnut butter and push it through a fine mesh strainer with the back of a wooden spoon or a pestle. Set the butter aside until needed.

2. In a bowl, toss the mushrooms with the lettuce, salt, pepper, and sugar.

3. In a small pot, bring ½ cup of water to a boil over high heat, then add the rice, cook for 1 minute, and drain.

4. In a large flame-proof casserole, melt the remaining butter over medium-low heat, then add the lettuce and mushroom mixture, stir, cover, and steam, stirring occasionally, for 30 minutes.

5. Add the veal, onion, rice, and mushroom powder, and then the water and milk. Bring to a near boil over high heat, making absolutely sure it does not come to a boil, then reduce the heat to low and simmer, partially covered, until the meat is nearly falling off the veal, about 2½ hours. Remove the veal and reserve for making Minestrone with Beef, Veal, and Pork Spareribs (page 275).

6. Strain the soup 3 times through a fine mesh strainer, pushing the solid pieces through with a pestle the first 2 times. The third and last time you strain, discard any bits that remain.

7. Pour into a clean pot, add the truffle oil, and correct the seasoning if necessary. Turn the heat to medium, but do not let the soup boil. Place the nut butter in the bottom of a soup tureen with the egg yolks and cream. Pour in the hot soup, stirring vigorously, and serve hot.

potato and leek soup # 1

LEEKS, ONIONS, AND POTATOES are all favorite vegetables in Croatia, and here they come together in a goose- and/or duck-based broth called *juha od poriluka*. After the leeks are cooked it is probably easier to liquefy them in a blender, rather than passing them through a food mill or using a food processor. If using canned chicken broth instead of homemade, taste for saltiness at the finish and adjust accordingly. **[Makes 6 servings]**

¼ cup unsalted butter
1½ pounds leeks, split in half lengthwise, washed well, and chopped
2 large onions, chopped
6 cups goose or duck broth (preferably) or chicken broth
Salt and freshly ground black pepper to taste
¾ pound potato, peeled and diced
½ cup sour cream

1. In a flame-proof casserole or large skillet, melt the butter over medium heat, then add the leeks and onions, reduce the heat to low, and simmer gently, stirring occasionally, until the onions are translucent and slightly caramelized, about 45 minutes.

2. Add the broth and cook until the leeks are very tender, about 1 hour. Strain, then put the leeks in a blender in batches with a cup of broth each time so the blender can work properly and run until liquefied, about 1 minute blending at the highest setting. Return the puréed leeks and broth to a large pot, season with salt and pepper, and bring to a boil. Add the potato and cook until tender, about 15 minutes. Correct the seasoning, add some sour cream to each individual serving bowl, ladle in some soup, and serve hot.

the best soups in the world

potato and leek soup # 2

***POTAGE PARMENTIER* IS ONE OF** the most famous and delightful French soups. It was named after Antoine-Augustin Parmentier, a French economist and agronomist, who was a prisoner of war in Hanover under the Prussians during the Seven Years' War. He survived on potatoes, then not at all popular in France, and upon his return was inspired to work for the reintroduction of the potato to France. He subsequently wrote *Sur la pomme de terre* (On the potato), published in 1789, and today any preparation called *parmentier* is one with potatoes. The soup is also known as *soupe à la bonne femme* (old wives' soup). When served cold it is known as a vichyssoise or *crème gauloise*. **[Makes 4 servings]**

6 tablespoons unsalted butter

3 leeks (1 pound in all), white part only, split lengthwise, washed well, and thinly sliced

1 pound baking potatoes, peeled and cut into chunks

4 cups water

Salt and freshly ground black pepper to taste

2 cups hot milk

1 large egg yolk

2 tablespoons crème fraîche or heavy cream

1 teaspoon finely chopped fresh chervil (optional)

Croûtons fried in butter (page 129) for garnish

smooth creamed soups

1. In a pot, melt 2 tablespoons of the butter over low heat, then add the leeks and cook, stirring, until softened, about 20 minutes. Add the potatoes and water. Season with salt and pepper and bring to a boil over high heat. Boil, covered, until the potatoes are softened, about 20 minutes. Mash the potatoes in the pot.

2. Pass the potatoes and leeks through a food mill into a clean pot. Add the milk to thin the soup and bring to a boil over high heat. Add the egg yolk, whisking constantly, then add the remaining 4 tablespoons butter and the crème fraîche and turn the heat off. Add the chervil, if using, and let heat for a few minutes. Serve hot with fried croûtons.

soup of upland cress

IN THE MORE RURAL AREAS of Provence, in the small valleys and foothills, away from the touristy coast, one finds cooks more willing than the bourgeois housewives of the cities to use wild salad greens in their preparations. Most such greens are rarely cultivated, although a few are. They appear for the most part in soups, salads, and omelets. This soup, called *potage de cresson Alénois,* is a wonderful way to use upland cress (*Barbarea verna*), which here is usually sold by gourmet greengrocers and at farmers markets. Some supermarkets sell it, too, but label it watercress (read the fine print and you can see it's upland cress). You can replace upland cress with watercress. **[Makes 4 servings]**

5 tablespoons unsalted butter
¾ pound upland cress (garden cress), heavy stems removed, washed well,
   and chopped
1 quart vegetable or chicken broth
10 ounces all-purpose potatoes, peeled and sliced
Salt and freshly ground black pepper to taste
¼ cup heavy cream
Croûtons (page 129, but fried in butter), for garnish

In a pot, melt 4 tablespoons of the butter over medium heat, then add the cress and cook, covered, until it wilts, 2 to 3 minutes. Add the broth and potatoes and cook over medium-low heat until tender, 20 to 25 minutes. Pass the broth through a sieve or food mill and return it to the pot. Season with salt and pepper, add the cream and remaining butter, heat thoroughly, and serve with croutons.

watercress soup

THIS BEAUTIFULLY COLORED SOUP, called *potage au cresson,* is found everywhere in France. It was adapted from a recipe in my friend Alexandra Leaf's *Impressionists' Table: Recipes and Gastronomy of 19th-Century France.* The soup is delicate without being creamy or heavy, and it's perfect served before roast veal or chicken. **[Makes 4 servings]**

1 medium-size all-purpose potato

2 tablespoons unsalted butter

1 small onion, finely chopped

2 bunches watercress (about 1 pound), leaves only

4 cups vegetable or chicken broth

½ cup heavy cream

2 large egg yolks

Salt and freshly ground black pepper to taste

1. Place the potato in a pot and cover with water by several inches. Turn the heat to medium-high and once the water comes to a boil, after about 15 minutes, reduce the heat to medium and cook until easily pierced by a skewer, about another 20 minutes. Drain, peel, crumble, and set aside.

2. In a flame-proof casserole or pot, melt the butter over low heat, then add the onion and cook, stirring, until it is translucent, about 10 minutes. Add the watercress and cook, stirring, until it has wilted. Add the broth and cook for 10 minutes. Transfer to a blender with the crumbled potato and purée for 3 minutes. (Don't worry, the potato will not become gummy as it would if you processed it alone.)

3. Blend the cream and egg yolks in the pot or casserole and then add the soup. Cook over low heat, seasoning with salt and pepper, until hot, about 10 minutes, without ever letting it come to even a near boil. Serve hot.

smooth creamed soups

cream of cauliflower soup

IN THE 1950S, when I was a child, my father was stationed in France with the U.S. Air Force, and we lived for some time in Beaumont-le-Roger in Normandy. Although I don't remember the food from those halcyon days of my rural French childhood, I have made many subsequent trips to the area and am quite fond of Norman food. The region is famous for its duck, apples, and Camembert cheese. Norman soups, especially cream soups, have a lusciousness I always associate with French cuisine. **[Makes 4 to 6 servings]**

4 cups chicken broth

1 cauliflower (about 2 pounds), trimmed and broken into florets

1 small boiling potato (5 ounces), peeled and diced

Bouquet garni, tied in kitchen twine, consisting of 2 tarragon sprigs

¾ cup heavy cream

⅛ teaspoon curry powder

⅛ teaspoon ground nutmeg

2 tablespoons fresh lemon juice

1 tablespoon salt

2 teaspoons freshly ground white pepper

2 teaspoons finely chopped fresh chives

2 teaspoons finely chopped fresh tarragon

1. In a large pot, bring the chicken broth to a boil over medium-high heat, then add the cauliflower and potato with the bouquet garni, cover, and cook until very tender, about 15 minutes.

2. Transfer the vegetables to a blender and blend until puréed. Return the purée to the pot, add the cream, and stir. Add the curry powder, nutmeg, lemon juice, salt, and pepper and heat over medium heat until hot. Serve in individual bowls sprinkled with the chives and tarragon for garnish.

purée of root vegetable soup

THE FRENCH SEEM TO BE MASTERS of the puréed soup, and their vegetable soups are some of the best. The combinations are infinite, of course, but in this instance the flavors are based on root vegetables. There is very little fat used, and as a result the taste is light and refreshing, yet satisfying.   **[Makes 4 servings]**

3 tablespoons unsalted butter

1 leek, white and light green part only, split lengthwise in quarters,
   washed well, and chopped

1 large garlic clove, finely chopped

1 tablespoon finely chopped fresh parsley

1½ cups (½ pound) coarsely chopped carrots

1 cup (6 ounces) coarsely chopped turnips

6 cups water

1½ cups (½ pound) peeled and diced potatoes

¼ cup crème fraîche or heavy cream

2½ teaspoons salt or more to taste

½ teaspoon freshly ground black pepper or more to taste

1. In a pot, melt 2 tablespoons of the butter over low heat, then add the leek, garlic, and parsley and cook, covered, until they sweat, about 5 minutes. Add the carrots and turnips, stir, cover, and cook, stirring, for 5 more minutes. Pour in the water and bring to a boil over high heat. Add the potatoes, reduce the heat to low, cover, and simmer until very tender, about 45 minutes.

2. Remove the soup from the heat and strain the broth. Return the liquid to the pot and place the vegetables in a blender with a little of the liquid to help the blades turn. Blend until puréed, then return to the pot. Bring to a boil over high heat, then remove from the heat, and whisk in the remaining tablespoon of butter and the crème fraîche. Season with the salt and pepper and serve hot.

artichoke velouté

THE NAME FOR THIS northern Italian soup, *vellutata di carciofi,* comes from the French word *velouté,* meaning "velvety." This creamy, smooth, and elegant soup made of artichokes typically is served as a first course. Because it is rich it is best followed by a simple second course, such as grilled fish. **[Makes 4 to 6 servings]**

½ cup (1 stick) unsalted butter, at room temperature
¼ cup all-purpose unbleached flour
5 cups chicken broth
8 large cooked fresh artichoke hearts or 16 canned
    artichoke hearts (two 14-ounce cans)
4 large egg yolks
1 cup heavy cream
Croûtons (optional, page 129)

1. In a pot, melt ¼ cup butter over medium-high heat. Using a wire whisk, stir in the flour and cook, stirring, until the flour becomes light brown and smells nutty, about 3 minutes. Slowly pour in 4 cups chicken broth, whisking all the time until smooth and creamy.

2. Place the artichoke hearts in a food processor and process until finely puréed, stopping the machine and scraping down the sides when necessary. You should have about 2 cups artichoke purée. Beat the egg yolks and cream together.

3. Remove the artichoke purée from the food processor and blend into the broth, stirring in the remaining 1 cup chicken broth. Return the artichoke broth to the food processor in batches and process until completely smooth and a little frothy, transferring it to a pot as you process each batch.

4. Bring the soup to a boil over medium heat. Remove from the heat and vigorously and constantly whisk in the egg yolk and cream. Return to very low heat and whisk in the remaining ¼ cup of butter 1 tablespoon at a time until completely melted. Serve immediately, with croûtons, if desired.

the best soups in the world

Smooth legume soups are those in which legumes are puréed with other ingredients. I am using "legume" in its culinary, not its botanical sense. In culinary terms, legumes include peas and beans. Botanically, a legume is a pea but not a bean. None of this will matter to you once you start making such delicious soups as the first one offered here, the Tarascan Bean Soup, with its puréed red kidney beans flavored with chipotle chiles, tomatoes, and onion. There are familiar classics, too, such as split green pea soup, which so many of us remember from our childhood, although this recipe is flavored with a smoked ham hock, leek, and onion and is correspondingly more satisfying. The best of the smooth legume soups is here too. It's Najwa's Lentil Soup. Najwa, my former wife, says it's nothing really. Oh, yeah? Well, it was chosen one of the 150 best American recipes ever!

smooth legume soups

tarascan bean soup

SOPA TARASCA **IS** *THE* **SOUP** from the home of the Tarascan (or P'urhépecha) people in the Mexican state of Michoacan. These Native Americans spoke a language with little relation to any other, and their origins remain unknown. They flourished from 1100 to 1530. When the Spanish arrived in the sixteenth century the Tarascan were unable to forge an alliance with the Aztecs, their enemies on their eastern border, and subsequently by 1530 both empires had succumbed to the Spanish. The center of their culture was Lake Pátzcuaro, and nearby Tzintzuntzan is now a much-visited archaeological site. It was the Spanish who named them Tarascan and who recognized their excellent craftsmanship. **[Makes 4 servings]**

1 cup (½ pound) dried red kidney beans

2 sprigs fresh epazote, finely chopped or 2 teaspoons dried (optional)

2 teaspoons dried oregano

1 teaspoon salt and more as needed

Water as needed

1 pound plum tomatoes, cut in half and seeded

2 large garlic cloves

1 tablespoon extra-virgin olive oil

½ large white onion, sliced

½ cup peanut oil

2 dried pasilla chiles

2 tablespoons chopped canned chipotle chile in adobo

½ pound Monterey Jack cheese, cut into 4 slices

the best soups in the world

1. Place the beans in a pot with the epazote, if using, the oregano, salt, and enough water to cover the beans by 3 inches. Bring to a boil over high heat. Reduce to medium heat and simmer until the beans are softened, about 1½ hours. Add more water if it is evaporating too rapidly and the beans are exposed. Drain, saving 1 cup of the cooking water.

2. Preheat the oven to 350°F.

3. Place the tomatoes and garlic in a baking tray and roast until the garlic is softened, about 25 minutes, and the tomatoes are softened and their skins can be pulled off, about 45 minutes. Peel the tomatoes and garlic and set aside.

4. Meanwhile, in a skillet, heat the olive oil over medium-high heat, then add the onion and cook, stirring, until it softens just a little bit, about 3 minutes. Remove the onion from the skillet, add the peanut oil, and let heat for 3 minutes. Add the pasilla chiles and cook until they soften, about 30 seconds, then remove and cool a bit. Once they are cool enough to handle, seed them and cut into strips. Set aside until needed.

5. Transfer the tomatoes and garlic to a blender with the beans, onion, and chipotle, and blend using the reserved cup of cooking water to help the blades turn. Add a little water if it seems too thick. Pass the purée through a food mill or fine-meshed sieve to remove seeds and skins.

6. Transfer the blender mixture to a pot and heat over low heat until it starts to bubble slightly. Add the slices of cheese and the chile strips to the soup, season with salt, and stir until the cheese has melted, then ladle the soup into heated bowls.

cream of
black bean soup

BEFORE I MOVED TO CALIFORNIA, I thought Mexican food was Mexican food. Now, I have a much better understanding of that country's regional cuisines and their differences. In my neighborhood, many Mexican-Americans trace their families to the state of Oaxaca, the home of moles. This soup is not a mole, but it is a delicious purée of flavored black beans that is garnished with roasted chile, crumbled cheese, and tortilla chips, called *totopos* in Oaxaca. It is called *crema frijolito* and is a dish served at the Temple restaurant on García Vigil 409-A, in downtown Oaxaca, Mexico. **[Makes 4 servings]**

½ pound (about 1 cup) dried small black beans, soaked in water to
    cover for 8 hours or overnight and drained

1 large garlic clove, coarsely chopped

¾ cup coarsely chopped white onion

2 teaspoons dried epazote or 2 tablespoons chopped fresh epazote or
    1 fresh sage leaf (optional)

8 cups water

2½ teaspoons salt or more to taste

2 tablespoons butter

½ cup Mexican *crema,* crème fraîche, or sour cream

Chopped fresh epazote (optional)

FOR THE GARNISH

2 ounces crumbled Mexican *queso fresco* or farmer's cheese

1 roasted fresh pasilla chile or Anaheim (New Mexico) chile, seeded and
    cut into 4 strips

Chopped fresh parsley or coriander (cilantro) leaves

1 ounce tortilla chips

1. Place the beans, garlic, onion, epazote, if using, and the water to cover in a large pot and bring to a boil over high heat. Reduce the heat to medium-high and boil until the beans are softened, about 1 hour. Season with the salt. Let the beans cool for 5 minutes, then transfer to a blender and purée with their liquid until smooth, in batches if necessary.

2. In a pot, melt the butter over medium heat, then add the bean purée and the *crema*. Stir until well blended, then add the fresh epazote, if using, and continue to heat until hot. Serve with the garnishes sprinkled and crumbled on top.

rick bayless's black bean soup

MY FIRST INTRODUCTION to the regional cuisines of Mexico was when I moved to California. Before that all I knew was that there was real Mexican food, which I probably never had had, and Tex-Mex, which I thought of as heartburn food. But in Los Angeles, Mexican-American communities could be identified by the state from which the immigrants came. Around my neighborhood, Oaxacan immigrants founded churches and restaurants, and theirs became the food from Mexico I liked the most. This Oaxacan soup, called *sopa de frijoles negros,* was one of my favorites. It's different from the preceding recipe; the two give you a sense of how much Oaxacans love black beans.

This recipe is from chef and cookbook author Rick Bayless, who has helped Americans understand the real Mexico and get past the Tex-Mex concept. I've adapted it from his book *Mexican Kitchen.* He asks you to fry your own corn tortilla strips, but you can cut a corner by buying already fried tostadas or high-quality corn tortilla chips to use as a garnish. When buying the chorizo sausage, make sure you get the pure pork sausage in natural casing and not the pork parts in plastic casing. The chipotle chiles in adobo are sold in small cans in most supermarkets. **[Makes 4 servings]**

¾ pound (1½ cups) dried black beans, picked over

12 cups water

6 ounces (about 1 link) Mexican-style chorizo sausage, casing removed and crumbled

1 stalk fennel, chopped

1 medium onion, chopped

3 chipotle chiles in adobo, chopped

4 teaspoons salt or more to taste

½ teaspoon freshly ground black pepper

12 medium shrimp, peeled and deveined if necessary

5 corn tostadas, broken up or a handful of corn tortilla chips

½ cup crumbled *queso fresco* or cheddar cheese

1. In a large pot, place the beans and cover with 6 cups of the water. Bring to a boil over high heat, then turn the heat off and let the beans sit for 1 hour. Drain.

2. Return the beans to the pot and cover with the remaining 6 cups of water. Bring to a boil over high heat, then reduce the heat to low, stir in the chorizo, fennel, onion, and chipotle chiles in adobo, partially cover, and simmer until the beans are tender, about 2 hours.

3. Transfer the soup to a blender, in batches if necessary, and blend until it forms a smooth purée. Return the soup to the pot, add the salt and pepper, stir, and heat over medium heat until hot, then add the shrimp and cook until they are orange-red, 3 to 4 minutes. Serve the soup in individual bowls garnished with the tostadas and crumbled cheese.

legume velouté

A LEGUME IS NOT A BEAN, technically. A pea, however, is one kind of legume. Legumes are, specifically, the dry, one-celled fruit that develops from a simple superior ovary and splits into two halves, with the seeds attached to the ventral suture. This splitting into two halves along natural lines is called dehiscing. Legumes tend to have very earthy tastes and are very satisfying eating. The best-known legumes include split green peas and all the dals of India, *dal* being a generic Hindi term for legumes. The cuisines of the Indian subcontinent are the greatest users of legumes—again, mostly in the form of the prepared dish called dal, a kind of spiced legume stew.

This recipe is not spiced, but gets its flavor from the particular fats used and from the variety of legumes. Many of those used in this soup will be found in Indian markets, and for these I have provided the Hindi name in parentheses. I do suggest substitutes, though. (All the legumes are dried.)   [**Makes 4 servings**]

the best soups in the world

2 ounces (¼ cup) black gram (*urad dal*) or black lentils
2 ounces (¼ cup) green gram (*moong dal*) or yellow split peas
2 ounces (¼ cup) red gram (pigeon pea or *toor dal*) or brown lentils
2 ounces (¼ cup) split green peas
2 ounces (¼ cup) mung beans
2 ounces (¼ cup) red lentils
1 unsmoked ham hock (about 1 pound)
2 ounces salt pork with skin side or one 6 × 3-inch piece pork skin or 1 pig's ear
6 sprigs fresh parsley
6 sprigs cilantro (fresh coriander)
8 cups chicken broth
Salt to taste
2 tablespoons walnut oil

1. Place the black gram, green gram, red gram, split green peas, mung beans, and red lentils in a large pot with the ham hock, salt pork, and sprigs of parsley and cilantro. Pour in the chicken broth and bring to a boil over high heat. Reduce the heat to low and simmer until the meat on the ham hock is falling off, about 3 hours.

2. Remove the skin, parsley, and cilantro and discard. Remove the ham hock and remove the meat. Discard the bone and chop the meat. Pour the soup into a blender and blend until very smooth. Return to a clean saucepan with the chopped meat and heat. Season with salt if necessary and add the walnut oil. Serve hot.

english pea soup

THE FAMOUS LONDON "PEA SOUPER," an idiom meaning a very thick fog, as thick as pea soup, is often used in England for any thick fog. But the phrase originally referred more particularly to a yellowish smog produced by the soft coal burned prior to the passage of the United Kingdom's Clean Air Act in 1956. Such fogs were prevalent in British cities, particularly London, during the rise of the industrial era in the nineteenth century. A *New York Times* article from 1871 refers to "London, particularly, where the population are periodically submerged in a fog of the consistency of pea soup . . ." An English pea soup is made with split yellow, not split green, peas. This recipe is the purest version of the soup you'll encounter.

[Makes 4 servings]

1 cup (½ pound) yellow split peas
¼ cup (½ stick) unsalted butter
1 large onion, finely chopped
1 quart vegetable broth
Bouquet garni, tied in cheesecloth, consisting of 5 sprigs fresh parsley,
    3 sprigs thyme, 2 sprigs marjoram or tarragon, and 1 bay leaf
2 teaspoons salt or more to taste
1 teaspoon freshly ground black pepper or more to taste

1. Place the peas in a large pot, cover by a couple of inches with cold water, bring to a boil over high heat, and boil for 5 minutes. Remove from the heat, cover, and leave to soak for 2 hours. Drain well.

2. In a large pot, melt the butter over medium-high heat, then cook the onion, stirring occasionally, until softened, about 4 minutes. Add the vegetable broth, drained peas, bouquet garni, salt, and pepper and let it return to a boil, then reduce the heat to low, partially cover, and simmer for 2 hours.

3. Remove and discard the bouquet garni. Transfer the soup to a blender and purée. Return it to the pot and heat a bit, correct the seasoning if necessary and serve hot.

smooth legume soups

split green pea soup

GREEN PEAS AND PEA SOUP have a long history, as we know from Aristophanes' play *The Birds,* in which Trochilus says, "Again he wants some pea-soup; I seize a ladle and a pot and run to get it." In America, split green pea soup was more popular in the early twentieth century than it is today, but one taste of this old-fashioned soup and you'll see why it was so popular back then. Formerly it was made so that you could see and taste the chunky pieces of peas. Today, it's smoother, which is the way I like it. In California, drivers passing through Buellton have for decades seen the billboards for Pea Soup Andersen's, a restaurant established in 1924 whose split green pea soup was so popular that Anton Andersen renamed his restaurant to reflect its specialty. It's likely that split pea soup was brought to America by the Dutch settlers in New York, who used green peas rather than the yellow cultivated by English settlers. But its popularity is not in doubt, as we are reminded by a familiar English nursery rhyme:

> *Pease porridge hot,*
> *Pease porridge cold,*
> *Pease porridge in the pot*
> *Nine days old.*

When I was a kid my mom always added cut-up frankfurters, which I still love and think of as comfort food. I think you will find a combination of croûtons and chives a bit more adult—but perhaps you shouldn't ignore your inner kid.   **[Makes 4 servings]**

234

the best soups in the world

1 cup (½ pound) split green peas

1 smoked or unsmoked ham hock (about 1 pound) (optional)

1 medium onion, chopped

1 celery stalk, chopped

1 small carrot, peeled and chopped

1 small leek, white part only, split lengthwise, washed well, and chopped

1 garlic clove, sliced

Bouquet garni, tied in cheesecloth, consisting of 5 sprigs fresh parsley,
    3 sprigs fresh thyme or 1 teaspoon dried, 1 bay leaf, and
    2 allspice berries

6 cups water

2 teaspoons salt

½ teaspoon freshly ground black pepper

¼ cup heavy cream

1 tablespoon unsalted butter

FOR THE GARNISH (CHOOSE ONE OR TWO)

½ cup small toasted croûtons (page 129)
2 cooked frankfurters, split lengthwise, sliced
¼ pound cooked ham, diced and sautéed in butter
¾ cup whipped cream
2 tablespoons chopped fresh chives

1. Place the split peas in a pot with the ham hock, if using, the onion, celery, carrot, leek, garlic, and bouquet garni. Cover with the water and bring to a near boil over high heat, skimming the surface of foam as it appears. Reduce the heat to low and simmer, partially covered and stirring occasionally, until the peas are tender and the meat on the ham hock is almost falling off, about 3 hours.

2. Remove the ham hock and the bouquet garni. Scrape the meat off the ham hock if desired, then discard the bone and the bouquet garni. Set the ham hock meat aside. Transfer the soup, in batches, to a blender and blend until a smooth purée.

3. Return the soup to a clean pot, season with salt and pepper, and reheat over medium heat with the ham hock meat. Stir in the cream and butter. Once the butter melts serve with a garnish of your choosing.

spring pea soup

THE FRESH GARDEN PEAS of spring are like the candy of the vegetable world. Spring is the season for English garden peas, whose plump pods open like a zipper when you pull the string and spill them out with a flick of the thumb. Look for the plumpest pods, the ones that appear to be filled with air and about to burst. Don't pod them until you want to make this soup. Restaurant chefs like to fancy up this dish by using chicken broth for the liquid and bacon or prosciutto as a garnish. My recipe takes a different approach. It is all about peas—even the broth is from the pea pods—and results in an intense and utterly delicious soup. **[Makes 4 to 6 servings]**

2 pounds fresh English pea pods (about 2½ cups peas)

10 cups water

Salt to taste

1 tablespoon unsalted butter

1 tablespoon extra-virgin olive oil

1 small onion, chopped

2 scallions, chopped

1 carrot, peeled and chopped

1 celery stalk, chopped

3 tablespoons chopped fresh parsley

¼ teaspoon dried summer savory

½ teaspoon freshly ground black pepper or more to taste

1½ teaspoons freshly squeezed lemon juice or more to taste

4 to 6 fresh mint sprigs

Crème fraîche to garnish the toast points

4 to 6 toast points

the best soups in the world

1. String the pods, remove the peas from the pod, and set aside. You should have about 2½ cups of peas. Place the pods in a large pot and cover with the water. Discard the strings. Bring to a boil over high heat, salt lightly with about 2 teaspoons salt, then reduce the heat to medium and cook until the pods are softened, about 1 hour. Drain and reserve 6 cups of broth. Discard the pods.

2. In a large pot, melt the butter with the olive oil over medium-high heat, add the onion, scallions, carrot, celery, parsley, and summer savory, and cook, stirring, until softened, about 6 minutes. Add the peas and cover with the 6 cups of pea broth. Bring to a boil over high heat, then reduce to low and simmer 20 minutes.

3. Remove from the heat, transfer the soup to a blender in batches, and purée until very smooth, about 1½ minutes of blending. Return the soup to the cleaned pot, season with 2 teaspoons salt and the pepper and heat over medium heat until just beginning to bubble on the edges. Season with the lemon juice and stir, then taste to see if you need more salt, pepper, or lemon juice. Serve immediately with a sprig of mint and a small dollop of crème fraîche smeared on top of a toast point.

Variation: You can turn this recipe into a chilled pea soup by refrigerating the soup until cold and serving it in small demitasse cups as an appetizer with a small dollop of crème fraîche and a mint leaf.

HERCULES AND PEA SOUP

In *The Frogs* of Aristophanes (c. 448–c. 388 BC), Dionysius illustrates for Hercules, whose appetite was as prodigious as his strength, man's desire for poetry and art by comparing it to a craving for pea soup.

DIONYSIUS: **Don't mock me, brother: on my life I am**
                    In a bad way: such fierce desire consumes me.

HERCULES: **Aye, little brother? How?**

DIONYSIUS: **I can't describe it . . . only illustrate.**
                    Have you ever felt a sudden passion for pea soup?

HERCULES: **Thousands of times!**

DIONYSIUS: **Am I clear, or must I tell you in another way?**

HERCULES: **About pea soup? No, *that* I understand.**

DIONYSIUS: **Such is the longing that devours my soul**
                    For lost Euripides.

Dionysius's longing is for a poet who can *write,* unlike the hacks of the day. This longing is like a longing for a pea soup.

velouté of fava beans

IN THE PERIGORD REGION of France one enters the land of duck, truffles, and foie gras, and in the spring delicious fava bean dishes like this *velouté de fèves,* a smooth soup with finely grated cooked turnip, carrot, and celery root (celeriac) as a garnish. You will need 2½ pounds of fava bean pods to yield 1 pound (3 cups) of single-peeled fava beans. You can peel them by plunging the beans in boiling water for four minutes, then draining and pinching off the skins. That makes them "double-peeled." Once they are peeled they will weigh about ¾ pound, which is just right for this recipe.   [**Makes 6 servings**]

2 tablespoons goose or duck fat (preferably) or unsalted butter

2 leeks, white part only, washed well and sliced into very thin rounds

1 large onion, chopped

1 large garlic clove, finely chopped

¾ pound double-peeled fresh fava beans (from 2¼ pounds of pods; see headnote)

½ teaspoon dried thyme

1 small bay leaf

6 cups chicken broth

1 tablespoon salt or more to taste

½ teaspoon freshly ground black pepper or more to taste

¾ cup crème fraîche

2 medium carrots, peeled and finely grated

1 large turnip, peeled and thinly grated

1 ounce celery root (celeriac), peeled and thinly grated

1. In a pot, melt 1 tablespoon fat over medium heat, then add the leeks, onion, and garlic and cook, stirring, until a bit softened, about 3 minutes. Add the fava beans, thyme, and bay leaf, cover, reduce the heat to low, and simmer, stirring occasionally, for 15 minutes.

2. Add the chicken broth, salt, and pepper and bring to a boil over high heat. Boil for 8 minutes, then turn the heat off and transfer to a blender, in batches if necessary, and blend until smooth. Return the soup to the pot, then add the crème fraîche and whisk it in to blend well. Keep the pot over low heat until you finish the next step.

3. In a skillet or flame-proof casserole, melt the remaining tablespoon of fat over low heat, then add the carrots, turnip, and celery root and cook, covered and stirring occasionally, until softened and tender, 15 minutes. Transfer the vegetables to the soup and stir. Let them heat for a minute or two, then serve hot.

tuscan white bean soup

THIS SMOOTH SOUP OR VELOUTÉ is the height of simplicity, but count on diners to ask you for the recipe nevertheless, because its taste is so soothing and delicious. Tuscans favor a variety of small white navy beans, called cannellini, and also use these to make a thicker version, which is spread on *crostini* (toast points) and served as an antipasto. If you leave the carrot out, the soup will be whiter. **[Makes 4 servings]**

1 cup (½ pound) dried white beans

1 leafy sprig fresh sage

Salt to taste

¼ cup extra-virgin olive oil

½ small onion, finely chopped

1 celery stalk, finely chopped

1 small carrot, peeled and finely chopped

¼ cup finely chopped fennel bulb (optional)

2 large garlic cloves, finely chopped

FOR THE GARNISH (CHOOSE ONE)

Twelve 1-inch squares thinly sliced pancetta, cooked until crispy

1 cup croûtons, fried in olive oil until golden

½ cup cooked tiny shrimp

1 tablespoon finely chopped fresh parsley

1. Place the beans in a pot. Remove 2 leaves of sage from the sprig to use later, then add the sprig to the beans with water to cover by several inches. Bring to a boil over high heat, salt lightly, then cook at a boil until tender, about 1½ hours, replenishing the water when necessary.

2. Meanwhile, heat the olive oil in a skillet over medium-high heat, then add the onion, celery, carrot, fennel, if using, and garlic and cook, stirring, until softened, about 6 minutes.

3. Drain the beans, saving 4 cups of the cooking liquid. Place the beans in a blender with the vegetables from the skillet and 4 cups of the cooking liquid. Blend until smooth. Transfer to a clean pot, add the 2 leaves of sage, and set over low heat. Cook until bubbling and hot, about 5 minutes. Serve hot with one of the garnishes.

chickpea purée with shrimp

THIS SICILIAN SOUP called *zuppa di ceci e gamberi* is made with dried chickpeas that are cooked a long time with flavoring vegetables: tomatoes, onion, carrot, and celery. This preparation is puréed and then the flavors are adjusted with olive oil, garlic, and rosemary. It's quite easy to make and can be prepared long ahead of time and then finished at the last minute by sautéeing the rock shrimp briefly before adding them to the soup. Most people find the result unique and delicious. If you decide you don't want to use dried chickpeas, remember that the canned ones still need to be flavored, so put them in a pot as in Step 1 and cook twenty-five minutes. The dried chickpeas, though, will provide a deeper, richer taste.

[**Makes 8 first-course servings**]

the best soups in the world

1 pound (about 2½ cups) dried chickpeas, soaked overnight in
   cold water to cover, drained

1 large carrot, chopped

1 celery stalk, chopped

1 large onion, halved

3 ripe tomatoes (about 1 pound), cut in half, seeds squeezed out, and grated
   against the largest holes of a standing grater down to the peel

3 quarts water

1 tablespoon salt or more to taste

1 teaspoon freshly ground black pepper or more to taste

6 tablespoons extra-virgin olive oil and more for drizzling

1 large garlic clove, finely chopped

1 sprig fresh rosemary

½ pound shrimp, peeled

1. Place the chickpeas in a stockpot with the carrot, celery, onion, and tomatoes, cover with the water, and bring to a boil over high heat. Boil, stirring occasionally, for 30 minutes, then reduce to low and simmer until tender, 2 to 2½ hours.

2. Transfer the mixture to a blender, in batches if necessary, and purée. Return to a clean pot and stir in enough additional water to make the chickpeas much creamier and looser than a hummus. Return to medium heat and bring to a boil, stirring constantly. Season with the salt and pepper.

3. Meanwhile, in a skillet, heat 5 tablespoons of the olive oil over medium heat, then add the garlic and rosemary and cook, stirring, for 1 minute. Transfer this mixture to the soup. The soup can be made up to this point and reserved to finish later, bringing it to a near boil before you serve.

4. In a skillet, heat the remaining tablespoon of olive oil over medium-high heat, then cook the shrimp until they turn white or orange-red (depending on the kind of shrimp) and are firm, 2 to 3 minutes. Ladle the soup into individual bowls, transfer the shrimp to the soup bowls, and serve with a drizzle of olive oil.

smooth legume soups

najwa's lentil soup

THIS LENTIL SOUP is one of my favorites, period. The recipe is from my former wife, Najwa al-Qattan, who makes it with such modesty. She always says, "It's really nothing." Well, she's wrong: it's really amazing. So much so, in fact, that after I published it in my book *A Mediterranean Feast,* it was discovered there and chosen for the book *The 150 Best American Recipes: Indispensable Dishes from Legendary Chefs and Undiscovered Cooks,* published by Houghton Mifflin in 2006. *Shūrbat al-ᶜadas,* as the soup is called in Arabic, is very popular among Lebanese and Palestinians and has a long history in the Middle East, as we know from the biblical story of Esau, who renounced his birthright for a pottage of lentils (Genesis 25: 29–34). Although that lentil soup was made with red lentils, this one uses brown lentils and begs for a homemade chicken broth (page 14). The oil used for frying the flatbread can be any inexpensive olive or olive pomace oil. **[Makes 4 to 6 servings]**

2 cups (1 pound) brown lentils

8 cups chicken broth

1 large onion, grated

2 teaspoons ground cumin

Salt and freshly ground black pepper to taste

2 tablespoons freshly squeezed lemon juice

2 cups olive oil

1 large Arabic flatbread or pita bread, cut into ½-inch squares

Extra-virgin olive oil for drizzling

1. Wash the lentils under cold running water, picking out any stones. Bring the broth to a boil in a large pot and add the lentils and onion. When the broth returns to a boil, reduce the heat to low, cover, and simmer for 1 hour. Do not stir.

2. Pass the lentils and broth through a food mill. Add the cumin and season with salt and pepper. Return the soup to the saucepan and stir. Taste to check the seasonings. Stir in the lemon juice and heat until the soup starts to bubble slightly. Taste again to check the seasoning and add whatever it needs.

3. Meanwhile, heat the olive oil for frying to 375°F in a medium-size pot or skillet. Fry the pieces of bread until golden, about 1 minute. Serve the soup with the fried croûtons of Arabic bread and extra-virgin olive oil passed at the table.

smooth legume soups

rasam

RASAM, A TAMIL WORD, names a spicy soup from South India known also as *chaaru* in Telugu and *saaru* in Kannada, two more of the many languages of India. There are tens of different kinds of *rasam,* although there aren't really a wide variety of soups in Indian cuisine. Maybe that's because of the popularity of curries and dals, which are thick, stewlike dishes that can be thought of as very thick soups. The tamarind water can be replaced with 3 table-spoons of fresh lime juice. The tamarind paste, black mustard seeds, fenugreek, curry leaves, and asafetida can be purchased online at www.adrianascaravan.com.   [**Makes 6 servings**]

3 garlic cloves

1-inch cube fresh ginger, peeled

2 teaspoons salt and more as desired

1 cup (½ pound) red lentils

½ teaspoon turmeric powder

6 cups water

2 tablespoons vegetable oil

½ teaspoon black mustard or brown mustard seeds

1¼ teaspoons cumin seeds

1 cup tomato purée, canned or fresh

½ teaspoon ground chile powder

½ teaspoon freshly ground black pepper

¼ teaspoon ground fenugreek

¼ teaspoon asafetida (optional)

½ cup tamarind water (see Note)

3 tablespoons chopped or crumbled curry leaves or mint leaves

1. In a mortar, mash the garlic, ginger, and salt with a pestle until it forms a paste. Set aside.

2. Place the lentils in a saucepan with the turmeric and cover with 3½ cups of the water. Bring to a boil over high heat, then boil until tender, about 25 minutes. Set aside without draining.

3. In a pot, heat the oil over medium-high heat, then add the mustard and cumin seeds and cook, shaking the pan occasionally, until popping, about 1 minute. Add the tomato purée, chile powder, pepper, fenugreek, asafetida, if using, and reserved ginger and garlic paste and cook, stirring constantly, until dense, 3 to 4 minutes.

4. Add the tamarind water and 2 tablespoons of the curry leaves to the pot. Stir well, increase the heat to high to bring to a boil, then reduce the heat to medium and cook, stirring, for 2 minutes.

5. Place the lentils and their remaining liquid in a blender and blend until puréed. Transfer the lentils to the pot. Pour the remaining 2½ cups of water in the blender to collect the remaining purée, shaking a bit, then transfer to the pot with the soup and bring to a boil over high heat. Once it reaches a boil, turn the heat off and serve hot, garnished with the remaining 1 tablespoon of curry leaves.

Note: To make tamarind water, place a 1-inch cube of tamarind paste or the cut-up beans from 2 tamarind pods in ½ cup of hot water. Let steep for 1 hour, then drain.

smooth legume soups

pigeon pea and chile soup

FROM THE INDIAN STATE of Andhra Pradesh, this soup is a kind of *rasam,* a type popular in south India. It's called *nimmkaiya charu* and utilizes the pigeon pea, a legume probably native to Africa that migrated to India in prehistoric times. The Portuguese took it to the New World. It is a familiar pulse in the tropics and has always been associated with poor people. This soup is certainly not poor, though, as it is spicy hot and very satisfying in winter. Pigeon peas are most likely to be found in whole food markets, and certainly in Indian markets, or they can be ordered through www.indianfoodsco.com. In the United States, pigeon peas are grown only as a forage crop for animals. In their place you can use split green peas. The curry leaves, black mustard seeds, and asafetida can only be found at Indian markets, or via the Internet at www.adrianascaravan.com.   **[Makes 6 servings]**

the best soups in the world

1 cup dried pigeon peas or split green peas

½ teaspoon turmeric powder

3 dried red chiles

1 teaspoon coriander seeds

1 teaspoon yellow split peas or red lentils

½ teaspoon black peppercorns

½ teaspoon cumin seeds

Pinch of asafetida (optional)

1 teaspoon black mustard or brown mustard seeds

2 ripe tomatoes (about ¾ pound), cut in half, seeds squeezed out, and
    grated against the largest holes of a grater down to the peel

3 fresh green finger-type chiles or 4 fresh green jalapeño chiles,
    seeded and chopped

1 teaspoon salt

Juice from ½ lemon

4 curry leaves (optional)

1. Preheat the oven to 450°F.

2. Bring a pot of water to a boil, add the pigeon peas with ⅛ teaspoon of the turmeric, and cook, stirring frequently, until almost tender, about 15 minutes. Drain, saving ¾ cup of the water, and set aside.

3. Lay the dried red chiles, coriander seeds, yellow split peas, peppercorns, cumin seeds, and asafetida, if using, on a baking tray, then roast in the oven until crispy, about 3 minutes. Grind coarsely in a spice mill or mortar and set this spice mix aside. Place the mustard seeds in the pan and roast them too until a few begin to crackle and pop, about 4 minutes. Set them aside separately from the spice mix.

4. In a pot, bring 2 cups of water to a boil and add the remaining turmeric, the tomatoes, and the green chiles. Once the water comes to a boil, reduce the heat to medium-low and cook until slightly reduced, about 15 minutes. Add the spice mix and salt, reduce the heat to low, and cook, stirring occasionally, for 10 minutes. Add the reserved pigeon peas and water, plus another ¼ cup of water, and leave it to simmer gently until very tender, about 20 minutes. Remove from the heat and pour in the lemon juice. Serve very hot garnished with fresh curry leaves, if using, and the roasted mustard seeds.

five dal soup

DAL **IS THE HINDI WORD** for "dried pulse," as well as for a curried legume porridge. Pulses are the dried edible seeds of leguminous plants. A legume is more or less the same thing as a pulse; more technically, it's a plant whose seeds form in a pod that splits in two—a dehiscent seedpod. Peas and lentils are examples of legumes. Gram, used in this recipe, is a legume from the *Vigna* genus. Grown in India for its seeds, "Gram" was originally the Portuguese *grão,* meaning "grain," later picked up by the British colonial rulers of India. India is the world's largest producer of pulses, and they have been eaten there since ancient times. All the legumes used in these dals belong to the Fabaceae (Leguminosae) family. In this recipe I use black gram (*Vigna mungo*), mung beans (*Vigna radiata*), lentils (*Lens culinaris*), pigeon peas, also called red gram (*Cajanus cajan*), and yellow and green split peas (*Pisum sativum*). Indian dal soups, sometimes known by the generic *rasam,* are earthy, soul-satisfying dishes that everyone loves.

This recipe is adapted from Yamuna Devi's *The Art of Indian Vegetarian Cooking.* The legumes' Indian names are in parentheses below, and it is in Indian markets that you will find them, along with any unfamiliar spices. Large whole/natural food markets such as Whole Foods may have these peas, too. In any case, I find the convenience of buying these ingredients on the Internet at sites such as www.indianfoodsco.com and, for the spices, www.adrianascaravan.com, too easy to pass up. Garam masala can be bought from www.penzeys.com.   [**Makes 6 servings**]

3 tablespoons dried red lentil (*masoor dal*) or mung beans

3 tablespoons dried pigeon peas (*toor dal*)

3 tablespoons dried yellow split peas (*chana dal*) or split green peas

3 tablespoons dried split green peas or green gram (*moong dal*)

3 tablespoons dried black gram (*urad dal*) or brown lentils

6 cups vegetable or chicken broth

1 tablespoon freshly ground coriander

1 tablespoon freshly grated ginger

1 teaspoon turmeric powder

1 teaspoon salt

¼ pound fresh spinach leaves, coarsely chopped

1 tablespoon mustard oil or vegetable oil

2 teaspoons cumin seeds

¼ teaspoon black mustard or brown mustard seeds

1 serrano chile, finely chopped

½ teaspoon garam masala

¼ teaspoon cayenne pepper
⅛ teaspoon asafetida (optional)
1 bay leaf
2 tablespoons finely chopped cilantro (fresh coriander)

1. Soak the dried pulses in a bowl covered with hot water for 1 hour.

2. Drain the pulses and place in a large pot with the broth, coriander, ginger, and turmeric and bring to a boil over high heat. Reduce the heat to low and simmer, covered and stirring occasionally, until very tender, about 1½ hours.

3. Add the salt and whisk the soup vigorously with a wire whisk until quite smooth, about 2 minutes. Add the coarsely chopped spinach and simmer for 10 minutes.

4. In a small nonstick pan, heat the oil over high heat, then add the cumin seeds, black mustard seeds, and chile and cook for 20 seconds. Add the garam masala, cayenne, asafetida, if using, and the bay leaf, stir a few times, then add 3 tablespoons water and cook for 1 minute, stirring constantly. Pour into the soup and stir well. Sprinkle with the cilantro and serve.

smooth legume soups

Minestrone is the Italian name, literally meaning "big soup," for a thick soup, chock-full of vegetables, meat, pasta, and herbs. There isn't one minestrone but many, depending on the region of Italy. Around the world are many minestrone-like soups, and they are also to be found in this chapter.

minestrone
and minestrone-like soups

soupe au pistou

THIS FAMOUS SOUP from Provence is literally "soup with pesto." But, oh my, how much more it is than that. Rich with vegetables, in the late spring and summer it's one of the most satisfying of soups. And that dollop of pesto is what truly makes it remarkable, and so much more than vegetable soup. *Pistou* is the Provençal word for "pounded," derived, just as the *pesto* of Liguria, from the Latin *pestare,* meaning the same. In fact, pesto and *pistou* are more or less the same thing: a condiment of pounded basil, pine nuts, garlic, and olive oil. One of the earliest descriptions we have of something similar comes from the Roman poet Virgil, who writes in verse in his *Ecolgue* II:

> *Now even the cattle court the cooling shade*
> *And the green lizard hides him in the thorn:*
> *Now for tired mowers, with the fierce heat spent,*
> *Pounds Thestilis her mess of savory herbs, wild thyme and garlic.*

La soupo-pistou in the local dialect, this is the French version of Genoese-style minestrone (page 272), the mother soup, except that here it is basically a vegetable soup with pesto. It's lighter, relatively, than the minestrone. You will first have to make the pesto (page 274) before serving this popular soup. The Provençal sometimes put tomatoes in their pesto. Some people like to grate Swiss cheese on top of the soup once it's cooked.   [**Makes 8 servings**]

the best soups in the world

1 cup dried small white beans, soaked in water to cover for 6 hours, drained

6 quarts water

2 tablespoons salt and more as needed

1 pound green beans, trimmed and cut into ½-inch-thick pieces

¾ pound tomatoes, peeled (page 273), seeded, and chopped coarsely

½ pound boiling potatoes (such as Yukon Gold), peeled and cut
  into ½-inch dice

½ pound carrots, peeled and cut into ¾-inch dice

½ pound zucchini, cut into ½-inch dice

2 leeks, white and light green part only, split lengthwise, washed well,
  and thinly sliced

4 sprigs fresh thyme

2 bay leaves

2 teaspoons freshly ground black pepper

3 tablespoons extra-virgin olive oil

½ cup *ditali* or any small tubular soup macaroni

1 recipe Pesto (page 274), or 1½ cups store-bought pesto with the addition
  of 1 peeled, seeded, and mashed small tomato

1. Place the white beans in a pot and cover with 3 quarts of the water. Bring to a boil over high heat, then reduce to medium, salt the water a bit, and cook until tender, 1 to 1¼ hours. Drain and set the beans aside.

2. Meanwhile, in a large stockpot, bring the remaining 3 quarts of water to a boil over high heat, then add the green beans, tomatoes, potatoes, carrots, zucchini, leeks, thyme, and bay leaf. Reduce the heat to medium-low, then stir in the 2 tablespoons salt, the pepper, and olive oil, and simmer, stirring occasionally, until tender, about 15 minutes. Add the pasta and reserved beans and continue cooking until the pasta is soft, too, about 15 minutes more. Serve hot with the pesto passed at the table, as everyone likes to put in his or her own quantity of pesto.

minestrone and minestrone-like soups

corsican country soup

THIS IS THE MOST FAMOUS of all the Corsican soups. Country folk simply call it *minestra* (soup), while city folk call it *soupe paysanne* (country soup). Shepherds would take some left-over soup with them into the mountain pastures to eat cold for their midday nourishment. Besides the vegetables in the recipe below, some cooks also use carrots, celery, zucchini, leeks, and dandelion, depending on the season. The pork fat can be cut off any pork you happen to have—the strip of fat surrounding a pork chop or shoulder, for example.

[Makes 8 servings]

¼ pound pork fat or bacon (see Note), chopped

2 pounds boiling potatoes (such as Yukon Gold), peeled and diced

1 small green cabbage (about 1½ pounds), cored and chopped

¾ pound Swiss chard, stem removed and chopped

1 medium onion, chopped

2 large garlic cloves, finely chopped

6 cups water

1 cup (about ½ pound) dried red kidney beans

One ½-pound piece cooked ham or smoked bacon, preferably on the bone

1 large tomato (about 10 ounces), peeled (page 273), seeded, and chopped

6 slices day-old French or Italian country bread, or ¼ pound lasagne sheets

1 tablespoon salt

Freshly ground black pepper to taste

Extra-virgin olive oil for drizzling

1. In a large flame-proof casserole or stockpot, cook the pork fat over medium-high heat, stirring, until there is some fat in the bottom of the pot, about 5 minutes. Add the potatoes, cabbage, chard, onion, and garlic and cook, stirring, until the greens are wilted, about 5 minutes. Pour in the water and bring to a boil. Reduce the heat to low, add the beans, ham or smoked bacon, and tomato, and cook until the beans are tender, 2 to 3 hours.

2. Add the slices of bread and continue to cook until a spoon can stand straight up in the center of the soup and, if using lasagne, the pasta is tender, about 15 minutes. Season with the salt and pepper, drizzle with olive oil, and serve.

   Note: If using bacon in place of pork fat, blanch it first by bringing a pot of water to a boil and boiling the bacon for 5 minutes; then drain and dry it.

fasting soup

THIS RECIPE, CALLED *POTAJE DE VIGILIA*, is from Huelva in Andalusia, Spain's southern-most region. It is a hearty soup with lots of flavor, but no meat—hence the name "fasting" soup—yet it is substantial and very nicely spiced with paprika, saffron, and black pepper. I call it "substantial" because of the marriage of the chickpeas, potatoes, and spinach, which not only provides body but is colorful, too.   [**Makes 6 servings**]

6 tablespoons extra-virgin olive oil

4 slices French or Italian bread

3 tablespoons sherry vinegar

1 medium onion, chopped

2 tomatoes, peeled (page 273), seeded, and chopped

2 teaspoons hot paprika

2 cups canned chickpeas (about 1 pound), with its liquid

1 pound spinach, heavy stems removed, washed well, and
  ripped into smaller pieces

3 potatoes (about 1 pound), peeled and cut into small pieces

4 cups water

½ cup dry white wine

2 teaspoons salt

1 teaspoon freshly ground black pepper

1 large hard-boiled egg, chopped

3 large garlic cloves, finely chopped

¼ cup finely chopped fresh parsley

3 tablespoons pine nuts

Pinch of saffron

1. In a pot or deep flame-proof casserole, heat 4 tablespoons of the olive oil over medium heat, then fry the bread until golden brown and crispy on both sides, 4 to 5 minutes. Remove the bread, rip into smaller pieces, place in a bowl, and douse with the vinegar.

2. In the same pot, add the remaining 2 tablespoons olive oil, then add the onion, tomatoes, and paprika and cook, stirring occasionally, until a thick sauce is formed, 10 to 12 minutes.

3. Add the chickpeas, spinach, potatoes, water, wine, salt, and pepper. Increase the heat to high, and once the spinach wilts and the broth is beginning to boil, reduce the heat to low and cook until the potatoes are very nearly tender, about 45 minutes.

4. Add the hard-boiled egg, garlic, parsley, pine nuts, saffron, and fried bread. Turn the heat off, let rest for 10 minutes, then serve.

LA RIBOLLITA

This famous soup from Tuscany, about which so many people said to me "certainly you'll have a recipe for *ribollita* in the book," is nothing but warmed-over bean soup. Of course, as with any well-known but simple dish, it's a bit more than that, but there really aren't any recipes for it, strictly speaking, because it's a leftover. But here's how to make it. Prepare the Black Kale Soup (page 260) with 2 cups white beans rather than red, a prosciutto or ham bone, 2 cups more water than called for in that recipe, a sprig of rosemary, and without the pumpernickel. The next day, place the soup in a deep baking casserole. Preheat the oven to 375°F. In a skillet, heat ¾ cup of extra-virgin olive oil over medium-high heat with 2 crushed garlic cloves and a pinch of dried thyme and cook until the garlic turns light golden, about 1 minute. Discard the garlic and pour half the oil over the soup. Layer 8 slices of Italian bread toast and 1 thinly sliced onion over the top of the soup. Pour the remaining oil over the onion and bake until golden, about 30 minutes.

black kale soup

BLACK KALE, *CAVOLO NERO* in Italian, is a kind of kale popular in central Italy. It is called *toscano* in Tuscany. In this soup, the black kale—and it is not actually black, just very dark green—is a natural accompaniment to the substantial texture of the potatoes and beans and the flavors of the aromatic herbs. For me, this is a very warming wintertime *zuppa di cavolo nero,* and I'll use canned tomatoes if I have to. Black kale is most commonly found in farmers markets, although sometimes in better supermarkets such as Whole Foods. One can make a *ribollita* soup with leftovers (see box, page 259). **[Makes 6 servings]**

6 tablespoons extra-virgin olive oil plus extra for drizzling

1 celery stalk, finely chopped

1 small onion, finely chopped

1 carrot, peeled and finely chopped

10 large fresh basil leaves, finely chopped

3 ripe tomatoes (about 1 pound), peeled (page 273), seeded, and
    finely chopped

2 boiling potatoes (about ¾ pound), peeled and cut up into pieces

1 tablespoon fresh thyme leaves

¾ pound black kale (or regular kale), washed well and sliced crosswise
    into strips

⅓ cup dried *borlotti* or red kidney beans

2 quarts warm water

Salt to taste

4 to 6 slices toasted pumpernickel bread, rubbed with
    a cut garlic clove

1. In a flame-proof casserole or pot, heat the olive oil over medium-high heat, then add the celery, onion, carrot, and basil (called the *trito* in Italian) and cook, stirring, until almost softened, about 8 minutes. Add the tomatoes and cook, stirring occasionally, until the tomatoes are somewhat dry, about 20 minutes. Add the potatoes and thyme and cook until they are slightly browned, 4 to 5 minutes, then add the kale and the beans.

2. Reduce the heat to low and cook until the kale has wilted, 8 to 10 minutes. Add the water and salt, turn the heat to high, and once small bubbles begin to form, reduce the heat to very low (or use a heat diffuser) and cook until the potatoes and beans are tender, about 3 hours. Serve with toasted bread and a drizzle of olive oil.

ITALIAN SOUPS

Strictly speaking, *zuppa,* commonly translated as "soup," is not so generic a term, but rather names one category of Italian soups: those containing vegetables but not pasta or rice. *Zuppa* is a thicker mixture than a clear bouillon. In a *zuppa* the vegetables are integral to the soup, which might appear creamy, although no cream is used. A *zuppa di verdure,* or "vegetable soup," is actually a kind of minestrone (a word that means "big soup") in which the vegetables are cooked in stock or water without any fat. This is a very simple preparation, usually without the addition of either pasta or rice, although the rules are not fast, and some cooks might add pasta, rice, or bread. The vegetables used for a *zuppa* might first be cooked in butter or pork fat.

The closest thing to a generic term for soup in Italian is *minestra,* which actually means "the first course"—that is, a soup containing pasta, rice, or gnocchi: a *minestra in brodo.* (The difference between a *minestra in brodo* and a *zuppa* is that the former consists of pasta, rice, or vegetables, separate and distinct and cooked in a stock base.) A famous *minestra* from Rome is *stracciatella,* a broth with eggs and cheese beaten into it. In Italy, a person who laughs easily is said to have eaten rice soup, *che aveva mangiato la minestra di riso,* a play on words, as *riso* means "rice" and "laughter." The number of *minestre* are endless, and include the renowned *pasta e fagioli* (pasta and bean soup). In northern Italy *minestra*
(continued)

usually means vegetables or legumes cooked in water with aromatics, perhaps a little meat such as cured pork, and the addition of rice. (In the south the addition would be pasta.) Another kind of soup, once considered a dish for invalids, is *minestrina,* a thin soup with pastina (a kind of soup pasta) or barley cooked in stock.

From *zuppa* and *minestra* we move to minestrone, for some the apex of Italian soups. A minestrone is a very thick vegetable soup, nearly a stew, with wide variations. Minestrones are simmered for a long time. One kind has as its starting point a *soffritto,* a mix of finely chopped vegetables such as onion, celery, and carrot, and cooking fat—perhaps olive oil, lard, pancetta, or some mixture of these—that is sautéed before the addition of other vegetables, stock, or water. Another way of making minestrone is to put all the vegetables and other ingredients in a pot, fill it with water or stock, and simmer it a long time. In the summer, minestrones are often served at room temperature.

This is not the end of the Italians' confusing soup classifications. We must also include the classic broth, or *brodo.* A *brodo* is a clear soup or, more accurately, a stock that is fundamental for other soups, stews, risottos, and some sauces. A *brodo* might be garnished with vegetables or other ingredients and served as the basis to consommé or *brodo ristretto,* a reduced bouillon (*brodo*) that might be flavored with other ingredients before being strained.

Another whole category of soups are those based on purées. They might be called *purées; potages* or *veloutés* (the French words); *passato* (meaning strained or puréed), referring to creamed or puréed soups; or *crema,* referring to smooth soups. A puréed soup might be based on a single vegetable or a mix of vegetables, and served either alone or with an appropriate garnish, such as croûtons or a starchy vegetable. A *crema* is a soup based on a purée but perhaps flavored with butter or a thickener such as béchamel sauce or cream. The *vellutate,* from the French word *velouté,* meaning "velvety," are fancy puréed soups that require some care in their preparation, as they are suited for fine cooking.

tuscan cabbage soup

TODAY WE DON'T THINK OF CABBAGE as a popular Mediterranean vegetable. But in the medieval Mediterranean it was ubiquitous, and the most common dish was cabbage soup. A fine example is this Tuscan *minestrone di cavolo,* which Pisans claim as their own. It is a delicious, rich, and complex minestrone that everyone will find satisfying in an elemental way, yet it began as nothing more than cabbage cooked in water.

[**Makes 4 servings**]

½ cup extra-virgin olive oil
1 medium onion, finely chopped
1 carrot, peeled and finely chopped
1 celery stalk, finely chopped
2 ounces pancetta, finely chopped
1 ounce prosciutto fat or ham fat, finely chopped
½ cup finely chopped fresh parsley
3 tablespoons finely chopped fresh basil leaves
1 pound green cabbage, outer leaves removed, cored, and chopped coarsely
½ pound red cabbage, outer leaves removed, cored, and chopped coarsely
1½ quarts water
½ pound (1 cup) dried cannellini or other white beans, soaked in cold water to cover
    for 2 hours and drained
1 pound boiling potatoes (such as Yukon Gold), peeled and diced large
Salt and freshly ground black pepper to taste
¼ pound *pennine* or other small tubular macaroni
¼ cup freshly grated Parmesan cheese (preferably imported Parmigiano-Reggiano)

minestrone and minestrone-like soups

1. In a stockpot, heat the olive oil over medium heat, then add the onion, carrot, celery, pancetta, prosciutto fat, parsley, and basil and cook, stirring occasionally, until the onion is softened and some fat is rendered, about 10 minutes.

2. Add the cabbages and toss with the vegetables until all the leaves are coated. Add the water and beans. Cover, reduce the heat to medium-low, and cook until the beans are slightly softened, about 1 hour, with the soup only gently bubbling. Add the potatoes and cook just until tender, 25 to 30 minutes.

3. Season the soup with salt and pepper and add the pasta. Cook the pasta, uncovered, until it is al dente, 12 to 15 minutes. Serve with the cheese and more olive oil if desired.

pasta and bean soup

THIS HEARTY AND DELICIOUS ITALIAN *minestra di pasta e fagioli* is so full-bodied that you only need a green salad to accompany it if you decide to serve it as a main course. In Italy it would be served as a first course instead of a pasta dish. The prosciutto skin is used for flavoring. It's a nice addition and can be bought from the deli counter of many Italian markets (some will even give it to you for free). Some supermarkets, such as Whole Foods, also sell prosciutto skin and hocks. If you decide to eat the prosciutto skin, cut it into strips; otherwise, leave it in one or two pieces that can be discarded after the soup is cooked.

[Makes 6 to 8 servings]

3 tablespoons extra-virgin olive oil

1 pound pork stew meat, diced

¼ pound pancetta, cut into strips

¼ pound prosciutto skin, whole or cut into strips (optional)

1 large onion, chopped

1 fennel bulb (about ¾ pound), chopped

1 celery stalk, chopped

6 garlic cloves, chopped

10 cups chicken broth

1½ cups (about 10 ounces) dried white beans

1 cup (½ pound) canned chickpeas

¼ pound Parmesan crusts (optional)

1 cinnamon stick

1 bay leaf

1 sprig fresh rosemary

Salt and freshly ground black pepper to taste

¼ pound *tubetti, ditali,* or other short tubular macaroni

Extra-virgin olive oil for drizzling

Freshly grated Parmesan cheese for sprinkling

1. In a large pot, heat the olive oil over medium-high heat, then add the pork, pancetta, and prosciutto skin, if using, and cook, stirring, until they turn color, about 5 minutes. Add the onion, fennel, celery, and garlic and cook, stirring occasionally, until softened, 12 to 15 minutes.

2. Add the chicken broth, white beans, chickpeas, Parmesan crusts, if using, cinnamon stick, bay leaf, and rosemary, bring to a boil over high heat, then reduce to medium-low, season with salt and pepper, and cook until the white beans are al dente, about 1¼ hours. Add the pasta and cook, stirring, until they, too, are al dente, 12 to 15 minutes. Remove and discard the cinnamon stick, bay leaf, and rosemary sprig. Both the prosciutto skin and Parmesan crusts can be eaten if desired. Serve with a drizzle of olive oil and the grated Parmesan cheese.

minestrone and minestrone-like soups

pasta and pea soup

THIS SPRINGTIME SOUP from Italy is called *minestra di pasta e piselli.* As the pasta swells during the cooking the soup becomes denser, so you will want to eat it as soon as it's done. Leaving it in the saucepan means the pasta will continue to swell and absorb the liquid until there is none left. This is a yeoman recipe that serves a hungry family of four well.

[Makes 4 servings]

¼ cup pork lard, pork fat, or extra-virgin olive oil

1½ ounces prosciutto, in one piece

1 medium onion

1 large garlic clove

10 large fresh basil leaves

1 tablespoon tomato paste

8 cups boiling water

3 cups beef broth

10 ounces shelled fresh peas (from about 2 pounds fresh pea pods) or frozen peas

Salt and freshly ground black pepper to taste

1 cup (½ pound) *semi di melone* or other small soup pasta

Freshly grated Parmesan cheese

the best soups in the world

1. Finely chop the lard, prosciutto, onion, garlic, and basil together or process them in the food processor until all the pieces are minuscule, scraping down the sides occasionally. Dissolve the tomato paste in 1 cup of the boiling water.

2. In a large pot, combine the remaining 7 cups of water with the beef broth over high heat, bring to a boil, then reduce the heat to low and let simmer while you continue the preparation.

3. In a flame-proof casserole or a large pot, cook the pork and onion mixture over medium heat, stirring frequently, until the onions are softened and everything looks mushy, 8 to 10 minutes. Add the tomato paste mixture and the peas to the casserole and cook for 5 minutes.

4. Transfer the pork and onion mixture to the pot with the soup, season with salt and pepper, and cook over medium heat until the peas are softened, about 35 minutes. Add the pasta and cook until tender, about 11 minutes for *semi di melone*. (Follow the package instructions for other soup pastas.) Serve immediately with Parmesan cheese.

A MINESTRONE POEM

In Calabria, the toe of the Italian boot, the most important dish is usually minestrone, a thick vegetable soup with pasta. A Calabrian poem sums it up about soups:

Sette cose fa la zuppa	Seven things does soup do
Cura fame e sete attuta	it cures hunger, slakes thirst
Empie il ventre	fills your stomach
Netta il dente	cleans your teeth
Fá dormire	makes you sleep
Fá smaltire	helps you digest
E la guancia colorire	and puts color in your cheeks

The most common soup eaten by the Calabrian fieldworker and his family in the nineteenth and early twentieth centuries was called *licurdia,* which is prepared with onions fried in lard and served with bread and lots of sweet red peppers. Perhaps that explains the rosy cheeks of a well-fed soup eater.

"married" soup

THIS SOUP FROM THE ITALIAN REGION of Campania is called *minestra maritata,* or "married soup." It's an old preparation considered by some Neapolitan gourmets a classic of their cooking. But there are versions throughout the south, and no one region can claim it absolutely. The Neapolitan variant originated at the tables of the bourgeoisie around the turn of the nineteenth century. So what, exactly, is married here? Probably the name has nothing to do with the actual institution of marriage but rather refers to the "marriage" of the common ingredients, such as vegetables, to the richer or more noble ingredients, be they eggs in the north or pork sausages, *lardo,* or pancetta in Campania. The meat used might include a lean pork sausage and a pork *andouillette,* as well as sow vulva and other parts. Over the years this heavy dish changed as cooks began to use veal or chicken in the broth instead of the fatty sausages and pork skin. To make this in the best possible way, you will want to procure a prosciutto bone, usually available from an Italian deli, although supermarkets such as Whole Foods sell, not the bone, but end pieces, which work OK. If the bone doesn't have much skin you can use a piece of pork skin, available from a butcher. Failing that, use an unsmoked ham hock. **[Makes 4 to 6 servings]**

¼ pound Parmesan, provolone, or caciocavallo cheese crust or end piece

6 ounces prosciutto skin or pork skin

1 pound ground pork

2 teaspoons salt and more as needed

1 prosciutto bone (preferably) or unsmoked ham hock (about 2 pounds)

1 pound mild Italian sausages

1 carrot, chopped

1 medium onion, chopped

1 celery stalk, chopped

Bouquet garni, consisting of 4 fresh parsley sprigs and 1 fresh marjoram sprig,
    tied with twine

8 black peppercorns

1 dried red chile, broken in half and seeded

10 cups cold water

1¾ pounds assorted green vegetables (at least 3 of the following:
    Savoy cabbage, chicory, escarole, leafy endive, spinach,
    romaine lettuce, borage leaves)

¼ cup freshly grated pecorino cheese

Freshly ground black pepper to taste

1. The day before you plan to serve, scrape the cheese crusts well to remove the imprimatur ink or wax, if any, and soak in water to cover overnight.

2. Bring 1 quart of water to a boil in a pot over high heat, then add the prosciutto skin, boil for 10 minutes, drain, and cut into strips if using prosciutto skin (leave whole if using the pork skin).

3. In a bowl, season the ground pork with 1 to 2 teaspoons salt and form into 2 big meatballs.

4. In a large flame-proof casserole (preferably earthenware), place the prosciutto skin, pork meatballs, prosciutto bone, drained cheese crusts, sausages, carrot, onion, celery, bouquet garni, peppercorns, chile, and 1 teaspoon of salt. Pour in the water. Cover the casserole and turn the heat to high. Once the water begins to boil, reduce the heat to low and cook 1¼ hours.

5. Wash the assorted vegetables and plunge them into a pot of boiling water for 5 minutes. Drain and cut into large pieces.

6. Strain the broth in the casserole through a cheesecloth-lined strainer into a large pot. You should have 1½ quarts; add water if needed. Slice the meat off the prosciutto bone and chop. Chop the sausage meat and crumble the two pork balls. Add to the saucepan with the strained broth and assorted vegetables. Turn the heat to medium and cook until done, 30 minutes to 1 hour. Serve with the pecorino and freshly ground black pepper.

briny cheese soup

THIS MINESTRONE IS A MOUNTAIN FARMER'S SOUP and is called *minestrone di viscido* in Sardinia. In the town of Ogliastra, *viscido* is the name of a kind of sour Sardinian cheese made from goat's milk that is cut into slices and brined. In the sparsely populated mountainous region of Nuoro, the cheese is called *merca*. A Greek or Balkan feta cheese or, if you can find it, a dry Sardinian pecorino, should be substituted. The Sardinian cheese is really quite something, but I have not yet seen it imported into this country. The taste is vaguely like a fermented feta cheese. *Fregula* is a typical Sardinian durum wheat pasta formed into coarse lumps that resemble couscous. *Fregula* is possible to find commercially made now, usually in Italian markets. An Internet source for *fregula* is www.gourmetsardinia.com.

[**Makes 4 servings**]

2 quarts cold water

3 boiling potatoes (about 1¾ pounds), peeled and cut into small cubes

⅓ cup dry white navy beans, soaked in water to cover overnight
    and drained

1 to 2 ounces pork fatback, rind removed and fat cut into ¼-inch-thick,
    4-inch-long strips

1 small garlic clove, peeled and crushed

1 teaspoon salt

¼ pound feta cheese, cut into 2 slices, or pecorino cheese, grated

¼ cup *fregula* or any small soup pasta

1. Put the water, potatoes, beans, pork fat, garlic, and salt in a large pot and bring to a boil slowly over medium heat. Once it begins to bubble gently, reduce the heat to a simmer and cook until the beans are half done, about 1 hour.

2. Wash the salt off the feta cheese, crumble or cut it into pieces, and add to the soup. Let the soup cook until the cheese melts, about 1 hour. Add the *fregula* or other pasta until it is cooked, about another 20 minutes. Stir well and often so the pasta doesn't stick, then serve immediately.

the best soups in the world

favata

THIS OLD SICILIAN PREPARATION, an elemental one, began as the simple gruel of fava beans in water. The soup, a thick, stewy minestrone-like dish found also in other regions of Italy's south, is very easy to make, and its powerful and delicious flavor is somewhat surprising given how little effort is required on the part of the cook. You can also use brown fava beans if the yellow variety is not available. (You can find dry fava beans in an Italian or Middle Eastern market.) The wild fennel is easily found by roadsides in California, but elsewhere, use the stems and leaves of a Florence fennel, that is, the common bulb fennel found in your supermarket. **[Makes 4 servings]**

1¼ cups (about ½ pound) dried yellow fava beans, soaked in water to
   cover overnight and drained
2 ounces pancetta, diced
1 medium onion, chopped
1 bunch wild fennel (about 10 stalks) or 1 common bulb fennel, chopped
6 cups water
2 mild Italian sausages (about ½ pound), casing removed and meat crumbled
1 tablespoon tomato paste dissolved in ½ cup water
2 teaspoons salt or more to taste
2 tablespoons finely chopped fresh parsley
6 slices French or Italian bread, toasted
Freshly ground black pepper to taste

Put the fava beans, pancetta, onion, and fennel in a large pot or flame-proof casserole and add the water. Bring to a boil over high heat, then add the sausages and dissolved tomato paste. Reduce the heat to low, season with the salt, and simmer until tender, about 1½ hours. Serve with parsley, toast, and pepper.

minestrone and minestrone-like soups

minestrone
alla genovese

DON'T BE INTIMIDATED by the long list of ingredients. This is, after all, what a minestrone is supposed to be—big! In Italy, a minestrone, a word that means "big soup," is usually served as a first course. This one from Genoa is hearty, loaded with all kinds of vegetables and flavors, and is made during the winter and spring. Pesto is an important ingredient. Remember that there isn't one minestrone but many, differing from region to region and even from family to family. This is the Genoese original that influenced the Provençal *Soupe au Pistou* (page 254). The rock Cornish game hen called for is an American breed that only goes back to the 1960s and is meant to replace the young chicken, called *pollastro* in Italian and *poussin* in French, that would be used by a Genoese cook. Simply leave out all the meat for a vegetarian minestrone. **[Makes 6 to 8 servings]**

the best soups in the world

½ cup extra-virgin olive oil

2 ounces salt pork, chopped

1 medium onion, chopped

1 leek, white and light green parts only, split lengthwise, washed well, and chopped

1 celery stalk, chopped

4 large garlic cloves, finely chopped

2 quarts water

½ pound beef shank

1 rock Cornish game hen (about 1½ pounds), cut in half

1 medium tomato, peeled (page 273), seeded, and chopped

Bouquet garni, tied with twine, consisting of 6 sprigs fresh parsley, 3 sprigs basil,
     1 sprig each of rosemary and thyme

¾ pound Hubbard or other winter squash, cut up

½ pound mustard greens, cut into strips

½ pound green cabbage, cut into strips

1 large parsnip (about ½ pound), sliced in chunks

1 large carrot, cut up

1 large turnip, cut up

1 potato, peeled and cut up

¼ cup dried red kidney beans

¼ cup dried black beans

Salt and freshly ground black pepper to taste

½ cup Pesto (page 274)

1. In a large stockpot or flame-proof casserole, heat the olive oil with the salt pork over medium-high heat, then add the onion, leek, celery, and garlic and cook, stirring, until translucent, about 10 minutes.

2. Add the water, beef, game hen, tomato, and bouquet garni. Bring to a boil over high heat, skim the surface of foam, then reduce the heat to low. Partially cover and cook until the meats are slightly tender, about 1½ hours. Add the squash, mustard greens, cabbage, parsnip, carrot, turnip, potato, and red and black beans. Simmer, partially covered, until everything is tender, about 3 hours. Season with salt and pepper.

3. Meanwhile, make the pesto and when you are ready to serve, ladle the minestrone into individual bowls and place a dollop of pesto on top for individual diners to stir into their soup.

SOUP

by Carl Sandburg

I saw a famous man eating soup.
I say he was lifting a fat broth
Into his mouth with a spoon.
His name was in the newspapers that day
Spelled out in tall black headlines
And thousands of people were talking about him.
When I saw him,
He sat bending his head over a plate
Putting soup in his mouth with a spoon.

PESTO

There are several pestos in Italian cooking, but the famous one known the world over is *pesto alla Genovese,* a mixture of fresh basil, garlic, cheese, pine nuts, and olive oil, all pounded together into a paste. It is native to the city of Genoa and used throughout the province of Liguria. Pesto is traditionally tossed with a kind of pasta called *trenette* (also called *bavette*), which is like fettuccine, and also finds its way into lasagne; it is also stirred into minestrone (page 272).

[Makes 1½ cups]

1 bunch fresh basil (about 80 medium-size leaves), washed and dried
2 large garlic cloves
2 tablespoons pine nuts, toasted until golden
Pinch of salt
3 tablespoons freshly grated Parmigiano-Reggiano cheese
3 tablespoons freshly grated pecorino cheese
¾ cup extra-virgin olive oil

1. The basil leaves used for making pesto must be completely dry. Use a salad spinner to remove the water from the washed basil, then dry them with paper towels. Leave the basil leaves spread out on top of paper towels for 1 hour to dry thoroughly.

2. Place the basil, garlic cloves, pine nuts, and salt in a large mortar and begin gently pushing with the pestle. Once the basil begins to mush, pound it more, pressing the leaves clinging to the sides down into the center of the mortar. Pound gently so that you turn the pesto into a paste and not a liquid. Slowly add the cheeses about a tablespoon at a time every minute and continue pounding. You will be pounding for 9 to 12 minutes. This can also be done in a small food processor with slightly different results.

3. If your mortar is not very large, scrape the pesto (once it is a thick paste) into a large, deep, and heavy ceramic bowl. Slowly begin pouring in the olive oil, stirring constantly with the back of a wooden spoon, or using the pestle gently. The pesto can now be used or jarred, topped with olive oil and refrigerated, always retopped with olive oil as you use it. It will keep for up to 6 months in the refrigerator as long as you continually replenish the topping of olive oil as you use the pesto, which prevents air exposure that would lead to spoilage.

minestrone with beef, veal, and pork spareribs

I FIND IT INTERESTING that Italian restaurants in the United States list "minestrone" on their menus. Imagine if they labeled a menu item "spaghetti"? Well, you would want to know: spaghetti with what? It's the same with minestrone. There are many minestrone, and you should be told which one. This particular minestrone is rich with mixed meats, a popular way of making a hearty big soup. It's flavorful and a perfect soup for late autumn.

[Makes 6 servings]

5 tablespoons extra-virgin olive oil

1½ pounds pork spareribs, cut into individual ribs

½ pound veal stew meat, cubed small

½ pound beef brisket or chuck steak, cubed small

10½ cups water

Parmesan cheese crusts (optional; use whatever you have on hand)

½ medium onion, finely chopped

1 leek, white part only, split lengthwise in quarters, washed well, and sliced

1 carrot, diced small

2 ounces prosciutto, diced small

4 large garlic cloves, finely chopped

1 tablespoon finely chopped fresh basil

3 tablespoons tomato paste

1 tablespoon salt

1 teaspoon freshly ground black pepper

½ pound potato, peeled and cubed small

½ pound butternut squash, peeled and cubed small

1 small fennel bulb, bulb and stalks, diced and leaves chopped

¾ cup (3 ounces) *ditalini* or other short, tubular soup pasta

1. In a large flame-proof casserole, heat 3 tablespoons of the olive oil over high heat, then add the spareribs, stew meat, and beef and cook, stirring occasionally, until browned all over, about 5 minutes. Add 10 cups of the water and bring to a boil over high heat. As it boils, skim the surface to remove all the foam. Reduce the heat to low, add the Parmesan crusts, if using, and simmer for 1½ hours.

(continued)

minestrone and minestrone-like soups

2. Meanwhile, in a skillet, heat the remaining 2 tablespoons olive oil over medium-high heat, then add the onion, leek, carrot, prosciutto, garlic, and basil and cook, stirring, until the onions are softened and sticking to the skillet, about 5 minutes. Add ½ cup water to deglaze the skillet, stir, and turn the heat off.

3. After the meat has been simmering for 1½ hours, add the tomato paste, season with the salt and pepper, and stir to blend. After 30 minutes, add the potato, squash, and fennel bulb and cook until nearly tender, about 1 hour. Add the contents of the skillet to the casserole, stir, and then add the pasta and cook until it is tender, about 15 minutes. Bring the minestrone to a boil, then turn the heat off and serve hot.

ch'airo paceño

SOUP IS BASED ON TRUST, and I hope you trust me when I tell you that this most famous soup of the Andes, with its odd and complicated-looking ingredient list, is worth a try.

When I first had this Bolivian soup and decided to include it in this book, I worried that no one would make it. Admittedly, I found myself collecting the various ingredients over several days, but the result was a delicious and intriguing soup with a story. In their book *Cocina Tradicional Boliviana,* Emilia Romero de Velasco and Carola Guttentag de Muzevich tell us that the soup is served in La Paz for Alasitas, a harvest festival of the native Aymara Indians of Bolivia that centers on Ekeko, the Aymara god of fertility, happiness, and prosperity. *Ch'airo* is also found in Peru, but this version has its roots in the cooking of the Aymara and Quechua peoples, who are native to Bolivia.

A number of ingredients will be difficult to find in the United States, but I provide you all the necessary information in case you want to try. Many of these foods can be ordered on the Internet at sites such as www.amigofoods.com.

The first unusual food you will need is *chalona,* or lamb jerky. I replace it with beef jerky. The *locoto* (or *rocoto*) is a native Peruvian-Bolivian chile of the *Capsicum pubescens* species. It is a very piquant, with thick fruit walls and black seeds. It is cultivated throughout the Andes and matures to a variety of colors. I substitute habanero chile; even though it is a different species, it will provide the intense floral piquancy needed.

The *ají colorado* is a finger-type chile of the species *Capsicum baccatum,* and for this recipe it is in its dried and powdered form. You can substitute the *ají amarillo* sold at www.adrianascaravan.com, or you can use the commercial chile powder blend found in the supermarket or cayenne.

You might like to try some of the *wakataya* (*Tagetes minuta* L.) called for in the original recipe. *Wakataya* is the Quechua word for an annual herb native to the temperate grasslands and montane regions of southern South America. In northern Chile it is called *suico,* and it is used there and in Bolivia and elsewhere in South America as an herbal tea or as a condiment in cooking. When the leaves of *wakataya* are crushed they exude an aroma reminiscent of licorice, and that's what I recommend as a substitute. Its essential oils are used in perfumery.

Another typical product of the Andes used here is *chuño negro,* which is a freeze-dried purple potato. Although you might find *chuño* in a South American market, I suggest in its place fresh purple potatoes sold at farmers markets, gourmet greengrocers, and some supermarkets, such as Whole Foods; you can even use red potatoes.

The dried seaweed is not a mistake. It is a substitute for the dried algae known by the Quechua word *llulluch'a* used in this dish. The *chicharrón* are pork cracklings, and those should be easy enough to find; they are sold in bags near the tortilla chips in a supermarket. Well, after reading all that, think you want to give it a try? It's delicious!

The ingredients in parentheses are not the translation of the English but the native Bolivian ingredients, which you can try finding on the Internet if you like—start at the web site mentioned above.   [**Makes 10 servings**]

¼ cup whole wheat berries

¼ cup corn kernels

1½ pounds lamb leg, cut into ¾-inch cubes

3 ounces plain beef jerky, diced

3 quarts water

1 medium onion, chopped

1 small tomato, chopped

1 turnip, peeled and cut into 8 wedges

1 stick (34 grams) black licorice (1 small branch or sprig *wakataya*),
    crushed with a rolling pin

¼ habanero chile (¼ *locoto* chile), chopped

1 sprig mint

1 tablespoon cayenne pepper (*ají colorado*)

1 tablespoon salt

5 fingerling potatoes (about 1 pound), peeled and sliced

½ cup diced purple potatoes (*chuño negro*)

¼ cup crumbled dried seaweed

¼ cup fresh or frozen peas

¼ cup double-peeled fava beans (see Note)

¼ cup finely chopped scallion

1 teaspoon oregano

10 pieces (2 ounces) pork cracklings (*chicharrón*)

5 slices (¼ pound) mozzarella (*queso fresco*), each cut in half

Finely chopped fresh parsley for garnish

Finely chopped mint for garnish

1. Bring a pot of salted water to a boil over high heat, add the wheat berries, and cook until almost tender, about 15 minutes. Add the corn and cook until both are tender, another 10 minutes. Drain and set aside.

2. In a large stew pot or flame-proof casserole, place the lamb leg and the jerky, cover with the water, then bring to a boil over high heat, skimming the surface of foam as it appears. Reduce the heat to low and add the onion, tomato, turnip, licorice, habanero chile, mint, cayenne, and salt and cook for 1 hour.

3. Add the wheat berries and corn, the fingerling potatoes, purple potatoes, and sea-weed and cook until the potatoes are almost tender, about 1¼ hours. Add the peas, fava beans, scallions, and oregano and cook until tender, about 12 minutes. Serve in individual bowls with the pork cracklings, cheese slices, and chopped parsley and mint.

Note: Double-peeled fava beans have been removed from their pod (first peel) and then plunged in boiling water for 5 minutes so you can pinch off each individual bean's skin (second peel).

SHORT SURVEY OF SOUTH AMERICAN SOUPS

Many South American soups, such as *potajes,* which are hearty soups; *pucheros,* soups like the French stew called pot-au-feu; and *cocidos,* thick meat and vegetable soups like stews, were introduced by the Spaniards. The more indigenous New World soups are found in Chile, Argentina, Uruguay, Bolivia, and Paraguay, all of which have *locros,* thick soups made with hominy, beans, squash, and sweet potatoes. The Andean *locros,* though, are like cream soups. In Bolivia, Chile, Peru, and Ecuador, thick stewlike soups called *chupes* are popular. In the north of the continent, Colombians and Venezuelans transformed the *chupe* into a thick soup that they call *ajiaco,* made with chicken and three kinds of potatoes. Finally, stretching the soup category quite a bit are the *sancochos*, which are really boiled dinners.

ajiaco bogotano

THIS FAMOUS SOUP FROM BOGOTÁ, COLOMBIA, is often made as a main course for lunch. It is thick and stewy, spicy, and delicious. The classic recipe calls for white, yellow, and purple potatoes. Nowadays, that's not so hard, as many supermarkets and farmers markets carry the less familiar varieties. In Colombia, the yellow potatoes are known as *papas criollas;* they are the wild potatoes still used by the natives of Columbia and surrounding Andean countries. Those, of course, you will not find, although you might be able to find them canned in Latin American markets. An essential ingredient, so a Colombian cook would say, is an herb called *guasca.* It's found in North America too, where it is treated as a weed. It's called gallant soldier (*Tridax parviflora* syn. *Galinsoga parviflora*) and absolutely necessary, they say, to make this soup more than just a potato chowder. It would be too hard to describe it well enough for you to find it in a field, but the picture at www.b-and-t-world-seeds.com/86392.html should help you out if you want to get real serious about this. Some cooks make this soup with yucca (cassava) instead of potatoes. Do not cut or prepare the avocado garnish until the moment of serving. **[Makes 8 servings]**

1½ pounds bone-in chicken breasts with their skin

10 cups chicken broth

1 medium onion, sliced

1 large garlic clove, lightly crushed

2 scallions, white and light green parts only, left whole

1 large russet baking potato (about 14 ounces), peeled and sliced ¼ inch thick

2 medium carrots, peeled and left whole

4 sprigs cilantro (fresh coriander)

5 sprigs fresh thyme

1 bay leaf

¼ teaspoon ground cumin

1 teaspoon cayenne pepper

2 teaspoons sweet paprika

10 black peppercorns

¾ pound small Yukon Gold potatoes, peeled

¾ pound small purple potatoes or red potatoes, peeled and halved if larger than the Yukon Gold

1 cup fresh or frozen peas

1 tablespoon salt or more to taste

FOR THE GARNISHES

2 cooked corn cobs, each cut into 4 pieces
½ cup crème fraîche, sour cream, or Mexican *crema*
¼ cup capers, drained or rinsed
2 ripe, firm avocados, peeled, pitted, and sliced
4 limes, cut in half
½ cup finely chopped cilantro (fresh coriander) leaves

1. In a large flame-proof casserole, place the chicken breasts, chicken broth, onion, garlic, scallions, russet potato, carrots, cilantro, thyme, bay leaf, cumin, cayenne, paprika, and black peppercorns and bring to a near boil over high heat. Reduce to medium and cook, partially covered and turning occasionally, until the chicken is tender, about 20 minutes. Make sure the broth never reaches a boil but only shimmers on the surface.

2. Remove the chicken, potato, and carrots. Slice the carrots into thin rounds. On a plate, mash half the potato slices and set the remaining slices aside. When the chicken has cooled enough to handle, remove the skin and bones and discard. Cut the chicken meat into strips about 1 inch long and ¼ inch wide.

3. Strain the broth into the cleaned casserole or a large pot, pushing the liquid out of the vegetables with the back of a wooden spoon. Discard all the remaining vegetables and herbs in the strainer.

4. Add the yellow and purple potatoes and the sliced and mashed russet potato to the casserole, then bring to a near boil over high heat. Reduce the heat to medium and cook, partially covered, until the potatoes begin to fall apart, about 30 minutes. Add the reserved chicken and carrots to the casserole, along with the peas, and simmer, turning gently, for 5 minutes, adding up to 2 cups of water if it is looking more like a stew than a soup. Season with salt. Serve with the garnishes on the side.

minestrone and minestrone-like soups

grain-based
soups

So many soups, especially in peasant traditions of old, were based on stale bread. In fact, these soup-soaked stale bread soups were called "sops," a word from which our modern "soup" is derived. Those bread soups and all soups based on wheat, such as those with pasta, as well as those based on other kinds of grains, are found here. This is a chapter with filling and soul-satisfying soups popular with everyone, including several soups you've probably never seen and that will undoubtedly enter your repertoire once you've tasted them.

bread soup

WHEN I FIRST HAD AN OPPORTUNITY to go to Albania, it was under the rule of the orthodox Communist ruler Enver Hoxha—and I was unable to visit because I was in a car accident in Greece that abruptly ended my trip short of the border. Since then I've always said that I would have been turned back at the border anyway. Albania, even today, is the least known Mediterranean nation. It is a poor country, mostly mountainous and hilly, but with a few small coastal plains. Wheat is one of its major agricultural products, so the bread soup called *buke mevaj me kripe* would not be unexpected at the table of Albanian peasants on a winter's night. Some cooks might use yogurt instead of sour cream, but in either case it is a rib-sticking meal. This recipe is adapted from Inge Kramarz's *Balkan Cookbook*.

[Makes 4 servings]

¼ cup extra-virgin olive oil
1 medium onion, finely chopped
½ teaspoon hot paprika
1 potato (about ½ pound), peeled and grated
1 quart beef broth
4 to 6 ounces croûtons (page 129)
½ cup sour cream or plain whole yogurt

In a large pot, heat 2 tablespoons of the olive oil over medium-high heat, then add the onion and cook, stirring occasionally, until softened, about 4 minutes. Stir in the paprika, then add the grated potato and broth. Reduce the heat to medium and cook until the potato is tender, 20 to 25 minutes. Add the croûtons to the soup, bring to a boil over high heat, then turn the heat off. Whisk in the sour cream or yogurt, drizzle with the remaining olive oil, and serve.

le mourtaïrol

LE MOURTAÏROL is an oven-baked chicken broth and bread soup seasoned with saffron that is one of the oldest dishes in European cuisine. The name indicates how the dish was originally prepared: in a mortar, each ingredient pounded to the desired consistency. There are recipes for this preparation—with this name more or less—in two anonymous fourteenth-century European cookery manuscripts, the Italian *Liber de coquina* and the Catalan *Libre de Sent Soví*. There is an old recipe that appears in the late fourteenth-century French cookery work *Le ménagier de Paris* as well as in the fourteenth-century English compilation of the master chefs of King Richard II known as the *Forme of Cury,* where it appears as "mortrews of Fyssh." In Chaucer's *Canterbury Tales* it is a "mortreux." Perhaps this broth is originally related to the tenth-century Arab *lubābiyya,* a preparation made with unleavened bread crumbs, saffron, pistachios, and rose water. Even with all this history, it's just a peasant soup and a perfect use of stale bread. A rich homemade chicken broth is required for this soup to stand out.

[Makes 4 to 6 servings]

1 pound stale French or Italian country bread
Pinch of saffron threads, crumbled
2 quarts chicken broth

1. Preheat the oven to 325°F.

2. Break up the stale bread in a high-sided baking casserole. Add the saffron to the chicken broth and stir. Pour half the chicken broth over the bread. Keep the casserole in the oven for 30 minutes or until it is as hot as you like your soup, moistening with additional chicken broth every once in a while until the broth is used up.

portuguese bread and purslane soup

BREAD IS THE FOUNDATION of many Portuguese soups. Typically, the bread used is home-made. This soup from Alentejo, called *sopa de beldroegas com queijinhos e ovos,* is also based on bread, which is natural enough since the area is considered the granary of Portugal. (Interestingly, Alentejo is also the source of half of the world's cork.)

You will want to use small, three-inch-diameter rounds of fresh sheep's cheese or any small cylindrical sheep's or goat's milk cheese to place on top of the soup at the end of its cooking. The name of this cheese is also Alentejo; it is a very soft, cylindrical cheese made in three sizes weighing about two ounces, one pound, and four pounds. The smallest ones, the ones used in this soup, are usually made from both sheep's and goat's milk. You are unlikely to find this cheese in a store, although you can order Portuguese cheeses from www.igourmet.com. In its place you might find a Miticrema. It is a soft fresh sheep's milk cheese from Spain that comes in a jar; it can be purchased at Whole Foods Markets. And in a pinch you can use a one-inch-thick slice of any soft cylindrical goat cheese sold in most supermarkets.

Purslane is a succulent vegetable with fleshy leaves usually used in soups and salads. When you sauté it in this recipe you may hear some of the leaves pop. Purslane is usually available at farmers markets and some gourmet greengrocers. If purslane is impossible to get, try making the soup with escarole. My recipe is adapted from Maria de Lourdes Modesto's *Traditional Portuguese Cooking* (1982). The Portuguese will pour the broth over the bread and eat the potatoes, eggs, cheese, and purslane from a side dish, but I like it as one big soup, almost like a minestrone.   [**Makes 6 servings**]

½ cup extra-virgin olive oil

2 medium onions, thinly sliced

2 large bunches purslane (about 1½ pounds), leaves only, washed well

2 quarts water

4 boiling potatoes (such as Yukon Gold, about 1 pound), peeled and
    cut into ¼-inch-thick slices

1 bulb garlic, outer white skin rubbed off, but cloves left attached

1 tablespoon salt

6 large eggs

¼ pound fresh or soft sheep's or goat's milk cheese

6 slices hard-crust country bread

the best soups in the world

1. In a large flame-proof casserole, heat the olive oil over medium heat, then add the onions and cook, stirring occasionally, until translucent, about 8 minutes. Add the purslane leaves and cook, tossing and stirring, until well blended. Add the water and bring to a boil over high heat, then add the potatoes, garlic bulb, and salt, reduce the heat to medium, and cook until the potatoes are tender, about 20 minutes.

2. Carefully break the eggs into the broth so the yolks don't break and leave them to poach, without stirring or stirring very gently, until the whites solidify but the yolks are soft, about 5 minutes. Add 6 soupspoonfuls of the cheese, placing them in separate areas of the casserole so they don't touch each other. Place the bread in individual soup bowls and ladle the soup over the bread, giving each diner an egg and a piece of cheese.

A SOUP FROM THE ROMAN EMPIRE

Apicius, who flourished in the first century AD in Rome, wrote our only extant cookbook from the Roman period. Here is a recipe for a soup called Julian Pottage (*Pultes Iulianae*). Spelt is a kind of soft wheat, and *liquamen* or *garum* is a kind of ancient fish sauce like the contemporary Thai fish sauce.

Julian pottage is made in the following way. Soak hulled spelt, cook, and bring to a boil. When boiling, add oil. When it thickens, stir to a creamy consistency. Take two previously cooked brains and half a pound of meat, minced as for rissoles. Pound the meat together with the brains, and put into a saucepan. Then pound pepper, lovage, and fennel seed, moisten with *liquamen* (*garum*) and a little wine, and put into the saucepan over the brains and the meat. When this has cooked enough, mix it with stock. Add this mixture gradually to the spelt, mixing it in by the ladleful, and stir until smooth, to the consistency of thick soup.

pappa al pomodoro

THE SECRET TO THIS CLASSIC tomato and bread soup from Florence is using the ripest garden tomatoes and good-quality artisanal bread. You cannot use supermarket tomatoes or sourdough bread. There are different versions of this soup, but the ones with lots of garlic are not typical in Florence, as Tuscans aren't as garlic crazy as, for example, Neapolitans. The ginger might just be a vestige of medieval spice use, because it is quite uncommon in the contemporary Tuscan pantry. The soup is usually eaten warm, with a drizzle of extra-virgin olive oil and a sprinkle of Parmesan cheese.　　　　　**[Makes 4 servings]**

¼ cup extra-virgin olive oil plus more to drizzle
1 small leek, white part only, finely chopped
1 garlic clove, finely chopped
Pinch of ground ginger
1 pound very ripe tomatoes, peeled, seeded, and chopped
1 teaspoon tomato paste
3 cups chicken or light vegetable broth
1 teaspoon salt
Freshly ground black pepper to taste
½ pound rustic Italian or French bread, without crust, ripped into small pieces
Freshly grated Parmesan cheese

1. In a pot, heat the olive oil over medium heat, then add the leek, garlic, and ginger and cook, stirring, until softened, about 3 minutes. Add the tomatoes and tomato paste and increase the heat to high. Once it starts to sputter, reduce the heat to medium and cook, stirring occasionally, for 5 minutes.

2. Add the broth, season with salt and pepper, and bring to a boil again over high heat. Add the bread and cook for 2 minutes. Remove from the heat, cover, and let sit for 1 hour. Stir, reheat a bit, and serve warm or at room temperature. Serve with extra olive oil to drizzle on top and some Parmesan cheese.

hasū

BREAD BAKERS SET ASIDE a portion of yeasted dough to act as a starter for the next batch of bread. This starter is called a sponge, poolish, *levain de boulanger* in French, and *biga* in Italian. In this medieval recipe of the Jews of North Africa, it is the foundation for a soup. The ethnologist Joëlle Bahloul tells us that this soup, called *hasū,* although eaten by the population at large, was especially associated with the Jews of Ain Beida on the eastern Algerian steppe, who often ate it in place of coffee on winter mornings when it was very cold or snowing.

Hasū is rare, unknown to outsiders, and nearly forgotten among Jews of North African extraction themselves, except for the elderly. It is a kind of piquant velouté, a soup made from semolina bread starter and spicy with *harīsa,* chile, and caraway. Some of the starter is mixed with ground coriander seeds and spoon-dropped into hot olive oil. These tiny fried beignets are used as a garnish. They are a little larger than hazelnuts and are called *thumniyya,* or they are made as one makes the little pasta balls, like couscous, called *muhammas.*

There is a long history to *hasū,* as we know from the descriptions left by the great twelfth-century Arab geographer al-Idrisi, who seems to indicate that *hasū* means very soft boiled eggs that are almost liquid. It's possible that eggs were once a prominent part of the dish—or that the dish should resemble thickly beaten eggs. *Hasū* also derives from the word for "to sip," so we know that it refers to a soup. There is a recipe for *hasū* (or *hasa*) in the thirteenth-century Hispano-Muslim cookbook probably written in the Spanish province of Murcia by Ibn Razīn al-Tujībī and called the *Kitāb fadālat al-khiwān fī tayyibāt al-tˁam waʾl-alwān,* which translates roughly as "The excellent table composed of the best foods and the best dishes." But in that recipe there is no egg. Even though this soup has many steps and is complex, the result is very much worth the effort. **[Makes 6 servings]**

¼ teaspoon active dry yeast

8 ½ cups water

2 cups unbleached all-purpose flour

1½ teaspoons ground coriander seeds

1 cup extra-virgin olive oil

6 large garlic cloves

1½ teaspoons caraway seeds

1 tablespoon tomato paste

1 tablespoon *harīsa* (page 62)

1½ teaspoons cayenne pepper

3 teaspoons salt

¼ cup dried mint

1. The day before you plan to serve the soup, in the bowl of an electric mixer, add the yeast, pour in ¼ cup warm water (about 105°F) and let stand until creamy, about 10 minutes. Stir in ¾ cup water and then the flour, 1 cup at a time. If you don't have an electric mixer, you can do this step in a bowl, and then use a food processor in Step 2.

2. Attach the paddle attachment to the mixer and run at the lowest speed for 2 minutes. (In a food processor, run until a sticky dough is formed in a few seconds.)

3. Transfer this starter dough to a lightly oiled bowl, cover with plastic wrap, and let rise for 24 hours. The starter will triple in volume and still be wet and sticky when ready. Cover and refrigerate until ready to use. You will need 200 grams, about 7 ounces or ¾ cup, of starter for this recipe. The remainder you can save for bread baking.

4. In a bowl, knead together 3 ounces (about ¼ cup) of the starter with the ground coriander.

5. In a skillet, heat ¼ cup of the olive oil over medium heat, then drop hazelnut-size spoonfuls of starter into the oil and cook until light golden, about 2 minutes. Remove with a skimmer and set aside.

6. To make the soup, in a mortar, pound the garlic and caraway together with a pestle until crushed. Add the tomato paste, *harisa,* cayenne, and 1 teaspoon salt and continue pounding and crushing until mushy.

7. In a pot, heat ¾ cup olive oil over medium-high heat, then add the garlic-tomato mixture and cook, stirring, for 1 minute. Stir in the 1 cup of warm water, let it come to a boil, then reduce the heat to low, cover, and cook for 5 minutes.

8. Meanwhile, dissolve the remaining 4 ounces (about 6 to 8 tablespoons) starter in ½ cup of water until homogenous and smooth. Stir into the soup. Add the remaining 6 cups of warm water and the remaining 2 teaspoons salt. Mix well and cook for 20 minutes.

9. Place the dried mint in a spice grinder, food processor, or mortar and blend until very fine, almost a powder. Stir into the soup, correct the seasoning, and serve.

semolina ball soup

THIS STUNNING SOUP from Tunisia is made with a large couscous ball called *sidir,* which you won't be able to find, although you could make your own. In its place it's perfectly fine to use the very typical North African–style ball of semolina known as *muhammas* in Tunisia and *burkukis* in Algeria. It's often described as a large couscous, and one Israeli firm markets it as "Israeli couscous," which it is not. It is sold in Middle Eastern markets and through various Internet sites with the label "toasted pasta ball," *mougrabieh,* or *moghrabiye,* the last two names being, curiously, what they call these in Syria—far from the home of couscous. In fact, the meaning of the two words is "from the Maghrib," that is, North Africa. This recipe is based on the one served to me by Hechmi Hammami, the executive chef of the Abou Nawas Hotel in Tunis, who used *qadīd,* a spiced lamb jerky, for his flavoring. Although it is a hot soup, one can also say it's intriguingly delicate.   [**Makes 4 servings**]

½ teaspoon caraway seeds

5 large garlic cloves, peeled

1 teaspoon salt

¼ cup extra-virgin olive oil

2 tablespoons tomato paste dissolved in 1 cup water

1 tablespoon *harīsa* (page 62)

½ teaspoon freshly ground black pepper

6 cups water

¼ pound (about ½ cup) toasted pasta balls (sometimes sold as "Israeli couscous")

1 Preserved Lemon (page 293), cut into small dice without the peel

1 tablespoon capers, rinsed

1 tablespoon finely chopped fresh mint leaves (optional)

1. Grind the caraway seeds in a mortar, then pound in the garlic and salt until the mixture forms a paste.

2. In a large nonreactive casserole or pot, heat the olive oil over high heat, then add the garlic-caraway paste, tomato paste dissolved in water, *harīsa,* and black pepper. It will sizzle violently for a second, so remember to keep your face away. Reduce the heat to medium, stir well to mix, cover, and cook, stirring a few times, for about 5 minutes.

3. Add the water, pasta balls, preserved lemon, and capers and simmer, uncovered, until the pasta balls are soft but not mushy, about 20 minutes. Sprinkle on the mint, if using, and serve immediately.

PRESERVED LEMONS

Preserving lemons is not only a great way to use the bounty of lemon trees; it also yelds an amazing condiment especially important to North African cooking. You'll want to use thin-skinned Meyer lemons. [Makes ½ pint]

2 Meyer lemons, washed well, dried well, and cut into 8 wedges each
⅓ cup salt
½ cup fresh lemon juice
Extra virgin olive oil to cover

1. In a medium-size bowl, toss the lemon wedges with the salt, then place in a half-pint jar. Cover the lemons with the lemon juice, screw on the lid, and leave at room temperature for a week, shaking it occasionally.

2. Pour in the olive oil to cover and refrigerate; they will keep for up to 1 year.

vermicelli and turmeric soup

VERMICELLI MEANS "LITTLE WORMS" in Italian, and in Tunisia vermicelli pasta is called *duwayda,* which means "inchworm" in Arabic. In this spicy hot preparation called *duwayda zarrā,* which means "farmer-style vermicelli," the pasta is indeed broken into one-inch inchworm lengths. This soup is a typical midday winter lunch dish in rural Tunisia. We have a record of this form of macaroni in North Africa appearing as early as the time of the Hafsids (1228–1574), the most important dynasty in late medieval Tunisia.   **[Makes 4 servings]**

½ cup extra-virgin olive oil
1 medium onion, finely chopped
2 tablespoons tomato paste dissolved in 1 cup water
2 tablespoons finely chopped celery leaves with a little stalk
1 tablespoon hot paprika
½ teaspoon turmeric powder
½ teaspoon cayenne pepper
½ teaspoon freshly ground black pepper
3 bay leaves
Salt to taste
5 cups water
6 to 8 ounces vermicelli or spaghetti, broken into 1-inch lengths

1. In a large flame-proof casserole, heat the olive oil over medium-high heat. Add the onion and cook, stirring frequently, until softened, about 4 minutes. Add the tomato paste dissolved in water, along with the celery leaves and stalks, paprika, turmeric, cayenne, black pepper, bay leaves, and salt. Reduce the heat to medium and cook, stirring, for 4 to 5 minutes.

2. Add the water and the vermicelli to the casserole and cook over medium heat until the pasta is soft, about 25 minutes, stirring occasionally. Serve hot.

korean chicken and rice soup

IN KOREAN COOKING, the difference between a *kuk* and a *chigae* is that a *kuk* is made with more water, so it's properly a soup, while a *chigae* is more like a stew. A *kuk* is also milder in taste, while a *chigae* is more boldly flavored. Another word for soup in Korean is *t'ang,* which is the Chinese word of the same meaning. This wonderfully simple soup is perfect in the winter. If you have a little leftover chicken breast, that makes it even easier. But if you don't, just poach the chicken breast in some water for 15 to 20 minutes, then let it cool and shred it with two forks. The Korean chile paste, known as *koch'ujang,* can be ordered though www.kgrocer.com or www.ikoreaplaza.com if you don't happen to have a Korean market in your neighborhood. **[Makes 6 servings]**

1 tablespoon sesame seeds
8 cups chicken broth
2½ tablespoons finely chopped garlic
2½ tablespoons finely chopped fresh ginger
½ cup short grain rice
1 tablespoon soy sauce
1 teaspoon sesame oil
1 tablespoon Korean chile paste (*koch'ujang*)
¼ pound shredded cooked chicken breast
2 scallions, finely chopped

1. In a small cast-iron skillet, toast the sesame seeds over medium-high heat without any fat, shaking the skillet often until the seeds are lightly browned, about 1 minute. Transfer to a small bowl and set aside.

2. In a large pot, add the chicken broth, garlic, and ginger and bring to a boil over high heat. Add the rice, reduce the heat to medium-low, and simmer until the rice is tender, about 12 minutes. Stir in the soy sauce and sesame oil. Add the chile paste and stir to blend. Add the shredded chicken and as soon as it is heated, ladle the soup into bowls and garnish with the scallions and reserved sesame seeds.

old-fashioned chicken noodle soup

CHICKEN NOODLE is surely the quintessential American soup. The Campbell's Soup Company certainly thought so and put it into a can back in 1934. For several generations now Americans have eaten the canned soup, thinking it's just fine. But this old-fashioned recipe is the proper chicken noodle soup. It is, as I like to say, chicken noodle soup circa 1933.

In fact, chicken noodle soup is one of the earliest soups for which we have a written record in any language. It is first recorded in the tenth-century Arabic cookbook *Kitāb al-tabīkh* (Book of cookery) by Ibn Sayyār al-Warrāq, in which a recipe called *nibātiyya* is a chicken broth with vermicelli. Of course, this tenth-century recipe is a far cry from my recipe here, as it consisted of a chicken broth cooked with chickpeas and onion and seasoned with a paste made of coriander, pepper, cassia, galangal, spikenard, cloves, nutmeg, long pepper, and ginger and finished with rose water, cheese, and hard-boiled eggs. In a fourteenth-century Italian cookery book called *Libro della cocina* (Book of cookery), by an anonymous Tuscan, a chicken noodle soup is called *de le lasagne*. There lasagne noodles are cooked in chicken broth and served with grated cheese.

My chicken noodle soup recipe is true slow food and is not concerned with quick cooking. As far away from a can as you can get, it's about magnificent tastes coaxed from simple ingredients—and it's all homemade. I believe you'll be startled at the difference in taste from the canned version. You can, off course, use commercial bouillon cubes and a package of egg noodles, but if you do, then why bother reading this recipe—why not just use a can? I hope you give this a try, as it's truly worth the effort.   [**Makes 6 servings**]

296

the best soups in the world

FOR THE NOODLES

1 cup all-purpose flour
1 large egg and 1 large egg yolk
¼ teaspoon salt

FOR THE SOUP

2 chicken breast halves (about 1½ pounds), on the bone
1 pound chicken parts (preferably a roasted carcass, or wings, feet, legs)
2 carrots, peeled and diced very small
2 celery stalks, finely chopped
2 large garlic cloves, finely chopped
6 tablespoons finely chopped fresh parsley
2 tablespoons finely chopped fresh basil

10 cups water

4 teaspoons salt

1 teaspoon freshly ground black pepper or more to taste

1. To prepare the noodles: in a bowl, pour the flour and make a well like a volcano crater in the center. Crack the egg into the well, add the egg yolk, season with the salt, and form into a ball, using the addition of water or egg white from your wet hands only, if necessary, to make it form. Once the ball of dough is formed, move it onto a lightly floured surface and begin to knead until you have a smooth, pliable ball, about 8 minutes. Wrap in plastic wrap and let rest for 1 hour.

2. Flatten the ball of dough and cut it into two. Roll each half thinner with a rolling pin. Roll the dough through a pasta rolling machine until about 1 millimeter thick. Roll again through the fettuccine cutter if you have one and cut it off into 3-inch-long segments. If you don't have a cutter attachment, cut the pasta with a knife into 3 × ⅜-inch strips. Arrange the fresh pasta on a table to rest and dry for 4 hours. Store the pasta until needed or continue with the preparation. (If you don't have a pasta rolling machine, cut the dough into 4 pieces and roll thin on a floured surface with a rolling pin.)

3. To prepare the soup: in a large pot, place the chicken breasts, chicken parts, half of the diced carrots and celery, both garlic cloves, 4 tablespoons of the parsley, and 1 tablespoon of the basil and cover with the water. Bring to just below a boil over medium heat, making sure the water never bubbles but only shimmers on top, then reduce the heat to low and simmer until the chicken is tender, about 45 minutes.

4. Remove the chicken from the broth and let cool. Remove and discard the bones and skin and shred the breast flesh with your fingers. Set the chicken meat aside. Strain the broth through a cheesecloth-lined strainer and then return it to the pot. Any meat from the chicken carcass or parts not used in this recipe can be saved for another purpose.

5. Add the remaining carrots, celery, parsley, and basil to the broth, bring to a boil over high heat, season with salt and pepper, and add the noodles. Cook until the noodles are tender, about 4 minutes. Reduce the heat to low and add the reserved shredded chicken breast. Simmer until the chicken is hot, about 3 minutes. Serve hot.

chicken soup with matzo balls

CHICKEN SOUP WITH MATZO BALLS is considered by American Jews to be the quintessential Jewish soup. Although traditional for Passover, the Jewish holiday commemorating the Hebrews' liberation from slavery in Egypt, and Purim, the celebration of the deliverance of the Persian Jews from massacre by Haman, as told in the Book of Esther, it is in fact enjoyed at any time. It was originally a soup of the Central and Eastern European Jews sometimes called the Ashkenazi. The chicken Passover soup eaten by Sephardic Jews, those of the Middle East and the Mediterranean, would be unrecognizable to Ashkenazic Jews, as it is gastronomically unrelated. In American Jewish tradition chicken soup is sometimes called the Jewish penicillin in recognition of the fact that it acts as a mother's cure-all for everything from nasal congestion to broken hearts.

As with all home-based soups, there are many different recipes and many different "secrets." I subscribe to several of these secrets. For instance, using chicken feet is almost required, but since they cannot always be found, using a beef bone or turkey wing will help, as will adding parsnip and/or parsley root, all of which improves the broth immeasurably. Making sure the broth never comes to a boil and removing the layer of fat that forms when it cools insures a nice clear broth that is not cloudy. (Of course, this is an open secret, and true for any broth.)

The one tricky part is making and cooking the matzo balls—*knaidlach* in Yiddish. Use a light hand when mixing and treat the matzo balls like the delicate dumplings they are; let them cook without disturbing them and keep them covered at all times while they cook. Some cooks make stuffed dumplings called *kreplach,* made from matzo meal, semolina, or wholemeal flour and stuffed with meat and chicken fat. Matzo meal can be bought, but I simply crush a box of matzo until it looks like dry rolled oatmeal. I usually make this soup over a period of two days—the broth the first day, refrigerating it overnight so a layer of fat forms, and the soup the second day. **[Makes 8 servings]**

FOR THE BROTH

One 4-pound chicken, wrapped in cheesecloth and tied off with kitchen twine

1 pound chicken feet or 1 turkey wing

1 pound beef soup bones with a little meat on them, split if possible

One 4-inch-long beef marrow bone

3 bouquets garni, each tied in cheesecloth and kitchen twine, and consisting of:

1) 2 small halved onions; 2 stalks celery, cut into 1-inch pieces; and 1 garlic clove

2) 3 carrots, peeled and cut into ½-inch pieces; ½ celery root (celeriac) or parsley root, peeled and cubed small; and 1 large parsnip, peeled and diced

3) 6 sprigs fresh parsley, 6 sprigs dill, 6 peppercorns, and 1 whole nutmeg

6 quarts water

FOR THE MATZO BALLS

4 large eggs, separated

½ pound matzo meal

½ teaspoon salt

½ teaspoon freshly ground white pepper

5 tablespoons rendered chicken fat (see Note)

2 tablespoons seltzer (club soda) or more if needed

FOR SERVING

2 tablespoons finely chopped fresh parsley

grain-based soups

1. In a large stockpot, place the chicken, chicken feet, beef bones, and the 3 bouquets garni and cover with the water. Bring to a near boil over high heat, then reduce the heat to low and simmer until the chicken is tender, about 3 hours.

2. Remove the chicken and when it is cool enough to handle, remove the cheesecloth and bone the chicken, discarding the cheesecloth, bones, skin, fat, and cartilage.

(continued)

Shred both chicken breast halves with your fingers and set the meat aside; the meat should be very tender and shred easily. Reserve the remaining chicken for another purpose. Discard the chicken feet and beef bones, but remove the marrow from the marrow bone and set aside with the shredded chicken meat. Discard the bouquet garni with the parsley and dill. Unwrap the carrot bouquet and dice some carrots, parsnip, and parsley or celery root to equal 2 cups. Discard the remaining vegetables. Strain the chicken broth through a fine mesh strainer, then refrigerate until a layer of fat forms on top. Remove the fat and save it, as you will need it to make the matzo balls. Set aside 3 quarts chicken broth for this soup and freeze the remainder for another purpose.

3. Prepare the matzo balls about 3 hours before you wish to serve the soup. In a bowl, beat the egg whites until stiff and set aside. In a large bowl, combine the matzo meal, salt, and pepper and mix well. Mix in the reserved chicken fat, seltzer, and egg yolks. Fold in the egg whites and form into a loose dough. Cover with plastic wrap and refrigerate for 2 hours so the dough can stiffen and the matzo can absorb the fat.

4. About 1 hour before you want to serve the soup, remove the matzo meal dough from the refrigerator and form into balls no bigger than 1 inch in diameter. You should have about 40 matzo balls. In a heavy soup pot with a heavy lid, bring the reserved chicken broth to a boil over high heat. Reduce the heat to low, gently place the matzo balls in the soup, cover, and simmer undisturbed, without any stirring or lifting of the lid, until firm and cooked through, about 35 minutes. It is important that the pot stay covered the whole time the matzo balls are cooking. About 7 minutes before the matzo balls are cooked and the soup is ready, add the shredded chicken breast and diced reserved vegetables and let them get hot in the soup. Serve hot garnished with parsley if desired.

FREEKEH OR GREEN WHEAT

Farīk, the classical Arabic spelling, but known in colloquial Arabic from Syria to Algeria as *fireek, freekeh, freeky, freek, freeka, fareek,* or *frikeh,* is an immature hard wheat (durum wheat or semolina, *Triticum turgidum* var. *durum*) that goes through a roasting process in its production. *Freekeh* has a higher nutritive value than rice, being especially high in protein, vitamins, and minerals. Because *freekeh* can only be found in Middle Eastern markets, Whole Foods supermarkets, or from Internet sources, I always call for bulgur as a substitute in these recipes.

The food is commonly prepared from immature grains of durum wheat when they are still milky. The stage at which *freekeh* is prepared is very critical. The moment the leaves start to turn yellow and the seeds are still soft and creamy is ideal. The wheat is harvested and arranged in small piles and left to dry in the sun for a day. The piles are set on fire and the blaze carefully controlled so only the straw and chaff burn and not the seeds. It is the high moisture content of the seeds—unique to hard wheat—that prevents them from catching fire. The supervisor of the burn must pay close attention to the location of the fire, the wind, and the progress of the burn to ensure a perfect final product. The roasted wheat then undergoes further thrashing and sun-drying to make the flavor, texture, and color uniform. It is this thrashing or rubbing of the grains that gives this food its name—*farīk* means "rubbed." The seeds are now cracked into smaller pieces so they look like a green bulgur. The resulting food is earthy, smoky, and has a distinct flavor. It is popular in Syria, Palestine, and Jordan, and one finds famous *freekeh* dishes in Turkey, Egypt, Tunisia, and Algeria.

The making of a dish called *farīk* is quite old, as we know from an early thirteenth-century Baghdad cookery book that contained a recipe called *farīkiyya*—although we can't be sure this was made from green wheat, let alone durum wheat. In that dish, meat is fried in oil and braised with water, salt, and cinnamon bark. Then dried coriander is stirred in with young wheat, and it is cooked until done and served with cumin, cinnamon, and fresh lamb tail fat.

In Tunisia, *farīk* also refers to young barley grains and is the name of a kind of almond that will split into two with only the slightest rubbing pressure. Another North African dish called *farīkiyya* is a kind of *harīsa* (the porridge, not the spicy condiment) made with green wheat instead of the regular hard wheat. *Farīqiya* is a gruel made with dates or rice and milk that is fed to pregnant women.

To clean the *freekeh* before using, spread the grains on a baking sheet and pick out any stones or chaff. Place in a strainer and give it a rinse under running water.

You can find out more about, as well as purchase, *freekeh* online at www.surfas online.com/products/33999.cfm and www.palestinianfairtrade.ps/freekeh.php. *Freekeh* is found in this country in Middle Eastern markets and, to a much lesser extent, whole food stores.

najwa's freekeh soup

FREEKEH **IS THE COLLOQUIAL** Palestinian expression for what's known in classical Arabic as *farīk*, a product made with the grains of immature durum wheat, otherwise known as green wheat. This is an earthy tasting soup, called *shūrbat al-farīk*, made regularly for me and our kids by my former wife Najwa. We all think of it as comfort food, especially Najwa, who grew up on this soup. (Come to think of it, so did my kids.) Najwa is an excellent soupmaker, and you'll want to try her lentil soup too (page 244). Although Najwa uses Crisco to fry the chicken, admitting that it isn't as healthy as oil, I used vegetable oil and was completely satisfied. The green wheat, or *freekeh*, can be purchased online at www.surfasonline.com/products/33999.cfm. You can read more about green wheat on page 301.   **[Makes 5 servings]**

2 tablespoons vegetable oil

1¾ pounds chicken thigh and legs on the bone with their skin

1 very large onion, thinly sliced

2 quarts water

1 cinnamon stick

6 whole cardamom pods

1 tablespoon *bahārāt* (page 303)

3 teaspoons salt

½ teaspoon freshly ground black pepper

½ pound (1 cup) *freekeh* (green wheat) or coarse bulgur #4,
      picked over for stones and chaff and rinsed well

Juice from ½ lemon

1. In a large flame-proof casserole, heat the vegetable oil over medium-high heat, then add the chicken and sliced onion and cook, turning the chicken and stirring the onion, until the chicken is golden brown on both sides, 10 to 12 minutes.

2. Cover the chicken with the water and add the cinnamon stick, whole cardamom pods, *bahārāt*, salt, and pepper. Bring to a near boil over high heat, making sure the water never actually reaches a boil. Reduce the heat to very low and simmer until the chicken is falling off the bones, about 2 hours. The surface of the broth should only be shimmering, never bubbling, otherwise the chicken will toughen. Skim the surface of foam as it appears.

3. Remove the chicken from the broth and when it is cool enough to handle, remove and discard the skin and bones. Pull the meat off the bones and shred thinner with your fingers. Set the meat aside. Remove and discard the cinnamon stick and cardamom pods.

4. Increase the heat for the broth to medium, then return the chicken meat to the broth along with the freekeh or bulgur. Cook until the *freekeh* or bulgur is tender, about 40 minutes. Stir in the lemon juice and serve hot.

BAHĀRĀT

Bahārāt means "spice" in Arabic, derived from the word *bahār*, which means "pepper." It is an all-purpose mix used in Lebanon, Syria, Jordan, and Palestine and found in many prepared savory dishes. *Bahārāt* can be bought at Middle Eastern groceries and markets, but it is also quite easy to make fresh for yourself and keep stored in a spice jar. There are many different variations, all based on the basic ingredients of black pepper and allspice. Some mixes might include paprika, coriander seeds, cassia bark, sumac, nutmeg, cumin seeds, or cardamom seeds. This recipe is basic; if you like, you can fiddle with it by adding some of the other spices mentioned.　　　　　　　　　　　　　　　　　**[Makes about ½ cup]**

¼ cup black peppercorns
¼ cup allspice berries
2 teaspoons ground cinnamon
1 teaspoon freshly grated nutmeg

Grind the peppercorns and allspice together and blend with the cinnamon and nutmeg. Store in a jar in your spice rack, away from sunlight. It will lose pungency as time goes by, but properly stored, it will remain good for many months.

tharīd

I FIRST PUBLISHED THIS RECIPE in my book *A Mediterranean Feast,* but I would like to also offer it here because this particular version is a Tunisian soup and, besides being delicious, it has an interesting history. The references in all the classical lexica describe *tharīd* as a kind of bread soup or a large earthenware bowl. It has been described as one of the Prophet Muhammad's favorite dishes, in reference to his saying that his wife Aishah held a place among women that *tharīd* held among food. *Tharīd* was a food of the Quraysh tribe of the Arabian Peninsula in pre-Islamic times and, in what might be an apocryphal story, Hāshim, Muhammad's great-grandfather, on a visit to Syria, cooked this dish, which was unknown to non-Arabs, for the Byzantine emperor, who liked it so much that he was persuaded to grant the Quraysh mercantile privileges. Al-Muqaddasī, the famed Arab traveler who was born in Jerusalem in AD 947, says that he ate *tharīd(a)* with the monks, probably meaning the Chaldean monks of Iraq, so the word may originally be Aramaic, Syriac, or Chaldean. The dried rose petals needed in this Tunisian *tharīd* can be ordered online through www.adrianascaravan.com.   [**Makes 8 servings**]

1 young chicken, quartered or 2 Cornish hens (about 3½ pounds total)

2½ quarts water

¼ cup canned chickpeas, drained

2 tablespoons clarified butter or butter

Bouquet garni, tied with kitchen twine, consisting of 1 celery stalk
    and 5 sprigs fresh parsley

Salt and freshly ground black pepper to taste

½ teaspoon ground cinnamon

½ teaspoon ground dried rose petals (optional)

2 large eggs

Juice from 1 lemon

½ cup extra-virgin olive oil

About ½ loaf day-old French baguette, cut into small cubes

1. Put the chicken, water, chickpeas, clarified butter, bouquet garni, salt, and pepper in a large pot and bring to a gentle boil over medium heat. Reduce the heat to medium-low, cover, and simmer, with the water only shimmering on the surface, for 1 hour.

2. Remove and discard the bouquet garni. Remove the chicken from the pot. When it is cool enough to handle, separate the meat from the bones. Lightly sprinkle the chicken meat with the cinnamon, rose petals, if using, ½ teaspoon of black pepper, and salt to taste and set aside. Discard the bones and skin.

3. Beat the eggs in a bowl with one-quarter of the lemon juice. Whisk a few table-spoons of hot soup into the beaten eggs to warm them. Transfer the beaten eggs back to the soup, whisking quickly so they don't curdle. Keep the soup warm over very low heat.

4. In a large skillet or flame-proof casserole, heat ¼ cup of the olive oil over high heat, then add the chicken meat with the remaining lemon juice and cook, turning to brown all sides, for 1 to 2 minutes. Transfer to a serving platter as the pieces finish cooking. Add the remaining ¼ cup of olive oil to the pan, reduce the heat to medium, and cook the bread cubes in the olive oil and leftover juices until lightly golden on all sides, 3 or 4 minutes.

5. Place the cubes at the bottom of serving bowls and ladle the soup on top. Serve the chicken on the side or with the soup.

algerian green wheat soup with meatballs

ALGERIAN SOUPS have remained rather unchanged since medieval times, with the exception of the use of New World foods such as the tomato and chiles. Soup is served in every home on a regular basis. There are different names for soups. In the eastern portion of Algeria they are usually called *jāry,* while in the center they are known by the more common Arabic word, *shūrba,* and in the west there are a variety of *harīra,* a name more often associated with the famous soup of the same name made in Morocco during Ramadan. During the month of Ramadan, the daily fast is often broken at sunset in Morocco and neighboring Algeria with one of these three soups. This soup, called *shūrbat al-farīk,* contains green wheat, a hard wheat product made by threshing the grains when they are young, and smoldering them over open fires. The grain is then sun-dried until parched. Green wheat is sold in Middle Eastern markets under the name green wheat, *fireek, freeky, freek, freeka, freekeh, fareek,* or *frikeh.* The cooking time of green wheat may vary because of its age, so allow extra time, and add water to the broth to keep it soupy. The Palestinian green wheat soup is quite different (page 302).

Green wheat or *freekeh* can also be purchased online at www.surfasonline.com/products/33999.cfm. You can read more about green wheat on page 301. Because *freekeh* can only be found in Middle Eastern markets or through Internet sources, I recommend substituting bulgur for it.   **[Makes 4 to 5 servings]**

2 chicken breast halves on the bone (about 1½ pounds)

7 tablespoons clarified unsalted butter or unsalted butter

2 medium onions, chopped

2 pounds ripe tomatoes, cut in half, seeds squeezed out, and
    grated against the largest holes of a standing grater down to the
    peel, or one 28-ounce can crushed tomatoes

1 teaspoon cayenne pepper

1 teaspoon salt and more as needed

Water as needed

½ pound (1 cup) *freekeh* (green wheat) or coarse bulgur #4,
    picked over for stones and chaff and rinsed

2 tablespoons tomato paste

1 pound ground lamb, beef, or veal

2 tablespoons finely chopped fresh parsley

1 tablespoon cornstarch

1 large egg yolk

Freshly ground black pepper to taste

1 celery stalk, finely chopped

1 bunch cilantro (fresh coriander), leaves only, finely chopped

1. Place the chicken breast in a large pot with the clarified butter, turn the heat to low, and cook, stirring, for 5 minutes. Add the onions, tomatoes, cayenne, and salt and cook, stirring, for 10 minutes. Pour in 6 cups of water, increase the heat to medium, and cook until tender, about 20 minutes.

2. Remove the chicken breasts, leaving the chicken broth in the pot, and when the breasts are cool enough to handle remove the meat from the bones and discard the bones and skin. Chop the meat into small pieces and set aside.

3. Pass the chicken broth through a food mill into a clean pot, setting aside in another pan about 2 cups of the broth in order to poach the meatballs you'll make in Step 4. (If you don't have a food mill, pour the broth through a strainer into a blender. Then add about half of the solids in the strainer to the blender and purée, discarding the remaining solids in the strainer. Add this blender broth to the large pot.) Heat the broth over medium heat, then add the *freekeh* or bulgur and tomato paste and stir until the tomato paste is blended. Cook, stirring occasionally, until the *freekeh* or bulgur is tender but chewy, 45 to 60 minutes.

4. Meanwhile, in a bowl, mix together the ground lamb with the parsley, cornstarch, egg yolk, salt, and pepper. Form into little balls about ¾ inch in diameter with wet hands so they don't stick. Add the meatballs to the reserved 2 cups of broth in a pot with the celery and cilantro and cook over medium heat until firm, about 15 minutes.

5. Place the chicken meat in a soup tureen and ladle the *freekeh* or bulgur soup over them. Then add the meatballs and the broth they cooked in and serve hot.

peruvian creole soup

THE CUISINE OF PERU is quite diverse, not only because of the country's many ethnic groups but also because of the great variety of edible plants that grow there and provide the raw materials for inventive cooks. "Creole" is an apt expression for all of Peruvian cuisine and not just this soup, although the appellation *criolla* tends to be applied to dishes that come from Lima, where populations mix more readily. This creole soup is called just that, *sopa a la criolla.* **[Makes 4 to 6 servings]**

2 tablespoons vegetable oil

¼ pound beef sirloin or flank steak, cut into 2-inch strips

1 medium tomato, cut in half, seeds squeezed out, and grated against
    the largest holes of a box grater down to the peel

1 small onion, separated and cut up in ½-inch squares

Salt and freshly ground black pepper to taste

10 cups water

3 sprigs fresh parsley

3 sprigs cilantro (fresh coriander)

3 sprigs fresh thyme

1 sprig fresh rosemary

1 tablespoon garlic salt

¼ pound angel hair pasta (capellini)

2 large eggs

One 12-ounce can evaporated milk

1 red or green jalapeño chile, seeded and sliced

4 to 6 small toast points

the best soups in the world

1. In a medium-size skillet, heat the oil over medium-high heat, then add the beef and cook until it turns color on both sides, about 1 minute. Add the tomato, onion, and salt and pepper and cook, stirring, for 2 minutes. Set aside, leaving it in the skillet.

2. In a pot, add the water, parsley, cilantro, thyme, rosemary, and garlic salt, bring to a boil over high heat, and boil for 5 minutes. Remove and discard all the herbs, then add the pasta and cook until al dente, about 2 minutes. Drain the pasta through a strainer, returning the liquid to the pot. Transfer the pasta to the skillet with the meat and toss well.

3. Bring the cooking liquid from the pasta to a boil over high heat, then turn the heat off. Break the eggs into the soup without stirring. When the eggs are firm, after about 5 minutes, add the can of evaporated milk and stir gently. Add the contents of the skillet to the soup and stir gently. Add the chile and stir again. Serve the soup in individual bowls, breaking the eggs up or leaving them whole if serving just a couple of people, and then place a small piece of toast to float on top.

grain-based soups

bolivian corn soup

CALLED *LAGUA DE CHOCLO,* meaning "fresh corn kernel soup," this soup from La Paz results in a thick and creamy soup (although there is no cream in it) that is delicious and easy to make. The corn will look very creamy after you grind it in the food processor. The secret is fresh corn scraped off the cob. **[Makes 6 to 8 servings]**

1 pound beef chuck, diced

1 medium onion, chopped

1 turnip (6 ounces), peeled and diced

8 cups water

5 teaspoons salt

8 small Yukon Gold potatoes (about 1 pound), peeled and sliced

Kernels from 6 large corn cobs, ground in a food processor

2 teaspoons dried oregano

¾ teaspoon cayenne pepper

1 tablespoon finely chopped fresh parsley

1. Place the beef, onion, turnip, water, and salt in a saucepan and bring to a boil over high heat. Reduce the heat to low and simmer, partially covered, skimming foam when it appears, until the beef is nearly tender, about 1 hour.

2. Add the potatoes and simmer over low heat until tender but firm, 25 to 30 minutes. Add the ground corn, ½ cup at a time, stirring with each addition, and adding a little water if it is getting too thick, until all the corn is added. Add the oregano and cayenne, bring to a boil over medium heat, and boil until it thickens and has a creamy consistency, about 15 minutes. Sprinkle with parsley and serve.

drunkard's soup

THIS FRENCH-CANADIAN SOUP is called *soupe à l'ivrogne,* or "drunkard's soup," and is a Québécois version of an onion soup, although with all that bread in it, bread soup might be the more appropriate description. It is said that the soup is quite nice when nursing a hangover. It's actually nice anytime, and particularly in the winter. Keep in mind when serving this soup that there are some people who might not like the soaked bread, known as sops in the Middle Ages, that bulks up the soup. Why they wouldn't like it is beyond me, except for it's soppy. **[Makes 8 servings]**

¼ pound salt pork, diced

3 large onions, chopped

6 thick slices (about 10 ounces) dense country-style white bread,
    cubed with its crust

8 cups beef broth

2 tablespoons finely chopped mixed herbs (equal amounts fresh
    parsley, thyme, tarragon)

Salt and freshly ground black pepper to taste

1. Preheat the oven to 350°F.

2. In an oven-proof cast-iron skillet, cook the salt pork over medium heat, stirring, until crisp, 6 to 7 minutes. Add the onions and cook, stirring, until golden brown, about 20 minutes. Add the bread cubes and toss well to coat with the salt pork fat.

3. Place the skillet in the oven to toast the bread lightly, about 15 minutes. Transfer the mixture to a large pot. Add the beef broth and herbs and simmer over low heat for 1 hour. Season with salt and pepper and serve.

wild rice and
mushroom soup

THIS CANADIAN SOUP comes from an anonymous cook in Saint-Henri-de-Lévis, a rural community south of Quebec, Canada. It's a quite variable soup, in that you can make it in several different ways, all of which are pleasing. First, I call for shiitake mushrooms, which give the soup a vaguely Japanese taste and appearance, but you could use the less overwhelming button mushrooms. Second, the onion can be sautéed first so that it is not as al dente as in this recipe. Third, one can bulk up the soup considerably by adding leftover pieces of roast game or more wild rice. Whatever you decide to do, the final result is a full-flavored soup that leaves you feeling light and nourished. [**Makes 8 servings**]

¼ pound slab bacon, diced

1 small carrot, diced small

1 small leek, white part only, split lengthwise, washed well,
 and thinly sliced

1 celery stalk, diced small

1 large red onion, thinly sliced

3 quarts chicken broth

½ pound shiitake or button (white) mushrooms,
 sliced (about 2 cups sliced)

¼ cup very dry sherry

3 tablespoons finely chopped fresh parsley

3 tablespoons finely chopped fresh chervil

3 tablespoons finely chopped fresh tarragon

2 cups cooked wild rice, cooked according to the
 package instructions

1. In a large flame-proof casserole, cook the bacon over medium heat, stirring frequently, until crispy, about 10 minutes. Remove and set aside. Add the carrot, leek, and celery to the casserole and cook in the bacon fat, stirring, until softened, about 5 minutes. Add the red onion and cook, stirring, until softened, about 5 minutes. The bottom of the casserole will now be encrusted brown, which is fine, as you will shortly deglaze this flavor-giving crust with the chicken broth.

2. Add the chicken broth, mushrooms, dry sherry, parsley, chervil, and tarragon and stir for 1 minute, stirring and scraping the bottom of the casserole. Reduce the heat to medium-low and simmer until the mushrooms are cooked through, 20 to 25 minutes. Stir in the wild rice and bacon and serve hot.

   Note 1: Be careful that you do not use cream sherry or medium dry sherry because both are too sweet. Use vermouth if you don't have sherry.

   Note 2: If there are no instructions for cooking the wild rice, place ½ cup of raw wild rice in a saucepan with 4 cups cold water and 1 teaspoon salt. Bring to a boil over high heat, then reduce the heat to medium-low, cover, and cook for 30 minutes. Turn off the heat and let it rest, covered, for 30 minutes. Drain the wild rice and it is ready to use. One-half cup raw wild rice will result in about 1½ cups cooked.

   Variations: You can cook the sliced onion separately in butter until completely soft before adding it to the soup. You can also add 1 cup of diced cooked turkey, quail, rabbit, or venison and another cup of cooked wild rice for a more substantial soup.

griddled fenugreek pasta and green wheat soup

THIS UNIQUE AND UNUSUAL WINTER SOUP from Algeria uses durum wheat, also called semolina, in two forms: as squares of fresh pasta made with fenugreek mixed into the dough that are first cooked on a griddle before going into the soup, and as the roasted young or green wheat called *freekeh* (page 301). I admit this recipe is labor intensive and that *freekeh* is hard to find, but I include it in this collection because it is so satisfying and will definitely be a topic of conversation for your guests.

It is called *jishīsha farīk,* and it can also be made with barley or bulgur. *Jishīsha* is derived from a word meaning "coarsely ground grains." *Freekeh*'s unique smell and taste is the result of the smoldering of the grain during its processing. It is a very old form of wheat product, first mentioned in the thirteenth-century Hispano-Muslim cookbook by Ibn Razīn al-Tujībī called *Fadālat al-khiwān,* in which a recipe called *jashīsh* appears to be a large semolina ball, or perhaps at least the part of the semolina that didn't get crushed in medieval mills. It is mixed with fenugreek to form the *jashīsh.* Another Hispano-Muslim cookbook of the thirteenth century, the anonymous *Kitāb al-tabīkh fī al-Maghrib wa'l-Āndalus* (Cookery book of the Maghrib and Andalusia), also called the Almohad cookbook, has two recipes for *jashīsh,* which one English translator called "grits."

Freekeh can be found in Middle Eastern markets or purchased online at www.surfasonline .com/products/33999.cfm. You can read more about green wheat on page 301. Bulgur is a fine substitute for *freekeh.* If you have leftovers, you'll need to add water to reconstitute the soup because the pasta will absorb the broth. **[Makes 4 servings]**

FOR THE PASTA

½ pound (1 cup) fine semolina flour
2 tablespoons ground fenugreek
¼ teaspoon salt
6 tablespoons water and more as needed
1½ teaspoons extra-virgin olive oil

FOR THE SOUP

¾ pound beef top loin, cut into ½-inch cubes
8 garlic cloves, finely chopped
1 tablespoon tomato paste
1 tablespoon extra-virgin olive oil

1½ teaspoons cayenne pepper

1½ teaspoons salt

½ teaspoon *rās al-hanūt* (page 316)

¼ teaspoon freshly ground black pepper

¼ pound (½ cup) *freekeh* (green wheat), or coarse bulgur #4,
   picked over for stones and chaff and rinsed well

½ bunch cilantro (fresh coriander), leaves only, chopped

1. To make the pasta: in a bowl, mix the semolina flour with the fenugreek and salt and add the water, then form into a ball of dough, adding water only by the tablespoon to help it form a ball. Turn out the ball of dough onto a lightly floured surface and knead, wetting your hands to help the dough stick together, until it forms a soft, malleable ball, after about 8 minutes of kneading. Divide the ball of dough into 2 smaller balls about the size of a tangerine. Wrap in plastic wrap and let rest for 1 hour.

2. Preheat a cast-iron griddle over low heat for 10 minutes.

3. Unwrap each ball of dough and press flat, using slightly oiled hands. When the dough is flat enough to run through the roller of a pasta machine, roll it out into a sheet of dough about 1 millimeter in thickness. Cut the dough into ½-inch squares or any shape. (If you don't have a pasta roller then you'll need to use a rolling pin and some elbow grease).

4. Spread a light film of olive oil on the griddle with a paper towel. Working quickly, space the raw pasta dough squares close to each other on the griddle and cook until light golden, about 5 minutes, turning them at least once. Set aside.

5. To make the soup: in a pot, preferably earthenware, add the beef, garlic, tomato paste, olive oil, cayenne, salt, *rās al-hanūt,* and black pepper. Add 1½ cups water, turn the heat to medium, then cook, stirring, and adding another 3 cups water as it cooks, until the beef is almost tender, about 45 minutes.

6. Add the *freekeh* or bulgur slowly, then add 4 cups water and leave it to cook over medium heat, stirring occasionally, until the *freekeh* or bulgur is tender, about 40 minutes. Sprinkle on the cilantro and stir. Add the pasta, let it sit, covered, off the heat for 10 minutes, then serve.

RĀS AL-HANŪT

Rās al-hanūt, literally "head of the shop," is a complex spice blend used mostly in Moroccan cooking, with versions also used in Algeria and Tunisia. Spice shops employ experts who concoct the mixture, using up to twenty-seven different spices. This is the basic recipe. The most typical additions to it are cumin, coriander seed, and ginger. But it can also contain powdered oregano, powdered rose petals, and another fifteen spices. If you want to use other spices, make sure they are powdered and add them in ¼-teaspoon increments.

[Makes about 4½ teaspoons]

2 teaspoons ground cinnamon
1 teaspoon turmeric
½ teaspoon freshly ground black pepper
¼ teaspoon ground nutmeg
¼ teaspoon ground cardamom
¼ teaspoon ground cloves

316

Mix all the ingredients and store in a spice jar. It will keep indefinitely but lose its pungency over time.

armenian barley yogurt soup

THIS SOUP CALLED *SPAS* IN ARMENIAN is easy to make, but tricky in that you must whisk constantly so the eggs don't congeal and the yogurt doesn't separate. It sounds complicated, but it's not—if you whisk constantly—so pay attention to the instructions in Step 3. *Spas* is also not as heavy as it sounds; in fact, its taste is refreshing in a satisfying way. The soup can be served cold, too, in which case don't finish it with the herbs right away. Let the cooked soup cool at room temperature, refrigerate for 4 hours, then sprinkle on the herbs and serve. The chilled soup is refreshing in summer.   **[Makes 4 to 6 servings]**

10 cups cold water

¼ cup pearl barley

2 cups (16 ounces) plain whole yogurt

4 large eggs

2 tablespoons all-purpose flour

2 tablespoons finely chopped onion

2 tablespoons unsalted butter

2½ teaspoons salt or more to taste

1 tablespoon finely chopped fresh mint

3 tablespoons finely chopped cilantro (fresh coriander)

1. In a pot, bring 6 cups of the water to a boil over high heat, then add the barley and cook, stirring occasionally, until tender, about 45 minutes. Drain the barley through a strainer and set aside.

2. In a large bowl, combine the remaining 4 cups water with the yogurt and stir until dissolved and smooth.

3. In a large pot, break the eggs and beat with a whisk, then add the flour, 1 tablespoon at a time, while whisking. Slowly whisk in the yogurt mixture and once it is blended with the eggs, turn the heat to high and bring to a near boil while whisking constantly, 8 to 9 minutes; never let it come to a boil or even bubble on the edges: immediately reduce the heat to low or remove from the heat entirely if you see bubbles on the edges. Simmer or stir until the mixture thickens slightly, 2 to 3 minutes. Make sure you incorporate any flour that has collected at the bottom of the pot.

4. Stir in the cooked barley, raw chopped onion, butter, and salt and simmer for another minute. Check the seasoning. Serve in individual bowls with the chopped mint and cilantro sprinkled on top.

armenian trahana soup

THIS RECIPE IS A TWO-STEP PROCESS because you must first make the *trahana,* which needs about a week. The amount of *trahana* you will make in this recipe is enough to make this soup and the Greek Trahana Soup of Chios (page 324). Although this is an Armenian recipe, the grain product known as *trahana* (*targhana* in Armenian, *tarhana* in Turkish, and *trahanas* in Greek—and even more spellings!) has a long history and is found through-out many Turkic-speaking regions as well as in the Balkans, Hungary, and to the east as far as Iran.

The first record of *trahana* can be found in the writing of the fourteenth-century Persian poet Bushaq-i At′ima. What is *trahana*? It is a leavened (usually) wheat flour and yogurt mix-ture that is sun-dried and left to ferment for up to seven days and is then stored and used for soups and stews. In the Turkish version of *trahana,* vegetables such as cooked onion, red bell pepper, or tomato are added to the fermenting flour-yogurt mixture. The final version of Turkish-style *tarhana* soup might contain ground meat and tomatoes. In Cyprus, a *tarhana* soup is made with the addition of halloumi cheese. The Lebanese *kishk* is a similar product. In this version, coarse bulgur is added to the flour and yogurt mixture.   [**Makes 8 servings**]

FOR THE *TRAHANA* (MAKES 3 TO 4 CUPS)

1½ teaspoons active dry yeast

1 cup water

½ teaspoon salt

1 cup (8 ounces) plain whole yogurt, preferably slightly sour

2 cups all-purpose flour, sifted

1⅓ cups coarse bulgur #3 or #4

FOR THE SOUP

8 cups beef broth

¼ cup unsalted butter

1 medium onion, finely chopped

1 tablespoon dried mint

Salt to taste

2 cups (16 ounces) plain whole yogurt, at room temperature

1. To make the *trahana*: several days before you plan to serve, in a bowl, dissolve the yeast in ¼ cup of the water, about 5 minutes. Add the salt and remaining water. Stir in the yogurt, then the flour and bulgur. Mix well. Cover with a kitchen towel and let stand overnight on a kitchen counter.

2. The next day, form the dough into egg-size pieces and flatten them in your hands until about ⅛ inch thick; you can keep your hands floured so the dough doesn't stick too much. Set them on a tablecloth or kitchen towels to dry on one side, then turn them over until thoroughly dried, perhaps 2 days in all. Leave for another 2 to 4 days until completely dry, then break and crumble into smaller pieces and store in a tight jar until needed. You'll have about 3 to 4 cups of *trahana*.

3. To make the soup: in a pot, bring the beef broth to a boil over high heat, then add 1 cup of the crumbled *trahana*, reduce the heat to medium, and cook until tender, about 40 minutes.

4. Meanwhile, in a small skillet, melt the butter over medium-high heat, then add the onion and cook, stirring occasionally, until golden, about 5 minutes. Mix in the mint and salt and remove from the heat.

5. Once the *trahana* is cooked, stir the onion mixture into it, reduce the heat to low, and cook for 5 minutes. Remove from the heat, stir in the yogurt, and serve hot.

grain-based soups

libyan soup

CONTEMPORARY LIBYA can be divided into the historical regions of Tripolitania to the west and Cyrenaica to the east. Libyans will tell you that their region was always too poor to have developed a cuisine. Everything appears vaguely familiar to cuisine in surrounding regions. The Italian influence is strong, especially in restaurants, and Libyans eat lots of pasta. Whether this was the result of the Italian occupation in the twentieth century or an addition to a pre-existing substratum of macaroni cookery is uncertain. If any dish can be considered a "national" dish, it is either *bazīn* or this soup called *shūrba libiyya. Bazīn* is a kind of polenta made with semolina and water and sometimes yeast, found along the southern Tunisian and Libyan littoral. This recipe was given to me by Professor Lisa Anderson, a scholar of modern Libya at Columbia University, who tells me that it "summarizes Libyan cuisine, such as it is."

[**Makes 4 servings**]

½ cup extra-virgin olive oil

1 tablespoon clarified unsalted butter or unsalted butter

1 large onion, finely chopped or grated

1 pound beef chuck or boneless lamb shoulder or leg,
    trimmed of fat and cubed

6 very ripe plum tomatoes (about 1 pound), peeled (page 273),
    seeded, and chopped

2 tablespoons tomato paste

5 cups water

½ cup canned chickpeas, drained

½ cup finely chopped fresh parsley (from about ½ bunch parsley)

1 teaspoon ground chile powder or cayenne pepper

1 teaspoon *bzar* (see Note)

1 teaspoon salt

¼ teaspoon ground cinnamon

½ cup pastina (soup pasta)

1 teaspoon dried mint

1. In a medium-size casserole, heat the olive oil with the clarified butter over medium-high heat, then add the onion and cook, stirring, until translucent, about 5 minutes. Add the beef or lamb and cook, stirring, until browned on all sides, 2 to 4 minutes.

2. Stir in the tomatoes, the tomato paste dissolved in 1 cup of the water, the chickpeas, parsley, chile powder, *bzar*, salt, and cinnamon and cook for 10 minutes. Add the remaining 4 cups of water and cook, covered, until the meat is tender, 1 to 1¼ hours. Add the pasta and cook, uncovered, until done, about 10 minutes. Just before serving stir in the mint. Serve hot.

Note: The Libyan spice mix known as *bzar* is usually made of equal parts of black pepper, cinnamon, cloves, nutmeg, turmeric, zedoary (*Curcurma zedoria*) or galangal, ground ginger, and a smaller part of cumin. Use whatever of the spices mentioned that you have.

grain-based soups

kazakh noodle and lamb soup

THE COMBINATION OF NOODLES AND YOGURT among Turkic-speaking peoples is quite old. An eleventh-century Turkish lexicon describes a now forgotten thick soup of noodles, lentils, and yogurt called *tutmaç.* In Kazakhstan, a Turkic-speaking Central Asian country, mutton and horsemeat are very popular, but this soup can be made with beef or lamb. This Kazakh soup called *kespe,* or noodles, is quite nice if you can personalize your noodles by making them at home. It's not hard to do, but there's also nothing wrong with store-bought noodles. Skip Steps 1 and 2 if using store-bought pasta, in which case you will need 6 ounces of fettuccine. I've called for the soup to be flavored with fresh dill, but a Kazakh cook might use a variety of greens and not just herbs. *Kespe* is served in a special bowl called a *kese,* which looks like a Japanese soup bowl, and is drunk from the bowl along with *katyk,* a sour yogurt product. **[Makes 6 servings]**

FOR THE NOODLES

1 cup plus 2 tablespoons all-purpose flour
1 large egg
2 tablespoon water
½ teaspoon salt

FOR THE LAMB SOUP

2½ pounds lamb shoulder on the bone or beef shank
4 bay leaves
Water as needed
2 carrots, peeled and finely chopped
1 onion, finely chopped
Salt and freshly ground black pepper to taste
½ cup coarsely chopped fresh dill
Plain yogurt for garnish (optional)

1. To prepare the noodles: mix the flour, egg, water, and salt together in a bowl, then form into a smooth and firm ball. Turn the dough ball out onto a floured work surface and knead for about 5 minutes, using a little more flour if it is sticky. Wrap the ball in a kitchen towel or plastic wrap and let rest for 30 minutes.

2. Roll the noodle dough out with a rolling pin until it can fit into the largest opening of a pasta roller. Put it through the roller just once. (If you don't have a pasta roller, roll the dough out with a rolling pin on a large, uncluttered work surface until you have a thin lasagna-like sheet of dough.) Cut the dough into strips as wide as fettuccine and 3 to 4 inches long. Arrange on a kitchen towel to dry while you continue the preparation.

3. Meanwhile, to prepare the soup: with a sharp paring or fillet knife, remove the meat from the lamb, place the bones in a pot with 2 of the bay leaves, and cover with 6 cups of water. Bring to a near boil over high heat, then reduce the heat to medium-low and simmer with the water bubbling gently, skimming the surface when foam arises, until you have a fragrant lamb broth, about 1½ hours.

4. Remove the big chunks of excess fat from the lamb meat, cut the meat into ¾-inch cubes, and set aside.

5. Remove the lamb bones and bay leaves from the broth and discard the bones. Add the cubed lamb and the remaining 2 bay leaves to the broth along with 4 cups of water, bring to a boil over high heat, then reduce the heat to medium-low and simmer until tender, about 1½ hours.

6. While the lamb is cooking, bring a few cups of water to a boil in a small pot, add the carrots and onion, blanch for 5 minutes, then drain and set aside.

7. Bring the lamb broth to a boil over high heat, then add the noodles and reserved carrots and onion. Taste, season with salt and pepper, and cook, stirring occasionally, until the noodles are tender, about 7 minutes if using freshly made. (Follow the package instructions if using store-bought.) Ladle into deep soup bowls, sprinkle with the dill, and serve. Serve the yogurt on the side, if desired.

trahana soup of chios

THIS SOUP FROM THE GREEK ISLAND of Chios in the Aegean, very near Turkey, is called *trahanosoupa*. *Trahana* is a species of the dried alimentary pastes of the Mediterranean (another being pasta) made by mixing durum wheat flour with eggs and sour milk called *xynogala,* or sometimes sweet milk; the mixture is then dried in the sun. It probably was invented as a means of preserving milk and eggs before refrigeration.

 Trahana is also known in Turkey and Armenia, where it is more likely to be made with bulgur instead of flour and yogurt instead of milk. Bulgur, another durum wheat food product, is cracked sun-parched hard wheat. In Turkey, tomatoes and bell peppers are sometimes stirred into the *trahana* dough before drying. On Chios, an island that was ruled by the Genoese during the Middle Ages, there is also a Turkish culinary influence, a result of the islands' proximity to the great city of Izmir. This is a traditional family recipe usually made during winter. It is usually made with tomatoes, eggs, cheese, and milk curds. This is a rich soup and best finished in the oven with oven-proof soup bowls and eaten with flatbread.

[**Makes 4 servings**]

the best soups in the world

1 quart water

1½ cups tomato purée, fresh or canned

¾ cup extra-virgin olive oil

2 cups (6 ounces) *Trahana* (see Steps 1 and 2 on page 319)

3 tablespoons vegetable oil

4 slices feta cheese (about 6 ounces), soaked in water until needed and drained

1 cup fine semolina flour

4 large eggs

1½ teaspoons salt or more to taste

1. Preheat the oven to 500°F.

2. Pour the water into a pot and whisk in the tomato purée. Add the olive oil, bring to a vigorous boil over high heat, reduce to medium, and cook, covered, for 15 minutes. Add the *trahana* and cook, stirring gently, for 5 minutes.

3. Meanwhile, in a nonstick skillet, heat the vegetable oil over medium-high heat. Dredge the feta cheese slices in the semolina on all sides, tapping off any excess, then cook on both sides until golden brown, turning once, for about 3 minutes. Turn the heat off and leave in the skillet until needed.

4. Crack the eggs into the soup and cook, stirring in one direction very gently, for 3 minutes. Season with the salt.

5. Transfer the soup to an oven-proof tureen or stew pot or 4 oven-proof soup bowls, add the fried cheese slices on top, and bake until bubbling, about 3 minutes. Serve hot.

pho

IT IS REMARKABLE how quickly *pho* (pronounced fuh), described as the national soup of Vietnam, became an American favorite, especially in California, where most Vietnamese immigrants have settled. It's just a beef and rice noodle soup, but with extraordinary delicacy and flavor. This version of *pho* is a Vietnamese-American version, so described to reflect the wealth found in this country, because the original soup comes from a poor country. Andrea Q. Nguyen, writing for the *San Jose Mercury News,* tells us that *pho* was probably invented in Hanoi sometime in the early twentieth century, as it shows both Vietnamese and French influences. In fact, some have argued that *pho* is a corruption of the French *feu,* as in the famous French stew *pot-au-feu.* Nguyen also tells us that the addition of beef must have been an attempt to satisfy French customers, as cows were more for labor than food in Vietnam a hundred years ago. After the split of Vietnam into north and south in 1954, many northerners moved south with their *pho,* only to find southerners adding all kinds of ingredients to the soup. A rule of thumb for this soup, in case you make a small portion, is 1 tablespoon of fish sauce for every quart of broth. *Pho* is considered a main course. **[Makes 8 servings]**

FOR THE BROTH

1 tablespoon peanut oil

2 large onions, cut into ¼-inch slices

2½ pounds meaty beef soup bones

2½ pounds cooked chicken carcass or chicken wings, backbone, and/or feet

5 quarts water

2 carrots, peeled and julienned

4 slices fresh ginger, peeled and julienned

1 small stick cinnamon

Seeds from 5 pods cardamom, lightly crushed

2 star anise

2 whole cloves

2 garlic cloves, crushed with their peel left on

1 teaspoon black peppercorns

FOR THE SOUP

½ pound beef sirloin, sliced very thin across the grain in bite-size pieces

Salt and freshly ground black pepper

1 large onion, sliced as thin as paper

2 scallions, trimmed and thinly sliced

2 cups (½ pound) fresh bean sprouts

6 tablespoons chopped cilantro (fresh coriander) leaves

4 fresh red or green serrano chiles, seeded and sliced in rings or julienned

2 limes, quartered

6 to 8 ounces rice sticks (thin rice noodles), soaked in hot water for
30 minutes, drained

¼ cup Vietnamese or Thai (*nuoc mam* or *nam pla*) fish sauce or
more to taste

1. To make the broth: the day before you plan to serve the soup, in a large stockpot, heat the peanut oil over high heat, then add the sliced onions and cook, stirring, until browned on the edges, 8 to 10 minutes. Remove the onions and set aside.

2. Place the beef and chicken pieces in the stockpot and cover with the water. Bring to a near boil over medium heat, then reduce the heat to low and simmer, skimming the surface of foam, for 15 minutes. Add the reserved cooked onion slices and the carrots, ginger, cinnamon, cardamom, star anise, cloves, garlic, and peppercorns. Bring to a boil over high heat, then reduce to low and simmer, partially covered, for 6 hours, skimming the surface of foam when needed. Strain the stock through a strainer into a large bowl. Strain again through a cheesecloth-lined strainer back into the cleaned stockpot or bowl. Refrigerate overnight or until the layer of fat forms on top, then remove and discard the fat. You will use 12 cups of broth. (The broth can be frozen at this point if you wish.)

3. When you are ready to serve, attractively arrange the sliced beef sirloin, seasoned with salt and pepper, on a platter and garnish the platter with the paper-thin-sliced onion and scallions. On another platter or plate, attractively arrange the bean sprouts, cilantro, chiles, and limes.

4. Thirty minutes before you want to serve the soup, bring a pot of water to a boil over high heat. Turn the heat off, then add the rice sticks and let sit for 30 minutes. Drain the rice noodles and place equal portions in each of the 8 soup bowls. Cover to keep warm.

5. Meanwhile, bring the beef broth to a boil over high heat and add the fish sauce and 1 teaspoon of black pepper; taste and add more of both if necessary. Pour the broth in a chafing dish or soup tureen and place over a portable warmer to keep hot in the center of the table for diners to serve themselves. Serve the soup, allowing each diner to add some beef and onion to a bowl. Ladle the hot broth over the meat, stirring to cook the meat. Add the bean sprouts, cilantro, chiles, and a squeeze of lime to taste.

filipino noodles in broth

HERE IS THE FAMOUS *PANCIT MAMI,* or noodles in broth soup, that Filipinos so love. *Pancit* are noodles, in this case made from rice. This is a quick-cooking dish, one of the reasons for its popularity among Filipino cooks. In fact, the word *pancit* is said to derive from the Hokkien (Fujian) words *pian i sit,* which mean "something conveniently cooked fast." Hokkien is the Chinese language spoken in Fujian province in southeastern China on the China Sea, from which many Filipinos of Chinese extraction come. The first *pancit* probably came to the Philippines as a result of trade with China.

In the Philippines, the topping for a noodle soup is an indicator of its provenance, so, for example, one will find shellfish in a coastal town or pork cracklings in pig-raising areas. The *mami* suffix to *pancit* means the noodles are fat, like Japanese udon noodles, which is what I call for here. The Filipino travel web site www.cockatoo.com tells us that the word *mami* is not a Tagalog word, but a Fujian Chinese word introduced to the Philippines by a popular Chinese restaurant and noodle factory called Ma Mon Lok, whose owners came from Fujian. If you decide to use the wheat-based fresh udon noodles, they are, surprisingly, sold in many supermarkets, usually on the perimeter of the store in a cold section where you'll also find other Asian products such as wonton noodle sheets, tofu, and sliced pickled turnips used for sushi. Although Filipinos generally don't spice up a soup like this, you can add a few squirts of Thai chile sauce if you like it piquant. **[Makes 4 servings]**

3 cups water

¼ pound boneless pork loin, fat removed

¼ pound boneless and skinless chicken breast

1 teaspoon salt and more to taste

2 tablespoons vegetable oil

1 medium onion, finely chopped

3 large garlic cloves, finely chopped

Freshly ground black pepper to taste

14 ounces flat rice noodles (pad thai) or fresh Japanese udon noodles

2 tablespoons finely chopped scallions

1. In a pot, bring the water to a boil over high heat, then reduce to low and add the pork and chicken, both in one piece. Season with 1 teaspoon salt and cook until firm and tender, about 18 minutes; the water should never be bubbling. Remove the meat from the water, saving the cooking liquid, and let cool. Cut the pork into thin strips, shred the chicken with a fork, and set aside.

2. In another pot, heat the oil over medium-high heat, then add the onion and garlic and cook, stirring, until softened, about 5 minutes. Add the pork and chicken and stir, then add the reserved cooking liquid, turn the heat to high, and cook for 2 minutes. Season with more salt, if necessary, and pepper.

3. Meanwhile, divide the raw uncooked noodles into the serving bowls, then ladle the hot soup over each to fill the bowls and let sit for 8 to 10 minutes. The hot broth will cook the noodles. Garnish each bowl with minced scallions and serve hot.

grain-based soups

There's nothing in the world finer than Cape Cod clam chowder. The best one you'll ever have is here. But you may not realize chowders and their cousins, bisques, are found in many places other than New England. The lobster bisque from Brittany you'll encounter is so extraordinary that when you taste it you'll marvel that it was made by your own hands. But try the others: they're all amazing.

chowders
and bisques

brazilian cod soup

THIS SOUP from the northwestern Brazilian city of Bahia is called *moqueca de peixe*. Bahian cooks often like their food quite spicy, typically using the habanero chile, called locally *meleguetta* pepper. But this soup is not spicy hot. Traditionally, the cook would use freshly grated coconut, but you can use unsweetened coconut flakes to make the coconut milk (page 191). Coconut milk is also sold in cans, usually in the Thai or Asian section of the super-market, although a lot of gourmets consider that a poor substitute. Not all supermarkets sell the unsweetened coconut flakes, so you may need to seek out an Asian market or order them from www.kingarthurflour.com. Sources for the red palm oil, called *dendê* oil in Brazil, which gives the dish an essential taste, are www.afrikan-food.com, www.jbafricanmarket.com, and www.goldencoastfoods.com. If you like you can serve the soup with some cooked white rice, on the side or stirred in.   **[Makes 4 servings]**

the best soups in the world

1 cup unsweetened coconut flakes

4 cups of boiling water

1 medium-size tomato, quartered

1 small green bell pepper, seeded and cut up

1 medium onion, quartered

Leaves from 8 sprigs cilantro (fresh coriander)

Salt and freshly ground black pepper to taste

1½ pounds cod or haddock fillets, cut up into cubes

2 tablespoons red palm oil (*dendê* oil)

2 tablespoons peanut oil

1 tablespoon fresh lemon juice

1. Place the unsweetened coconut flakes in a bowl, pour the boiling water over them, and let steep for at least 15 minutes. Squeeze the liquid out through a strainer. This is the coconut milk.

2. Place the tomato, pepper, onion, and cilantro (fresh coriander) in a food processor and run until the mixture forms a coarse paste. Transfer the paste to a skillet and heat over low heat, stirring. Season with salt and pepper and cook, stirring, until softened, about 15 minutes. Add the fish fillets to the mixture and continue cooking until the fish turns pale white, about 8 minutes. Add the coconut milk, red palm oil, peanut oil, and lemon juice and simmer until hot, about 8 minutes. Serve hot.

peruvian shrimp chowder

THIS PERUVIAN *CHUPE DE CAMARONES* is a shrimp chowder typical of Arequipa, one of southern Peru's largest cities which, although near the coast, is also at 7,550 feet elevation. This is a great recipe in which to use the powdered South American chile called *ají amarillo,* which I buy at www.penderys.com. **[Makes 6 servings]**

3 tablespoons vegetable oil

1 large onion, chopped

2 large garlic cloves, finely chopped

2 large tomatoes, peeled (page 273) and cut into eighths

1 small potato, peeled and cut in sixths

½ teaspoon ground chile powder (*ají amarillo*)

¼ teaspoon red chile flakes

1½ teaspoons seasoning salt

2½ teaspoons salt

4 drops Tabasco sauce

4½ cups water

1¼ cups whole milk

2 ounces cream cheese (about ¼ cup), at room temperature

2 corn cobs, kernels removed

½ pound medium shrimp, shelled

3 flounder, fluke, red snapper, rex sole, or sole fillets (about 1½ pounds), cut into 6 pieces

6 sprigs mint

1. In a flame-proof casserole, heat the oil over medium heat, then add the onion and garlic and cook, stirring frequently, until golden, about 10 minutes. Stir in the tomatoes, potato, chile powder, chile flakes, seasoning salt, 2 teaspoons of the salt, and Tabasco. Add 3 cups of the water and 1 cup of the milk, then bring to a near boil over medium-high heat, stirring occasionally, 5 to 6 minutes. Reduce the heat to low and simmer until the potatoes are almost tender, about 15 minutes.

2. In a bowl, beat the cream cheese with the remaining ¼ cup milk until very smooth. Stir the cream cheese mixture into the casserole. Add the corn kernels and cook until softened, about 15 minutes. Add the shrimp and continue to cook, stirring, until the shrimp are firm and orange-red, about 5 minutes.

3. Meanwhile, bring the remaining 1½ cups water and ½ teaspoon salt to a boil in a skillet over high heat, then reduce the heat to medium-low and poach the fish fillets until fork-tender, about 6 minutes. Remove the fillets and place one in each of 6 soup bowls. Spoon the soup over the fillets, garnish with the mint, and serve hot.

parsnip chowder

ALTHOUGH THE PARSNIP is originally from the Mediterranean, it hasn't been terribly popular there since the Renaissance, when Maestro Martino da Como gave a recipe for deep-fried parsnips in his *Libro de arte coquinaria* (*Book of the art of cookery*), written in 1450. Subsequently, the parsnip made the voyage to the West Indies, where in 1564 it was introduced to Margarita Island off the coast of Venezuela. It didn't grow well in the tropical climate, but by 1609 it was being grown in Virginia. From there it was dispersed by Native Americans, for the most part, and from 1629 appeared in Massachusetts, where it became a popular vegetable and whence this chowder hails.

Westfield, Massachusetts, became the capital of the parsnip, and when I grew them in my garden in Arlington, I would leave them in the ground to overwinter, digging them up in the spring. The most remarkable thing about a parsnip for most people is how naturally sweet and spicy they are. This is both a drawback and and an advantage of the plant—a drawback in that blander root vegetables usually win out in popularity because they combine easily with more foods (as, for example, the potato does). The parsnip is also a plant that doesn't produce much food given the room it takes up in the garden. But its advantage is its taste, which you will experience in this delicious chowder.   [**Makes 4 servings**]

2 ounces salt pork, cut into ½-inch dice

2 tablespoons unsalted butter

1 medium onion, chopped

½ pound parsnips, peeled and diced

½ pound boiling potato (such as Yukon Gold or white rose), peeled and diced

2½ cups chicken broth

1½ cups whole milk

½ cup heavy cream

½ teaspoon salt or more if desired

Freshly ground black pepper to taste

Oyster crackers or pilot crackers for garnish (optional)

2 teaspoons finely chopped fresh parsley or chervil

1. Place the salt pork in a pot or flame-proof casserole and turn the heat to medium-low. Once it starts sizzling, about 4 minutes, reduce the heat to low and cook, stirring occasionally, until slightly crispy and golden, about 10 minutes. Remove and set aside.

2. Increase the heat to medium, add 1 tablespoon of the butter to the pot and once it has melted, add the onion and cook, stirring, until softened and golden, about 5 minutes. Add the parsnips, potato, and 1½ cups of the chicken broth, increase the heat to high, and bring to a boil. Cook at a boil, covered, until tender, about 15 minutes. If the chicken broth is evaporating too fast, add the remaining chicken broth. Reduce the heat to low.

3. Remove about 1½ cups of the chowder and pass through a food mill back into the pot (or run for a few seconds in a food processor). Add the milk, cream, the remaining butter, the salt, and pepper and heat over medium heat, stirring occasionally, making sure it does not come to a boil, about 5 minutes. Serve hot with crackers, if desired, and parsley or chervil.

cape cod clam chowder

AS THIS IS THE PERFECT RECIPE for the perfect clam chowder, I'm adapting it from my book *Real Stew* (Harvard Common Press, 2002), where it was first published. Forgive me for rattling on here, but this is important for chowders, for soupmaking, for life. To paraphrase one writer, a properly made New England clam chowder is a dish to preach about, a dish to sing hymns over, to fight for. I, too, feel very strongly about clam chowder. If one doesn't feel strongly, if one doesn't defend a particular way of cooking something, I believe one is not really interested in food and therefore allowed to ignore my ranting and raving here. Many fine cooks make many different fine chowders, from coastal Maine down to Virginia, and this one wouldn't be worth writing about if I didn't dogmatically claim that this recipe, this recipe right here, is the only true clam chowder.

This is a Cape Cod clam chowder, and I believe the best clam chowder is made on Cape Cod. Although I lived in Cambridge, Massachusetts, for fifteen years, the clam chowder there, which is Boston clam chowder, is just too thick, creamy, and floury, and I'll bet it became that way because of tourists. Just as a proper chili con carne never has beans or tomatoes in it, for me a true clam chowder should never contain flour or cream, certainly never fish broth (might as well call it fish soup), and God forbid a tomato. A true clam chowder is very simple, but rarely gotten right. Adding flour, popular with restaurant chefs, turns the elixir into an unappetizing and gummy white mud. Clam chowder is made with milk, not cream, although I use cream to approximate the old-time taste of unhomogenized milk. Adding a tomato means you're from below the chowder Mason-Dixon Line to New England chowdaheads.

A clam is a delicate creature and gets easily lost in too much starchy thickening, acidic vegetables, herbs, seasoning, or smoky bacon (as opposed to salt pork flavor). A true clam chowder is made with live quahogs with their liquor (*Mercenaria mercenaria* L.), and never canned clams, and with diced lean salt pork, onion, potatoes, butter, salt, white pepper (not black pepper, so the kids won't try to pick it out), and if you can manage it, raw fresh creamery milk. In the early twentieth century, Cape Codders could easily get raw milk, which had a creamier taste than today's pasteurized and homogenized milk. It's therefore proper to mix whole milk with half-and-half or a little heavy cream to approximate this taste. Clam chowder can also have a potato, a little celery, and a little sprinkle of thyme—but that's it. Some cooks use a combination of baking potatoes and boiling potatoes; the baking potato crumbles a bit to provide a thickness to the chowder. Chowder is always served hot—but not piping hot—with common crackers. And clam chowder is always "aged"—that is, it is best when it sits on a warm, turned-off stove for some hours, or if it is reheated.

What about shucked clams versus steamed clams? Well, normally one doesn't need to shuck quahogs because they're only used for chowder, whereas littlenecks and cherrystones (two names for smaller versions of quahogs) are usually eaten raw, so if you're not proficient at shucking you can steam the clams slightly to open them.

"Chowder" appears to derive from the French *chaudière,* a cauldron used by the fishermen of Brittany to cook up a fish chowder. It seems that these Breton fishermen were responsible for bringing their *chaudière* to Newfoundland, where it was used to make a dish with fish or clams. From there chowder spread to Nova Scotia and New England, probably via fishermen who fished the Grand Banks and would regularly put into local ports when severe storms arose. In John R. Bartlett's *Dictionary of Americanisms* published in 1848, a chowder is described as a dish from New England made of fresh fish, especially cod or clams, and stewed with slices of pork or bacon, onions, and biscuits, with the addition at times of cider or champagne.

The earliest chowders were fish chowders, and they were always made in a clear broth. They were also layered, and "chowder" was also used as a verb, meaning to cook like a chowder, that is, layering all the ingredients. There is no record of clam (as opposed to fish) chowder before the mid-nineteenth century; the first written mention of clams being used in chowder is from 1829, in Lydia Marie Child's *The Frugal Housewife.* But we know that the clam was thriving along the New England shore when the Pilgrims arrived in the early seventeenth century, and we know from their letters that clams and mussels were foods described as "at our doors." So it's possible they made clam chowder.

The first mention of a chowder in print—and it was a fish chowder—was in 1732. In 1751, the Boston Evening Post published a recipe for chowder containing onions, salt pork, marjoram, savory, thyme, ship's biscuit (hardtack), and fish, to which was added a bottle of red wine. All of the chowders mentioned before the mid-nineteenth century were made with water and not with milk, although they did contain salt pork. By 1880, clam chowder had become a regional dish from Maine to Virginia. The dividing lines between chowder made with milk and chowder made with tomatoes were also starting to form about this time, and they seem to be in southwestern Connecticut, south of which tomatoes are used, and Cape Cod, north of which milk is used. The no-man's-land here seems to be Rhode Island and southeastern Connecticut, where a clear broth is used.

Every ingredient is important in chowder. First, the quahogs (pronounced ko-hogs). They should be live. Quahogs are too big and tough to be eaten raw; that's why they are used for chowder. Some cooks use littlenecks, razor shell, or soft-shell clams, but if you do, you're making a different chowder. On Cape Ann and on Cape Cod, soft-shell clams are used for fried clams, not chowder. In Maine, though, they'll use any kind of clam. Surf clams (*Spisula*

(continued)

[*Hemimactra*] *solidissima* Dillwyn) are large, deep-water clams that get washed up with the surf on the ocean side of Cape Cod. They can be used in chowders, too. Second, the milk. Whole milk with half-and-half and/or cream will approximate the old-time taste. Third, the potatoes. They should be waxy boiling potatoes such as Yukon Gold or red rose that can handle boiling and still retain their shape. Don't use baking potatoes; they will disintegrate and make your chowder too potatoey (although some people do like it that way). For the onion, I like to use any large yellow onion. I always use salt pork rather than bacon in chowders, because bacon is too strong a flavor.

Cooks have many secrets for making a good clam chowder; one of them is to cook the onions very gently so they caramelize a bit and disappear into the chowder. Doctoring your finished chowder with parsley or chives is a restaurant innovation to give the chowder "color." Just remember: chowda don't need no color—it's already got one: white. One last warning: be very careful when heating the milk, or it will curdle. This recipe makes a good-size batch of chowder, which is just fine, because leftovers are heavenly.   [**Makes 10 servings**]

the best soups in the world

20 pounds quahogs or large cherrystone clams or 5 cups chopped clams

1 tablespoon baking soda

2 quarts water

2 pounds boiling potatoes (such as Yukon Gold), peeled and diced

½ pound lean salt pork, diced

1 large yellow onion (about 14 ounces), finely chopped

Salt, if necessary

Freshly ground white pepper to taste

½ teaspoon dried thyme

2 cups whole milk

3 cups half-and-half

1 cup heavy cream

6 tablespoons unsalted butter

12 split common crackers or oyster crackers

1. Prepare the clams by letting them soak in cold, clean seawater (preferably) or tap water for 1 hour with the baking soda. You can do this in a plugged-up kitchen sink. Remove the clams and rinse, then place them in a large 20-quart stockpot filled with an inch or two of water. Cover, turn the heat to high, and steam the quahogs until they all open, 25 to 30 minutes. Discard any clams that remain firmly shut. Remove the clams from their shells once they are cool enough to handle and discard the shells but save all the liquid. Strain the liquid through a strainer into a smaller stew pot. Strain again through a cheesecloth-lined strainer

if necessary. Chop the clams. (You can do this in a food processor in pulses.) You should have about 5 cups of chopped clams.

2. Add all the collected clam juice to the water you steamed the clams in. If you have less than 2 quarts of liquid in the stockpot add enough water to the collected juices to make up the difference, although you will probably have more than 2 quarts.

3. Bring the reserved clam liquor to a boil, then cook the potatoes until three-quarters cooked and nearly tender, 8 to 10 minutes. Add the reserved chopped clams, cook at a boil for 5 minutes, then turn the heat off and let the chowder sit. If scum forms, skim it off at once.

4. Meanwhile, in a large skillet add the salt pork and cook over medium-low heat, stirring, until nearly crispy, about 15 minutes. Remove the salt pork with a slotted spoon and set aside. Reduce the heat to low, add the onion, and cook, stirring occasionally to deglaze the skillet, until golden and very soft, about 30 minutes. Add the salt pork and onion mixture to the potatoes and stir. Check the seasoning and add salt if necessary (it shouldn't be necessary if you've used quahogs from Wellfleet) and the pepper and thyme. Let the chowder age in the refrigerator for 24 hours.

5. Remove the chowder and reheat over low heat. Once it is hot, add the milk, half-and-half, and cream. Cover and heat the chowder until it is about 140°F. The broth should never even come close to a boil though, or the milk will curdle. Stir in the butter, and remove the stew pot from the burner, but leave on the stove, covered, to stay warm for 1 hour or more. Serve with common or oyster crackers.

mr. paca's oyster soup

WILLIAM PACA OF MARYLAND, a signer of the Declaration of Independence, was married to Ann Chase, whose father, Samuel Chase, a colleague of Mr. Paca and also a signer of the Declaration, was appointed to the Supreme Court by George Washington. In 1811, Ann Chase began writing a recipe book in which she recorded some of the favorite recipes of her husband, who had died in 1799, so we can assume that this recipe dates from his lifetime. William Paca loved a very thick oyster stew. This was a rich soup course served in the home of the chief magistrate of Maryland, but it was a popular even among ordinary denizens of Baltimore, probably only lacking the richness and spice of the kitchens of the upper classes. It's possible that either a slave or a servant opened the oysters, or that they were authorized to pay the oysterman to shuck them.

Oysters were far more popular in late eighteenth- and nineteenth-century America than they are today. The harvest was vast and stories of oyster eating prodigious. Oysters were packed in barrels of ice and shipped on rivers and canals on the Eastern seaboard, and later in the nineteenth century railroads brought oysters to the rest of the country. Since oysters were larger in the eighteenth century than they are today, I have changed the directions slightly to thicken the soup before adding the oysters. This recipe is from Ann Chase's manuscript, as reprinted in the book *Maryland's Way*, published by the Hammond-Harwood House Association in 1964. The original recipe, which yields twelve servings, instructs, "Take half a gallon of oysters opened new with their liquor and stew them: when half done take a piece of butter the bigness of a teacup and rub in with as much flour as will thicken them. Season with pepper, salt, and mace. Just before you take them up add half a pint of cream."

[**Makes 4 servings**]

2 dozen oysters, scrubbed and washed well, soaked in cold water to cover
    with 1 tablespoon baking soda for 1 hour, and drained
¼ cup water
¼ cup unsalted butter (½ stick)
¼ cup all-purpose flour, at room temperature
⅛ teaspoon ground mace or nutmeg
¼ teaspoon freshly ground black pepper
1 cup hot heavy cream
Salt to taste if necessary
Oyster crackers for garnish

1. Place the oysters in a stockpot with the water, cover, and turn the heat to high. Once the oysters have opened slightly, after 1 to 2 minutes, turn the heat off, remove the oysters, pry them open with an oyster knife, and remove the oysters. Strain the oyster liquor through a fine mesh sieve into a clean saucepan and discard the shells. Set the oysters aside.

2. In a bowl, cream together the butter and flour with a fork.

3. Heat the pot containing the oyster liquor over low heat and once it starts bubbling around the edges add the mace, pepper, and butter-flour mixture, stirring to incorporate the flour. Cook until it thickens, about 2 minutes. Add the oysters and simmer until they begin to curl at the edges, 4 to 6 minutes. Remove from the heat, stir in the cream, and season with salt if necessary. Serve with oyster crackers.

anne kearney's oyster-fennel soup

THIS MAGNIFICENT SOUP comes from Anne Kearney, former chef of Peristyle, a well-received New Orleans restaurant then serving a French-inflected bistro cooking with Creole overtones. One can see the Provençal inspiration in her recipe in the use of fennel, garlic, tarragon, and anise liqueur. The oysters should be cooked only until their edges curl up. You want them plump, juicy, and soft as pillows. Herbsaint is a typical anise liqueur of New Orleans, but any pastis such as Pernod, Ouzo, or Arak will do. A quart of oyster juice may be difficult to come by, so what I do is put two fat oysters in a blender with a quart of water and liquefy it; this also contributes to an interesting texture.

CAUTION: the amount of alcohol called for during the flambéing in Step 2 may be more than your stove top and range hood can handle, although it wouldn't be in a restaurant kitchen. Run the range hood at full blast, make sure the work area and kitchen is clear of objects and people, and add the liqueur. Shake the pan gently to ignite it. It will burst alarmingly into flames, so be prepared to immediately remove the pan from the burner, as it will flame up quite high—possibly three feet—so it doesn't scorch the hood. Lower the pan a bit away from the stove until the flames die down in about 10 seconds, then return it to the burner. I'm making this sound scarier than it is so you will know what to expect and can handle it all calmly. **[Makes 4 servings]**

the best soups in the world

FOR THE BROTH

1 tablespoon peanut oil

²/₃ cup diced onion

¹/₃ cup diced fennel bulb

¹/₃ cup diced celery

¾ teaspoon finely chopped garlic

½ cup Herbsaint, Pernod, Ouzo, Arak or other pastis

1½ tablespoons all-purpose flour

1 quart oyster juice or fish broth

FOR THE OYSTERS AND FINISH

24 shucked oysters

½ cup heavy cream

1 tablespoon chopped fresh tarragon

1 tablespoon chopped fresh chives

1 tablespoon chopped fresh parsley

1 teaspoon salt or more to taste

Freshly ground black pepper to taste

1. In a large skillet, heat the oil over medium heat, then add the onion, fennel, and celery and cook until softened, about 6 minutes. Add the garlic and cook for 1 more minute.

2. Add the liqueur carefully; with a slight, short jerk of the pan it will flame up alarmingly (see caution in headnote). Remove the pan from the stove until the flames die down in a bit, then stir constantly while the liqueur burns off to prevent it from burning the vegetables. Once the flame is extinguished, sprinkle on the flour and cook, stirring, for 2 to 3 minutes. Add 1 cup of the oyster juice, scrape the bits from the bottom of the pan, and transfer the contents of the pan to a pot.

3. Add the remaining oyster juice to the pot and bring to a boil over high heat, then reduce to a simmer and cook for 30 minutes. The soup can be kept warm at this point and reheated later.

4. When you are ready to serve, bring the broth to a boil over high heat, then add the oysters and cook until their edges begin to curl, about 2 minutes. Stir in the cream, tarragon, chives, parsley, salt, and pepper, turn the heat off, and serve.

maryland crab soup

THE BLUE CRAB used in a Maryland crab soup has the scientific name *Callinectes,* which is Greek for "beautiful swimmer." The earliest recipe of a precursor to Maryland crab soup that I'm familiar with is from 1820; it is for "gumbo soup with crab," from the Baltimore "receipt" book of Mary Galloway Maxcy, the wife of the solicitor of the U.S. Treasury. I think there is a strong argument to be made that the roots of Maryland crab soup rest in the gumbo made by African slaves in the South, because of the tomatoes, spices, and variety of diced vegetables. The Maxcy's were slave owners, and it's possible that the soup was learned from one of the domestic slaves.

In Maryland there are two basic crab soups: this one, which is spicy and tomato based, and cream of crab soup, which is usually made with milk, chicken broth, and sometimes sherry. There is a huge range in recipes for this summer soup—some cooks using fish broth, others water, some more vegetables—but in the end most all Maryland crab soup recipes are thick soups meant to feed a large number of people. I've scaled this recipe down just a bit, but it is still a summer party dish that will feed about twelve people. Typically, the crabs for the broth would be the leftover carcasses from a steamed crab dinner the day before, but I use fresh crabs and keep the carcasses and shells to make another crab broth.

In putting together this recipe I've consulted a number of sources: "Wayne's Award-Winning Maryland Crab Soup" from Paula Deen's television show "Paula's Home Cooking, Episode: Weekend House Guest"; David Ansel's *The Soup Peddler's Slow & Difficult Soups,* published by Ten Speed Press; *Canton Cooks,* a cookbook compiled by the Canton neighborhood library in Baltimore; and Chef Nancy Longo of Pierpoint Restaurant in Fell's Point, Baltimore. But most importantly, my friend Boyd Grove, denizen of Baltimore and connoisseur of crab soup, tells me that it's meant to be thick, and not served as a first course. **[Makes 12 servings]**

the best soups in the world

½ pound thick-cut bacon, cut into ½-inch squares

1 medium onion, chopped

8 quarts water

One 35-ounce can plum tomatoes

12 fresh blue crabs (about 3 pounds) or 2 Dungeness crabs,
   cut in half (or 12 blue crab carcasses)

1½ cups chopped celery

1½ cups fresh corn kernels (about 3 cobs)

1½ cups ¼-inch-dice green beans

1½ cups fresh or frozen peas

1½ cups fresh or frozen lima beans

1½ cups diced potatoes

3 tablespoons Old Bay seasoning
1 tablespoon red chile flakes
3 tablespoons salt
1 pound fresh crab claw meat, picked over

1. In a skillet, cook the bacon and onion over medium-high heat, stirring, until half-cooked and not yet crispy, about 8 minutes. Set aside.

2. In a large stockpot, add the water and tomatoes and bring to a boil over high heat. Add the live crabs and boil for 12 minutes. Remove the crabs and set aside to cool. (If using carcasses, leave them in the pot.) Reduce the heat to low and simmer for 1 hour.

3. Meanwhile, remove the meat from the crabs and set aside. As this is mysteriously complicated unless you are from Maryland, see the box below for guidance on how to shell a crab.

4. After the soup has been simmering for 1 hour, add the celery, corn, green beans, peas, lima beans, potatoes, Old Bay seasoning, red chile flakes, and the reserved bacon and onion; if you have used crab carcasses and shells, strain the soup before adding the vegetables and discard the shells. Simmer until the vegetables are cooked, about 30 minutes. Season with salt. Add the reserved crab meat and the fresh claw meat, stir, and serve.

PICKING CRABS

There are eight steps to removing the crab meat from a cooked blue crab:

1. Twist off the claws and legs.

2. Place the crab on its back and pull the apron up and off.

3. Cut the bottom shell just under the mouth with a knife.

4. Press your thumbs into this space you've created and lift off the top shell.

5. Remove and discard the spongy white gills, which are inedible.

6. Snap the crab body into halves.

7. Twist off the back fins.

8. Crack the claws with a mallet to remove the claw meat. Remove the meat from other parts with a nut pick.

maine lobster stew

FIRST, BE AWARE THAT LOBSTER STEW, like clam chowder, is a two-day affair. The first day is for preparing it; then it goes overnight in the refrigerator for its "seasoning." It's hard to believe that this simple soup was once considered poor people's food in Maine. The great Maine writer Stephen King, whose family was poor, describes how his mother kept lobster stew on the stove but out of embarrassment would hide it away when company came. The scene appears in his short story "The Reach."

As best I can make out, lobster stew is what they call lobster chowder in Maine. But one should be careful about a proper Maine lobster stew, because many recipes are called Maine lobster chowder or stew simply because they have lobster from Maine in them. *Those* are not Maine lobster stews. Although all those fanciful recipes might taste just fine, it is important that we make this stew as a Downeaster would, and that means simply. The Pulitzer Prize–winning Maine poet Robert P. T. Coffin (1892–1955) advised that lobster stew should be half lobster and half liquid. Sometimes you will find white wine or sherry in lobster stew. This harks back to the first lobster stew recipe I'm familiar with, the one in the *Accomplished Cook* by Robert May, published in London in 1685, which uses claret.   **[Makes 4 to 5 servings]**

Two 2-pound live lobsters (yields about 18 ounces lobster meat)

6 tablespoons unsalted butter

2 cups heavy cream

1½ cups whole milk

3 tablespoons very dry sherry

Salt and freshly ground black pepper to taste

Oyster crackers for garnish (optional)

1. The day before you plan to serve, in a stockpot, bring 1 inch of water to a boil over high heat, then add the live lobsters, partially covered, and steam for 15 minutes. Remove the lobsters and when they are cool enough to handle, crack them and remove all the meat from the arms, claws, body, legs, and fan tail. Chop into pieces not larger than ¾ inch. Set aside along with any tomalley and coral you find in the lobster, reserving the shells.

2. Place the shells in a large pot and cover with water. Bring to a boil over high heat and boil for 1 hour. Remove and discard the lobster shells and strain the broth, setting aside 1 cup.

3. In a large pot, melt 5 tablespoons butter over high heat, then add the lobster meat and cook, stirring, until bubbling vigorously, about 2 minutes. Slowly stir in the cream and milk. Add the reserved 1 cup of lobster broth and the sherry and season with salt and pepper. Cook over high heat until tiny bubbles appear on the edges. Turn the heat off. Stir in the reserved lobster tomalley and coral, let cool, and place in the refrigerator overnight.

4. Bring water to a boil over high heat in the lower portion of a double-boiler. Pour the lobster stew into the top part of the double-boiler and heat over medium heat, stirring occasionally, until very hot but not bubbling, 10 to 15 minutes. Add the remaining tablespoon of butter and once it has melted, serve with crackers, if using.

lobster and corn chowder

WHEN I LIVED IN NEW ENGLAND, this favorite was one we made once a year, usually with leftovers from our August lobsterfest. After such a feast is the easiest time to make it, because you will have leftover lobster meat, shells, and corn. But it's spectacular enough to make anytime. You will see recipes for this soup with twice the amount of lobster I use. I feel that's overindulgence, because there is so much flavor in the chowder as it is. It also should be simple, like all chowders; it doesn't need a thousand ingredients.

[Makes 4 to 6 servings]

One 2-pound live lobster

6 tablespoons unsalted butter

½ cup diced salt pork

2 boiling potatoes (about ¾ pound), peeled and diced

1 medium onion, chopped

1 quart half-and-half

4 cooked corn cobs, kernels scraped off (about 2 cups)

Salt and freshly ground black pepper to taste

⅛ teaspoon cayenne pepper

1. In a large pot, bring a couple of inches of water to a boil over high heat, then cook the lobster covered with just a little opening for steam to escape, about 12 minutes. Remove and let cool. When cool enough to handle, remove the meat, cut into ¾-inch pieces, and set aside; you should have about 14 ounces of meat. Save the shells, place in a pot with 2 quarts water, and bring to a boil. Boil for 30 minutes, strain the broth, and set aside.

2. In a large saucepan, melt 4 tablespoons of the butter with the salt pork over medium-low heat, then cook, stirring, until the salt pork is crispy, about 10 minutes. Add the potatoes and onion and cook, stirring, until the onion is translucent, about 10 minutes. Add the half-and-half and 2 cups of the strained lobster broth and bring to a simmer over medium-high heat. Reduce the heat before anything begins to boil and cook until the potatoes are tender, about 6 minutes. Add the lobster meat, corn, salt, pepper, and cayenne and simmer until the lobster meat is hot, about 10 minutes. Add the remaining 2 tablespoons butter and once it melts, serve immediately.

norwegian fish soup

THIS CREAMY, CELERY-FLAVORED FISH CHOWDER is called *fiskesuppe* in Norwegian, meaning, simply enough, "fish soup." It's interesting to speculate whether the *chaudière* or chowder from Brittany that is thought of as the progenitor of the chowders of New England may have its roots in some kind of Viking food. We know that Viking raids in Normandy and Brittany were common in the ninth century and that the Northmen ate lots of fish—dried, salted, and fresh—and lots of milk products, such as sour milk, buttermilk, and *skyr,* a kind of cheese curd, but there is no mention of chowders (and, in fact, no mention of any actual dishes at all) in the historical record. In any case, this delicious chowder is adapted from a recipe in *Ekte Norsk Mat* by Astrid Karlsen Scott.   **[Makes 4 to 6 servings]**

the best soups in the world

2 cups water

4 celery stalks, chopped

½ cup diced salt pork

¼ cup (½ stick) unsalted butter

3 tablespoons all-purpose flour

1 cup whole milk

1 cup heavy cream

2 teaspoons salt or more to taste

½ teaspoon freshly ground black pepper or more to taste

2 cups fish broth

1 medium onion, chopped

1½ cups (about ½ pound) cut-up fish fillet (such as flounder, fluke, or cod)

2 tablespoons finely chopped chives

1. Bring the water to a boil in a large pot over high heat, then add the celery and cook until tender, about 7 minutes. Set aside with the water it cooked in.

2. In a skillet, cook the salt pork over medium-low heat, stirring, until crispy, 8 to 10 minutes. Set aside.

3. To prepare the white sauce, in a pot, melt the butter over medium-high heat, then stir in the flour to form a roux and cook, stirring, for 1 minute. Remove the saucepan from the heat, slowly whisk in the milk and cream, return to medium heat, and cook, stirring, until the white sauce becomes thicker, 7 to 8 minutes. Season with the salt and pepper.

4. Add the fish broth to the cream sauce to make it thinner and reduce the heat to low. Add the cooked salt pork, chopped onion, and celery and cooking water to the broth, stir, then add the fish fillets and cook over low heat for 20 minutes. Serve the soup hot with chives.

frisian mustard soup

THIS SOUP IS ALWAYS SURPRISING because of the sharp bite of the mustard, a wonderful flavor for the shrimp and fish broth. It's called *Amelander mosterdsoep* in Dutch and is an old Frisian recipe from the island of Ameland. The Frisian Islands are a string of long and narrow sandy barrier islands in the North Sea running along the northeast coast of Holland, the northwest coast of Germany, and a portion of Denmark. The people speak Frisian, a Germanic language that is the language closest to English.

To prepare the mustard, stir together 2 tablespoons of powdered mustard seed with some water, then add more mustard or water until it is the consistency of a Dijon mustard from a jar. Many supermarkets sell the small shrimp required for this soup, already cooked and shelled, in the frozen foods section; they will work fine. **[Makes 4 servings]**

4 tablespoons (½ stick) unsalted butter

1 large onion, chopped

6 tablespoons all-purpose flour

4 cups boiling fish broth

6 tablespoons heavy cream

3½ tablespoons powdered mustard, mixed with a little water to form
   a smooth consistency

3 tablespoons white wine vinegar

4 teaspoons nonpareil capers, rinsed

1½ teaspoons salt

¾ teaspoon freshly ground black pepper

6 ounces small shrimp, shelled

3 tablespoons very thinly sliced white part of leek

1. In a large pot, melt the butter over medium-high heat, then add the onion and cook, stirring occasionally, until translucent, about 6 minutes. Stir in the flour to form a roux, stirring for about 1 minute, then slowly add the fish broth, stirring, until well blended and smooth.

2. In a bowl, stir together the cream and blended mustard. Add to the soup with the vinegar, capers, salt, and pepper and cook over medium-high heat, making sure it doesn't come to a boil, until bubbling lightly on the edges of the saucepan, about 3 minutes. Add the shrimp and heat, without letting the broth boil, until cooked through and orange-red, about 5 minutes for fresh shrimp and less if using cooked shrimp. Check the seasoning. Sprinkle on the leeks, cook for 1 minute, and serve.

shrimp bisque

THIS BISQUE IS ADAPTED FROM a recipe by Taunt Nit of Forked Island, Louisiana, who says that it is sometimes called white shrimp stew. Make sure the milk never comes to a boil, or it may curdle. If it does you can correct it somewhat by blending in some *beurre manié,* a blend of equal parts soft butter and flour, to thicken it again. You can serve this with corn bread or oyster crackers. Crab, crayfish, or lobster may be substituted for the shrimp.

[Makes 4 to 6 servings]

5 tablespoons unsalted butter

1 small onion, finely chopped

1 celery stalk, finely chopped

2½ pounds fresh shrimp with their heads or 1¼ pounds defrosted headless shrimp, heads and/or tails removed and saved for making broth if desired or ¾ pound raw shelled shrimp

¼ cup unbleached all-purpose flour

1 quart whole milk

1½ teaspoons salt

2 teaspoons Tabasco sauce

1 teaspoon hot paprika

½ teaspoon freshly ground white pepper

2 teaspoons freshly squeezed lemon juice

In a large pot, melt the butter over medium-high heat, then add the onion and celery and cook, stirring, until the onion is softened, about 5 minutes. Add the shrimp and cook, stirring frequently, for 2 minutes. Stir in the flour and once it is blended in, pour in the milk in a slow stream, whisking gently the whole time. Add the salt, Tabasco sauce, paprika, white pepper, and lemon juice. Bring to just below a boil, then reduce the heat to medium and simmer for 5 minutes. Serve immediately.

prawn bisque

AS PRAWNS ARE NEARLY IMPOSSIBLE to get in the United States, you can use shrimp: although prawns look like miniature lobsters, their taste is closer to shrimp. This Australian soup is creamy and delicious. Australian cooks also make this soup with yabbies, the name of a local crayfish (*Cherax destructor*) that typically is four to eight inches long.

[Makes 4 to 6 servings]

2 pounds large shrimp

4 cups water

1 medium onion, chopped

1 celery stalk including the green tops, chopped

2 tablespoons unsalted butter

2 tablespoons all-purpose flour

1 tablespoon salt

¾ teaspoon freshly ground black pepper or more to taste

½ cup dry white wine

1 tablespoon tomato paste

½ teaspoon paprika

½ cup heavy cream

1 tablespoon brandy

1 cup whipped cream for garnish

Zest from ½ lemon, very thinly julienned for garnish

1. In a large saucepan, bring 3 quarts of water to a rolling boil, salt the water abundantly, then cook the shrimp until they turn orange-pink, 2 to 3 minutes. Remove and let cool. Remove the shells and set the shells aside. Devein the shrimp if necessary. Set aside 6 shelled shrimp for garnish.

2. In a pot, add the shrimp shells, water, onion, and celery, bring to a boil over high heat, then reduce the heat to medium and cook, covered, for 20 minutes. Remove from the heat and cool slightly. Strain and set the broth aside.

3. In a pot, melt the butter over low heat, stir in the flour, salt, and pepper to form a roux, then cook, stirring, for 2 minutes. Slowly add the shrimp broth and stir until thickened and bubbling, about 10 minutes. Stir in the wine, tomato paste, and paprika and cook gently, stirring, for 10 minutes.

4. Transfer the soup, in batches if necessary, to a blender, add the shrimp and cream and blend until smooth. Pour back into the pot with the brandy and heat through gently over medium-low heat. Do not allow this mixture to boil. Serve garnished with a dollop of whipped cream, the reserved shrimp, and the lemon zest.

lobster bisque

LOBSTER BISQUE is one of the great soups of the world. It's hard to say where it originally comes from, but Brittany is a good guess, as the word *bisque,* although its origin is unknown, may derive from the Bay of Biscay. Another thought is that it derives from *bis cuit,* "twice-cooked." In any case, although its origins may be obscure, the word is indeed French. Today, a bisque is a cream soup made with shellfish. In the eighteenth century, though, *bisque* was used for all manner of soups made from pigeons or game and not necessarily creamed or puréed. This *bisque de homard* is labor intensive, but it is lightly creamy, with a wonderful lobster flavor coming from the broth, and a very memorable experience. Make it on a special occasion for special people. **[Makes 12 servings]**

the best soups in the world

FOR THE LOBSTER BROTH

3 quarts water

Three 1½-pound live lobsters

2 bottles dry white wine

3 ripe tomatoes, chopped

1 leek, white and light green parts only, split lengthwise, washed well, and thinly sliced

½ celery root (celeriac), peeled and diced

1 celery stalk, chopped

1 carrot, peeled and chopped

3 garlic cloves, finely chopped

Grated zest of ½ orange

Bouquet garni, tied in cheesecloth, consisting of 12 sprigs fresh parsley and 4 sprigs tarragon

FOR THE BISQUE

6 tablespoons (¾ stick) unsalted butter

4 shallots, finely chopped

1 small carrot, very finely chopped

2 garlic cloves, finely chopped

One 6-ounce can tomato paste

¾ cup dry white wine

Salt and freshly ground black pepper to taste

¼ teaspoon cayenne pepper

4 tablespoons unbleached all-purpose flour

1 tablespoon finely chopped fresh tarragon
4 tablespoons cognac
1 cup heavy cream

1. To make the broth: bring the water to a boil in a large stockpot, add the lobsters, and cook for 20 to 25 minutes. Remove the lobster and cool, reserving the cooking water. Remove all the meat from the lobsters and save any tomalley and coral. Cut up the lobster meat and set aside. Return the empty shells to the stockpot with the cooking water and add the white wine, tomatoes, leek, celery root, celery, carrot, garlic, orange zest, and bouquet garni. Bring to a boil over high heat, then reduce to low and simmer, uncovered, for at least 1 hour. Drain through a fine wire mesh sieve and reserve, discarding the vegetables and shells.

2. To make the bisque: in a large pot, melt 3 tablespoons of the butter over high heat, then add the shallots, carrot, and garlic and cook, stirring, until softened, about 4 minutes. Add the tomato paste and cook, stirring, for 2 minutes. Add the wine and cook for 3 minutes, then add the reserved lobster broth and simmer for 15 minutes. Season with salt and pepper and the cayenne. Continue to simmer the broth for another 15 minutes.

3. Meanwhile, melt the remaining 3 tablespoons butter in a small saucepan over low heat. Whisk in the flour to form a roux, then add 2 teaspoons of the chopped tarragon, reserved lobster tomalley and coral, and a little lobster broth. Stir until smooth. Add 1 tablespoon of the cognac and stir. Turn this mixture into the lobster broth, now called a bisque. Bring to a boil and continue to whisk until thickened. Reduce the heat to medium, season with salt and pepper, and simmer for another 15 minutes.

4. Whisk the cream into the bisque, then add the remaining 3 tablespoons cognac. Add the lobster meat, heat until very hot, then serve immediately, garnished with the remaining 1 teaspoon tarragon.

velouté joinville

A VELOUTÉ IS CLASSICALLY DEFINED as a thick soup that is roux based, meaning a liaison of flour and broth (or milk) enriched with another liaison of cream and egg yolk. In modern restaurants, roux-based sauces and soups are unfashionable, but there is no reason they should be, and at home we home cooks can use them without constraint because we seek good food, not fashion. But you do need to be careful with roux, because they can make a soup taste heavy rather than thickened—this is probably why they became unfashionable.

The name of this classic seafood velouté, rich with fish broth, shrimp, mussels, and mushrooms, derives from Francots de Joinville (1818–1900), the duke of Orleans and son of the nineteenth-century French king Louis-Philippe. In classic French cooking there are a number of preparations called à la Joinville, and many of them have the shrimp and mushroom combination. If you have to use large shrimp, slice them so they are about a half inch long.

[**Makes 4 to 6 servings**]

16 mussels, debearded and washed well

4 cups fish broth

5 tablespoons unsalted butter

½ pound very small shrimp, shelled

Salt to taste

¾ cup sliced button (white) mushrooms

¼ cup thinly sliced white part of leek

3 tablespoons all-purpose flour

1 cup heavy cream

1 large egg yolk

1 teaspoon lemon juice

Freshly ground white pepper to taste

1. Place the mussels in a pot with ½ cup of the fish broth. Bring to a boil, covered, over high heat, and steam until all the mussels have opened, 5 to 8 minutes. Discard any mussels that remain firmly shut. Remove the shells from the pot and extract the mussels, setting them aside. Strain the remaining broth through a fine mesh strainer and add this mussel liquid to the rest of the fish broth.

2. In a pot, melt 3 tablespoons of the butter over medium heat, then add the shrimp and a little salt and cook, stirring, until orange-pink, about 2 minutes. Remove with a slotted spoon and set aside with the mussels.

3. Add the mushrooms and leek to the pot, cover, and cook for 5 minutes. Remove the leek and mushrooms with a slotted spoon and set aside with the shellfish, keeping both warm.

4. Melt the remaining 2 tablespoons of butter in the pot over medium heat, then stir in the flour to form a roux and cook, stirring, for 2 minutes until it turns golden. Add the remaining fish broth and bring to a boil over high heat, stirring or whisking constantly to remove any lumps. Reduce the heat to low and simmer for 15 minutes.

5. Meanwhile, combine the cream and egg yolk, then add to the broth, stirring vigorously, and simmer for 3 more minutes, making sure it does not boil. Add the reserved mussels, shrimp, and mushrooms and leek, stir in the lemon juice, season with salt and white pepper, and serve.

icelandic curried
langoustine soup

LANGOUSTINES, OTHERWISE KNOWN as Dublin Bay prawns, are more closely related to lobster than shrimp. They are what the Italians call scampi. Prawns are not the easiest thing to find, so I substitute jumbo shrimp or lobster in this recipe called *humarsúpa úlfars* or *karríkrydduð humarsúpa* in Icelandic. It is adapted from one published in Reykjavik's *Morgunbladid* newspaper that was translated for me by my friend Gudrun Magnusdottir, who tells me that this is considered a modern soup, perhaps no more than seventy-five years old. That's obvious from the use of garlic, curry, and paprika, which I don't think anyone would associate with Iceland.

Langoustines are usually sold frozen in this country and can be replaced with lobsters (for a closer taste), crayfish, or jumbo shrimp. In Icelandic, the butter-and-flour ball is called *smjörbolla* and is used as a thickener for sauces. Most professional kitchens call it *beurre manié*, following the French. If you are using lobster instead of langoustines, it will be easiest to steam it before preparation. Some cooks add a splash of brandy at the end. In place of the fish base paste you can reduce the water to 4 cups and add 2 cups of lobster or shrimp broth.

[**Makes 4 servings**]

the best soups in the world

12 langoustines, 12 extra jumbo shrimp (about ¾ pound), or
    one 2-pound live lobster
3 tablespoons unsalted butter
1 small onion, finely chopped
5 garlic cloves, finely chopped
2 large button (white) mushrooms, finely chopped
¾ cup tomato purée
1 teaspoon sweet paprika
½ teaspoon curry powder
6 cups water
¾ cup white wine
1 teaspoon fish base paste or 1 fish bouillon cube
1 teaspoon beef base paste or 1 beef bouillon cube
¼ cup flour blended with ¼ cup (½ stick) room temperature unsalted butter
¾ cup heavy cream
2½ teaspoons salt
1½ teaspoons freshly ground black pepper

1. If using langoustines, steam in 1 inch of water for 3 minutes. If using shrimp, boil in salted water until orange-pink, about 2 minutes. If using lobster, steam in several inches of water for 15 minutes. Let the cooked shellfish cool.

2. Split the langoustines down the middle and remove the innards. Remove the tail meat, cut into ¼-inch strips, and set aside, reserving the shells. If using shrimp, remove the shells, split them in half lengthwise, and reserve the shells. If using lobster, remove all the meat from the shells, slice into strips, and reserve the shells.

3. In a large pot, melt the butter over low heat, then add the langoustine, shrimp, or lobster shells and cook for 15 minutes. Add the onion, garlic, mushrooms, tomato purée, paprika, and curry and continue to cook, stirring, for 2 minutes. Stir in the water, white wine, fish and beef base paste or bouillon cube and continue to simmer for 1 hour. Strain the broth through a strainer and return to a clean pot, discarding all the shells and vegetables. Add the flour-butter mixture and whisk until everything is blended and thickened.

4. Pour the cream into the broth and stir. Season with the salt and pepper. Bring the broth to a furious boil over high heat, add the reserved shellfish meat, and cook until firm and curled up, 2 to 3 minutes. Reduce the heat if it is welling up over the edge of the pot. (If using cooked lobster it only needs to be heated for about 1 minute.) Ladle the soup into individual soup bowls and let rest 5 minutes before serving.

chowders and bisques

fish and chile chowder

THIS IS ONE OF THE MOST SATISFYING CHOWDERS you'll ever eat, quite perfect in winter but great anytime if you like chiles. The two different chiles have different floral bouquets resulting from their nature and their preparation. This a great soup for a make-ahead dinner, as it actually improves in taste if you can leave it to sit and age a bit. The pasilla (sometimes misnamed poblano) chiles can be replaced with long green chiles (peperoncini).

[Makes 4 servings]

2 pasilla (poblano) chiles
2 tablespoons peanut oil
1 small onion, chopped
1 large garlic clove, finely chopped
½ celery stalk, chopped
2 habanero chiles, seeded and finely chopped
2 ounces salt pork, diced small
4 cups fish broth
1 medium Yukon Gold potato (6 ounces), peeled and diced
Kernels from 1 corn cob (about 1½ cups)
1 cup cream
¾ pound mixed fish fillets, such as cod, flounder, fluke, haddock, or hake,
    cut into bite-size pieces
2 teaspoons salt
¾ teaspoon freshly ground black pepper
2 tablespoons chopped cilantro (fresh coriander) leaves

1. Preheat the oven to 450°F.

2. Place the pasilla chiles in a baking pan and roast until the skin blisters black all over, about 30 minutes. Remove and when cool enough to handle, peel and remove the seeds. Cut the chiles into strips or smaller pieces.

3. In a large saucepan, heat the peanut oil over medium heat, then add the onion, garlic, celery, habanero chiles, and salt pork and cook, stirring frequently, until crispy, about 12 minutes.

4. Add the fish broth, potato, and corn, reduce the heat to low, and simmer until the potato is tender, about 30 minutes. Add the cream and roasted pasilla chiles and cook until heated in a few minutes. Add the fish, salt, and pepper and cook until the fish starts to flake, about 20 minutes. Turn the heat off, cover, and let sit to mellow for 1 hour. Reheat a little if necessary and serve with a sprinkle of the cilantro.

cheese soups

and egg soups

There's no such thing as a category of soups called dairy soups, but in this chapter that's more or less what you've got. Here you'll find soups whose primary or star ingredient is cheese (the first grouping) or eggs (the second). Some of these, such as Egg-Drop Soup, you may know very well, even if you've never made them. There are some real winners here that you'll make over and over—they're simple too—such as Cheddar Ale Soup, and real zingers for spice lovers, such as Tunisian Spicy Egg-Drop Soup.

venezuelan creole soup

CALLED *CHUPE CRIOLLO*, this is a chicken and cheese soup. In Venezuela, *queso bianco*, a soft white cheese, is used. If you think you're going to have leftovers don't use all the cheese: it will sink to the bottom of the pot and congeal, and it doesn't remelt well.

[**Makes 4 to 6 servings**]

1 tablespoon vegetable oil

1 medium onion, finely chopped

1 bunch cilantro (fresh coriander), stems removed and leaves chopped

4 large garlic cloves, finely chopped

1 teaspoon ground cumin

2 boneless and skinless chicken breast halves (1 pound), cubed

6 cups water

Salt to taste

3 boiling potatoes (about 1 pound), peeled and diced

1 corn cob, kernels removed

2 cups whole milk

6 ounces fresh mozzarella cheese, diced or shredded

1. In a large pot, heat the oil over medium heat, then add the onion, half the cilantro, the garlic, and cumin and cook, stirring occasionally, until the onion is mushy, about 8 minutes. Add the chicken and cook, stirring occasionally, until it turns color, about 5 minutes. Add the water, season with salt, and cook over medium heat without letting the water come to a boil for 15 minutes; reduce the heat to low if it is bubbling.

2. Remove the chicken with a slotted spoon, shred it into very small pieces using two forks, then return it to the pot together with the potatoes. Bring to a near boil over high heat, then reduce the heat to low and simmer, stirring, until the potatoes are tender, about 15 minutes. Add the corn, milk, and the remaining cilantro, mix well, and check the seasonings. Return the broth to a simmering point over low heat, making sure it does not boil, then remove it from the heat, top with the cheese, and serve immediately.

mexican roasted poblano and three cheese soup

THIS RECIPE IS CALLED *sopa "no te rajes Adelita"* in *La tradicional cocina Mexicana y sus mejores recetas* (1994), from which it is adapted. It's a delicious soup made so appealing by the roasted poblano chile. Poblano chiles are dark green, heart-shaped, and mildly hot—much less hot than a jalapeño. In some supermarkets they are labeled pasilla chiles, which they are not; pasilla chiles are very dark green, nearly black, long, and thin, though they nevertheless make a fine substitute. Because supermarkets increasingly carry a variety of Mexican cheeses, I give you the names of those used here, but the substitutes are excellent, should you not find the Mexican ones. **[Makes 4 servings]**

1 pound poblano chiles
¼ cup (½ stick) unsalted butter
2 cups whole milk
2 ounces Mexican *queso chichuahua* cheese (or muenster cheese)
2 ounces Mexican *queso oaxaca* cheese (or hard mozzarella cheese)
2 ounces Mexican *queso amarillo* cheese (or Dutch Gouda or Edam cheese)
½ cup Mexican *crema* or sour cream
Salt and freshly ground black pepper to taste

1. Preheat the oven to 425°F.

2. Place the chiles on a baking tray and roast until their skins blister black, about 40 minutes. Remove the chiles from the oven and when they are cool enough to handle, peel and seed them. Cut the chiles into strips.

3. In a large pot, melt the butter over medium heat, then add the milk, chiles, cheeses, and *crema* and cook, stirring constantly in a figure-8 pattern, until the mixture is homogenous and the cheese melted, about 8 minutes. Season with salt and pepper and serve.

cheddar ale soup

THIS SOUP, PROBABLY ADAPTED IN VERMONT from an old English recipe, is popular throughout northern New England. You can use either orange or white cheddar, although orange cheddar provides a more appetizing color. Don't buy cheddar that is aged more than two years, as it doesn't melt as it should for this soup. It's also best to use top-quality ale and not a lager. Once you put the cheese in make sure the broth does not come to a boil.

[**Makes 8 servings**]

¼ cup (½ stick) unsalted butter
1 small onion, finely chopped
1 small carrot, finely chopped or grated
¼ cup all-purpose flour
½ teaspoon powdered mustard
½ teaspoon paprika
½ pound mild orange cheddar cheese, shredded or grated (2 cups)
7 cups chicken or vegetable broth
1¼ cups half-and-half
One 12-ounce bottle ale
2 tablespoons chopped chives

In a pot, melt the butter over low heat, then add the onion and carrot and cook, covered and stirring occasionally, until the onion is softened, about 5 minutes. Add the flour, mustard, and paprika, stirring until well blended. Add in the cheese and broth, stirring slowly until the cheese is melted in, about 5 minutes. Add the half-and-half and ale and simmer over low heat, stirring occasionally, for 30 minutes. Serve, garnishing each bowl with some chives.

leek, mushroom, and stilton cheese soup

THIS ENGLISH SOUP begins humbly, with sautéed leeks and mushrooms, but once it's finished, with the blue-veined Stilton cheese and the horseradish and sour cream garnish, it's quite memorable. It's best to use freshly grated horseradish, but if you can only find prepared horseradish, then that's what you use. **[Makes 4 servings]**

FOR THE GARNISH

¼ cup sour cream
¼ cup freshly grated horseradish
1 small gherkin, finely chopped

FOR THE SOUP

¼ cup (½ stick) unsalted butter
4 leeks (about 1 pound), white part only, split lengthwise, washed well,
    and finely chopped
½ pound button (white) mushrooms, coarsely chopped
3 cups vegetable broth
1 cup whole milk
½ pound boiling potatoes (such as Yukon Gold), peeled and diced small
3 ounces Stilton cheese
1 teaspoon finely chopped fresh parsley

1. Prepare the garnish by mixing together the sour cream, horseradish, and gherkin in a bowl.

2. To make the soup: in a pot, melt the butter over medium heat, then add the leeks and mushrooms and cook, stirring occasionally, until softened, about 10 minutes. Add the broth, milk, and potatoes and bring to a boil over high heat, then reduce the heat to low and simmer until the potatoes are tender, about 20 minutes.

3. Add the Stilton cheese by crumbling it into the soup. Stir for 1 to 2 minutes, then ladle into individual bowls and serve with a tablespoon of the garnish and a sprinkle of parsley on top.

tibetan blue cheese and beef soup

IT'S POSSIBLE THAT THE KIND OF CHEESE used in this soup is very old. In the thirteenth century, as the famous Venetian traveler Marco Polo passed through Tartar country in the far western part of today's Xinjiang province of China, he wrote in his travel diaries of the making of a "kind of milk paste." The Tartars and Afghans called this kind of milk paste *kurút,* while the Tibetans called it *ch'ura.* Today, *churu* is a mold-ripened cheese from Tibet for which Roquefort or any blue cheese would be a fine substitute, the point being that it should be sourish. This exotic mixture combines hot chile with the pungent blue cheese, using a spice called *emma* in Tibetan that is a variety of Sichuan peppercorn. Because a wide variety of spices are not available in Tibet, cooks use cheese for spicelike flavoring. This Tibetan , also called *churu,* is adapted from Alka Didi, restaurant reviewer for MyBindi.com. **[Makes 4 servings]**

the best soups in the world

1 tablespoon vegetable oil

½ small onion, chopped

¼ teaspoon hot paprika

¼ teaspoon ground Sichuan peppercorns or black pepper

¼ teaspoon finely chopped garlic

¼ teaspoon finely chopped fresh ginger

¼ pound beef top sirloin, finely chopped

1 jalapeño chile, seeded and finely chopped

2 to 3 tablespoons blue cheese

5 cups water

1 large ripe tomato (about 10 ounces), peeled (page 273), seeded, and diced

1½ teaspoons salt or more to taste

¼ cup cornstarch mixed with ¼ cup water

In a large pot, heat the oil over medium-high heat, then add the onion and cook, stirring occasionally, until golden, about 4 minutes. Stir in the paprika, Sichuan peppercorns, garlic, and ginger. Add the beef and cook, stirring constantly, until browned, 1 to 2 minutes. Add the chile, reduce the heat to low, and add the cheese. Cook, stirring, until the cheese melts, 2 to 3 minutes, then add the water, tomato, and salt, reduce the heat to low, and simmer for 30 minutes. Stir in the cornstarch mixture and bring to a boil over high heat. Cook until the mixture thickens a bit, about 5 minutes, then let rest 10 for minutes and serve.

french garlic soup

IN THE SOUTHERN FRENCH regions of the Languedoc and Provence, garlic is thought of as a vegetable as well as a spice. This *soupe à l'ail,* "garlic soup," uses a lot of black pepper, but its opulence comes from the eggs. Pepper was expensive in the Middle Ages, where this soup has its origins, and when it appeared, it was usually on the table of a noble family or for special occasions, as with this heavily peppered soup that consummates the rite of marriage in traditional ceremonies in Languedoc. The copious use of both garlic and black pepper in this dish that the wife presents to her husband on their first day as a couple must represent the hopes for the lives ahead of them—that they be spiritually, if not materially, rich. This soup needs hard-toasted bread and lots of black pepper, so be liberal. **[Makes 8 servings]**

2 quarts water

1 cup extra-virgin olive oil

15 garlic cloves (about 1 head), finely chopped

Bouquet garni, tied in cheesecloth, consisting of 8 sprigs fresh parsley,
    8 sprigs fresh thyme, and 1 bay leaf

Salt to taste

6 large egg yolks

Abundant freshly ground black pepper

8 slices French bread, toasted golden

1. In a large pot or flame-proof casserole, bring the water, olive oil, garlic cloves, bouquet garni, and salt to a boil over high heat and boil for 5 minutes. Reduce the heat to low and simmer for 1 hour.

2. In a bowl, beat the egg yolks. Remove the soup from the heat and pour a ladleful of it slowly into the bowl with the yolks to warm them, beating constantly.

3. When the broth has cooled for 5 minutes, pour the egg mixture into the soup, beating or whisking the whole time. Pepper the soup generously. I leave it up to you the exact amount to use, but it should be heavily peppered. If the soup tastes bland after you've added the pepper, it needs more. Leave to thicken a bit over low heat, making sure the soup does not boil. Divide the bread among individual soup bowls, ladle the soup on top, and serve.

zuppa pavese

AN IMPORTANT MOMENT IN FOOD HISTORY was the great battle at Pavia in northern Italy in 1525 between Charles V of Spain (1500–1558) and the defeated King Francis I of France (1494–1547). The French historian Fernand Braudel suggests that the Battle of Pavia, besides being a triumph of the harquebusiers, was also the triumph of empty stomachs because Francis's army was too well fed, while the Spaniards and Lombards he fought could make do with a simple broth.

Legend has it that Francis took refuge in a nearby farmhouse after the battle. The embarrassed yet deeply honored housewife was preparing some soup. She had to turn her humble soup into a dish fit for a king, so she fried some stale bread, put it into the soup, cracked in two newly laid eggs, and ladled some boiling broth over the eggs. The whites curdled gently and the yolks remained soft. She served it with *grana padano* cheese, and the king approved, asking that the recipe be given to one of his servants. And so was born, the culinary apocrypha goes, *zuppa pavese,* the famous egg-drop soup from Pavia. The crucial elements here are the broth and the eggs. The broth should be clear and flavorful and homemade. The eggs must be at room temperature. **[Makes 4 servings]**

2 tablespoons unsalted butter

4 slices French or Italian bread with crust

¼ cup freshly grated Parmesan cheese (preferably, imported Parmigiano-Reggiano cheese)

1½ quarts Rich Veal Broth (page 12)

4 small or medium eggs, at room temperature

1 tablespoon finely chopped fresh parsley

Freshly ground white pepper to taste

1. Preheat the oven to 200°F and warm four oven-proof soup bowls for at least 30 minutes.

2. In a large skillet, melt the butter over medium heat, then cook the bread on both sides until golden, making sure you do not blacken the edges. Place a slice of bread in each bowl. Sprinkle a tablespoon of Parmesan on each slice of bread.

3. In a pot, bring the broth to a rolling boil over high heat. Without breaking the yolk, crack 1 egg onto each slice of bread and carefully ladle or pour the boiling broth over the egg until the bowl is filled. Sprinkle with parsley and a pinch of white pepper and serve immediately. Add more Parmesan at the table if desired.

Note: The broth must be boiling furiously before you pour it into the bowls, so the eggs, which should be small or medium and not large, can cook a bit.

cheese soups and egg soups

tunisian spicy egg-drop soup

THIS SOUP CALLED *MASHALWISH* is a kind of Tunisian egg-drop soup. Quite nice and very spicy, it is perfect for a winter's day. It can be made with meat or without, but it always contains eggs, whisked in at the end. This is the meat version, using a typical dried meat product of North Africa called *qadīd,* which is nothing but a spiced lamb jerky, and the lamb or beef sausage known as *mirkās* or *merguez.* I usually use a "peppered" or "hot" beef jerky that is sold in supermarkets to replace the lamb jerky. *Merguez* sausage is being sold in more and more places in this country, and you can also always find it online at www.gourmetfoodstore. com or www.dartagnan.com. If you want to try and make your own, I have a recipe on my web site, www.cliffordawright.com. In a pinch, linguiça sausage, Cajun andouille sausage, or even hot Italian sausage can be used, although you would never find a sausage made of pork in a Tunisian dish. For the vegetable version, just leave out the meat. Although no Tunisian cook suggested it to me, following the instructions for adding eggs as in Chinese Egg-Drop Soup might be nice (page 379). **[Makes 6 servings]**

4 large garlic cloves

1½ teaspoons caraway seeds

1 teaspoon salt and more as needed

¾ cup extra-virgin olive oil

6 ounces lamb or beef jerky (use "peppered" or "hot"), cut into 1-inch pieces

6 ounces *merguez* sausage, cut into ½-inch slices

2 tablespoons tomato paste

2 tablespoons *harīsa* (page 62)

1 teaspoon cumin seeds

1 teaspoon aniseeds

1 teaspoon cayenne pepper

6 cups water

4 large eggs

2 cups croûtons (page 129)

1. In a mortar, pound the garlic, caraway, and 1 teaspoon salt with a pestle until mushy.

2. In a large pot or flame-proof casserole, heat the olive oil over medium heat, then add the jerky, merguez sausage, tomato paste, *harīsa,* cumin, aniseeds, cayenne, and the garlic and caraway mixture and cook, stirring, for 1 minute. Add 2 cups of the water, cover, and cook, stirring occasionally, until the jerky is soft and the sausage cooked through, 18 to 20 minutes.

3. Add the remaining 4 cups water and bring to a boil over high heat. Break the eggs into the soup, then quickly whisk. Season with more salt if desired and cook until the eggs are cooked and form little pieces, about 4 minutes. Place the croûtons in individual serving bowls, ladle the hot soup over them, and serve.

kazakh lamb and omelet soup

KAZAKHSTAN IS A HUGE CENTRAL ASIAN country four times the size of Texas. The Kazakhs are a mix of Turkic and Mongol nomadic tribes who migrated into the region in the thirteenth century. The area was conquered by Russia in the eighteenth century and became a Soviet Republic in 1936. Today, the population is just over 50 percent Kazakh, 30 percent Russian, and also includes minority groups of Ukrainians, Germans, Uzbeks, and others. Kazakhstan is bordered by the Caspian Sea in the west, Russia in the north, and China in the east. This recipe comes from the city of Alma-Ata, now known as Almaty, very close to the Kyrgyzstan border to the south. Horse is the most popular meat in Kazakhstan, but mutton runs a close second. I use lamb in this soup, called *ashshy-sorpa*. I've adapted the recipe from the one served at the restaurant Zheruik on Seifullin Prospect 500 in Almaty. This soup is a wonderful representation of a taste popular on the Central Asian plains; it's delicious, yet you won't quite be able to put your finger on its uniqueness. **[Makes 6 servings]**

1 pound lamb bones, with some meat on them (such as shank)

12 cups water

¼ cup unsalted butter or rendered lamb fat

1¼ pounds boneless lamb stew meat, diced

¼ pound radish or daikon, chopped

1 large onion, chopped

1½ teaspoons freshly ground black pepper or more to taste

1 medium tomato, cut into 6 wedges

4 large garlic cloves, chopped

1 bay leaf

¼ cup white wine vinegar

Salt to taste

FOR THE OMELET AND GARNISH

4 large eggs

¼ cup whole milk

1 tablespoon unsalted butter

Pinch of salt

2 tablespoons chopped cilantro (fresh coriander)

2 tablespoons chopped fresh dill

1. Place the lamb bones in a large pot, cover with the water, and bring to a boil over high heat, skimming the surface of foam as it appears. Boil for 1 hour, then strain, discarding the bones. Set aside 4 cups of the broth.

2. In another pot, melt the butter over medium-high heat, then cook the diced lamb, stirring, until browned, about 7 minutes. Add the radish, onion, and black pepper and cook, stirring, until the onion is softened, about 8 minutes. Add the tomato, garlic, and bay leaf and stir. Add the wine vinegar along with the 4 cups of reserved broth, reduce the heat to medium, and cook until the meat is tender, about 1½ hours. Season with salt.

3. Meanwhile, to prepare the omelet, in a bowl, beat together the eggs and milk. In a large nonstick skillet, melt the butter over medium heat. Add the egg mixture and salt and cook, covered, until the top is dry, then flip with a spatula to cook the other side, about 4 minutes in all. Remove the omelet and cool. (If you think turning such a large omelet may be difficult, make 2 small omelets instead.) Roll the cooled omelet into a large cigar shape and cut into ¼-inch-thick slices.

4. Bring the soup to a boil over high heat. Once it starts bubbling, add the sliced omelet, correct the seasoning, and serve in individual bowls. Sprinkle the top of each soup bowl with the chopped cilantro and dill.

omelet soup

THE NAME OF THIS THAI SOUP is transliterated in various ways, so you might see it as *gaeng jeut kai jiaw* or *kaeng chud* or *kŭaytĭaw* or *gwaytio* on a restaurant menu. Whatever you see, it's a very simple omelet soup that you can make at home in a flash. The Thais consider this a bland, Chinese-style soup. Perhaps compared with some of their incendiary dishes it is bland, but I find it full of flavor. I've adapted the recipe from David Thompson's *Classic Thai Cuisine* (1993). If you decide to double the recipe, then make two omelets rather than one large one. **[Makes 2 to 3 servings]**

2 large eggs
Salt to taste
2 tablespoons vegetable oil
2 large garlic cloves, finely chopped
1 shallot, chopped
2 cups chicken broth
2 tablespoons oyster sauce
1 teaspoon palm sugar or granulated sugar
2 tablespoons cilantro (fresh coriander) leaves, coarsely chopped
½ teaspoon freshly ground white pepper

1. In a bowl, beat the eggs with some salt.

2. In a wok, heat the oil over medium-high heat, then cook the garlic until sizzling vigorously, about 15 seconds. Increase the heat to high. Add the shallot to the wok and cook, stirring, for another 15 seconds. Add the beaten eggs, tilting the wok so they spread a bit. Cook until the edges have set and the center is not loose and somewhat dry, then carefully turn with a spatula so the omelet doesn't break. (If it does break, don't worry). Cook for another minute, then remove and set aside to cool. Roll the omelet into a cigar shape and slice into ¼-inch-thick slices.

3. Pour the chicken broth into the wok and bring to a boil over high heat. Add the oyster sauce and sugar and cook for 1 minute. Add the omelet slices and cook for 30 seconds. Add the cilantro and white pepper and serve.

the best soups in the world

egg-drop soup

I JUST LOVE EGG-DROP SOUP in Chinese restaurants and thought it would be the simplest thing to make at home. Surprise! It's not. Well, I should say that everything is easy until the eggs go in. Your goal is thin, silky ribbons of egg that melt in your mouth. You want to avoid rubbery eggs and globs of congealed egg. The problem is easily solved with two people: one to hold the fork and pour the egg through it, and the other to stir simultaneously. But this recipe assumes you're alone in the kitchen, and it will guide you in appreciating egg-drop soup, a soup whose name is literal. (In Chinese it's called *don tong*). Some people like to add a splash of chile oil at the end, but I don't care to make the soup piquant.

[Makes 4 to 6 servings]

3 large eggs

2 teaspoons water

1 tablespoon cornstarch blended with 3 tablespoons water

6 cups chicken broth

1 tablespoon soy sauce

1 teaspoon rice wine or dry sherry

¾ teaspoon salt or more to taste

½ teaspoon sugar

2 scallions, trimmed and finely chopped

1. In a bowl, beat the eggs lightly with the water, making sure you don't beat so much that bubbles appear. In another bowl, blend the cornstarch and water.

2. In a pot, bring the chicken broth to a boil over medium-high heat, reduce the heat to medium, and stir in the soy sauce, rice wine, salt, and sugar. Stir in the cornstarch mixture and cook, stirring, until the soup thickens and is smooth, about 5 minutes.

3. Turn the heat off, then immediately but slowly pour half the eggs through the tines of a fork held about 5 inches above the soup. When you've poured half the eggs, stir once in one direction with a two-pronged fork or 2 chopsticks held in one hand. Continue pouring the remaining eggs through the tines of the fork. Stir for 1 minute in one direction with the two-pronged fork or chopsticks until the eggs congeal and form ribbons. Add the scallions and serve immediately.

All the soups made with shellfish or fish are found in this chapter except for chowders and bisques, which you'll find on pages 331 to 364. So if it's clam chowder you're looking for, that's on page 338. But here you'll find some favorites, such as the many different Italian *zuppe di pesce* or the memorable Provençal *soupe de poisson.* Here also are amazing if less familiar soups, ranging from a Peruvian seafood soup called *parihuela* to Thai Hot and Sour Shrimp Soup. What's the rarest soup here? Probably the Niger River Fish Soup of the Songhai, which I ate on the banks of the river a few miles from Timbuktu. The tribesmen, believe it or not, told me how to make it, and now I tell you.

seafood
soups

fish tea

THIS SPICY-HOT SOUP FROM Jamaica is called fish tea, a name that reflects British influence. (Any nonalcoholic drink or broth is called tea in Jamaica.) In the south of the country turbot is used, while on the northern shores snapper or parrotfish would be used, producing a thinner broth. The soup could also have pumpkin, okra, or spinners, which are elongated dumplings, added to it.   [**Makes 4 servings**]

One 1½-pound whole fish (such as red snapper, sea bass, or striped bass),
     filleted, fillets cut into 3 pieces each, carcass saved
3 large garlic cloves, lightly crushed
2½ quarts water
1 small ripe plantain, cut into 1-inch slices
1 small sweet potato, left whole
½ green bell pepper, chopped
1 medium onion, chopped
2 scallions, trimmed and chopped
1 small carrot, peeled and sliced ¼ inch thick
1 small chayote, peeled and diced
1 small habanero chile, finely chopped
2 sprigs fresh thyme
¼ teaspoon aniseed
1 tablespoon salt
½ teaspoon freshly ground black pepper

1. Place the carcass of the fish in a large pot with the garlic, cover with the water, and bring to a boil over high heat. Reduce the heat to low and simmer for 1 hour without stirring, replenishing the water with up to a ½ cup if needed.

2. Discard the fish carcass and add the plantain and sweet potato. Cover and cook for 30 minutes, then add the bell pepper, onion, scallions, carrot, chayote, habanero, thyme, and aniseed and cook until the sweet potato is tender, about 1 hour. Remove the sweet potato, peel, mash, and set aside.

3. Increase the heat to high and once it reaches a near boil, reduce the heat to medium and add the fish fillets. Cook, stirring often but gently, until it begins to flake, about 5 minutes. Season with the salt and pepper. Return the mashed sweet potato to the soup, cook for 3 minutes, then serve.

the best soups in the world

niger river fish soup of the songhai

THE SONGHAI, a West African people who live mostly in Mali and Niger, are the prominent ethnicity, along with the Tuareg, around the remote legendary town of Timbuktu. About five miles to the south of Timbuktu is a ferry landing on the banks of the wide Niger River. It was here while waiting for the six-car ferry to arrive from the distant shore that some Songhai men sitting under a tent offered us a fish soup they were making for themselves over an open fire. It was very kind of them, the soup was really delicious, and I decided then to try to replicate it. I didn't get exact translations because of language difficulties, but here goes. The fish was a small river species in the carp family, but I use trout here because it's easy to get. The fish also contained chopped chile leaves or potato leaves, but I've replaced them with parsley. The Songhai flavor their dishes with baobab, chile, peanuts, dried okra, and a mixture called *gebu,* which is a seasoning of onion flour and ground sesame seeds. We ate the soup with Tuareg bread, something like a two-inch-thick Arabic bread.

[**Makes 4 servings**]

One 1-pound trout, gutted and cleaned, head and tail removed and
   saved, cut into 4 pieces
1 cup chopped fresh parsley
3 tablespoons *gebu* spice mix (see Note)
2 teaspoons salt
1 teaspoon freshly ground black pepper
5 cups water
¼ cup peanut oil

1. In a bowl, toss the fish pieces, including the head and tail, with the parsley, *gebu* spice mix, salt, and pepper.

2. In a saucepan, bring the water and peanut oil to a vigorous boil over high heat. Add the fish mixture and cook over high heat until the fish starts to fall off the bone, about 6½ minutes in all. Serve hot.

   Note: To make the spice mix known as *gebu,* mix together 4¼ teaspoons dried onion powder, 4½ teaspoons powdered sesame seeds, and ½ teaspoon ground coriander.

ghana fish soup

FISHERMEN IN GHANA will make a fish soup called *nsaswia* right on the shore where they land their boats. It's a simple soup of cut-up fresh whole fish such as red mullet cooked with lots of scallions and superhot African bird chiles. Usually it is eaten with *kenkey* or *banku*. *Kenkey* is a kind of African tamale made with fermented fine corn meal steamed in a banana leaf, while *banku* is closer to a polenta. This soup is a bit more complex and uses the hot sauce known as *kpakpo shito* in the Ga language of Ghana. If you use three different types of fish for this soup it will taste more interesting. The red palm oil is a necessary ingredient for achieving an authentic African taste. It, as well as the dried crayfish, can be ordered on the Internet at www.jbafricanmarket.com or www.asiamex.com (click on "Nigeria"). Powdered dried shrimp can also be found in supermarkets in the Latino foods aisle. You will have more hot sauce than you need for this recipe, but it can be refrigerated for two weeks and is very nice with some grilled pork chops or beef steaks. I would serve the soup with cut-up pieces of flatbread. [**Makes 4 servings**]

FOR THE HOT SAUCE

2 medium tomatoes, peeled and chopped

1 medium onion, chopped

14 fresh or pickled red and/or yellow chiles

½ teaspoon salt

FOR THE SOUP

4 small mixed fish pieces or steaks (about 1 pound), such as sea bass, black cod, or blue mackerel

Juice from 1 lime

1 large garlic clove, very finely chopped

1 teaspoon ground ginger

½ teaspoon salt to taste

½ cup red palm oil or walnut oil mixed with ½ teaspoon paprika

4 medium onions, 2 ground in a food processor and 2 thinly sliced

4 fresh red chiles (any kind), seeded and finely chopped

1 teaspoon tomato paste

4 ripe fresh tomatoes (1 pound), peeled (page 273), seeded, and ground in a food processor or 3 cups crushed canned tomatoes

2 teaspoons powdered dried crayfish or shrimp

1½ cups water

1. To make the hot sauce, place the tomatoes, onion, chiles, and salt in a blender and blend for 30 seconds. Pour the mixture into a bowl and set aside for 15 minutes before using.

2. To make the soup, rinse the fish steaks. Lay them in a ceramic or glass pan and sprinkle the lime juice over them. Sprinkle the fish with the garlic, ginger, and salt and set aside in the refrigerator until needed.

3. In a large pot, heat the red palm oil over medium-high heat, then add the ground onions, chiles, and tomato paste and cook, stirring, until softened, 4 to 5 minutes. Add the tomatoes and powdered dried crayfish or shrimp, reduce the heat to medium-low, and simmer, stirring, until soupy, about 15 minutes.

4. Add the water, increase the heat to high, and boil for 5 minutes. Add the fish, sliced onions, and 2 tablespoons of the hot sauce and turn the fish several times to coat. Reduce the heat to low and simmer gently until the fish is cooked and beginning to flake, about 15 minutes. Serve hot.

kainuu fish soup

THIS FRESHWATER FISH SOUP called *kainuulainen kalakeitto* is from Kainuu, a region of central Finland bordering Russia to the east. Kainuu is filled with many lakes and is a popular destination for hikers and fishermen. Although any mixture will do, the Finnish cook would typically use freshly caught salmon, perch, pike, or whitefish. The soup is at its best when eaten with fresh rye bread. You can also use saltwater fish if you like.   [**Makes 4 servings**]

1 large yellow onion, quartered

6 allspice berries

6 cups water

2 medium potatoes, peeled and diced

1 pound mixed boneless freshwater fish steaks or fillets, cubed

2 teaspoons salt

¼ cup chopped fresh dill

¼ cup finely chopped fresh parsley

2 tablespoons melted butter

1 medium red onion, finely chopped

1. Place the yellow onion and allspice berries in a pot and cover with the water. Bring to a boil over high heat and boil until reduced to about 4 cups, about 18 minutes. Remove and discard the onion and allspice.

2. Bring the broth back to a boil, then add the potatoes and cook at a boil until almost tender, about 10 minutes. Add the fish and cook until it flakes, about 6 minutes. Season with the salt. Add the dill and parsley, stir, then serve with melted butter and raw onions at the table.

zuppa di pesce siracusana

A *ZUPPA DI PESCE* should need no introduction—it's Italian fish soup, literally. But there are hundreds of different ones, each usually associated with a particular town. Syracuse is one of the most beautiful cities in Sicily, and it is home to clear waters and delicious fish dishes, such as this soup. The gastronomy of Syracuse has been notable since ancient times. Even the Greek philosopher Plato weighed in, criticizing the city's culinary excesses. Syracuse was also home to one of the earliest known writers on food, Archestratus, whose only surviving work is a gastronomic poem written about 348 BC called the *Hedypatheia,* which can be translated as "Life of luxury." In the twelfth century, the famed Arab geographer al-Idrisi wrote about the richness of the city's port and markets.

As with all fish stews, the more kinds of fish you use, the better. Choose what is locally obtainable and fresh if the fish I call for are not available. Some possibilities are wolffish (ocean catfish), hake or cod, grouper or red snapper, redfish (ocean perch), monkfish, dogfish, shark, sea bass, halibut, striped bass, dolphinfish (mahimahi), pompano, bluefish, and ocean pout (ling). **[Makes 4 servings]**

2 pounds mixed fish fillets or steaks (see above), cut into large chunks

1 medium-size onion, thinly sliced

1½ stalks celery, finely chopped

1 ripe tomato (about 10 ounces), peeled (page 273), seeded, and chopped

3 tablespoons finely chopped fresh parsley

3 garlic cloves, crushed

1 bay leaf

3 cups water

1 cup dry white wine

6 tablespoons extra-virgin olive oil

Salt and freshly ground black pepper to taste

4 slices toasted or grilled Italian bread

1. Preheat the oven to 350°F.

2. Place the fish, onion, celery, tomato, parsley, garlic, and bay leaf in a large, deep casserole. Add the water, wine, and olive oil, then season with salt and pepper and stir well to mix everything. Bake until the fish is about to flake when tugged with a fork, 45 minutes, and serve with some toasted or grilled bread in each serving bowl.

zuppa di pesce alla catanese

OLIVES, SULTANAS (golden raisins), and capers are an ingredient mix typical of the baroque style of cooking one finds in Catania, Sicily's second biggest city, on the eastern side of the island in the shadow of the active volcano Mount Etna. As is true with any fish stew, the more kinds of fish you can manage to put into it, the more delicious it will be. For the "mixed fish" below, try to use at least three of the following: bluefish, mackerel, Spanish mackerel, king-fish, mahimahi, yellowtail, and shark. If not, use some other types of dark-fleshed fish. Serve with slices of Italian bread fried in olive oil. **[Makes 4 servings]**

¼ cup extra-virgin olive oil
2 large garlic cloves, lightly crushed
2 tablespoons tomato paste
¼ cup golden raisins
¼ cup capers, drained and rinsed
8 imported green olives, pitted and cut in half
¼ cup finely chopped fresh basil
¼ cup finely chopped fresh parsley
2 salted anchovy fillets, rinsed and chopped
Salt and freshly ground black pepper to taste
4½ cups water
1 pound redfish (ocean perch), scorpion fish, sculpin, rockfish, or red snapper
1 pound mixed fish (see headnote)

1. In a large flame-proof casserole (preferably an earthenware one in which case use a heat diffuser), heat the olive oil over medium-high heat. Add the garlic and cook, stirring, until it begins to turn light brown, less than 1 minute. Discard the garlic and reduce the heat to medium. Add the tomato paste, stir it into the olive oil, then add the raisins, capers, olives, basil, parsley, anchovy fillets, salt, and pepper, then ½ cup water, and cook until the liquid is reduced by half or a little more, about 10 minutes.

2. Add the fish, cover with the remaining 4 cups of water, and increase the heat to high. Cover and cook until the more delicate fish begin to break up, about 12 minutes. Serve immediately.

zuppa di pesce dalle isole eolie lipari

THE AEOLIANS ARE AN ARCHIPELAGO of volcanic islands off the north coast of Sicily and a popular summer destination for Italians and other Europeans. Lipari, the largest of the islands, although still small, is the one that most people visit. I arrived in the early 1980s with my then wife and remember it well, because we had chosen to visit during the hottest summer in a hundred years. The food of the island is simple, as we can see from this fish soup, almost more a stew than a soup. The wine is the cook's choice. I've heard Sicilians say never and I've heard others say always. So I use a little in this recipe to thin the broth. The chile was not in the original dish that I had in Lipari, but I like it in moderation.   **[Makes 4 servings]**

1½ pounds boneless mixed fish cubes (at least 4 kinds of fish, such as swordfish, mahimahi, yellowtail, halibut, cod, monkfish, sea bass, striped bass)
½ cup (8 tablespoons) extra-virgin olive oil
1 cup dry white wine
4 large garlic cloves
One 28-ounce can diced San Marzano plum tomatoes
½ cup water
¼ teaspoon red chile flakes
Salt and freshly ground pepper to taste
¼ cup chopped fresh parsley

1. In a ceramic or glass bowl, toss the fish with 3 tablespoons of the olive oil, ¼ cup of the wine, and 1 chopped garlic clove and marinate in the refrigerator for 1 to 3 hours.

2. In a pot, heat the remaining 5 tablespoons of olive oil over medium-high heat with the garlic until sizzling. Add ½ cup of the wine and the tomatoes and cook until the wine is reduced somewhat, about 10 minutes. Add the remaining ¼ cup wine, the water, chile flakes, salt, and pepper and bring to a boil over high heat. Add the marinating fish and its marinade and cook until the fish can be pulled apart with a fork, about 8 minutes. Add the parsley, stir, and serve.

dubrovnik fish soup

THE PROXIMITY OF THE ITALIAN PENINSULA and the naval dominance of the Venetian Republic during the Middle Ages resulted in a perceptible Italian culinary influence along the Dalmatian coast, where fish soups are called *brodet* in Serbo-Croatian, from the Italian *brodetto*. But this recipe came to me by way of someone calling it *čorba* in Serbo-Croatian, deriving not from the Italian, but from the Turkish and Arabic words for "soup." It's a simple fish boil called *riblja čorba na Dubrovački način,* a soup from Dubrovnik that will be success-ful if you have a good mix of fish—at least four kinds—and a whole fish from which to make the broth. A good mix would be a whole striped bass, a whole porgy (scup), and fillets from bluefish, cod, and salmon. You can ask the fishmonger to fillet the whole fish for you, keeping the heads, tails, and carcass for the broth. **[Makes 4 servings]**

3½ pounds mixed fish steaks, pieces, heads, and carcasses (see headnote),
    including whole fish, cut-up

12 cups water

Sea salt to taste

1 cup dry white wine

1 large ripe tomato (about ½ pound), peeled (page 273), seeded,
    and chopped

¼ cup finely chopped fresh parsley

¼ cup extra-virgin olive oil

10 black peppercorns

1 bay leaf

½ cup medium grain rice

1. Place the fish heads, tails, and carcasses (1 to 1½ pounds altogether) in a large pot and cover with 6 cups of the water. Bring to a boil over high heat, reduce the heat to medium, and simmer for 1 hour. Strain the fish broth through a cheesecloth-lined strainer and set aside. You should have about 1 quart of fish broth.

2. Pour the remaining 6 cups of water into a large pot and season with sea salt. Add the wine, tomato, parsley, oil, peppercorns, and bay leaf and bring to a rolling boil. Add the fish pieces to the boiling broth one at a time and boil furiously for 8 to 10 minutes.

3. Meanwhile, bring the reserved fish broth to a boil in a medium-size saucepan, add the rice, and cook until almost tender (times vary, so keep checking). Turn the heat off.

4. Put about 2 or 3 tablespoons of the cooked rice in each individual serving bowl using a slotted ladle. Ladle the fish with broth over the rice and serve.

fish soup from the island of simi

THEO TSAKKIS AND HIS WIFE CONSTANCE own the Nireas Restaurant in the walled old town of Rhodes, on the island of the same name in the Aegean Sea. They took over the restaurant from Theo's parents some years ago, but it was when Theo's mom was in the kitchen that I learned how to make this extraordinary fish soup called *psarosoupa,* which only means "fish soup." It is sometimes called *kakavia* and is a dish Greeks like to call their bouillabaisse, even though it is quite different than the French fish stew. This method of making fish soup is typical of Simi, one of the Dodecanese islands north of Rhodes, very near the Turkish coast, whence the Tsakkis family migrated some years ago.

The first thing one noticed in the Nireases' kitchen is that the fish were extremely fresh—some still moving. Three kinds of fish—red gurnard, porgy, and red mullet—were cooked in water with diced potato, chopped onions, celery, garlic, salt, and pepper. Once the fish were cooked they were removed from the broth and set aside. The broth was boiled for several minutes with some rice, then egg whites were beaten with lemon juice and stirred into the broth for a few seconds. Normally egg yolks are used, but here it was the whites, which made the whole preparation lighter.

the best soups in the world

I learned much about the cooking of the islands of Simi and Rhodes from Theo and Constance, who are food enthusiasts, preservers of culinary tradition, and owners of one of very few authentic Rhodiot restaurants in the old town (the rest serve typical Greek tourist food). **[Makes 4 servings]**

1 pound boiling potatoes (such as Yukon Gold), peeled and cut up

1 medium onion, quartered and separated

2 celery stalks, quartered

½ cup extra-virgin olive oil

6 large garlic cloves, crushed

Salt and freshly ground black pepper to taste

3 quarts cold water

2 whole porgies (scup), sea bass, or striped bass (about 2 pounds in all),
   scaled, gutted, and cleaned

½ pound red snapper, red mullet, or fresh sardines (about 3 red mullet,
   1 red snapper, or 4 sardines), scaled, gutted, and cleaned

¾ pound haddock, halibut, sea bass, or cod fillet

½ cup long grain rice

3 large egg whites

Juice from 1 lemon

1. Put the potatoes, onion, celery, olive oil, garlic, and salt and pepper in a large pot and cover with the water. Bring to a boil, reduce the heat so the boil is gentle, and cook for 1 hour. Check the seasoning.

2. Bring the soup to a furious boil again and add the porgies. After 2 to 3 minutes, add the remaining fish and cook at a full boil, removing the fish with a spatula before they break up, 6 to 8 minutes. Reduce the heat of the soup to a gentle boil. The whole fish can be served as is, or you can fillet them by carefully pushing the meat off the bones. Set the fish aside and keep warm.

3. Boil the broth for another 2 minutes. Add the rice and cook until softened, 10 to 12 minutes. Beat the egg whites with the lemon juice. Add a little of the broth to the egg white mixture, continue beating, and then add to the broth in the pot and cook for 2 minutes, stirring once or twice.

4. Ladle the broth with some of the rice into each soup bowl, without the potatoes, celery, and onion, and serve the fish separately, or let each diner put his or her own mixture of fish into the bowl. Save the remaining broth with its vegetables and process into a purée to use as the base for a creamy soup.

seafood soups

arab gulf fish soup

THIS SAVORY FISH SOUP called *shūrbat al-samak* (fish soup) is popular along the Arabian side of the Persian Gulf (called the Arabian Gulf by Arabs). It is seasoned with a spice blend known as *kabsa,* which also gives its name to a famous dish of Saudi Arabia, *kabsa bi'l-dajāj,* a chicken, rice, and nut dish spiced with *kabsa.* The *kabsa* mix is described in the note below; you can use the excess spice to season some chicken for baking. The soup is also seasoned with the dried limes known as *loomi* (*lūmī*), popular in the cooking of Iran, Iraq, and the Persian Gulf states. They give prepared dishes a delightful tang and are available through www.daynasmarket.com. Aleppo pepper is available at www.penzeys.com and many Middle Eastern markets. The shrimp of the Gulf are famous, and before oil (the black kind) was discovered, the shrimpers and pearl divers of the Gulf drove the economies of the small, then-poor sheikdoms.   [**Makes 4 servings**]

the best soups in the world

3 tablespoons extra-virgin olive oil

6 tablespoons finely chopped onions

½ teaspoon Aleppo pepper

5 large garlic cloves, finely chopped

1 large ripe tomato, peeled (page 273), seeded, and chopped

Pinch of saffron, crumbled

1 dried lime (*loomi* or *lūmī*) or 1 small fresh lime left in a 200°F oven for 3 hours

1 teaspoon *kabsa* spice mix (see Note)

6 cups fish broth

1 tablespoon tomato paste

¼ pound large shrimp, shelled

½ pound red snapper or sole fillet, cut in half

2 tablespoons finely chopped cilantro (fresh coriander)

1. In a pot, heat the olive oil over medium-high heat, then cook the onions, stirring, until translucent, about 2 minutes.

2. Add the Aleppo pepper, garlic, tomato, saffron, *loomi,* and *kabsa* mix and cook, stirring, for 1 minute. Add the fish broth and tomato paste and bring to a boil over high heat. Add the shrimp and fish, reduce the heat to low, and cook until the shrimp are firm and orange-red and the fish is ready to flake, about 5 minutes. Correct the seasoning and serve with a sprinkle of cilantro.

Note: To make the *kabsa* spice mix, blend together 1½ teaspoons cayenne pepper, ¾ teaspoon ground cumin, ¾ teaspoon ground cinnamon, ½ teaspoon ground cloves, ½ teaspoon black pepper, ½ teaspoon ground cardamom, ½ teaspoon ground nutmeg, ½ teaspoon ground coriander, and, optionally, ½ teaspoon ground dried lime (*loomi*) or fresh and very finely chopped lime zest.

seafood soups

algerian fish and barley soup

IN ALGERIA THERE IS A UNIQUE FISH SOUP called *shūrbat al-hūt* (fish soup) made with barley that is traditionally served during the month of Ramadan after the sun has set. It is a quite popular soup. Some favorite fish of the Algerians are grouper, bream, dogfish, skate, monkfish, and sea bass. Of course, the more kinds of fish you use, the better.

[Makes 6 to 8 servings]

1 pound ripe tomatoes, cut in half, seeds squeezed out, and grated against the largest holes of a standing grater down to the peel

1 medium onion, finely chopped

1 medium boiling potato (such as Yukon Gold), peeled and diced

2 medium carrots, peeled and diced

2 small leeks, white and light green parts only, split lengthwise, washed well, and chopped

1 stalk celery, chopped

5 large garlic cloves, finely chopped

1 bouquet garni, tied together in cheesecloth, consisting of 1 small bunch fresh parsley, 1 small bunch cilantro (fresh coriander), 1 sprig fresh thyme, and 2 bay leaves

2 quarts water

Salt to taste

2 pounds mixed fish steaks, such as red snapper, sea bass, grouper, and mackerel, cut up into 2-inch pieces

½ pound (1 cup) pearl barley

¼ cup extra-virgin olive oil

1 tablespoon cayenne pepper

1 tablespoon tomato paste mixed with ½ cup water

1 tablespoon *harīsa* (page 62)

¼ teaspoon ground cumin seed

1 teaspoon freshly ground black pepper

½ teaspoon (2 pinches) saffron threads, crumbled

¼ teaspoon dried mint

1. In a large pot, add the tomatoes, onion, potato, carrots, leeks, celery, garlic, and bouquet garni, then pour in 1 quart of the water. Bring to a boil over high heat, then reduce the heat to medium and cook until the vegetables are softened, about 30 minutes. Pass the vegetables through a food mill and return them to the pot, discarding the bouquet garni, or process in a blender.

2. In another pot, bring the remaining 1 quart water, lightly salted, to a boil and add the fish. Reduce the heat to medium, cook for 4 minutes, then remove the fish with a skimmer and set aside, saving the fish broth.

3. Add the fish broth to the vegetable broth along with the barley, olive oil, cayenne, tomato paste mixture, *harīsa,* cumin, black pepper, saffron, and mint. Bring to a boil over high heat, then reduce to medium and simmer until the barley is tender, about 1 hour. Add hot water to the soup in ½-cup increments if it is becoming too thick. If the barley takes longer than an hour to cook, continue adding hot water to keep it soupy.

4. Meanwhile, remove the skin and bones from the fish, if any. Once the barley is tender, return the fish to the broth and cook until the fish begins to flake, about 5 minutes. Serve immediately.

seafood soups

VIETNAMESE HOT SAUCE

This condiment, called *nouc cham*, is put in soups and on vegetables, meats, and fish. Store in the refrigerator. **[Makes about ⅓ cup]**

1 large garlic clove, finely chopped

1 teaspoon finely chopped lime zest

¼ teaspoon red chile flakes, or more if desired

3 tablespoons water

2 tablespoons fish sauce (*nuoc mam* or Thai fish sauce)

2 teaspoons lime juice

2 teaspoons sugar

In a small bowl combine the garlic, lime zest, and chile flakes. Stir in the water, fish sauce, lime juice, and sugar. Whisk until well blended and the sugar is dissolved.

the best soups in the world

vietnamese fish and dill soup

THE VIETNAMESE HAVE DIFFERENT CLASSES OF SOUPS—some for breakfast, some for before a meal, some for snacks. Those soups known as *canh* are light and usually served as a first course. Diners spoon it out of a big bowl into smaller individual bowls and eat with rice on the side. This *canh* is quite fragrant, delicious, and light—perfect before something more substantial (although of course you are not required to follow it up in this way). The soup can be garnished with dill sprigs, fish sauce (*nuoc mam*), or a hot Vietnamese chile and garlic sauce available in a Vietnamese market, although it's extremely easy to make your own (see box). **[Makes 4 to 6 servings]**

1 tablespoon peanut oil

1 pound catfish, red snapper, perch, or redfish fillets, cut into 1½-inch squares

3 tomatoes, peeled and cut into eighths

1 medium onion, cut into eighths

2 tablespoons fish sauce (*nuoc mam* or Thai fish sauce)

2 quarts water

2 celery stalks, finely julienned into matchsticks

2 tablespoons finely chopped fresh dill

1 teaspoon freshly ground black pepper

4 to 6 fresh dill sprigs

Vietnamese Hot Sauce (optional, page 398)

1. In a large pot, heat the peanut oil over medium-high heat, then add the fish and cook, stirring immediately and then constantly, until it turns white on all sides, 2 minutes. Add the tomatoes, onion, and fish sauce, reduce the heat to low and simmer, stirring occasionally, for 5 minutes. Pour in the water and bring to a near boil over high heat. Reduce the heat to low and simmer until the onions are softened and the fish cooked, about 8 minutes.

2. Stir in the celery, dill, and black pepper. Cook for 1 minute, then ladle into one big bowl or individual bowls. Garnish each with a dill sprig and serve with fish sauce and Vietnamese Hot Sauce, if desired, on the side.

seaweed soup with egg and dried anchovies

I FOUND THIS MALAYSIAN-CHINESE SOUP so intruiging when I stumbled across it on a blog called Little Corner of Mine by Ching, a mother of two young children living in Colorado Springs, Colorado. It's obviously an overwhelmed-mom-friendly kind of recipe, but at the same time has very appealing tastes for adults. If you expect your children to eat this soup, do as Ching does by starting them very early. Ching says she makes it for her husband and kids because "it's delicious and the seaweed is nutritious." You can probably find the dried seaweed in the international aisle of your supermarket, and maybe the dried anchovies, too, but if not, you can certainly order them from either www.asianmerchant.com or www.templeofthai.com. Ching also uses Swanson's chicken broth and makes it with meatballs instead of the dried anchovies. **[Makes 2 to 4 servings]**

4 cups water

¼ cup (about ½ ounce) dried anchovies

1 teaspoon chicken bouillon granules or 1 teaspoon chicken base paste
     or 1 chicken bouillon cube

3½ × 2 × ¼-inch stack dried seaweed, separated, or 2 large dried
     seaweed sheets (nori)

1 large egg, beaten

½ teaspoon salt or more to taste

In a pot, bring the water to a boil over high heat, then add the anchovies and chicken bouillon granules and stir until the granules are completely dissolved. Add the seaweed and stir to break it up, cooking for 1 minute. Add the egg and stir in a figure-8 pattern until the egg is solid, like egg-drop soup, about 1 minute. Taste the soup, season with salt, and serve hot.

korean piquant fish soup

THIS RECIPE, CALLED *MAEUN-TANG,* is a hot spicy fish soup boiled with lots of *koch'ujang* (Korean chile paste), *koch'ukaru* (Korean chile powder), and various vegetables. As its main in-gredient, fresh- or seawater fish is cut into several pieces and boiled, in one of its variations, with ground beef and green vegetables, such as watercress, as well as garland chrysanthemum. In other variations cooks might add onion, radish, chile, crown daisy, garlic, and sometimes pumpkin and bean curd. The soup is also seasoned with garlic and soy sauce. Although you could use chicken or fish broth as a foundation, I use water and I still get a magnificent soup. Both the Korean chile paste and the powdered chile can be ordered from www.kgrocer.com or www.ikoreaplaza.com. Popular fish for this dish include red snapper, sea bass, yellow corvina, codfish, croaker, pollack, and even freshwater fish like carp and trout. A whole fish of about 1¼ pounds is ideal. I've used blue mackerel and black cod, which made an excellent soup. In addition, shellfish such as crabs, clams, and oysters can be added to provide a bit of sweet-ness and a nice counterpoint to all the piquancy. Serve with steamed rice if desired.

[Makes 5 servings]

seafood soups

6 cups water

6 tablespoons Korean chile paste (*koch'ujang*)

2 tablespoons Korean chile powder (*koch'ukaru*)

1 tablespoon soy sauce

½ cup thinly sliced daikon (white radish)

½ yellow summer squash, thinly sliced (1 cup)

3 green finger-type chiles or green jalapeño chiles, cut on the bias and seeded

2 whole fish (about 2 pounds in all), such as red snapper, corvina, porgy, or blue
   mackerel, heads and tails removed and saved for making fish broth, fish scaled,
   gutted, and cut into 1-inch steaks

12 littleneck clams

4 large garlic cloves, finely chopped

3 scallions, cut on the bias

5 fresh parsley sprigs, leaves only

1 tablespoon salt

In a large pot, bring the water to a boil over high heat. Add the Korean chile paste, Korean chile powder, and soy sauce and let the water return to a boil. Add the rad-ish, yellow squash, and half the chiles, reduce the heat to medium, and cook for 4 minutes. Add the fish, clams, and garlic and cook until the fish begins to flake and the clams open, about 8 minutes. Add the remaining chiles, the scallions, parsley, and salt and cook for another 2 minutes. Serve hot.

alexandre dumas' shrimp and tomato soup

ALEXANDRE DUMAS THE ELDER (1802–1870) is best known as the author of *The Three Musketeers* and *The Count of Monte Cristo,* but he himself believed he would be remembered for his *Grand dictionnaire de cuisine* (*Great Dictionary of Cuisine*), an ABC of culinary matters and recipe descriptions. This recipe appealed to me because of his introduction to it. I'll let Dumas speak for himself: "I love the sea. It is essential not only to our pleasure but to our very basic happiness. When I have not seen it for a long time I am seized with an irresistible longing, and on any convenient pretext I take the train to Trouville, Dieppe, Le Havre. This time I went to Fécamp. I had no sooner arrived than I was invited on a fishing party. I know these fishing parties. You don't catch anything, but on the way home you buy a fish for dinner."

This time he bought shrimp and made this *potage à la tomate et aux queues de crevettes* as part of a multicourse dinner he prepared, including lobster *à l'amércaine.* The soup is best served with a crunchy French baguette on the side.   [**Makes 6 servings**]

the best soups in the world

Salt

8 cups water

2 slices lemon

2 bouquets garni, wrapped in cheesecloth, consisting of several fresh
   sprigs each parsley, basil, thyme, and tarragon, and 1 bay leaf

½ pound large shrimp (about 24)

¼ cup (½ stick) unsalted butter

3½ pounds ripe tomatoes, cut in half, seeds squeezed out, and grated
   against the largest holes of a standing grater down to the peel

3 medium onions, thinly sliced

1 large garlic clove, finely chopped

1 teaspoon beef glaze (beef base)

½ teaspoon freshly ground black pepper

2 cups beef broth

1. In a large pot, salt the water and bring it to a boil with the lemon and 1 bouquet garni over high heat. Add the shrimp and boil for 2 minutes, then remove the shrimp, shell them (if not shelled already) and set aside. Discard the lemon slices and bouquet garni but save the cooking water.

2. In another pot, melt the butter over medium heat, then add the tomatoes, onions, garlic, and remaining bouquet garni and cook, stirring, until the liquid has evaporated a bit and the onions are softened, about 15 minutes. Pass this mixture through a food mill or purée in a blender, then return to a clean pot.

3. Add the beef base (glaze) and pepper and return to medium heat. Cook, stirring occasionally, until it is thick and dense, about 12 minutes. Add the beef broth and ½ cup of the reserved shrimp cooking water. Bring to a boil over high heat, add the shrimp, immediately turn the heat off, let sit 1 minute, and serve.

soupe de poisson

THIS IS THE FAMOUS FISH SOUP OF PROVENCE, and the original behind bouillabaisse. Soup fish, that is, those that disappear into a broth and are not actually eaten in any identifiable form, were used exclusively for the fish soups that are today found all along the small ports of Languedoc and Provence. This recipe is typical of Marseilles. In restaurants, *soupe de poisson* is ubiquitous, and some restaurant chefs use a *chinoise,* a small green orange preserved in brandy, to flavor the broth.

As with all fish soups and stews, a proper *soupe de poisson* requires a good mix of fish, such as a 1½-pound striped bass, a 1½-pound redfish, a small mackerel, and a few pieces of eel without the skin. In any case, there should be a minimum of four fish, preferably with heads (they provide so much flavor), and at least one of the fish should be an oily variety such as eel, bluefish, striped bass, kingfish, yellowtail, Spanish mackerel, blue mackerel, or mackerel. Ideally, since the fish are used for flavoring the broth and not eaten individually, you can get fish carcasses and heads from your fishmonger. **[Makes 4 to 6 servings]**

¼ cup extra-virgin olive oil

1 large onion, finely chopped

2 leeks, white part only, split lengthwise, washed well, and finely chopped

1 small fennel bulb and stalks, finely chopped

2½ quarts cold water

3 to 4 pounds whole fish (choose 4 from those mentioned above),
   cleaned and each cut into 3 pieces

1 pound ripe tomatoes, peeled (page 273), seeded, and finely chopped

1 tablespoon tomato paste

3 garlic cloves, finely chopped

Bouquet garni, tied in cheesecloth, consisting of 12 sprigs each fresh parsley
   and thyme and 1 bay leaf

½ teaspoon cayenne pepper

Pinch of saffron threads, crumbled

Salt and freshly ground black pepper to taste

1 teaspoon freshly grated orange zest or one 10-inch-long strip orange zest

1 teaspoon brandy or cognac

3 ounces vermicelli, broken in 3 pieces

¼ recipe Sauce Rouille et Croûtes (page 406)

¼ pound Gruyère cheese, freshly grated

1. In a large, deep, flame-proof casserole or earthenware soup pot, heat the olive oil over medium-high heat, then add the onion, leeks, and fennel and cook, stirring occasionally, until wilted, about 6 minutes. Add the water, fish, tomatoes, tomato paste, garlic, bouquet garni, cayenne, and saffron, season with salt and black pepper, and stir again. Bring to a boil and let boil for 45 minutes. Add the orange zest and brandy and boil for another 8 minutes; the fish will have disintegrated at this point.

2. Remove from the heat and pass the broth through a food mill, discarding all the vegetables and fish that do not pass through on the first several turns of the food mill, or process in a blender.

3. Meanwhile, bring a large pot of water to a rolling boil, salt abundantly, and add the vermicelli. Cook until very al dente and drain.

4. Return the fish soup to the casserole, bring to a gentle boil, add the vermicelli, and cook for 5 minutes. Ladle into individual serving bowls with a heaping tablespoon of *sauce rouille* and 1 or 2 croûtes, if desired. Serve with the grated cheese. Refrigerate any leftover *sauce rouille*.

Note: Normally the cook chooses either the vermicelli or the bread as the garnish, but I like them both.

seafood soups

SAUCE ROUILLE ET CROÛTES

This is a recipe for the famous Provençal saffron- and garlic-flavored mayonnaise and fried bread, traditionally used for *soupe de poisson* and bouillabaisse. But I think it's just great with everything. Some recipes suggest adding tomato paste for coloring, but I don't find this necessary because of the saffron and cayenne.

[Makes 1¼ cups sauce and 10 servings of *croûtes*]

1½ cups diced French bread, white part only
½ cup fish broth
4 to 6 large garlic cloves, to your taste
1 teaspoon salt
1 large egg yolk
½ teaspoon cayenne pepper
Pinch of saffron threads, crumbled
Freshly ground black pepper to taste
1¼ cups extra-virgin olive oil
5 tablespoons unsalted butter
40 to 50 slices French baguette bread (about 1 loaf)

1. Soak the diced bread in the fish broth. Squeeze the broth out. Mash all but 1 of the garlic cloves in a mortar with the salt until mushy. Place the bread, mashed garlic, egg yolk, cayenne, saffron, and black pepper in a food processor and blend for 30 seconds. Slowly pour 1 cup of the olive oil through the feed tube in a slow, thin, steady stream while the machine is running. Refrigerate for 1 hour before serving. Store whatever you don't use in the refrigerator for up to 1 week.

2. Meanwhile, prepare the *croûtes*. Crush the remaining garlic clove with the side of a knife. In a large skillet, melt the butter with the remaining ¼ cup olive oil and the crushed garlic over medium heat until the garlic begins to turn light brown. Remove and discard the garlic.

3. Lightly brush both sides of each bread slice with the melted butter and oil and set aside. When all the slices are brushed, place them back in the skillet and cook until they are a very light brown on both sides. Set aside until needed.

Variation: Another way to make the *croûtes* is to toast them first and then rub both sides with a cut piece of garlic.

Note: If the *rouille* is separating, add 2 to 3 tablespoons of the fish broth and whisk it in until smooth and re-emulsified.

the best soups in the world

AJÍ PANCA EN PASTA

Ají panca is the name of a mild Peruvian chile that is nearly purple in color when ripe, the time that it is picked and sun-dried. *Ají panca en pasta* is a Peruvian paste or *harīsa* (page 62) made with this particular chile and used as a condiment in cooking. It is made by soaking the dried chiles in water and then blending them into a paste. For Internet sources try www.penderys.com and www.worldspice.com. I make some suggestions for substitutes below.

[Makes about ½ cup]

5 dried *ají panca* chiles or a combination of 1 dried pasilla chile, 2 dried *guajillo* chiles, and 4 dried red *de arbol* chiles
1 fresh *ají panca* chile or fresh red jalapeño chile
¼ teaspoon freshly ground cumin seeds
¼ teaspoon salt
1½ teaspoons safflower oil

In a bowl, soak the dried chiles in warm water to cover until very soft, 3 to 5 hours. Remove, scrape out the seeds, and place in a food processor with the fresh chiles, cumin, salt, and safflower oil. Purée until smooth, about 2 minutes. Transfer to a jar or container and refrigerate until needed.

parihuela

IT'S A MYSTERY why this soup is not better known. It is, very simply, one of the world's great seafood soups. I would not call it a chowder or a gumbo; it's a soup. And although there might a temptation to call it a Peruvian bouillabaisse, that would be accurate only insofar as this and the French dish are both magnificent; their ingredients are entirely different. The South American chiles called for here have a floral bouquet, even in their dried state, that lends a unique flavor to the soup, which you might not be able to create with the typical Mexican-type chiles found in our supermarkets. Here are Internet sources for them: try www.penderys.com and www.worldspice.com. This recipe is derived from the *parihuela* served by Isabel Quispe Aquino, who has a stall called Cevichería Restaurante Isabel in the market at Chorrillos, a seaside district of Lima. Her *parihuela* is often called the best there is.

[**Makes 6 servings**]

3 pounds fish head and carcass (preferably) or ¾ pound chowder fish scraps

10 cups water

4 teaspoons salt and more as needed

16 mussels

8 littleneck clams, washed well

½ cup vegetable oil

2 medium onions, chopped

4 large garlic cloves, crushed

3 tomatoes (about 1 pound), peeled, seeded, and chopped

2 tablespoons hot paprika

1 tablespoon *ají panca en pasta* (sun-dried red chile paste) (page 407)

3 dried *ají mirasol* (sun-dried yellow chiles) or whole dried
    red chiles (see headnote)

1 teaspoon fresh oregano or ½ teaspoon dried

Freshly ground black pepper to taste

1 bay leaf

¾ cup dry white wine

2 tablespoons soy sauce

2 tablespoons chopped cilantro (fresh coriander)

2 tablespoons finely chopped fresh parsley

6 small fish fillets (about 1½ pounds), such as red snapper, flounder,
    fluke, or sole

10 ounces medium shrimp, shelled

10 ounces squid, cleaned, skin removed, and cut in rings, with tentacles

8 sea scallops

10 ounces shelled and cooked lobster meat, crayfish meat, or crab meat

Juice from ½ Key lime or ¼ regular lime

2 scallions, chopped for garnish

1. In a large pot, cover the fish head and carcass with the water and 3 teaspoons of the salt, bring to a boil over high heat, then boil furiously for 20 minutes. Add the mussels and clams and boil until they open, 5 to 10 minutes. Remove the mussels and clams and set aside. Turn the heat off, strain the broth through a strainer, and reserve the broth.

2. In another pot, heat the oil over medium-high heat, then add the onions and garlic and cook, stirring, until translucent, about 5 minutes. Add the tomatoes, paprika, *ají panca,* whole dried chiles, oregano, pepper, and bay leaf and cook, stirring, for 4 minutes. Reduce the heat to low and cook, stirring occasionally, for 5 minutes. Add the reserved fish broth, the wine, soy sauce, cilantro, and parsley and stir. Check the seasoning and add 1 teaspoon salt unless already salty enough. Add the fish fillets, shrimp, squid, scallops, and cooked mussels and clams, bring to a boil over high heat, then boil until the fish is about to fall apart, about 5 minutes; 1 minute before the fish look like they're going to fall apart, add the lobster meat. Serve immediately with a few drops of Key lime juice and the scallions.

sweet pepper and fish soup from almería

ONE TRAVEL WRITER described the city of Almería in Andalusia, where this fish soup called *caldo con pimientos de Almería* originated, as the "most African of Spanish towns." He referred, of course, to North Africa and its Muslim sensibilities, which we see reflected today especially in Almería's architecture. This fish soup has at its base *salsa de patatas,* potato sauce. *Mero* (grouper) is very popular along the coast, as popular as mutton is in the hills. A local proverb goes, "among the meats, mutton, among the fish, grouper." If grouper is unavailable, you can use halibut, sea bass, or red snapper in this stew. Traditionally, the fish would be served separately from the broth as a second course. **[Makes 4 servings]**

2 large red bell peppers

5 cups cold water

1 tablespoon salt

1 boiling potato (about ½ pound), peeled and cubed

½ pound grouper, halibut, sea bass, red snapper, or redfish (ocean perch) fillets or
    steaks without bones

1 teaspoon cumin seeds

2 large garlic cloves

2 teaspoons hot paprika

Pinch of saffron threads, crumbled

1 medium tomato, peeled (page 273), seeded, and chopped

1 cup beef broth or water

6 tablespoons extra-virgin olive oil

1. Preheat the oven to 425°F.

2. Place the bell peppers in a baking pan or tray and roast until the skins blister black on all sides, about 40 minutes. Remove from the oven and once they are cool enough to handle, remove the skins, stems, and seeds. Slice or chop and set aside.

3. Put the water in a pot with the salt and bring to a boil. Add the potato and boil for 12 minutes. Remove the potato with a slotted spoon and set aside. Add the fish and boil for 2 minutes. Remove the fish with a slotted spoon and set aside. Save the fish-potato broth.

4. In a mortar, pound the cumin seeds with the garlic, paprika, and saffron into a paste. Add the tomato and a few cubes of reserved potato and transfer to a food processor or blender (or continue pounding with a pestle) and process until smooth; while the processor or blender is running or you are pounding, add the beef broth or water. The sauce should be homogenous. Whisk in the olive oil in a slow stream, as if you were making mayonnaise.

5. Return the remaining potato cubes to the reserved fish-potato broth and bring to a boil. Add the red bell peppers and cook for 10 minutes over medium-high heat. Strain this broth through a fine-mesh strainer and pass the vegetables through a food mill back into the broth. Add the reserved fish and the contents of the food processor to the broth and heat gently. Serve hot.

algerian fish soup

THIS SOUP, CALLED *SHŪRBA BAHRĪYA,* is best made with strong fish, the kind you might use if you were making Soupe de Poisson (page 404), this being the Algerian version. When one sees this kind of velouté in Algerian dishes, you can bet it is a French influence. A typical fish for such a soup would be dogfish, a small shark sometimes available in fish stores on the East Coast of the United States. Its Algerian Arabic name is similar—*kalb al-bahr,* or seadog— but, curiously, this shark bears no resemblance to a dog at all. The best fish to use for this soup would be three of the following: dogfish, sardine, Spanish mackerel, blue mackerel, mackerel, mahimahi, yellowtail, grouper, mako shark, swordfish, and, in a pinch, salmon.

The cubeb pepper (*Piper cubeba* L.) called for in the ingredient list is a pungent and bitter spice made from the dried berries of a tropical vine. In the Middle Ages, cubeb pepper from southern West Africa was traded to Europe as an ersatz black pepper when the real thing was scarce. If you are interested in trying this spice, a small quantity can be ordered from www.adrianascaravan.com. Using a food mill, as called for here, is much easier than pushing the fish through a strainer, so consider a purchase if you don't already have one.

[**Makes 4 servings**]

1 pound fish steaks (3 kinds, see headnote)

4 ripe tomatoes (about 2 pounds), peeled (page 273) and cut in half

1 medium onion, chopped

2 celery stalks, chopped

Bouquet garni, tied with kitchen twine, consisting of 10 sprigs cilantro and
    10 sprigs fresh parsley

2 teaspoons salt and more to taste

4 cups water

3 tablespoons extra-virgin olive oil

1 tablespoon tomato paste

1 teaspoon freshly ground black pepper and more to taste

¼ teaspoon cubeb pepper (optional)

3 ounces vermicelli, broken into 1-inch lengths (yielding 1 cup broken)

1. In a large pot, add the fish, tomatoes, onion, celery, bouquet garni, and 2 teaspoons salt. Cover with the water. Bring to a boil over high heat and boil, stirring occasionally, until the fish flakes, 8 to 10 minutes. Pour the contents of the pot into a colander or strainer set over another pot or deep bowl. Remove and discard the bouquet garni and any fish bones.

2. Pass the fish and the contents of the pot through a food mill twice and discard any solid matter that does not pass through, or process in a blender. Return the fish purée to a clean pot. Add the olive oil, tomato paste, black pepper, and cubeb pepper, if using, and bring to a boil over high heat. Add the pasta and boil until tender, 8 to 9 minutes. Season with salt and pepper, if necessary, and serve hot.

seafood soups

sopa leão velloso

THERE ARE BARS IN RIO DE JANEIRO that specialize in this rich and spicy seafood soup typically made with whole grouper and shellfish. One normally makes the broth with the head of the grouper, but as whole grouper are so hard to find outside of Florida I've adapted this recipe so that you can make the soup without the whole fish. The taste will still be true to the original. This recipe is adapted from Margarette de Andrade's *Brazilian Cookery: Traditional and Modern*. Skip Step 1 if you're not using a whole fish. **[Makes 4 servings]**

One 2-pound whole fish or 1 pound grouper or cod fillet

10 cups water or fish or crab broth

1 tablespoon salt or more to taste

Bouquet garni, wrapped in cheesecloth, consisting of 1 celery stalk with leaves, 3 fresh parsley sprigs, 4 cloves, and 10 black peppercorns

½ pound medium shrimp, with their shells

12 littleneck clams, washed well

5 tablespoons extra-virgin olive oil

2 plum tomatoes, peeled (page 273), seeded, and chopped

3 scallions, trimmed and chopped

½ cup finely chopped fresh parsley

2 large garlic cloves, crushed

2 tablespoons finely chopped cilantro (fresh coriander) leaves

1 teaspoon ground coriander

½ teaspoon cayenne pepper

½ pound cooked crab meat, picked over

½ pound cooked lobster meat, cut up into small pieces

½ teaspoon fresh ground black pepper

the best soups in the world

1. Complete this step if using a whole fish. Gut, scale, and clean the fish. Remove the head and slice the fish into 1-inch-thick steaks. Set the fish steaks aside in the refrigerator until needed. Place the fish head in a large pot and cover with cold water. Bring to a boil over high heat, add the salt and bouquet garni, reduce the heat to low, cover, and simmer for 1½ hours. Strain the broth, discarding the fish head and bouquet garni. Return the broth to the cleaned pot.

2. Start with this step if using prepared fish broth. Place the bouquet garni in the fish broth (not necessary if you've completed Step 1). Bring the broth to boil over high heat, then reduce the heat to low and simmer for 30 minutes. Bring the broth back to a near boil over high heat, then add the shrimp, in their shells, and cook until orange-red, about 2 minutes. Remove the shrimp with a skimmer, remove the shells, devein if necessary, and set the shrimp aside in the refrigerator. Discard the shells. Keep the broth at a gentle boil.

3. Add the clams to the fish broth and cook, covered, until they open, 5 to 8 minutes. Remove from the broth and when they are cool enough to handle, remove the meat from the shells and reserve with the shrimp in the refrigerator. Discard any clams that remain firmly closed. Strain the broth through a cheesecloth-lined strainer to remove any particles or sand, then return to a clean pot.

4. In a nonstick skillet, heat 3 tablespoons of the olive oil over medium-high heat, then add the tomatoes, scallions, parsley, garlic, cilantro, coriander, and cayenne and cook, stirring frequently, until the vegetables have softened a bit, about 4 minutes. Transfer the vegetables to the seafood broth.

5. In the same nonstick skillet, heat the remaining 2 tablespoons of olive oil over high heat, then cook the fish steaks until light golden on both sides, turning only once, 4 to 5 minutes. Pull the meat off the bones with a fork and discard the skin and bones. Break the fish into smaller pieces and add to the broth. Add the reserved shrimp and clams and the crab and lobster to the broth. Season with the black pepper, correct the salt, if necessary, and cook over medium heat until all the seafood is heated through, about 5 minutes. Serve hot.

razor clam soup

I CAN GUARANTEE YOU that you will not find a recipe for razor clam soup anywhere else. Razor clams are rare, although they do occasionally appear in fish stores on both the East and West Coasts. When they do, buy them. Buy tons of them, because they are a rare treat and make for some very fine eating. There are several species of razor clam, so called because they look identical to a barber's straight razor. In Italian the razor clam is known as *cape longhe* or *cannolicchi,* and this recipe from Venice is called *cape longhe a la capuzzina.* The razor clam most likely to be sold in this country is the Atlantic version, distinguished by its scientific name *Enis directus.* There is a species from the West Coast, called the jackknife clam (*Tagelus californianus*), but it is not commercially viable. All you need to know is that they're called razor clams and should be soaked in cold water to cover with a little baking soda before using, just as you would with any clam. Some restaurants leave the clams in their shells, but for less messy eating, remove them. **[Makes 6 servings]**

3 pounds razor clams
¾ cup extra-virgin olive oil
¼ cup finely chopped fresh parsley
3 large garlic cloves, very finely chopped
6 slices Italian bread, fried in olive oil until golden

1. Wash and rinse the clams well or soak them in cold salted water.

2. In a large flame-proof casserole or stockpot, heat the olive oil over medium-high heat, then add the parsley and garlic and cook, stirring, until sizzling. Add the drained clams and cook, covered, until the shells open and the meat becomes firm, about 8 minutes. Remove the clams from their shells and arrange in a soup tureen or individual soup bowls. Pour the juice from the casserole over the clams and serve with the fried bread.

oyster soup

PLUMP FAT OYSTERS stewed in a tomato broth seasoned with basil or parsley, anchovies, and chile make this Italian *minestra di ostriche* a real treat for the oyster lover. The pasta used is a tiny seashell shape called *conchigliette piccole* no. 46 (or De Cecco brand no. 53). If it's not available from your Italian market it can be ordered it from the Barilla, Delverde or De Cecco companies, three huge Italian pasta-making firms whose products are in every supermarket in Italy and the United States. In its place you may use any tiny tubular pasta suitable for soups. **[Makes 4 servings]**

¼ cup extra-virgin olive oil

6 tablespoons finely chopped fresh basil or parsley leaves

2 large garlic cloves, finely chopped

4½ cups crushed tomatoes or tomato purée

1 pound shucked oysters with their juice (about 14 to 18 oysters)

4 salted anchovy fillets, rinsed and chopped

½ teaspoon red chile flakes

Salt and freshly ground black pepper to taste

6 ounces (about 1 cup) *conchigliette piccole* no. 46 (Delverde) or
   no. 53 (De Cecco)

1. In a pot, heat the olive oil with the basil and garlic over medium heat, stirring, then turn the heat off once everything has been sizzling for about 2 minutes.

2. Add the tomatoes and cook, stirring occasionally, until much of their liquid has evaporated, about 15 minutes. Add the oysters, anchovies, and chile flakes and season with salt and black pepper. Reduce the heat to medium-low and cook until the oysters have shrunk a little and their edges are curling up, 8 to 10 minutes.

3. Meanwhile, bring a large pot of abundantly salted water to a boil and add the pasta when the water is rolling. Drain when al dente and stir into the oysters. Salt if necessary and serve.

mussel and fish soup from lecce

THE BEAUTIFUL BAROQUE CITY OF LECCE in the province of Apulia sits in the middle of the heel of the Italian boot, also known as the Salento Peninsula, surrounded on three sides by the sea, which is just a few kilometers away. Market fish, although limited in variety, are extremely fresh, and that means Salentine fish cookery is quite enticing. In Lecce, a popular lunch dish is a simple soup of mussels and fish known as a *brodetto,* which means "broth."

[**Makes 6 servings**]

½ cup extra-virgin olive oil

2 fish heads or 1 pound fish pieces for soup or 1 fish carcass

2 onions, chopped

4 large garlic cloves, sliced

3 cups dry white wine

4 pounds mussels, debearded and washed well

1 pound red snapper or perch fillet, cut into ½-inch pieces

1 pound tomatoes, cut into ½-inch pieces

Salt (optional)

2 tablespoons chopped fresh mint

2 tablespoons chopped fresh basil

6 slices toasted Italian bread

1. In a large pot or casserole, heat the olive oil over medium-high heat, then add the fish heads or soup fish pieces or fish carcass, the onions, and garlic and cook, stirring and crushing the fish, until a crust has formed on the bottom of the pot, about 10 minutes. Pour in the white wine to deglaze the pot, scraping the bottom. Continue to boil for about 10 minutes.

2. Strain the broth through a fine mesh strainer and return it to the pot after wiping it clean with a paper towel. Bring to a boil and add the mussels, cover, and cook until the mussels just start to open, about 3 minutes. Add the fish and boil, covered, for 2 minutes, then add the tomatoes, cover, and cook for 2 minutes more. Taste the broth and salt if necessary. Finally, add the mint and basil, cook 1 minute, and serve in a bowl over toasted bread.

zuppa di aragosta trapanese

THIS IS A SOUP WHOSE DESCRIPTION I had for years but for which I could not find a recipe anywhere. Finally, I cobbled together some more descriptions, reinterpreted my insufficient notes, and wrote this recipe so that it yields exactly what I once ate in western Sicily—a magnificent soup of lobster from the port of Trapani on the island's west coast. For a really rich flavor you will want to have already prepared lobster broth, but you can start with water, too. **[Makes 8 servings]**

1 cup extra-virgin olive oil

16 slices French baguette

5 large garlic cloves, finely chopped, reserving 1 clove for rubbing on the bread

1 small onion, finely chopped

½ bunch fresh parsley, leaves only, chopped

2 pounds tomatoes, canned or fresh, peeled and chopped

2 teaspoons salt or more to taste

1 teaspoon freshly ground black pepper or more to taste

One 2¾-pound live lobster (or two 1½-pound live lobsters)

6 cups lobster broth (Step 2, page 349) or water

¼ teaspoon saffron, crumbled slightly

1. In a large skillet, heat ½ cup of the olive oil over medium heat, then cook the bread slices until golden on both sides, about 1 minute. Remove and set aside. Once they are cool, rub both sides of each bread slice with a cut garlic clove. (When you're done rubbing the bread, finish chopping the clove and set it aside with the others.)

2. In a large flame-proof casserole, heat the remaining ½ cup olive oil over medium-high heat, then add the garlic, onion, and parsley and cook, stirring frequently, until softened and translucent, about 5 minutes. Add the tomatoes, salt, and pepper and stir to mix well. Reduce the heat to low and cook until it forms a denser sauce, about 15 minutes.

3. Meanwhile, cut up the live lobster. (If you are squeamish about that, then steam the lobster for about 8 minutes first in a few inches of water in a large pot, then continue.) Remove the claws and arms and crack them so much of the meat is exposed. Separate the tail from the body and split it down the middle with a chef's knife. Split the body in half and crack and separate. Place the lobster body, legs, and any tomalley and coral into a large metal bowl and crush them a bit with a mallet (do this gently by pressing rather than hammering so you don't make a huge mess with splattering lobster parts). Place in the casserole with the tomato sauce and cook for 1 hour over low heat. Set the claws, arms, and tail aside in the refrigerator until needed.

4. Drain the contents of the casserole through a colander or strainer and return the liquid to a large pot. Turn the heat to medium and, as the soup begins to bubble slightly, add the reserved lobster claws, arms, and tail and cook until the lobster meat can be extracted easily, about 20 minutes. Remove all the lobster from the soup and set aside until cool enough to handle. Remove all the meat from the shells with a lobster pick and return the meat to the soup with the lobster broth and saffron. Cook over medium heat until the broth is flavorful, adjusting the seasoning if necessary, about 10 minutes. Serve in individual bowls with the fried bread.

hot and sour shrimp soup

THIS SIMPLE, LIGHT SOUP from the central and southern regions of Thailand, where freshly caught shrimp are plentiful, is called *tom yam gung* (also transliterated in several other ways). It is a name some version of which you are likely to have seen on a Thai restaurant menu, and it literally means "boil mix shrimp." You'll be thrilled to discover how easy it is to capture its very fresh taste from four main flavors—hot, sour, sweet, and salty. But there are several things you'll need to do for your soup to be memorable. First, use fresh shrimp with their heads, if at all available, and cook them as briefly as possible (if using defrosted shrimp the same rule applies). Second, use fresh ingredients if possible. And third, don't let the lime juice boil.

This soup can be made with ingredients other than shrimp, such as chicken, fish, or mushrooms. Some cooks use a combination of fresh and dried chiles, usually a good amount of *prik kee nu* (literally, mouse-dropping chiles, and also known as scuds or bird's-eye chiles) and fresh chiles such as *prik kee fa,* literally, "sky pointing chile," sold in American supermarkets as "Thai chiles." Thai fish sauce can be found in the international aisle of supermarkets. The more exotic ingredients listed below can be replaced with the substitutes I suggest, or you can order them on the internet at www.adrianascaravan.com and www.friedas.com.

[Makes 4 servings]

1 pound fresh jumbo shrimp with their heads, heads and shells
  removed and reserved, or ½ pound (about 10) headless defrosted
  jumbo shrimp, shells removed and reserved

4 cups lightly salted water

25 dried bird's-eye chiles or 3 dried finger-type red chiles

2 tablespoons Thai fish sauce

2 lemongrass stalks, tough outer portion removed, finely chopped or
  thinly sliced

1 tablespoon finely chopped fresh ginger or galangal

3 kaffir lime or lemon leaves, thinly sliced, or 1 teaspoon freshly
  grated lime zest

3 tablespoons fresh lime juice

4 tablespoons coarsely chopped cilantro (fresh coriander) leaves

10 fresh or canned straw mushrooms

1. Rinse the heads and/or shells of the shrimp. Place the heads and/or shells in a medium-size saucepan and pour the water over them. Bring to a boil, then reduce the heat to low and simmer for 20 minutes. If using fresh shrimp heads, small rivulets of orange-colored oil from the tomalley will rise to the surface—this is where so much flavor resides. Strain the broth through a strainer, pressing out liquid from the heads and/or shells with the back of a wooden spoon. Return the broth to a clean pot. Slightly bruise the bird's-eye chiles in a mortar with a pestle. (This is not necessary if using dried finger-type chiles.)

2. Bring the shrimp broth to a boil over high heat and season with 1 tablespoon of the fish sauce. Add the bird's-eye chiles, lemongrass, ginger, and lime leaves to the broth. Stir, cook for 1 minute, add the shrimp, and cook over medium-high heat for 2 minutes more. Reduce the heat to low and simmer until they turn pink-orange and are firm, another 2 minutes.

3. Meanwhile, in a soup tureen, stir together the remaining 1 tablespoon fish sauce, the lime juice, and cilantro. Pour the soup into the tureen and stir. Add the straw mushrooms and let sit for 2 minutes. Serve hot.

indonesian yellow squash and shrimp soup

RECIPES FOR THIS INDONESIAN DISH, called *sayur labu kuning,* do not always call for tiny dried shrimp to be crushed into the soup. If you decide to use them, you can find them in the international aisle of most supermarkets, or they and the shrimp paste can be ordered from www.adrianascaravan.com. I've adapted this recipe from one by Kokkie Blanda, an Indonesian cook, and have replaced the dried shrimp with tiny fresh shrimp. Use any Vietnamese or Thai fish sauce; it is available in the same supermarket aisle as the dried shrimp. See page 191 for the difference between coconut milk and coconut cream.

[**Makes 4 servings**]

FOR THE SPICE PASTE

6 small shallots, chopped

1 tablespoon chopped lemongrass

4 fresh red finger-type chiles

1 teaspoon palm sugar (preferably) or granulated sugar

½ teaspoon freshly ground white pepper

½ teaspoon shrimp paste

FOR THE SOUP

1 teaspoon fresh lime juice

1 pound yellow summer squash, cut into ¾-inch cubes

4 cups coconut milk (page 191)

1 cup water

¼ pound very small shrimp (120 count to a pound) or 2 ounces dried shrimp (about 1½ cups), both washed and ground coarsely in a food processor

1 cup coconut cream (page 191)

1 tablespoon Thai or Vietnamese fish sauce

Salt to taste, if necessary

¾ cup small fresh basil leaves

1. To make the spice paste: in a mortar or food processor, mash or process the shallots, lemongrass, chiles, sugar, white pepper, and shrimp paste together until mushy or a paste is formed.

2. To make the soup: in a bowl, sprinkle the lime juice over the squash and leave for 10 minutes.

3. In a pot, bring the coconut milk and water to a boil over high heat, then stir in the shrimp and the spice paste. Add the marinating squash to the pot and cook until the squash is half cooked, about 3 minutes. Pour in the coconut cream and stir a few times, then add the fish sauce and salt if needed, cover, and turn the heat off. Let rest for 30 minutes. Just before serving, add the basil, then serve hot.

scallop and ginger soup

THIS CHINESE SOUP is perfect as a light start to dinner. It's very simple to make, and the sea scallops used are shaved into thin slices that make for a delightful sensation when they slip down your throat. **[Makes 6 servings]**

4 cups water
1 ounce fresh ginger, peeled and finely julienned, peel reserved
1½ teaspoons soy sauce
2 scallions, trimmed and finely sliced on the diagonal
2½ cups fish broth
½ teaspoon cornstarch
½ teaspoon fresh lemon juice
Salt and freshly ground white pepper
12 sea scallops, cut in ⅛-inch-thick disks

1. In a pot, bring the water and julienned ginger to a boil over high heat. Reduce the heat to medium, add the soy sauce and scallions to the pot, and let the broth begin to bubble gently on the edges.

2. In another pot, add the fish broth and ginger peels and bring to a boil over high heat. Remove from the heat and let steep for 15 minutes. Remove the peels with a skimmer.

3. In a small bowl, mix the cornstarch with 1 tablespoon of water and the lemon juice and stir into the fish broth. Pour the fish broth into the ginger broth and season with salt and pepper. Over low heat, add the scallops and poach for 8 minutes; the surface of the broth should be completely still and not bubbling or shimmering. Serve hot.

426

the best soups in the world

korean clam soup

THIS SIMPLE SOUP is called *jo gae gook* in Korean. Its preparation involves almost nothing, yet it is beautiful to look at, and its tastes are hot and straightforward. This is a recipe I would recommend to someone who has never made Korean food, not only for its ease but also because it tastes very Korean and will be as good as anything you could order in a restaurant. The red chile powder can be found in Korean markets or ordered from www.kgrocer.com or www.ikoreaplaza.com.   [**Makes 2 to 4 servings**]

1 quart water

10 small littleneck or Manila clams, cleaned

3 ounces firm tofu, diced

1 scallion, white and green parts, cut on the bias in ¼-inch slices

2 teaspoons salt

1½ teaspoons ground Korean chile powder or 1 teaspoon ground red chile

1 fresh red jalapeño chile, chopped

Pour the water into a pot with the clams. Bring to a boil, reduce the heat to medium, and just after the clams open up, take them out with a slotted spoon. Add the tofu, scallion, salt, and ground chile powder and cook for another minute. Put the clams back in the pot and heat for 1 minute. Serve, garnished with the fresh chopped chile.

crab and miso soup

THIS IS A VERY SATISFYING SOUP, and I imagine it would be perfect on a cold day in the late fall. I use the more familiar Japanese word *miso* here for the fermented soybean paste, but in Korean the preparation is called *toenjang,* and this soup is *toenjang jiege keh.* One can find the soybean paste in Korean markets, but the Japanese miso may be more handy. In any case it's available, as is Korean chile, through Internet sources such as www.orientalpantry .com. This recipe comes from Kwangju, where cooks like salty and spicy-hot food. To prepare the crab, clip off the big claws, wash the body, turn it over so the bottom is facing up, and pull out the gills and inner viscera and discard (follow the instructions on page 347). Wash the crab again and crack the claws. The soup is served with the crabmeat in its shell. Serve in individual bowls with rice on the side if desired. **[Makes 4 servings]**

2 cups water

2 tablespoons miso (fermented soybean paste; *toenjang* in Korean)

½ pound firm tofu, cut into ½-inch cubes

2 live blue crabs or 1 Dungeness crab (about 1¾ pounds), prepared for cooking as
described in headnote

1 small zucchini, peeled and cut into ⅛-inch-thick slices

1 small onion, thinly sliced

2 large garlic cloves, crushed

1 tablespoon Korean chile powder or 2 teaspoons cayenne pepper

One ⅛-inch slice fresh ginger

2 teaspoons salt

1 fresh red jalapeño chile, sliced

1. Put the water and miso in a pot over low heat. Cover and simmer until blended, about 10 minutes, stirring occasionally. Add the tofu and cook for 5 more minutes.

2. Add the crabs, zucchini, onion, garlic, chile powder, ginger, and salt and bring to a boil over high heat. Turn with a spoon several times to blend the ingredients, being careful not to break the tofu. Cover, reduce the heat to low, and simmer until the crabs are cooked through and the vegetables are softened, 25 to 30 minutes. Garnish with the fresh red chile and serve hot.

chilled
soups

A chilled soup is not just something for a hot summer day, although that is when I most often make them. But chilled soups are refreshing at any time of year. My favorite chilled soup is gazpacho, the first recipe, but all the classics from borshch to vichyssoise are here. Give the Hungarian chilled cherry soup a try, and new worlds will open up. Two chilled soups appear elsewhere in the book: Armenian Barley Yogurt Soup on page 317 and Spring Pea Soup (the variation) on page 236.

gazpacho

THE SECRET TO GAZPACHO is not to allow any of the ingredients to stand out over the others. It should be a completely harmonious orchestra of flavors. And above all, you must use the sweetest, vine-ripened, height-of-the-season tomatoes—which means gazpacho is usually made only in the summer.

To create this recipe, I synthesized the two best gazpachos I've ever eaten. I had one at a country fair held at the Guillen family estate, the Hacienda Guzman, in rural Andalusia, about an hour's drive from Seville. I had the other at El Tablon restaurant, Cardenal Gonzalez, 75, in Córdoba. In both cases, the gazpacho was a creamy pinkish orange, very smooth and full of fresh vegetable flavor that was bursting with sweetness. Do not use all the garnishes listed below; choose four or five (and make sure they are at room temperature).

[**Makes 4 servings**]

4 large garlic cloves

2 teaspoons salt

2 slices week-old French bread, with or without crust

2½ pounds very ripe tomatoes (such as Carmelo tomatoes),
   peeled (page 273), chopped, and passed through a sieve to
   remove all seeds (save some of the juice to soak the bread in)

1 red or green bell pepper, roasted, peeled, and seeded

6 tablespoons extra-virgin olive oil

1 small cucumber, peeled, seeded, and chopped

4 tablespoons good-quality Spanish sherry vinegar

1 hard-boiled egg yolk

Salt and freshly ground black pepper to taste

¼ teaspoon ground cumin or more if desired

12 ice cubes

GARNISHES (CHOOSE FOUR OR FIVE)

Ripe, firm tomato, finely chopped

Green bell pepper, finely chopped

Hard-boiled egg, shelled and finely chopped

Cucumber, peeled, seeded, and finely chopped

Scallions, finely chopped

Sweet onion, finely chopped

Finely chopped fresh parsley leaves

Freshly ground cumin seeds

Croûtons (page 129), cut smaller than dice

Sweet paprika

Jamón serrano or prosciutto, chopped small

Homemade olive oil–based mayonnaise

Canned tuna in olive oil

Chopped imported black olives

Chopped imported green olives

A few drops of red wine

Finely chopped fresh tarragon leaves

Pine nuts

1. In a mortar, pound the garlic and salt until mushy. Transfer to a food processor and pulse until mushier.

2. Soak the bread in the juice from the tomatoes and a little water, then squeeze it out as if you were making a snowball. Add the bread to the processor and pulse a couple of times until well blended. Add the bell pepper and tomatoes and process for 5 seconds, then pour in the olive oil while running the food processor continuously. Add the cucumber and process some more. Drizzle in the vinegar and add the egg yolk while continuing to process. Season with salt, pepper, and cumin, if desired.

3. Transfer to a bowl and add the ice cubes. Leave in the refrigerator for several hours before serving, stirring occasionally, and serve when the ice cubes have melted with a selection of garnishes of your choosing.

chilled soups

ABOUT GAZPACHO

The home of the famous cold vegetable soup known as gazpacho is Spain's southern region of Andalusia; it is Andalusia's best-known dish. It probably originated during the Middle Ages, when Spain was part of the Islamic world, as a soup the Spanish today call an *ajo blanco,* which contained garlic, almonds, bread, olive oil, vinegar, and salt. *Ajo blanco* is today associated with the seaport of Málaga and is made with fresh grapes (see the recipe on page 434). Gazpacho is sometimes thought of as a liquid salad; indeed, it is served as a first course and is traditionally made with ripe tomatoes, bell peppers, cucumbers, garlic, and bread moistened with water that is blended with olive oil, vinegar, and ice water and served cold. There are several versions of gazpacho, some of which contain almonds, and others made without tomatoes or peppers.

Gazpacho is traditionally made in a mortar, and the bread is ideal when it is about a week old. The bread and vegetable mixture is pounded to a paste; then one begins to add the tomatoes, then the olive oil, and finally the vinegar, tasting after each step to make sure the soup is balanced. The tomatoes should always go through a sieve so there are no seeds in the finished dish.

The rise in the popularity of gazpacho in the rest of Spain beyond Andalusia is said, by Alicia Rios and Lourdes March, authors of Spanish cookbooks, to be the creation of Eugenia de Montijo, the wife of the nineteenth-century French emperor Napoleon III. Still, gazpacho was unknown, or little known, in the north of Spain before about 1930. According to Juan de la Mata's *Arte de reposteria,* published in 1747, the most common gazpacho was known as *capon de galera;* it consisted of a pound of bread crust soaked in water and left in a sauce of anchovy bones, garlic, vinegar, sugar, salt, and olive oil to soften. Then one added "some of the ingredients and vegetables of the Royal Salad [a salad composed of various fruits and vegetables]."

An American cookbook published in 1963 tells us that "gazpacho, the soup-salad of Spain, has become an American food fashion." The author, Betty Wason, goes on to tells us that in Mary Randolph's *Virginia Housewife,* published in 1824, there is a recipe for gazpacho. The Randolph recipe for gaspacho [*sic*], however, is not a soup, but more of a tomato and bread stew. The French poet and critic Théophile Gautier (1811–1872) wrote about gazpacho, too.

There are many variations of gazpacho, such as *gazpacho de antequera,* made with homemade mayonnaise blended with lemon juice and egg whites, pounded garlic, and almonds. *Gazpacho de Granada* is made with pounded garlic, cumin, salt, bell peppers, and tomatoes, with olive oil added until creamy; then water and bread go on top. *Gazpacho de la serrania de Huelva,* from the mountainous country around Huelva, is a purée of garlic, paprika, onions, tomatoes, and bell peppers, with sherry vinegar and olive oil stirred in until creamy; it is served with cucumber and croûtons. *Salmorejo Cordobés* (also translated as "rabbit sauce") is made with garlic, bell peppers, tomatoes, and moistened bread pounded into a paste, with olive oil stirred in until it has the consistency of a purée. It is served with eggs, oranges, and toasted bread. *Gazpacho caliente* uses hot chiles—there are also gazpachos made with green beans or pine nuts.

The origin of the word "gazpacho" is uncertain, but etymologists believe it might be derived from the Mozarab word *caspa,* meaning "residue" or "fragments," an allusion to the small pieces of bread and vegetables in a gazpacho soup. On the other hand, it may be a pre-Roman Iberian word modified by the Arabic. (One hears a lot about Mozarab when speaking of historic Andalusia. "Mozarab" is a corruption of the Arabic *mustʿarab,* "would-be Arab," those Hispano-Romans who were allowed to practice their religion on condition that they pledge their allegiance to the Arab caliph, as opposed to the *muwalladūn,* Hispano-Romans who in fact converted to Islam.) José Briz, who wrote a book on gazpacho, also suggests that the word derives from the Hebrew *gazaz,* meaning "to break into pieces," referring to the bread base.

Originally, gazpacho was nothing but bread, water, and olive oil, all pounded in a large wooden bowl called a *dornillo.* It was poor people's food, traditionally eaten by workers in the fields, whether they were vineyards, olive plantations, citrus groves, wheat fields, or cork farms.

ajo blanco

THIS COLD SUMMER SOUP comes from Málaga in the Spanish region of Andalusia and is a kind of white gazpacho with a medieval history. It is thought to have its roots in the era of Islamic Spain between the eighth and fifteenth centuries. This almond-flavored soup is usually served with Muscat grapes. A proper *ajo blanco* is a perfect emulsion of ground almonds, olive oil, bread, and garlic. Its whiteness comes from the almonds. Peel the grapes by dropping them in boiling water for about a minute and a half; peeling them is slightly tedious but it's for the better. **[Makes 4 servings]**

5 ounces Italian or French bread, crusts removed
1½ cups blanched whole almonds (about ¼ pound)
2 large garlic cloves
1 teaspoon salt or more to taste
²/₃ cup extra-virgin olive oil
1 tablespoon sherry vinegar
4 cups cold water
1 pound seedless green grapes, peeled (see headnote)

1. Soak the bread in some water for a minute, then squeeze dry.

2. In a food processor, crush the almonds with the bread, garlic, and 1 teaspoon salt until pasty. Pour the olive oil through the feed tube in a slow stream as the machine is running. Blend in the vinegar and ¾ cup of the water through the feed tube and run continuously for 1 minute. Transfer to a blender and process even finer at high speed for 2 minutes.

3. Transfer the almond mixture to a bowl and whisk in the remaining cold water. Refrigerate for a few hours. Remove from the refrigerator and add more salt or vinegar if needed. Serve very cold with the grapes sprinkled on top.

vichyssoise

IT'S ALWAYS A SURPRISE to people when they hear that this famous soup is not from France, although the inspiration is. This cold potato, leek, and milk soup was invented by the French chef Louis Diat (1885–1957) when he was chef du cuisine of the Ritz-Carlton Hotel dining room in New York. In a *New Yorker* magazine interview published in 1950, he relates how it came about. His brother and he would, during the summers, add cold milk to cool off their mother's and grandmother's potato and leek soup at their home near Vichy, then famous only for being a spa. He fancied it up a bit by straining it twice, adding heavy cream, sprinkling it with chives, and serving it on the menu as *crème vichyssoise glacée.* Even though most everyone agrees that Diat invented the soup, there are no written references to the soup before 1923, according to Manfred Höfler's *Dictionnaire de l'art culinaire français,* published in 1996. Remember, too, that the potato and leek soup it's based on, Potage Parmentier (page 219), goes back to the eighteenth century.   [**Makes 4 servings**]

½ tablespoon unsalted butter
2 leeks, white and light green parts only, split lengthwise, washed well,
    and coarsely chopped
1 small onion, chopped
½ pound potatoes, peeled and diced
2 cups water or chicken broth
1 teaspoon salt
1 cup whole milk
1 cup half-and-half
½ cup heavy cream
Freshly ground white pepper to taste
Fresh chives, chopped for garnish

1. In a large saucepan, melt the butter over medium high heat, then add the leeks and onion and cook, stirring occasionally, until softened, about 5 minutes. Add the potatoes, water, and salt, reduce the heat to low, and simmer, covered, until the potatoes are softened, about 40 minutes.

2. Add the milk and half-and-half and bring to just below a full boil, stirring. Turn the heat off, transfer in batches to a blender, and purée. Stir in the cream and white pepper and chill for 4 hours before serving. Garnish with chives.

tarator

THIS COLD SUMMERTIME SOUP is a favorite in Bulgaria and Macedonia. In fact, a thicker version is used as a meze dip in Greece and Turkey, where it is called *tzatziki* and *cacık,* respectively. In Arab countries of the Middle East, though, *taratur* is a sauce made with tahini and lemon juice. The blend of yogurt, walnuts, cucumber, and garlic seems so natural and the dish is made all the more appealing by stirring in a good quality olive oil. I once served *tarator* on a hot July 4th, followed by some yogurt-and-mint-marinated grilled lamb, and it was as perfect a meal as could be. For a slightly lighter taste, you can use vegetable or sunflower seed oil.

[Makes 4 to 6 servings]

1 pound (2 cups) plain whole yogurt

3 cucumbers, peeled and finely grated

8 large garlic cloves, pounded in a mortar with 1 teaspoon salt until mushy

2½ ounces (about ¾ cup) shelled walnuts

¼ cup extra-virgin olive oil

Water if necessary

1 bunch dill, stems removed, chopped

In a bowl, beat the yogurt until smooth. Add the cucumbers, garlic mixture, and walnuts and mix well. Add the oil and beat until well blended. If your yogurt was quite thick, add some water to thin it and make it soupy. Let rest in the refrigerator for 2 hours before serving. Stir the dill in at the last moment and serve.

the best soups in the world

cold borshch #1

MANY BELORUSSIAN SOUPS are served as a combination of first and second courses. They are rich and thick and smooth, a texture achieved through long boiling or braising. But in the summer, this cold borshch soup from Minsk called *khaladnik* is wonderfully flavorful and refreshing. Sorrel is a salad and soup green that has a distinctly lemony and biting taste. I usually find sorrel at farmers markets and specialty greengrocers. In its place you can make do with spinach or arugula leaves and several thin slices of lemon, which can be removed from the soup before serving. **[Makes 6 servings]**

10 cups water

3 teaspoons salt or more to taste

½ pound sorrel, chopped

2 red beets (about 14 ounces)

3 tablespoons white wine vinegar

2 large cucumbers, peeled, seeded, and shredded

7 scallions, trimmed and finely chopped

1 large egg, separated

2 cups plain whole yogurt

1 tablespoon sugar

2 tablespoons sour cream

1 tablespoon finely chopped fresh dill

1. In a large pot, bring 6 cups of the water with 2 teaspoons of the salt to a boil over high heat, then add the sorrel and cook for 5 minutes. Turn the heat off and let cool.

2. In a small pot, add the beets and cover with the remaining 4 cups of water and the vinegar. Bring to a boil over high heat and cook the beets until tender, about 40 minutes. Drain the beets, saving 2 cups of the liquid, then let cool, peel, and shred the beets and set aside.

3. In a bowl, mix together the shredded beets, the cucumbers, scallions, egg yolk, and remaining 1 teaspoon of salt. Add this mixture to the sorrel liquid. Mix together the beet cooking liquid, yogurt, egg white, and sugar and add to the sorrel liquid mixture. Whisk the soup well, refrigerate for 3 hours, and serve with a dollop of sour cream and a sprinkle of fresh dill.

cold borshch # 2

THIS LITHUANIAN BORSHCH is a bit different from the Belorussian one on page 438. It uses buttermilk instead of yogurt and is called *ðaltibarðèiai* (which frankly, I can't pronounce); it might be the most popular soup in Lithuania. Of the many cold borshch made in Eastern Europe, I found this Lithuanian one delicious and beautiful. It offers the contrast of the cold beet soup with the hot potatoes. I tried cataloging the varieties of hot and cold borshch and gave up when I got to about forty. Be careful when working with beets because they stain quickly. Yukon Gold are an excellent variety of boiling potatoes.

[Makes 6 to 8 servings]

2 red beets (about 14 ounces)

2 large hard-boiled eggs, shelled, whites finely chopped, and yolks left whole

1 cup finely chopped scallions

2 teaspoons salt

2 fresh cucumbers, peeled, seeded, and finely chopped

4 cups buttermilk

1 cup ice water

6 tablespoons sour cream

4 small boiling potatoes (about ½ pound), peeled

8 sprigs fresh dill, finely chopped

1. Place the beets in a large saucepan and cover by several inches with cold water. Bring to a boil over high heat and boil, replenishing the water if necessary, until a skewer glides easily to the center of the beet, about 50 minutes. Drain, and when cool enough to handle, remove the skin and grate the beet on the large openings of a box grater. Set aside until needed.

2. In a bowl, crush the egg yolks with the scallions and salt. Add the egg whites, beets, cucumbers, buttermilk, ice water, and sour cream. Refrigerate for 2 hours before serving.

3. When it is time to serve, place the potatoes in a saucepan and cover with cold water. Bring to a boil over high heat, then reduce the heat to medium and cook until a skewer glides easily to the center of a potato, about 45 minutes in all. Drain and dice, but keep the potatoes hot.

4. To serve, mix well and ladle the soup in individual bowls sprinkled with dill and a few of the hot potatoes.

the best soups in the world

chilled peach soup

THIS SOUP IS A TRUE CALIFORNIA DISH. I've only been served this preparation in California—and never in restaurants, at that. The peaches in California are amazingly delicious, and come June I slurp those luscious June Ladies while leaning over the kitchen sink, the juices running off my chin. But here is an interesting way to use up those peaches you haven't stuffed down your gullet. The soup is served as a first course, so you don't need much—or any—sugar. It's important that you use ripe peaches. Some people may be disappointed that this soup is not dessert, but think of it as a kind of gazpacho made with peaches instead of tomatoes. Put the mint in only at the last moment to ensure it doesn't begin to taste woody. Taste before serving and if you think something is off, then go ahead and add a little sugar. **[Makes 4 servings]**

4 large ripe peaches
2 cups dry white wine
½ cup water
1 cinnamon stick
3 cloves
Crème fraîche for garnish (optional)
6 large fresh mint leaves, cut into fine ribbon confetti with scissors

1. Bring a pot of water to a boil over high heat, then add the peaches and boil until their skins loosen, 1 minute. Remove the peaches, peel off the skins, and remove the pits. Cut up the peaches.

2. Place the peeled peaches in a blender with 1 cup of the wine and blend until smooth. Transfer to a saucepan with the remaining cup of wine, the water, cinnamon, and cloves. Bring to a near boil over high heat, stirring almost constantly, then reduce the heat to low and simmer, stirring, for 10 minutes. Remove and discard the cinnamon and cloves and chill the soup in the refrigerator for at least 4 hours before serving. Serve garnished with a small dollop of crème fraîche, if using, and the confetti of mint.

chilled watermelon soup

THERE ARE A GREAT MANY watermelon soup recipes, ranging from those that combine the watermelon with mangoes or berries to those that call for ginger or peaches. This recipe is Sicilian inspired, and I find it an amazing soup in the summer. It's served as a dessert soup.

[**Makes 4 servings**]

4 pounds ripe watermelon flesh, seeds removed

6 tablespoons sugar

¼ cup coarsely chopped unsalted pistachios

¼ cup semisweet chocolate bits

¼ cup candied orange peel, diced small (optional)

1 cinnamon stick

½ teaspoon rose water

½ teaspoon vanilla extract

4 jasmine flowers for garnish (optional)

1. Place the watermelon flesh in a food processor and process until almost smooth. Pass the watermelon through a food mill to make it smoother; you can also run it in a blender. You should have 5 cups of watermelon liquid. Transfer to a metal bowl (to keep it colder).

2. Stir in the sugar, pistachios, chocolate bits, candied orange peel, if using, cinnamon stick, rose water, and vanilla extract and refrigerate for 4 hours.

3. Remove the cinnamon stick. Ladle the watermelon soup into chilled bowls and garnish with jasmine flowers, if using.

chilled cherry soup

THIS HUNGARIAN SOUP is called *hideg meggyleves* (*hideg* = "cold," *meggy* = "cherry," and *leves* = "soup"), and although you can serve it as a dessert soup, in Hungary it would be a first course. It's traditionally made with sour cherries during the cherry season in late spring and early summer. Some cooks add red wine, use heavy cream rather than sour cream, or use corn starch as a thickener, but I like this recipe, which I've adapted from János Mohácsi of the Budapest University of Technology and Economics. It's a popular soup in Poland, too.

[Makes 4 to 6 servings]

6 cups water

¾ cup sugar

Grated zest from ½ lemon

½ teaspoon ground cinnamon

¼ teaspoon salt

1 pound fresh ripe cherries, pitted

6 tablespoons sour cream

1 tablespoon all-purpose flour

3 tablespoons heavy cream

1. In a large pot, add the water, sugar, lemon zest, cinnamon, and salt, bring to a boil over high heat, then boil for 4 minutes. Add the cherries, then reduce the heat to medium-low and simmer 5 minutes.

2. In a bowl, stir the sour cream and flour together. Slowly whisk in a ladleful of the cherry liquid. Stir this mixture back into the soup and boil over medium-high heat, stirring almost constantly in a slow figure-8 pattern, until it thickens a bit, about 10 minutes. Let sit in the pot until cool, then stir in the cream and refrigerate until cold. Serve chilled.

chilled apple soup (normandy)

THIS NORMAN SOUP, called *la pommeraie glacée,* is undoubtedly popular in this land famous for apples and apple liquor such as Calvados. It is not a sweet dish, but smooth and beguiling, with an intimation of something other than apples—and indeed, the apples are balanced by a leek and a potato. This recipe is adapted from Claude Guermont, chef-owner of Le Pavillon restaurant in Poughkeepsie, New York. It is quite different from the Polish cold apple soup on page 444, this soup being closer to a vichyssoise in taste and smoothness.

[Makes 4 servings]

3 tablespoons unsalted butter

1 leek, white part only, split lengthwise, washed well, and coarsely sliced

3 cups Granny Smith or Golden Delicious apples, peeled, cored, and diced into
 ¼-inch cubes

4 cups chicken broth

1 cup diced potatoes (in ¼-inch dice)

¾ cup heavy cream

1½ teaspoons Calvados or other apple or fruit liqueur

Pinch of ground cinnamon

Salt and freshly ground black pepper to taste

FOR THE GARNISH (OPTIONAL)

1 tablespoon unsalted butter

1 apple, any kind, peeled, cored, and cut into ¼-inch dice

the best soups in the world

1. In a pot, melt the butter over medium heat, then add the leek and cook, covered and stirring occasionally, until translucent, about 3 minutes. Add the apples and cook, uncovered and stirring occasionally, until glazed and slightly soft, 5 minutes.

2. Add the chicken broth and the potatoes, bring to a boil over high heat, then reduce the heat to medium-low and simmer until tender, about 30 minutes.

3. Transfer the soup to a food processor and purée in batches until smooth. Return the soup to a bowl and stir in the heavy cream, Calvados, and cinnamon. Season with salt and pepper. Refrigerate for 3 hours.

4. If using the garnish, melt the butter in a small skillet over medium-high heat, then add the apple and cook, stirring, until it begins to get pulpy, about 5 minutes. Transfer to paper towels to drain, then add to the soup as a garnish when serving.

chilled apple soup (poland)

MIROSŁAW MALISZEWSKI, president of the Association of Polish Fruit Growers, says, unsurprisingly, that Polish apples are the best in the world. But this isn't just puffery. The climate in Poland—especially around the region of Mazovia, where fifty percent of Poland's two million tons of apples are produced every year—is ideal because of its cold nights and warm days: what an apple would consider to be apple heaven. There are other places in the world with these conditions, of course, but not all offer apple soup in their cuisines. This chilled apple soup is called *jablecna polevka studena* in Polish, but don't worry about pronouncing it: just eat a deliciously thick and refreshing apple soup. The soup is very thick when done; if you like it soupier, thin it with a cup of water. **[Makes 4 to 6 servings]**

1¼ pounds Granny Smith, York, Rome Beauty, Winesap, or Gravenstein apples, peeled, cored, chopped or diced small

4 cups water

Juice from ½ lemon plus 4 thin slices of the other half

¼ teaspoon salt

2 cups sour cream

3 tablespoons all-purpose flour

3 tablespoons raisins

2 teaspoons sugar

1. Place the apples in a pot with the water, lemon juice, and salt and bring to a boil over high heat, then boil until the apples are softened, about 12 minutes.

2. Meanwhile, in a bowl, stir together the sour cream and flour. Add to the apples and bring to a boil over high heat. Add the lemon slices, raisins, and sugar. Turn the heat off and let cool, then refrigerator for 4 hours and serve cold.

internet food shopping

Modern home cooks have a world of food at their fingertips. Many of the ingredients I've used in this book came, in fact, from the sources below. This list consists of online food shopping sites that are reputable, have been around for at least five years (and many longer than that), and are (in most cases) easily navigable. If you've never ordered food products from an Internet site, you've just got to try it: it's amazing to have these wonderful foods arrive at your doorstep. And I've saved you all the research—all you've got to do is click (and pay). The foods are listed alphabetically, and I have tried not to include items easily found in local supermarkets.

African foods: www.afritaste.com; www.jbafricanmarket.com; www.afrikan-food.com; www.asiamex.com

Aleppo pepper: www.penzeys.com

Anchovies, dried: www.kgrocer.com; www.ikoreaplaza.com; www.asiamex.com; store.asianmerchant.com; www.templeofthai.com

Asafetida: www.adrianascaravan.com

Asian foods: www.asianfoodgrocer.com

Black gram (*urad dal*): www.indianfoodsco.com

Black mustard seeds: www.adrianascaravan.com

Bonito flakes, dried (*katsuobushi*): www.asianfoodgrocer.com

Cardamom pods: www.penzeys.com

Chana dal (see Yellow split peas)

Cheese, various kinds: www.igourmet.com

Chiles, *ají amarillo*: www.adrianascaravan.com; www.penderys.com

Chiles, *ají mirasol*: www.penderys.com; www.worldspice.com

Chiles, *ají panca*: www.penderys.com; www.worldspice.com

Chiles, ancho: www.adrianascaravan.com; www.myspicer.com; www.friedas.com

Chiles, dried Aleppo (see Aleppo pepper)

Chiles, dried bird's-eye: www.importfoods.com; www.friedas.com; www.adrianascaravan.com

Chiles, *locoto*: store.amigofoods.com

Chiles, poblano: www.friedas.com

Chiles, South American varieties: www.penderys.com; www.worldspice.com

Chiles, Thai: www.importfoods.com; www.templeofthai.com

Chuño negro (Peruvian freeze-dried potatoes): store.amigofoods.com

Coconut cream: www.asianfoodgrocer.com; www.importfoods.com; www.templeofthai.com

Coconut flakes, unsweetened: www.kingarthurflour.com

Coconut milk: www.asianfoodgrocer.com; www.importfoods.com; www.templeofthai.com

Coriander root: www.importfoods.com

Crayfish, dried: www.jbafricanmarket.com; www.asiamex.com.com

Cubeb pepper: www.adrianascaravan.com

Curry leaves: www.adrianascaravan.com

Fenugreek: www.adrianascaravan.com

Fermented soybean paste (see Miso)

Freekeh (green wheat): www.surfasonline.com

Fregula: www.gourmetsardinia.com

Galangal, fresh or dried: www.importfoods.com; www.friedas.com; www.adrianascaravan.com

Garam masala: www.penzeys.com

Green gram (*moong dal*): www.indianfoodsco.com

Green wheat (see *Freekeh*)

Kaffir lime leaves: www.importfoods.com; www.templeofthai.com

Kashk (or *kishk*): www.sadaf.com

Katsuobushi (see Bonito flakes, dried)

Kelp, dried (*kombu*): www.asianfoodgrocer.com

Koch'ujang (see Korean chile paste)

Kombu (see Kelp, dried)

Korean chile paste (*koch'ujang*): www.kgrocer.com; www.ikoreaplaza.com

Korean chili powder (*koch'ukaru*): www.kgrocer.com; www.ikoreaplaza.com

Korean red adzuki bean paste (*p'at komul*): www.kgrocer.com; www.ikoreaplaza.com

Lemongrass: www.importfoods.com; www.templeofthai.com

Lentils: www.indianfoodsco.com

Limes, dried (*loomi*): www.daynasmarket.com

Loomi (see Limes, dried)

Merguez sausage: www.gourmetfoodstore.com; www.dartagnan.com

Miso (fermented soybean paste): www.asianfoodgrocer.com

Moong dal (see Green gram)

Mung beans: www.indianfoodsco.com

Mustard oil: www.indianfoodsco.com

Ogbono seed: www.asiamex.com

Palm sugar: www.importfoods.com

Pigeon peas (*toor dal*): www.indianfoodsco.com

Plum jam: www.shakersprings.com

Polish foods: www.polisheats.com; www.janeksfinefoods.com

Polish sausage: www.polisheats.com; www.janeksfinefoods.com

Polish smoked bacon: www.polisheats.com; www.janeksfinefoods.com

Potatoes, Peruvian freeze-dried (see *Chuño negro*)

Red palm oil: www.asiamex.com; www.afritaste.com; www.jbafricanmarket.com

Rose petals, dried: www.adrianascaravan.com
Sbrinz cheese: www.igourmet.com
Shrimp, dried: www.adrianascaravan.com
Shrimp paste: www.adrianascaravan.com
Sichuan chile bean paste: www.asiamex.com; www.adrianascaravan.com
Sichuan peppercorns: www.adrianascaravan.com
Szalona sausage: www.polisheats.com; www.janeksfinefoods.com
Tamarind paste: www.adrianascaravan.com
Thai chile sauce: www.importfoods.com; www.templeofthai.com
Thai fish sauce: www.importfoods.com; www.templeofthai.com
Toor dal (see Pigeon peas)
Urad dal (see Black gram)
Winter melon: www.friedas.com
Yellow split peas (*chana dal*): www.indianfoodsco.com

internet food shopping

recipes by region

Basic broths are not listed here;
see the Index for them.

449

recipes by region

Europe, Eastern

Europe, Western, other

France

recipes by region

index

461

index

465

index

index

index